WE FACE THE DAWN

CARTER G. WOODSON INSTITUTE SERIES

Deborah E. McDowell, Editor

WE FACE THE DAWN

Oliver Hill, Spottswood Robinson, and the
Legal Team That Dismantled Jim Crow

Margaret Edds

University of Virginia Press | Charlottesville and London

University of Virginia Press
Printed in the United States of America on acid-free paper

First published 2018

9 8 7 6 5 4 3 2 1

Library of Congress Cataloging-in-Publication Data
Names: Edds, Margaret, 1947– author.
Title: We face the dawn : Oliver Hill, Spottswood Robinson, and the legal team that
    dismantled Jim Crow / Margaret Edds.
Description: Charlottesville : University of Virginia Press, [2018] | Series: Carter G. Woodson
    Institute series | Includes bibliographical references and index.
Identifiers: LCCN 2017026804 | ISBN 9780813940441 (cloth : alk. paper) | ISBN 9780813940458
    (ebook)
Subjects: LCSH: Segregation in education—Law and legislation—United States—History—
    20th century. | School integration—United States—History—20th century. | Hill,
    Oliver W., 1907–2007. | Robinson, Spottswood William, III, 1916–1998. | Civil rights
    lawyers—United States—Biography.
Classification: LCC KF4155 .E33 2018 | DDC 344.73/0798—dc23
LC record available at https://lccn.loc.gov/2017026804

Cover photo: Spottswood Robinson and Oliver Hill entering the Alexandria, Virginia, courthouse in the Arlington school-desegregation case, 1958. (Bettman Archive/Getty Images)

For Bob

I greet the dawn and not a setting sun,
When all is done.
—Paul Laurence Dunbar

CONTENTS

Illustrations follow page 160

ACKNOWLEDGMENTS

Of the many individuals who contributed to this portrait of Oliver Hill and Spottswood Robinson, none elicit greater gratitude than their surviving children, Oliver Hill Jr. and Nina Robinson Govan. Each graciously shared family keepsakes and memories. Although the list is fast dwindling of those who knew Mr. Hill and Judge Robinson in their prime, I am grateful to have had access—as a journalist or more recently—to several who did. Among them: James Benton Jr., Robert L. Carter, Stephen L. Carter, Joan Johns Cobbs, Clarence Dunnaville, James Dyke, Lucy Thornton Edwards, Jack Greenberg, Ruth Bader Ginsburg, Oswald Govan, Jack Gravely, Jack Greenberg, Robert Grey Jr., Leslie Griffin Jr., Linwood Holton, Henry Marsh, Ferguson Reid, Robert "Bobby" Scott, Douglas Wilder, and LaVerne Williams. Their combined observations illuminate the written record that forms the foundation of this book.

I spoke only once with Judge Robinson—at the fortieth anniversary of the *Brown v. Board of Education* decision. With characteristic politeness and caution, he weighed my request for an interview and declined, citing his desire to avoid any appearance of conflict while serving the federal courts as a senior judge. Fortunately, Hill was less reticent. Listening to his memories as he sat in the Richmond courtroom where he and Robinson argued *Davis v. County School Board of Prince Edward County* remains a highlight of my journalistic career.

Both Hill and Robinson were deceased before work on this book began. I am therefore grateful for access to interviews conducted and retained by several organizations: the Brown vs. Board of Education Collection, Yale University Library; The Ground Beneath Our Feet Project, Virginia Center for Digital History, University of Virginia; the Juan Williams Collection, Howard University School of Law Archives; the Voices of Freedom Digital Collection, Virginia Commonwealth University; the Virginia Project Foundation (Carolyn Oliver); and the William A. Elwood Civil Rights Lawyers Project Collection, University of Virginia Library.

Special thanks to the Virginia Foundation for the Humanities for support of this project and to the archivists and librarians who eased my path, especially Francine Archer and Lucious Edwards of Virginia State University; Seth Kronemer of Howard University School of Law; Selicia Allen of Virginia Union University; and the wonderful staff of the Library of Virginia. Four Virginia historians earned my enormous gratitude for their unwavering enthusiasm and generous attention to the manuscript: James Hershman, Brent Tarter, Peter Wallenstein, and James Sweeney.

My family remains my greatest source of learning and joy: Kate, Mark, and Harrison Garabedian; Sharon, Brett, and Lauren Halsey; Rachel Edds and Elliot Lieberman; Adam Lipper; Jerwaine and Margaret Simpson; Taylor Stojka and her family; and first and foremost, Bob Lipper.

The University of Virginia Press acknowledges the generous contribution of the Virginia Trial Lawyers Association to support the publication of this book.

WE FACE THE DAWN

INTRODUCTION

Gloucester County, 1948

> I want to tell you right now that if I have the power to
> stop it, there won't be any mixed schools in Virginia.
> —Governor William "Bill" Tuck

On the morning of September 9, 1948, Oliver Hill and Spottswood Robinson unleashed the most potent weapon of all in their struggle against racial oppression and apartheid. The children. Twenty-nine of them, outfitted in their Sunday-school best, gathered outside the Gloucester Training School, a rickety outpost of second-class education situated a crow's cry from the rich marshland and misty riverbanks that edged the secluded Tidewater Virginia county. Already that morning the two civil rights attorneys and a handful of black educators had toured school facilities. The visit confirmed what they instinctively knew to be true: local officials had failed to comply with a federal judge's groundbreaking order, issued less than two months earlier, to bring training-school standards up to par with those for local white schools in time for opening day.

The cluster of ramshackle buildings boasted a splash of fresh paint here, a cut of new linoleum there. But pot-bellied coal stoves still substituted for a central heating plant, and worn exhaust pipes exposed second-floor classrooms as a potential firetrap. A new combination drinking fountain and wash basin had replaced an outdoor pump (often broken) as the primary source of drinking water, but tin buckets nearby signaled that students would still have to haul water to several buildings. Long wooden tables serving as desks hinted at nineteenth-century schooling. Rotting outdoor cubicles passed as lavatories. And supplies for science classes amounted to a few test tubes, several bottles of acid, and—consistent with a school mission focused more on vocational training than on academics—a bottle of auto cleaner and polish.[1]

The hodgepodge came nowhere near to passing the equality test ordered by C. Sterling Hutcheson, a federal judge serving eastern Virginia. The time had come for Hill and Robinson to raise the stakes. First, they planned a brazen reminder that real children were being cheated by shoddy schools. Second, they intended to press in court to see just how far Hutcheson would go to hold school officials to account. Already the judge had surpassed expectations. Months earlier, some two dozen brave Gloucester County parents and guardians had filed suit with support from the state chapter of the National Association for the Advancement of Colored People and the all-black Virginia Teachers Association. Their lawsuit demanded that black children receive an education on par with that of their white peers. Surprisingly, given Hutcheson's conservative political tilt and his roots in Virginia's Southside, a tobacco and peanut region with demographic and cultural kinship to the Deep South, the judge had sided with the plaintiffs in the Gloucester case and three others. To the even greater dismay of many whites, he had done so with marked impatience. His late July order set an almost impossible deadline. Renovations in Gloucester were to be ready by the first day of school in September. Otherwise, school officials risked being held in contempt.[2]

Was Hutcheson prepared to carry through on that threat? No one knew. The two attorneys, little known outside Virginia in 1948 but destined to emerge as giants in the fight to eliminate Jim Crow segregation in America, were determined to find out. Confident, unfazed by confrontation, the forty-one-year-old Hill joined with his quieter, intellectually gifted younger partner, known to friends as Spot.[3] Together they intended to demonstrate to as large an audience as possible that opening day had arrived in Gloucester County and school officials had flunked the judge's test. Lest anyone forget that this foray into legal briefs and courtroom hearings was more than some dry, bloodless exercise, the two lawyers planned to put the children front and center. That day, Hill and Robinson contemplated nothing less bold than attempting to enroll students from the Gloucester Training School in the county's far superior white classrooms.

As the group, some three dozen strong, traveled along the shaded sidewalks of Gloucester Courthouse Village, past public buildings dating to prerevolutionary times, through a silent throng of white onlookers, and up the steps of the all-white Botetourt High School, Hill, Robinson, and J. Rupert Picott, of the teachers' association, led the way. Eighteen elementary-school students and eleven high-school students trailed, the boys in open-collared white shirts or jackets, the girls in prim dresses. The fifth grader Elizabeth Carter set the style in a striped cotton dress with scalloped collar. Frilly bows secured her neatly plaited braids.[4]

Standing six foot one and still basking in his celebrated election to the Richmond City Council just three months earlier, Hill commanded attention. His balding pate, angular nose, and hooded eyelids gave his face a distinctive, almost Middle Eastern cast. He stared straight ahead, frowning slightly. Beside Hill, nine years his junior, the reedy, dark-haired Robinson cast a less imposing physical shadow. Acquaintances knew that appearances were deceptive. The brainy attorney boasted the highest academic average of any Howard University School of Law graduate in memory, including Hill and the NAACP's chief legal counsel, Thurgood Marshall. In deference to that acumen, and with his eye on developing a school-equalization strategy for the entire South, Marshall had tapped Robinson the previous winter to go county by county in Virginia investigating school inequalities and preparing lawsuits.[5] As the group approached Botetourt High School, Robinson smiled faintly at a newspaper cameraman. "We didn't get no further than the auditorium," recalled George Booth, a Brooklyn, New York, retiree who was age ten at the time. He glimpsed a gymnasium outfitted with basketball hoops and trampolines. "It was nice, way better than ours."[6]

Moments later, Principal H. L. Secord greeted the visitors. Cordially but firmly, he dismissed the request to enroll the black students. "I'm very glad to have them register," he said, "but I can't accept them in classes due to the state segregation law." "Because they're Negroes?" inquired Robinson. Ignoring the question, Secord agreed to take the name, age, and address of each applicant. But if the children wanted an education, he suggested, they had best retrace the three miles to the Gloucester Training School. Hill and Robinson had expected no more. They were ready with a prepared response aimed less at school administrators than at the courts and the public: "We intend to pursue our remedies to the fullest extent until our clients receive the opportunities and facilities they are entitled to under the Constitution."[7] As for Booth, "I didn't know what was the outcome of it. When they got through talking, they loaded us up and brought us back to the Training School." All he knew was that "they sure didn't want us at their school."

Back in Richmond, Virginia's corpulent and pugnacious chief executive was preparing a statement of his own. Governor William M. "Bill" Tuck, whose home county abutted that of Judge Hutcheson's in the racially charged Southside, urged calm. He promised that unnamed radical forces seeking to undermine separation of the races would not prevail, and he leveled a swipe at the mounting civil rights advocacy of President Harry S. Truman, who—with reelection balloting two months away—was just beginning to campaign in earnest.

"Certain persons posing as leaders of the Negro race have shocked many people in Virginia by advocating and urging the violation of the constitution of our Commonwealth on the part of public school officials," Tuck said. "Segregation of the races in the public schools is called for in the fundamental law. It has been observed throughout the history of our Commonwealth and will continue to be observed. The advocates of the so-called 'civil rights' program sponsored by President Truman will not force upon the people of Virginia this curse of non-segregation in our schools, which would be offensive to the sensibilities of the better elements of the people of both races."[8] Soon it would be Judge Hutcheson's turn to choose sides.

While few realized it, that September morning and the events that soon followed in Hutcheson's courtroom foretold a tipping point in the nation's long struggle toward an integrated society. Hill and Robinson's foray soon would validate a prophecy made almost two decades earlier by Charles Hamilton Houston, the revered and visionary vice-dean at the Howard University School of Law. Houston had articulated a desegregation strategy hinged on the absurdity of trying to make separate facilities for blacks and whites truly equal. Once the cost and impracticality of that effort was clear, Houston predicted, integration would follow. Because of the universal need for education and its central importance to achieving the American dream, schools should serve as the proving ground. Houston saw the initial goals as integrating graduate and professional programs at southern public universities and equalizing the salaries of black and white teachers in elementary and secondary schools.[9]

"Charlie was wise enough in 1930, he said that that [challenging segregation per se] would be like batting our heads against a stone wall. He said what we need to do was challenge this wall at its weakest point. . . . So the weakest point was inequality. That's what we did," recalled Hill a few years after being awarded the nation's highest civilian accolade, a Presidential Medal of Freedom, in 1999.[10] If Houston was the architect, Hill and Robinson were to be among the master builders, shaping plans and putting them to the test.

By the late 1940s, advocates stood at the brink of fulfilling Houston's vision. After years of fighting school inequality paycheck by paycheck, brick by brick, NAACP attorneys were poised to battle for true integration. A year after the Gloucester case finished playing itself out in Hutcheson's courtroom in the spring of 1949, the US Supreme Court set the dominoes tumbling with decisions integrating graduate and professional schools at state universities in Texas and Oklahoma.[11] Within weeks, the NAACP had dropped all pretenses. Prodded by Robinson, among others, an all-out attack on segregated schools was under way. In the months to come, challenges in South Carolina, Kansas, Delaware, Virginia, and the District of Columbia would combine like separate tributaries into a mighty river of change. The two Virginia lawyers would respond to the passionate imperative of a student strike at R. R. Moton High School in rural Prince Edward County in April 1951 by filing one of the desegregation lawsuits that combined to form the seminal *Brown v. Board of Education of Topeka* ruling, striking down segregated public schools. In hindsight, the outcome of Robinson and Hill's Gloucester case proved a prophetic signal that separate but equal was destined to collapse under its own weight.

The 1954 *Brown* decision did not materialize out of thin air. Some two decades of meticulous groundwork, much of it laid in Virginia, preceded the court decision. Before integration could occur, "separate but equal" education had to be unmasked as a fraud. That painstaking exercise, conducted over many years, involved a slew of attorneys, educators, civil rights activists, and parents. None contributed more to the effort than Hill and Robinson. Hill, vibrant and combative, headed the legal committee of the NAACP's Virginia State Conference of Branches for more than two decades. Robinson, exacting and deliberate, served as the NAACP's chief legal representative for the southeastern United States throughout the 1950s. Together, they were simply "the best local civil rights lawyers that we had anywhere in the South," said former federal judge Robert L. Carter, a Marshall deputy who became chief counsel for the NAACP after the movement's legal apparatus split in the mid-1950s. The historian Patricia A. Sullivan echoed the tribute, calling the pair "the strongest team of civil rights lawyers working in the South."[12]

The Gloucester case was not an anomaly. The Virginians filed, or oversaw the filing of, more lawsuits demanding equal schools than any other grassroots legal team in the nation. "By the spring of 1951 no lawyer in America—with the possible exception of Thurgood Marshall—had logged more combat hours fighting for better schools for Negroes" than Hill or Robinson, wrote the historian-journalist Richard Kluger. At one point, the pair and their allies had legal actions pending in seventy-five Virginia school districts. The *Washington Post* estimated that the equalization campaign resulted in some $50 million (about $500 million in 2016 dollars) in increased spending on teacher salaries, school facilities, and transportation at black schools in the Old Dominion alone.[13] As the results resonated across the South, their fieldwork was the vital underpinning that made *Brown* possible.

Hill and Robinson's contribution to the *Brown* decision extended beyond their challenge to segregated schools in Prince Edward County. After a group of lawyers met in New York in September 1952 to cement arguments for the Supreme Court's crucial first hearing in *Brown*, they deferred to Robinson—as often happened—for the final edit. And when the high court set a rehearing in the historic case for December 1953, it was the painstaking Robinson who refined the arguments of the organization's brightest legal minds into a 235-page brief praised by Kluger as "an eloquent manifesto . . . [deserving of] a place in the literature of advocacy." Kluger deemed Robinson to be Marshall's "most valuable all-around associate."[14] Later, Hill and Robinson fought to reopen schools closed by massive resistance to integration in Norfolk, Charlottesville, Warren County, and Prince Edward. And when foes in Virginia and elsewhere across the South tried to strike a death blow to the NAACP by lashing out at the lawyers' professional ethics, the duo led in carrying the fight for survival to the US Supreme Court.[15]

Nor were those the only landmark cases involving the pair. In *Alston v. School Board of Norfolk* in 1940, a breakthrough in the equality movement, Hill helped establish the right of black teachers to equal pay. In

Irene Morgan v. Commonwealth of Virginia, decided more than a decade before Rosa M. Parks's more celebrated victory, Robinson helped cement the rights of black citizens to travel unencumbered. In *Hurd v. Hodge* and *McGhee v. Sipes*, he helped torpedo covenants barring home sales to blacks. The list goes on. Courtroom actions alone do not capture the full scope of Hill and Robinson's impact, however. Essential as they were to implementing the NAACP's ground game, the Virginians were equally pivotal in charting higher-level strategy, particularly in education, transportation, and housing. Throughout the 1940s and 1950s, they logged thousands of miles traveling to New York, Washington, Atlanta, and elsewhere to join small teams of lawyers hammering out court briefs and planning legal maneuvers. Together, Hill and Robinson helped form a tiny brotherhood of trusted intimates, led by Marshall and largely connected through Howard Law. The group debated theories, practiced arguments, boosted one another's confidence, mourned and mocked setbacks, stoked camaraderie with poker and bourbon (though the ascetic Robinson skipped the liquor), and provided the assembled courage and intellectual fortitude to challenge and defeat a white power structure determined to thwart them at every turn.

Hill brought energy, vision, and drive to the task; Robinson added penetrating legal analysis, scrupulous research and writing, and tenacity, even obstinacy, in the face of trials. Key assets included their proximity in the Upper South to the NAACP's national offices and staff and the strength of an unusually skilled supporting cast of dedicated Virginia attorneys and NAACP officers, particularly their law partner Martin A. Martin; the Alexandria/Emporia activist Samuel W. Tucker; the state NAACP president, J. M. Tinsley; and the executive secretary, W. Lester Banks. Their stubborn defiance of Jim Crow segregation came at considerable personal cost and spanned decades. It began with Hill's 1930s forays into school inequality in southwest Virginia, was joined by Robinson when he graduated from Howard Law and became a faculty member in 1939, and continued through mid-twentieth-century battles to escape a segregationist vortex determined to devour critics of the South's racially divided way of life. At times, the NAACP lawyers moved too fast, demanded too much to suit black community elders schooled in accommodation. At other times, their careful legal calculations frustrated grassroots firebrands impatient for change. But throughout they persisted, convinced that the law and the arc of the moral universe validated their path. Perhaps it is no accident that one or both often stand next to Marshall in photographs of the cadre of lawyers who shaped civil rights strategy in the 1940s and 1950s. "They were involved in all the important cases of that period. No more than a dozen to ten people in the whole country, the whole world" were similarly involved, said Jack Greenburg, who served as director-counsel of the NAACP Legal Defense and Educational Fund, Inc., from 1961 to 1964, succeeding Marshall.[16]

Hill and Robinson were not the only local lawyers to wage the NAACP's fight in the southern hinterlands. Arthur D. Shores of Birmingham, A. P. Tureaud of New Orleans, Colonel A. T. Walden of Atlanta, Z. Alexander Looby of Nashville, Harold R. Boulware of Columbia, J. R. Booker of Little Rock, and T. G. Nutter of Charleston, West Virginia, among others, formed a network of ground support for Marshall and the Legal Defense Fund during the critical years surrounding the mid-twentieth century. But even within that small fraternity of prominent southern black lawyers, Robinson and Hill stood out.[17]

Hill and Robinson's courtroom and community work is less familiar than the images of fire hoses dousing demonstrators in Birmingham in 1963 or police batons cracking the skulls of marchers on the Edmund Pettus Bridge at Selma in 1965. But long before those moments occurred, Hill and Robinson's courageous activism in a state that surpassed any other in restricting political control to a landed, moneyed elite helped launch the revolution. The civil rights movement did not begin in the 1960s. It did not emerge only from marches on Washington or the case files of Thurgood Marshall and the New York offices of the NAACP and its Legal Defense Fund. Important parts of its foundation were laid in Virginia in the 1940s and 1950s by Oliver Hill and Spottswood Robinson. Their little-known story forms a missing link in the long and still-unfinished chain leading from American slavery to racial equality. In bridging the perilous spaces between grassroots activists, top movement commanders, and the white jurists and legislators who often governed their fate, the Virginia duo stand without peer.

As the law firm of Hill, Martin & Robinson prepared to challenge Gloucester County's foot-dragging in contempt hearings before Judge Hutcheson in the fall of 1948, leading whites in the county contemplated the unthinkable. Surely, they reasoned, the courts and the NAACP did not expect them to move heaven and earth to equalize black schools overnight. In an editorial headlined "Time for Tolerance and Calm Thinking," the *Gloucester Gazette–Matthews Journal* applauded the magnanimity of local whites and suggested that black residents think twice before too impatiently challenging the status quo: "Most citizens [read: white citizens] have evidenced little or no resentment" to Hutcheson's equality order because they recognize the legitimacy of the push for equal schools, the editorialist noted. Even though white taxpayers would bear the brunt of any new spending for schools, the community was committed to righting the situation, the writer observed, ignoring the extent to which white wealth was tied to black labor.

Then came a warning: "There will be great resentment, however, against those responsible for any effort to require the localities to conform to these decisions before it is reasonably possible to do so." Lest anyone miss the point, the newspaper underscored the danger. "This resentment will inevitably be manifested by many toward the entire Negro race and not alone the leaders responsible for the unreasonable demands."[18] In an era when racial violence was no idle threat, in other words, Oliver Hill and Spot Robinson were messing with fire. Innocent parties stood to be burned.

Despite the ominous warning, as southern communities went, the county was less fractious than many. Nestled between the York River and the lower Chesapeake Bay in the middle of three scenic peninsulas that sculpt the Virginia shoreline, Gloucester was home to rugged watermen, small-acreage farmers, and a smattering of wealthy plantation owners. A ferry ride separated the county from more populous centers such as Newport News and Williamsburg, creating a sheltered world of creeks and oyster beds, wild daffodils and watermelon patches. "If you owned your own boat and a little piece of land, you were solidly in the middle class," said Frederick R. Carter, a minister and mortician whose father headed the local NAACP during the 1948 school-equalization crisis.[19] Still, neighborliness had its limits. Forced segregation was on ample display in the edition of the *Gazette-Journal* published just after the failed school-registration attempt. White schoolchildren would get free admission to an upcoming agricultural fair on Wednesday, black children on Thursday, the paper reported. The Matthews Cannery would be open on Friday for white patrons only. Church news carried a designated section: "Among the Colored." And a small *w* (white) or *c* (colored) appeared next to the names of those charged with crimes.[20]

When it came to the schools, however, neither the NAACP lawyers nor Judge Hutcheson intended to be swayed by custom. Rebuffed by Principal Secord on opening day, Hill and Robinson quickly regrouped. Years of activism had steeled them against intimidation. Shortly, the firm presented the court with papers accusing school officials of "maliciously, contumaciously, willfully, and contemptuously" ignoring the judge's equalization order—everything, it seemed, shy of tossing the document in a dumpster.[21] Staunchly, Hutcheson ordered a contempt hearing for October 22.

As the day approached, Governor Tuck weighed in on the impending crisis. Addressing the annual meeting of the Virginia commissioners of revenue, a center of support for the conservative political machine headed by US senator Harry F. Byrd, the governor tossed away his prepared remarks. According to the *Richmond Afro-American*, Tuck "wax[ed] vehement, his face becoming a deep crimson" as he roared into a microphone: "I want to tell you right now that if I have the power to stop it, there won't be any mixed schools in Virginia. . . . If the people of New Jersey or some other place want to eat with the colored people, sleep with them and marry them, it's all right with me, but I don't want anybody coming down here to tell this state how to attend to its business."[22]

It was not some carpetbagger, however, but a son of Virginia who was about to level a blow. One of seven sons born to a Southside circuit-court clerk who was a devotee and ally of Senator Byrd, the future judge had grown up in a world where blacks and whites kept to carefully delineated spaces. A brother, writing to the judge in 1954 while staying at a hotel in Live Oak, Florida, revealed his prejudice. "A colored chamber maid of the hotel today had the temerity to sit down in a chair in my room while I was discussing her washing for me," he sniffed. Whatever his family's private persuasions, however, Hutcheson had achieved an intellectual breakthrough by the time the Gloucester County case and its companions reached his courtroom. Legal precedent prescribed separate but equal schools for black and white children. "Equal," Hutcheson had come to believe, meant precisely that.[23] Several years later, in a far more momentous Virginia case overseen by Robinson and Hill, the judge would reveal the limits of his apostasy. But for now Hutcheson had lost patience with excuses.

Undemonstrative but not easily cowed, the somber jurist listened to a handful of witnesses at the October contempt hearing before stopping the proceedings. He had heard enough to know that compliance with his earlier order remained in doubt. Gloucester schools must offer equal courses, equal teaching materials, and equal facilities, he admonished. Lack of money was no excuse. "The court is not interested in how the funds are acquired," Hutcheson said. He ordered the parties to prepare for a December trial. That two-day affair at the stately federal courthouse in downtown Richmond exposed not only Gloucester's racial fissures but also, by extension, those of Virginia and the South. For the most part, Hutcheson listened impassively as white school officials described late-breaking efforts to improve black schools, including a recently approved 60 percent increase in the property tax rate to pay for equalizing teacher salaries and early steps toward a bond referendum for construction.[24] Twice, however, the judge's irritation surfaced. When the school board attorney, C. E. Ford, implied that the principal of the Gloucester Training School might be at fault for the failure to repair a drinking fountain, Hutcheson abruptly stopped testimony. The school board could not "shift its responsibilities" for conditions at the black school onto the principal, he warned. Later, Hutcheson appeared incredulous that in seven months the board had collected only about two-thirds of the 750 signatures needed to schedule a bond referendum. The school board member Wallace Fletcher tried to deflect blame for the anemic effort onto Robinson and Hill. "We were afraid it would backfire if we put too much pressure on it," Fletcher testified. "It hurt us when attorneys for the Negro pupils took Negro children to the Botetourt High School and attempted to register them for the opening of the fall term." "What do you mean?" asked Ford. "Well," said Fletcher, "the citizens just wouldn't sign."[25]

To the delight of Robinson and Hill, the consternation of white school officials, and the surprise of both, Hutcheson's ruling on January 13, 1949, cut through such malarkey to focus on the underlying disparities. Adopting arguments laid out by the NAACP attorneys, Hutcheson said that the Gloucester school officials had made progress, just not enough. Having set in motion preliminary plans for a new black school building, "they leisurely await developments, ignoring their liability under the injunction order," Hutcheson chided. "For nearly two years the defendants have been conferring with architects and not yet have they received even a draft of preliminary plans." The defense claim that the true motivation of plaintiffs was to eliminate segregation of the races was "beside the point," the judge continued. Having allowed black schools to be inferior to white ones, school officials must "exercise diligence and industry" in correcting that condition. He would review the progress of school officials in the spring and weigh punishment accordingly, Hutcheson said.[26]

Overjoyed, the *Richmond Afro-American* labeled the victory "a stunning rebuke" for school officials. The *Gazette-Journal* soberly assessed the options: "We are committed in Virginia to segregation. That fact is recognized by a majority of the better thinking Negroes of our state." With segregation came the responsibility to provide equal schools. "We believe the white citizens of Gloucester are willing to accept that responsibility."[27]

Not so much so. Two months later, by a vote of 591 to 368, Gloucester residents defeated a three-hundred-thousand-dollar bond issue for black schools. Responding in early May, Hutcheson delivered a startling and unprecedented rebuke. Underscoring his earlier contempt ruling, he imposed fines totaling one thousand dollars on four Gloucester school officials. Nor, the judge made clear, were the levies necessarily his last word. Lack of progress could result in even tougher penalties.[28] "This is the kind of talk for which we have been long waiting," exulted the *Afro-American*. An editorial-page cartoon pictured Judge Hutcheson spanking a Gloucester County school official. "They didn't think He'd Keep his Promise," read the cutline.[29]

Those in the know understood that something momentous had occurred in a federal courtroom in eastern Virginia. After almost a decade of laborious struggle spearheaded by Hill and Robinson, the ground had shifted. If a judge who could not be considered a natural ally had been persuaded that black and white schools must be equal under the Virginia constitution and higher-court rulings, and if the price tag of that equality was too onerous for many communities to bear, then there was only one place left to go. Speaking in January, Hill had denied that the purpose of the Gloucester lawsuit was to force school integration, insisting, "Injection of the segregation issue into the case has been a red herring." But Hill's language was carefully nuanced to leave open the possibility of pursuing that goal down the road.[30]

Now, in the wake of the fines, the true nature of the problem for white officials was revealed. Journalists correctly predicted a spike in similar lawsuits across Virginia. And while Gloucester County would struggle successfully over the next several years to patch state and local funding into a new brick school for blacks, a sobering report from the Southern Regional Council suggested just how daunting the segregationists' task would be. The biracial group estimated a cost of $545 million (more than $5.5 billion in 2016 dollars) to equalize school buildings alone, not including salaries and curriculum changes, in eleven southern states. The group's analysis put the value of school property for each black child at $63, compared with $221 for each white pupil. "The white South must either recognize this fact and act accordingly, or else face the prospect of yielding ungracefully to a series of court rulings," the council prophesized.[31]

What Judge Hutcheson had grasped in the elegant writings of Spot Robinson and the passionate pleadings of Oliver Hill was that implementation of the "equal" in Virginia's so-called separate but equal schools had been a travesty. If that was so, and if counties and cities had neither the means nor the will to maintain parallel and equal school systems, then it was only a matter of time until the "separate" part of the equation crumpled as well. Furthermore, Hill, Robinson, and their colleagues knew well that if those structures collapsed in Virginia, the vanguard state in the movement for equalization in elementary and high schools, the rest of the South could not lag far behind. After years of struggle, they had arrived at the cusp of the long-anticipated push for integrated schools.

Battle scarred as the duo were, the vitriol and conniving that awaited them in the 1950s and 1960s would prove a shock. That their dreams of equal and integrated education might elude millions of American children almost seven decades later was beyond imagining. On the long and tortured road to equality, untold miles remained. But on a crisp fall morning in 1948 all that mattered was the task at hand.

ORIGINS, 1907–1939

I went to law school to become a lawyer
so that I could challenge segregation.
—Oliver White Hill

ONE

A World Split by Law and Custom

The final weekend of May 1907 marked a milestone in one of history's most breathtaking reinventions. Forty-two years after General Robert E. Lee trudged toward Appomattox, with Richmond smoldering in ruin behind him, the survivors and offspring of that debacle gathered in the Confederacy's one-time capital to face the war's final challenge: contriving victory out of defeat. Thousands of officers, soldiers, and widows descended on the city for the largest reunion yet of the United Confederate Veterans. Some thirty-one special trains helped transport the small army, braced by a supporting cast of sons, grandsons, and southern belles. Unrepentant southerners served notice. The defiant phoenix known as the New South had no intention of shedding old feathers. Instead its future would be adorned in them.[1]

Before the gathering dispersed four fevered days later, the veterans had driven their stake deeper into the southern soil. Two war heroes joined a growing pantheon of Confederate deities on display in the city. An estimated ten thousand veterans paraded down Franklin Street to mark the unveiling of an equestrian statue of the dashing J. E. B. "Jeb" Stuart, fatally wounded at the tender age of thirty-one at the Battle of Yellow Tavern, just north of Richmond. A few days later, tens of thousands more watched as the dedication of a granite-and-bronze memorial to the late Confederate president, Jefferson Davis, marked the reunion's grand finale. Fireworks shimmered. Balloons hoisted Confederate flags high into sullen skies. And the sweet voices of schoolchildren trilled nostalgic anthems. "Until the end of time," the *Richmond Times-Dispatch* promised, "the glory of the day will live in history."[2]

For an African American baby born into a separate Richmond a few weeks earlier, on May 1, 1907, the reunion held far darker implications. For him, the hoopla could be taken as a threat, a sinister introduction to the zealotry and myopia of a world of which he was not a part and to which his very existence would one day pose a threat. That infant, Charles B. White, gained his name from an uncle, the younger brother of a father who quickly disappeared from the child's life. Soon, Charles would take a different name, although it would be thirty-five years before he petitioned a Richmond city court to make the change official. Oliver, after his mother, Olivia. White, for the paternal family into which he was born. Hill, from his stepfather, Joseph C. Hill, whom Olivia would marry when her son was four years old. It was by that name, Oliver White Hill, that the child would one day make his mark.[3]

Law and custom divided blacks and whites in the society into which Oliver Hill and, nine years later, Spottswood William Robinson III were born. Race relations in both Richmond and the Old Dominion were a mixed bag. On the one hand, an unusually large contingent of free blacks in the capital (nearly one-fifth of the city's black population before the war) helped create a postwar black entrepreneurial class that gratified civic boosters. Notables included the indomitable Maggie L. Walker, the first female president of a chartered bank in America; John Mitchell Jr., an intrepid newspaper editor who early in his career excoriated white powerbrokers for their injustices; and Giles Beecher Jackson, a more conciliatory lawyer who drew personal congratulations from President Theodore Roosevelt after engineering an eye-catching exhibit on black progress at the 1907 Jamestown Ter-Centennial Exposition. From 1890 to 1920 "Richmond was considered the most important center of Negro business activity in the world," a 1940 Works Progress Administration report proclaimed. For years, Virginia's white leaders smugly, and largely correctly, boasted that the state stood apart from much of the South by treating black citizens within the rule of law. Lynching, for instance, was comparatively rare, although that is not to say that no brutal racial killings occurred. Dozens did.[4]

On the other hand, the twin evils of slavery and prejudice pierced the very marrow of Richmond's and Virginia's bones. City fathers liked to cite tobacco manufacturing, flour mills, and ironworks as Richmond's primary antebellum industries. In fact, a far more sordid enterprise—slave markets—had emerged as the city's foremost economic driver by the 1850s. The historian Michael Chesson identified Richmond as "the center of the [slave] trade for the seaboard South," second only to New Orleans as the nation's slave mart. Human bondage, with its attendant suffering and degradation, lined city coffers. Moreover, to say that the state operated lawfully is faint praise given that many laws demeaned and debased blacks as second-class citizens. Revisions to the Virginia constitution adopted in 1902, five years before Hill's birth, had the unapologetic intent of whittling black voting to a sliver. Carter Glass, a future US senator and secretary of the treasury under President Woodrow Wilson, famously laid out the target: "Discrimination! Why that is precisely what we propose . . . with a view to the elimination of every negro voter who can be gotten rid of, legally, without materially impairing the numerical strength of the white electorate." Results mirrored intent. In Richmond's Jackson Ward, the boyhood neighborhood of both Hill and Robinson, the number of registered black voters dwindled from almost three thousand to thirty-three after the new constitution took effect.[5]

Significantly, the revised constitution also cemented the separation of black and white schoolchildren, an arrangement dictated since 1870 only by statute. "White and colored children shall not be taught in the same school," ordered article 9, section 140. Separate, most assuredly, did not mean equal as tacitly promised in the Supreme Court's infamous 1896 decision, *Plessy v. Ferguson*. In the 1920s, the state spent four times as much educating each white child as it did educating each black child. Localities maintained four hundred four-year high schools for white children and only eight for black youth.[6]

Efforts to legalize racial separation intensified in the years surrounding Hill's and Robinson's births and childhoods. Emboldened by *Plessy*, the Virginia General Assembly in 1900 passed the state's first Jim Crow transportation law, demanding separate railroad cars for blacks and whites. In fact, Jim Crow had long been the de facto policy of life in Richmond and elsewhere across Virginia in settings ranging from hospitals to cemeteries to streetcars. When the legislature authorized (but did not require) localities to make streetcar segregation mandatory in 1904, an outraged black community in Richmond took to the streets with a boycott. Rallied by the fiery John Mitchell, black travelers walked for months. The boycott helped nearly bankrupt the Virginia Passenger and Power Company, but the protest became moot when the legislature in 1906 ordered segregated streetcars statewide. In 1911 Richmond adopted the state's first ordinance requiring racially segregated neighborhoods. One observer called it "the most elaborate and comprehensive racial zoning law in the nation." The statute caused consternation among blacks until a Supreme Court decision six years later invalidated that ordinance and similar ones.[7]

Two particularly crude pieces of legislation underscored the determination of white elites to keep blacks separate and subservient. The false science of eugenics lent an aura of legitimacy to the scheme. Virginia's Racial Integrity Act of 1924 decreed that only those with "no trace whatsoever" of nonwhite blood could be deemed Caucasian. The single exception, in deference to blue bloods claiming descent from Pocahontas and John Rolfe, went to those with one-sixteenth or less American Indian blood. Zealously enforced by Walter A. Plecker, director of the Bureau of Vital Statistics and an unapologetic white supremacist, the law greatly expanded the number of Virginians deemed "colored." Those unfortunates paid a severe price in matters ranging from education to marriage to voting. Two years later, the legislature underscored its contempt for minorities with adoption of the Virginia Public Assemblages Act, mandating racial separation in public places. The white editor of the *Daily Press* of Newport News, outraged after he and his wife were seated beside black patrons during a dance recital at the Hampton Institute in February 1925, launched the protest that led to passage of the act.[8]

Black Virginians were not entirely impotent in the face of such assaults. In the 1921 gubernatorial election, after Democrats accused Republicans of favoring blacks by advocating repeal of the poll tax and Republicans fought the charge by proclaiming a "lily-white" party, John Mitchell rebutted the blatant racism by heading an all-black slate of candidates. He lost badly, garnering just over 5,000 out of about 210,000 cast in the gubernatorial race. Still, a protest had been registered. Black citizens also won occasional victories in the courts, as when a reinvigorated NAACP chapter in Norfolk successfully fought a 1925 residential segregation ordinance and James O. West of Richmond in 1929 established his right to vote in a Democratic primary run by the state.⁹ But for the most part, the city and state in which the future civil rights champions gained their start flaunted a racial caste system in which whites occupied superior roles and blacks lived, in effect, as an underclass of untouchables.

No law was needed to segregate Hill and Robinson's neighborhood. That had occurred already without formal prodding. Jackson Ward, located about a mile northwest of Capitol Square, served as the political, cultural, and economic center of black Richmond. Originally populated by a smorgasbord of free blacks, slaves, Jews, and other European immigrants, the ward became an almost entirely African American enclave as the twentieth century unfolded. In its nicer sections, two-story brick Italianate homes with narrow porches and postage-stamp yards encased by knee-high wrought-iron fences lined many of the streets. Robinson, who grew up there in the 1920s in relative prosperity, lived in one such house. Other buildings were subdivided into apartments or rooms for boarders, and a proliferation of absentee landlords contributed to a decline in upkeep. Italian-run confectionaries and small groceries, often owned by Jews, dotted many of the corners. Black-owned businesses, ranging from banks and insurance companies to small mom-and-pop operations, prospered as well, at least for a time. For a child, the segregated neighborhood fostered a sense of security and camaraderie that had little to do with economics. "It was a beautiful place to live. People knew each other," recalled Thelma Fant, a Richmond native who grew up in the ward.¹⁰

To other eyes, however, housing in portions of Jackson Ward constituted "dilapidated, unsanitary shacks," many lacking running water and indoor toilets.¹¹ A 1913 photograph of cluttered, ramshackle housing on a hillside dipping into nearby Shockoe Valley might well have captured the St. James Street address where Hill lived with his great-grandmother and grand-aunt for his first six years. "I'm sure we were poor as Job's turkey," Hill said, recalling the small home, but he retained fond memories of chicken-and-dumplings Sunday dinners and mischievous high jinks as he ran free with other young boys through streets and muddy alleyways. In wintertime, he enviously watched older boys sled down the north side of the Shockoe ravine past a historic African American burial ground, sail across railroad tracks at the bottom, and land partway up the hillside where he lived.[12] Not far beyond their starting point, St. James Street abruptly became North Avenue. There, the black world Hill knew just as speedily turned white.

Olivia Lewis White Hill was absent for most of her son's early life. Born in 1888, Hill's mother was the product of an illicit liaison between a young black woman, Nannie Lewis, and a white student at the Medical College of Virginia. Olivia, a pragmatic, no-nonsense woman who could easily have passed for white, learned early the vicissitudes of life. Raised by a single mother, she apparently retained some knowledge of her father, who practiced medicine in New York, because she once asked her son if he would like to visit him. Hill declined.

Olivia's first marriage ended badly. Her husband, William Henry White Jr., was the fifth child and first son of a stern, charismatic, and bristle-bearded Baptist minister who founded the Mount Carmel Baptist Church and whose congregants included Oliver's great-grandmother and grand-aunt. The senior White and his wife, Kate Garnett White, who was reputed to be part Native American, were baptized in the early 1880s into the membership of Ebenezer Baptist Church, one of Jackson Ward's venerable institutions. A few years later, in a service preached by Professor J. E. Jones of Virginia Union University, White received his ordination and was authorized to launch one of several churches seeded by Ebenezer. When Mount Carmel conducted its first baptism ceremony in October 1888, several thousand festive celebrants reportedly wound their way through city streets to Bacon's Quarter Branch, a small stream located near the northern edge of Jackson Ward.[13]

By the time of Oliver's birth, Mount Carmel and its parsonage were located on North First Street in Jackson Ward, a busy thoroughfare just a stone's throw from the Lewis home. It is reasonable to assume that Olivia met the roguish and tempting William Jr. at the church attended by her family. State records list William's age as twenty-one and Olivia's as twenty at the time of their marriage, April 15, 1906. But if the birth date on her death certificate is correct, she actually was just seventeen, still several months shy of her eighteenth birthday. Oliver was born a year later, and the marriage quickly collapsed. William left, returned briefly, and then abandoned the family for good. A printer by trade, "he was kind of a ne'er do well and an alcoholic," said Oliver White Hill Jr. of the grandfather he never met.[14]

Faced with calamity, Olivia packed her bags and set off in search of employment at the luxurious Homestead Hotel resort in the Allegheny Mountains town of Hot Springs, Virginia, west of Roanoke. Leaving her son with her grandmother, she found work dipping water for white guests from the mineral springs. She also caught the eye of a mild-mannered and reliable hotel bellman, Joe Hill. When Olivia's divorce became final in 1911, they married. A few years later, Nannie Lewis, who had been living in Scranton, Pennsylvania, became ill and returned to her mother's home in Richmond to die. Olivia and Joe traveled to Richmond for the funeral, and Oliver experienced his first conscious awareness of his mother. The relationship, he said, "jelled instantly." With her life stabilized, Olivia wanted her son at her side. She and Joe had moved from Hot Springs to Roanoke, where Joe had opened a pool hall. When they returned home after the funeral, Oliver accompanied them. At age six, he was about to begin the second, brighter phase of his childhood.[15]

When Hill arrived in Roanoke, the city was a mere three decades into its metamorphosis from a sleepy railroad stop to an industrialized boomtown of the New South. The transformation began with the 1882 decision of a Philadelphia investment company to locate the headquarters and machine shops of the Norfolk and Western and Shenandoah Valley railroads at the site. By 1910, with a population of about thirty-five thousand, the city was Virginia's third largest. Eight thousand or so of those residents were black.[16] Life for Roanoke's black population was characterized by the same bootstrap struggle to overcome enforced, second-class isolation that prevailed throughout the South. One of the worst episodes of racial violence in state history had occurred there two decades before Hill's arrival. The September 1893 robbery and severe beating of a white farmwoman who had come to town to sell produce had led to a confrontation between police officials and a white mob that left eight dead and thirty-one wounded. The black man accused of the crime had eventually been captured and horribly killed, and the mayor, blamed for early attempts to protect him, had been forced to temporarily flee town.[17] City fathers had strived to diminish the scars, but a wary distance between the races remained.

Fortunately for the young Hill, his parents found lodgings at the home of Bradford Pentecost, a Norfolk and Western Railway chef, and his wife, Lelia. The pair would become two of the most influential people in Hill's life. Accepting the American Bar Association's award for pro bono publico work late in life, Hill credited the Pentecosts, along with his mother and stepfather, for instilling "a sense of self esteem and respect for my own [self] and also respect for the human dignity of other person[s] irrespective of their economic or social status."[18] The Pentecosts became Oliver's surrogate parents after Prohibition closed Joe Hill's pool hall and the Hills returned to Hot Springs to work. Concerned about inadequate black schooling in Bath County, Virginia, Olivia had agreed to separate from her son once again. Later, when the couple moved to Washington, DC, so that Joe could work in the Navy Yard during World War I, she elected not to interrupt Oliver's education. Not until 1923, when he had finished the eight years of schooling then offered Roanoke's black students, did Hill rejoin his parents. In the meantime, the Pentecosts introduced Oliver to a black middle-class world he had barely glimpsed. The benefits extended well beyond economic comfort. The couple modeled attitudes and behavior that fortified Oliver for a lifetime—pride in his race, an insistence on respect from whites, and an expectation that he would attend college and make something of his life.[19]

"Between birth and fifteen, I lived on three different economic levels," Hill once noted. In his early years, "I was a poor folks' child, but a very happy one." Next, he lived an upper-middle-class life with the Pentecosts. And when he rejoined his parents to attend Washington's prestigious Dunbar High School, he dropped to lower-middle-class status. "So I went through the whole shebang of economic, social conditions," something he considered a fortunate life lesson.[20]

Oliver lived with the Pentecosts in a comfortable, two-story, white wood-frame home at 401 Gilmer Avenue in Roanoke's Gainesboro neighborhood. There, he absorbed valuable lessons. Lelia Pentecost, who in later years signed her letters "your other mother," was a full-cheeked, dignified woman with upswept hair who expected to be treated with the same respect as white matrons. She took pride in never having worked outside her home, and she cultivated a reputation for sending packing any traveling salesman who addressed her by her first name or failed to remove his hat upon entering her home. Naturally sociable, Hill acquired added confidence from Mrs. Pentecost's example. "From early childhood I developed personal esteem and expected white folks to treat me like they did one another in such settings," he said. That lesson was reinforced on a day when a white man rounded up a number of Gainesboro boys, including

Oliver, with the promise of a chance to make money. He took them across town, applied blindfolds, and set them to fighting one another in a make-shift boxing ring for the amusement of white gawkers. A strong, stocky youth, Oliver held his own. He returned proudly to Gilmer Avenue with fifty cents in his pocket. To his surprise, his reward was a whipping and an admonishment from Mrs. Pentecost to never again make a fool of himself for white folks.[21]

Bradford Pentecost possessed a more subdued temperament, but he too could be riled. A talented chef recruited by Norfolk and Western to upgrade its dining-car service, he was well paid and a respected community elder. Pentecost made frequent three-day trips to such cities as Birmingham, Alabama, and Columbus, Ohio. He often returned home with newspapers that introduced his young charge to a larger world. Oliver also benefited from witnessing the fearlessness with which Pentecost was prepared to take on several white men who had threatened and terrified the boy. Ever alert to opportunities to make money, Hill one day watched some older boys pick up discarded whiskey bottles and return them to a distillery for pocket change. He did the same, but when he got to the second floor of the building, someone yelled, "Get the little nigger and cut his balls out." Several men chased him around the floor until he escaped. Whether the episode was serious or in jest, Hill never knew. But the next day, a "mad-as-hell" Pentecost marched Oliver back to the distillery, ready to confront the abusers. The building was empty, and eventually Pentecost had to leave to go to work. Nothing came of the incident, but Hill knew he had a defender.[22] Oliver welcomed the bond because by then any dreams of reconciling with his own father had collapsed.

Back in Richmond to visit his great-grandmother a few years after his departure, Hill was surprised to receive a visit from his biological father. He was then nine years old, and so far as Oliver could recall, the two had never met. He described the disastrous encounter in his autobiography: "One day he took me out for a streetcar ride. Unfortunately, it wasn't a very enjoyable ride. I became nauseated by the odors emitted by the electric trolley. . . . To make matters worse, my father had the nerve to ask me did I want to come live with him. That was a stupid question to ask a nine-year-old kid who had never seen him before."[23] It was their last meeting. Years later, Hill tried to track down his father in New York, where he was reputed to be living. The effort failed. From childhood on, the two parental male figures in Oliver's life were his stepfather, Joe Hill, with whom he had a congenial relationship, and Bradford Pentecost.

The young Hill was good at sports and at games, and he was a natural leader among a pack of boys who roamed the streets, sometimes engaging in rock fights with similar bands of young white boys. One seldom-mentioned incident from that era instilled a lifelong lesson. As a civil rights crusader, Hill combined a capacity for outrage with a pragmatic ability to apply the brakes when tempers soared. An explosive moment that could have wrecked his life inspired years of struggle to tamp his emotions. "I had a terrible temper when I was a kid, but I ran into an incident one time, and it scared me so that I put forth extra effort to controlling it," Hill recalled. When he was about twelve years old, Hill found a stiletto knife, which he prized. He made a case for it, "used to carry it around," and practiced flinging it with accuracy into a board. One day he got into a heated argument with a boy named Herschel, the older brother of a good friend. Furious, Oliver chased Herschel down the street and into his house. As Herschel ran out the back door, he pulled the door shut behind him. At that very instant, Oliver—racing through the front door—pulled out his stiletto and flung it down the hall. The knife embedded, quivering, in the middle of the just-closed door. "Boy, it scared me to death, because I realized that if that knife had struck him in the back, it could have killed him. And I ran down there and got my stiletto, ran back home, grabbed the axe and broke it up, and never carried a knife, except on occasion, again. That was an experience I had that made me careful about my temper. I can get mad in a quick cent."[24]

Other memories of the Roanoke years focused on a series of jobs. His work began with house chores as a young boy and extended to ice-wagon deliveries and three-in-the-morning risings to hawk copies of Roanoke and New York newspapers. In school, he was a mediocre student, tripped up by poor grades in conduct. But there seems never to have been malevolence in the mischief or any question that his education would extend beyond the limit then offered to Roanoke's black children. Finishing eighth grade at the inaccurately named Harrison "High" School, Hill faced the choice of attending black academies in Richmond, Petersburg, and Lawrenceville— or moving to Washington, DC, to attend the excellent Dunbar High and live with his parents. That was an easy decision. He headed north.[25]

In the years that followed, as Hill completed high school and moved on to Howard, he studied moderately, played hard, and was employed steadily. He also found time for sports. A high-water mark at Dunbar came during his last football game in the autumn of 1926, when he threw for a game-winning touchdown and then kicked the extra point. The next year, as a Howard freshman, he repeated the feat before suffering a career-ending injury. He continued on the varsity basketball team. On campus, "I was a happy-go-lucky guy," an attitude reflected in his first-semester grades at Howard—Cs in English, history, and physical education and an incomplete in German. But if his classroom performance was spotty, he was gaining an astonishingly broad education in human nature and self-sufficiency. Beginning in high school, Hill worked summer jobs at resort hotels in Pennsylvania, Massachusetts, and Connecticut, glimpsing sophisticated worlds, partying late, and honing his mastery of poker and blackjack. In the summer of 1929, at age twenty-two, while a junior at Howard, he traveled across the continent as a Canadian Pacific Railway employee, taking in breathtaking scenery and interacting with an older, harder-boiled railroad crew. Despite temptations, he kept perspective: "One thing I was taught early in life was never to raise so much hell over the weekend that I couldn't go to work on Monday morning."[26] Throughout his college years, "there were occasions where I stayed up all night, went home, set the alarm, got in bed, slept for as short a period as half an hour, got up, got dressed, and went to work." But despite his extroverted, fun-seeking nature, "most of the time I functioned in a rather moderate and conventional manner."[27]

A dawning purpose now underlay that prudence. A seminal event occurred during his second year at Howard. Sam Hill, his stepfather's brother, died from a cerebral hemorrhage. Sam Hill worked primarily at the post office, but he maintained a small law practice on the side. After his death, Hill's widow passed his law books to Oliver. Reading those pages, he glimpsed for the first time how entwined the fortunes of his race were with the Constitution and the Supreme Court's interpretations of it. Years later, Hill recalled that *Plessy v. Ferguson* particularly had astonished him: "I thought they'd lost their cotton-picking minds. There wasn't any question in my mind. [Segregation] violated the Fourteenth and Fifteenth Amendments—the Fourteenth Amendment in particular."[28]

Whether Hill so early in life fully grasped the import of amendments that would not become central to the NAACP's antisegregation strategy until some years later is open to question.[29] But there is no doubt that he saw the gift of the law books and his early reading of them as a turning point in his personal evolution. He resolved to try to correct a terrible wrong. The path to that outcome, he realized, lay in a career in the law.

Young Spottswood Robinson also was moving toward a rendezvous with the Howard University School of Law, but by a different path. Nine years Hill's junior, born on July 26, 1916, Robinson grew up surrounded by the accoutrements of Richmond's black professional class. If it was not exactly a silk-stocking existence, there was little doubt that the family would be protected—in flush times and bad—by at least warm woolens. A good address in Jackson Ward, the business acumen of his father and grandfather, and a notable family pedigree ensured that status. According to family records, one of Robinson's great-great-grandmothers was the sister of James Payne, a Richmond native who became the fourth president of the Republic of Liberia. His grandmother, Nannie, was the granddaughter of Powhatan Roberts White, a mixed-race lawyer prominent in the city after the Civil War. White died spectacularly along with dozens of others in April 1870 when a balcony and second-floor courtroom in the capitol collapsed into the House of Delegates chamber below.[30]

The first Spottswood William Robinson was a slave who as a young boy reputedly walked away from his master's farm in Spotsylvania County, made his way to Richmond, and melded into the city's potpourri of free blacks and slaves. "I expect he changed his name and blended in," said Nina Robinson Govan, daughter of the civil rights attorney and great-granddaughter of the senior Robinson. "A young person could move to the city and start working, and no one would think twice." After emancipation, the enterprising Robinson opened a liquor store and bar at 19–21 North Eighteenth Street, near a downtown farmers' market. Letterhead stationery retained by the family advertises four "full quarts" of I. W. Harper Whiskey for five dollars and an equal amount of Shaw's Malt Tonic & Beverage for four dollars. When Prohibition jeopardized Robinson's livelihood, he regrouped, launching a Jackson Ward grocery that later became his son's real-estate office. An early photograph shows a nicely groomed, mustachioed Robinson in white apron and tie with well-stocked shelves of cans and tins behind him. His daughter Mamie, a raven-haired beauty, sits nearby.[31]

Robinson Sr. and his wife, Nannie, reared four children to adulthood.

A fifth died in infancy after swallowing a penny. The eldest was Spottswood W. Robinson Jr., father of the future civil rights attorney. Foreseeing the demise of his father's liquor business, Robinson Jr. cofounded a real-estate firm in 1916 at age twenty-three. He nurtured it into a thriving enterprise including rentals, sales, loans, and insurance. By the 1920s his business had become so demanding that he persuaded his father to give up the grocery store and become his chief assistant. Robinson Jr. surely valued the help, because by then he was pursuing a dream—study of the law. Unable as a black man to gain admittance to the state's white law schools, Robinson Jr. leapt at the opportunity when Richmond's Virginia Union University opened an evening law department in 1922. Founded by the American Baptist Home Mission Society in the aftermath of the Civil War, the school relished its mission of bringing education to previously deprived black citizens. Robinson Jr. proved to be a star pupil, graduating magna cum laude in 1926. He gained admittance to the Virginia bar that same year. From then until Union discontinued the law department in 1931, he taught courses in property and partnership law, areas that would also intrigue his son.[32]

In an admiring tribute to his father published in 1982, Spottswood Robinson III noted that "this Unionite ministered to his clientele as a respected member of the bar in Richmond." Among his clients were "the many small as well as the few large, and he gave them all his best." Adding to his ongoing success in real estate, Robinson Jr. served as vice-chairman and general counsel of the Virginia Mutual Benefit Life Insurance Company and as a vice-president of the Consolidated Bank & Trust Company, both black owned.[33]

Despite Robinson Jr.'s quick mind and esteem in prominent black circles, some family members believe that he could have accomplished more had it not been for a weakness for alcohol. "He grew up in the saloon. He had a problem with alcohol," acknowledged Govan, who recalled her grandfather with great fondness. As a child, she lived in a three-generation household, and she remembered warmly her grandfather's singing at the player piano, conducting word and spelling games at the dinner table, and treating her to cherry tarts and French twirls from a nearby bakery. But there was a darker side, including occasional phone calls informing the family that her grandfather needed to be escorted home. Much as he admired his father, but not wanting to enable the behavior, Spottswood III refused to go.

His resolve may have been strengthened by memories of his father being arrested twice in the early 1930s, once on disorderly charges and once for "reckless and careless driving of an automobile (drunk)." Both charges were dismissed, but the incidents likely made a deep impression on a son then in his mid-teens. Throughout adulthood, the future judge was a tee-totaler, underscoring his disciplined nature and perhaps his dismay at his father's weakness.[34]

Spottswood Robinson III—called William by his well-educated mother—was the first of three children born to Inez Clement Robinson and Robinson Jr. Inez Clement attended both Hartshorn Memorial College in Richmond, a women's school later incorporated into Virginia Union, and Howard before settling into the life of a homemaker.[35] The couple's middle child, Nancy Robinson Funn, married a New York funeral director and became a housewife. The youngest, Isadore Robinson Burke, rose to become supervising real-estate manager for the Housing and Development Administration of New York City. Robinson III began life in a household that included his parents and his paternal grandparents. While his immediate environs offered a secure cocoon, elsewhere the 1920s were a perilous time for blacks. Nationally, tensions smoldered.

A year after Robinson's birth, several thousand whites in East Saint Louis, Illinois, upset by black competition for jobs, went on a rampage that killed at least forty blacks and eight whites and left hundreds homeless. That was a forewarning of chaos to come. Two years later, when Robinson was three, the so-called Red Summer race riots of 1919 drenched the nation in a bloodbath of arson and violence. Rioting broke out in more than three dozen communities, from large cities such as Washington, DC, and Omaha, Nebraska, to smaller outposts such as Jenkins County, Georgia, and Elaine, Arkansas. In Chicago alone, a week of fury after the drowning death of an African American teenager left thirty-eight dead and more than five hundred seriously wounded. An estimated two thousand homes and apartments were damaged, and the mayhem cost millions in property damage and related bills. Two years after that, in the summer of 1921, when Robinson was about to turn five, violence decimated the African American community in Tulsa, Oklahoma. During a terrifying eighteen hours, spawned by unsubstantiated claims that a nineteen-year-old black shoeshine boy had accosted a white female elevator operator, furious whites burned the black section of town to the ground. Credible estimates of the number killed range as high as three hundred. Thousands were left homeless.[36]

Such harsh racial realities encroached minimally on Robinson's early life. His basic needs could be met within a few blocks of his home at the intersection of Leigh and Adams Streets in Jackson Ward. The castlelike Monroe Elementary School, housed in an old armory, and the more contemporary Armstrong High School, where he would graduate in 1932 at age fifteen, stood just to the west. He walked one block east to Booker T. Washington School for sixth and seventh grades. Across the street from the Robinson home were the sedate and upper-crust Saint Phillips Episcopal Church, which the men of the family attended, and, should the need arise, W. I. Johnson's Funeral Home. A private hall for dances and parties and an Italian confectionary for small sundries helped make up his block. Around the corner and one block up was the black library, affectionately known as the "Double O" because of its address at oo Clay Street, where East Clay ended and West Clay began. Not until the late 1940s would the city's main library open its doors to black citizens, including schoolchildren. Two blocks east lay Jackson Ward's busy Second Street commercial area. Attractions included the popular Hippodrome and Globe Theatres and the True Reformers Hall, operated by a leading beneficial society and the site of lectures and other community gatherings.[37]

The Robinsons' immediate neighbors were a cross section of black Richmond. Relatively well-to-do families, including the Robinsons, the owners of Johnson's Funeral Home, and the president of a fraternal society rubbed shoulders daily with an educational and economic hodgepodge. Close neighbors included a tobacco factory laborer, a janitor, a presser in a clothing store, a porter in a confectionary store, a peddler of fish and oysters, an elementary-school teacher, a box factory laborer, a cook at a private club, and a servant in a private home.[38] That segregated world had obvious disadvantages. Schools lacked gymnasiums and other staples of white education. Instructional books were secondhand castoffs from John Marshall High and other white schools. Clothes bought at white-owned stores on nearby Broad Street could not be tried on in advance of purchase. Even so, a quality teaching force instructed young minds, and for many residents of Jackson Ward, life was far from miserable. "There wasn't any fear in those days of being abducted. We had free rein," recalled W. Ferguson Reid, who lived near his friend Spot Robinson in the 100 block of

Leigh Street, known as "Quality Row." Prestigious residents of the Row included Maggie Walker. "Everybody in the block could tell you what to do. If you did anything wrong, they went straight to your mother. You had to be home when the street lights came on," said Reid, who became a physician and the twentieth century's first black member of the Virginia General Assembly.[39]

As a boy, Spot III foreshadowed his adult self—rail-thin yet able to hold his own at tennis and basketball; sociable but content to be alone. Reid recalled the future civil rights attorney as serious, patient, precise, and detail-oriented, all qualities that surfaced in his later work. By the age of twelve he had begun to help out at the real-estate office, first answering phones and sweeping up at day's end. Later, he graduated to more complex tasks. Once, the younger Reid happened into Robinson's bedroom and found him constructing a model of Charles Lindbergh's airplane, the *Spirit of St. Louis,* from plans in *Popular Mechanics* magazine. The challenge included magnifying the dimensions of the plans and creating a structure that would fly. "It was the first time I'd seen someone take two-dimensional paper and make a three-dimensional object," Reid said. The propeller had to be carved from wood, and a rubber band manipulated to produce movement. He recalled Robinson's exhaustive explanation of the process. "Spot had a way of, if you ask him a question, he's going to give you a long, detailed answer," Reid said. Years later, when Robinson designed his own home and built his own fishing boat, the engineer's mindset resurfaced. "Anything he went into, he went into methodically."[40]

If there was a major drawback to the Robinsons' Leigh Street address, it was traffic. Before the time of interstate highways, Route 1, a main north-south corridor, ran down Leigh Street. Noisy, smoky trucks and buses joined cars and the occasional horse-drawn delivery cart to congest the road in front of the family home. The inconvenience helped spur interest by Robinson Jr. when a group formed to create a subdivision for affluent, upper-class blacks about a mile and a half to the north of Jackson Ward. In what would become known as Frederick Douglass Court, in tribute to the nineteenth-century abolitionist leader, the University Realty Company in 1919 laid out 113 lots on land accessible by streetcar and adjacent to Virginia Union University. By 1930, census records show, the Robinsons had joined the exodus. Their new home at the corner of Dubois and Langston Avenues (named for the African American luminaries

W. E. B. Du Bois and Langston Hughes) was a two-story frame and stucco "foursquare" structure with an A-shaped roof, a sun parlor, hardwood floors, and steam heat.[41]

Spot III and other Douglass Court youth rode the trolley car or walked to Armstrong High School, competed for Boy Scout merit badges in an all-black troop, and persuaded their parents to let them build a tennis court on a vacant lot. Working together, they removed the topsoil to create a clay court. Several, including Robinson, became proficient players. He honed swimming skills and a lifetime passion for fishing at Echo Lake, a rural property northwest of Richmond that was owned by an African American farmer and preacher, Jacob E. Lewis. Over time, fishing and woodworking would become the pastimes that freed Robinson from the intellectually exhausting task of shaping legal briefs and courtroom strategies.[42] Graduating from Armstrong High, with ceremonies held at the city auditorium the evening of June 10, 1932, Robinson ranked eighth academically among 123 graduates. His grade-point average of 89.1 did not match his later achievement at the Howard School of Law, but it was respectably solid.[43]

When Robinson entered Virginia Union a few months later, just past his sixteenth birthday, his ambitions were as yet unformed. From childhood, he had been pressed by his father to become a lawyer. "That was drilled into me as soon as I was old enough to understand. I didn't have any inclination to be a lawyer. I resisted the idea clean up to the time that I went to law school," Robinson said. What he preferred was to become "an engineer of some sort. I like to use my imagination or I like to use my hands. I enjoy creating." Under his father's tutelage, however, he signed up for business courses, tacitly acknowledging that the real-estate firm was a future employment option as well.[44] At Union, Robinson encountered a school bound by tradition and propriety. The university catalog advised incoming students that conduct was expected to be "in harmony with the teachings of the Scripture, the spirit of the Golden Rule and the behavior of gentlemen." Liquor, pool, and gambling were strictly prohibited. Even card playing on campus was taboo. Attendance was required at daily chapel and Sunday-afternoon preaching.[45] None of that appears to have been a problem for the congenial and conscientious young man whose chief vice was having taken up smoking at age fourteen.

There was no hint that the Spot Robinson who entered Union in 1932 was destined to become a major force in the nation's drive for racial equality. Beyond engineering and possibly architecture, his passion was tennis. "My family was not by any means well-to-do, but even through the Depression years, we managed to be comfortable," Robinson said about his early life. "I was sensitive to the segregated society here in Richmond, but I was living within it. I never had—I was never caught in racial fights or anything of that sort. I was very resentful of it [segregation], but during that time—and this would have been up to 1936 when I got to law school—it was something, while not accepted, it was something that you just lived with. I think the philosophy of my time, [one] we had in common with a great many others, was that we have this condition of things, but we can still lead a good life."[46]

Meanwhile, some one hundred miles to the north in Washington, Robinson's future law partner, Oliver Hill, already was engaged in a personal metamorphosis from unformed youth to civil rights revolutionary. A similar evolution awaited Robinson, his transformation several years away.

TWO

A First-Class Law School

"Peace. It is truly *wonderful*." Hands hoisted in mock salute to the Reverend Major Jealous Divine, better known to thousands of devotees as Father, the two lanky, jovial Howard Law students boomed out the prescribed catchphrase as they ducked into the downtown Washington diner for lunch. The peace slogan and a quarter netted customers a plate of down-home cooking—pork chops or turkey, baked beans, potatoes, macaroni, peas, tomatoes, biscuits or corn bread, peaches, cake or pie, and tea. Thirty-five cents produced an extra large helping. Oliver Hill typically took the twenty-five-cent plate; his buddy Thurgood Marshall was a thirty-five-cent man. Neither of the young men subscribed to Father Divine's International Peace Mission Movement, with its emphasis on abstinence from liquor, tobacco, and even sex with a marital partner, but they shared at least one trait with the diminutive, gourd-faced Harlem evangelist: both liked to eat.[1] And in the first years of the Great Depression, when money was tight and every cent counted, the price was right at Father Divine's kitchen.

The lunchtime camaraderie was a welcome break for law-school best friends whose daily schedules in the fall and winter of 1930 were an exhaustive grind. Marshall was up before daybreak six days a week to catch the train from Baltimore to Washington's Union Station. Then a trek of some eight blocks took him to the three-story brownstone at 420 Fifth Street NW, which housed Howard Law. Meanwhile, Hill traveled across town from his home near Howard's main campus, arriving in time for the law school's eight o'clock opening. Classes continued until eleven thirty, followed by lunch at Father Divine's and a long afternoon of studying together in the law-school library. Next, Hill was off to his job as a waiter at the upscale Stoneleigh Apartments, home to a well-to-do, conservative white clientele. Any socializing happened after nine in the evening. Marshall retraced his route to Baltimore, where a crowded household including his parents, his wife, Buster, and assorted relatives awaited.[2] As Hill and Marshall launched their law studies, back in Richmond Spottswood Robinson's focus was on scouting, tennis, and the insular world of Armstrong High. For a mere boy, Howard Law lay on a distant, still invisible horizon.

By Hill and Marshall's second year, Marshall had secured a coveted job in the law-school library. Sometimes he worked late into the evening. As for Hill, when the Stoneleigh replaced its black servers with white waitresses, he scrambled to find employment in the House of Representatives dining room. He and several other students arranged for a taxi to race them from the law school to the Capitol after classes adjourned for the day.[3]

Hill trailed Marshall slightly in academics (Marshall ranked first in the class; the Virginian recalled that he wound up second).[4] Physically, socially, and politically, however, the pair were a near match. Their competitive passion and love of life made them "about as close friends as anybody has ever been," Marshall once told an interviewer. Both were natural-born leaders. Their height and energy drew attention when they entered a room. Hill called Marshall "Turkey" because of his strutting gate; Marshall referred to Hill as "Peanuts" because of his love of the snack. Marshall had done his undergraduate work at Lincoln University in Chester County, Pennsylvania; Hill had attended arch-rival Howard. As an undergrad, Marshall had joined the Alpha Phi Alpha fraternity; Hill, the rival Omega Psi Phi. So it was no surprise when the pair engaged in a friendly, spirited competition for the helm of their law-school class. Even the Washington edition of the *Afro-American* newspaper took note. "Struggling for class leadership, the 22 members of the second year at the Howard University law school have split into two equally divided factions each with its own set of officers, each claiming to be the real representatives," the newspaper reported in October 1931. "The double election followed several class meetings which ended in unusual disorder, one being halted by a member of the faculty."[5] The individuals named by the competing factions to the important post of student council representative? Hill and Marshall. "Anything Thurgood and I could agree on happened. If we didn't agree, it didn't happen," Hill chuckled over the matter.[6]

Hill never deviated in his motivation for turning to the law. "I went to law school to become a lawyer so that I could challenge segregation," he said in numerous interviews. What he did not know when he walked through the door of the Howard University School of Law was how fortunately timed his arrival would be. Founded in 1869, the school had provided a functional but undistinguished night-school education to a predominantly black clientele for just over sixty years. Classes were taught largely by white faculty, for whom teaching was a way to supplement their day income as lawyers, judges, or government workers. By one estimate, the school had produced more than three-fourths of the nation's black attorneys, but it was not accredited by either the American Bar Association or the Association of American Law Schools.[7] That was about to change. Robinson would benefit equally from the improved academic rigor when he entered the law school, six years after Hill.

The 1926 installation of Howard University's first black president, Mordecai W. Johnson, launched the transformation. Accused—for better or worse—of bringing a "messianic complex" to his new role, Johnson possessed a deep sense of vocation and commitment to black advancement. He saw no better place to begin the road to societal improvement than at the law school. As a first step, he asked an exceptional young faculty member, Charles Hamilton Houston, to conduct a survey of the experiences of black lawyers nationwide. Houston sent letters to clerks of court in southern states, asking how many black attorneys practiced in their jurisdictions. The replies were sobering, even shocking: "None—nor have been nor hope ever will be in our Court" (Page County, Virginia); "Thank the Lord, There are None" (Laurens County, Georgia); "None. Better spend your time on more profitable questions. Who ever heard of Negroes practicing law. They can't even read it" (Lafayette, Missouri).[8]

Those distressing results reinforced the more polite but equally harsh indictment of Supreme Court Associate Justice Louis D. Brandeis, who, in a perhaps apocryphal story, told Mordecai Johnson that he could always tell when a legal brief had been prepared by a black lawyer. Typically, such documents simply did not meet the standards necessary to receive proper consideration from the justices, even sympathetic ones, Brandeis supposedly said. He urged Johnson to correct the deficiency.[9]

Johnson apparently agreed with the sentiment, whether or not the particulars of the Brandeis story are true. To oversee an improvement campaign, Howard's president and trustees again turned to Houston, now thirty-three, whose youth belied his accomplishments. A Phi Beta Kappa graduate of Amherst College, Houston had distinguished himself at Harvard Law School, becoming the first black editor of the *Harvard Law Review*. His mentors were Dean N. Roscoe Pound and the future Supreme Court associate justice Felix Frankfurter, both progressive thinkers. After earning both an LLB and a doctorate in law at Harvard, Houston won a traveling fellowship to the University of Madrid. There, he completed a Doctor of Civil Laws degree. Returning to his hometown of Washington, DC, the handsome and serious-minded scholar began practicing law with his father and teaching part time at Howard. He told students that the key to eliminating discrimination lay in the Fourteenth Amendment to the Constitution, guaranteeing due process and equal protection of the law to all citizens, and that black lawyers must be the architects of change.[10] Only black lawyers would care deeply enough to endure the harrowing journey to equality, he argued. "Experience has proved that the average white lawyer, especially in the South, cannot be counted on to wage an uncompromising fight for equal rights for Negroes," he wrote.[11]

On June 4, 1929, the board installed Houston as resident vice-dean in charge of a new day program at Howard Law. He refused the title of dean, preferring that extra resources be spent on faculty.[12] The vice-dean's ambition for the school matched and even exceeded Johnson's. Demanding and disciplined, Houston foresaw a school whose graduates would do nothing less than transform America. After winnowing by a first-rate faculty, high standards, and hard work, graduates would scatter into the hinterlands to launch a revolution. But first, Howard Law had to be transformed. The old night school must go. New faculty—most of them black—needed to be hired and full accreditation achieved.

Moreover, all this must be accomplished against a backdrop of economic struggle and racial turmoil. In the fall of 1930, when Hill and Marshall became two of the first students to enter Howard Law's full-time day program, the nation was enmeshed in the worst economic depression in its history. Racial and regional politics were so fraught that even an antilynching bill could not make its way through a firewall of southern congressional opposition. Before the pair finished in the spring of 1933, Adolph Hitler would become chancellor of the Third Reich; a newly inaugurated Franklin D. Roosevelt would launch the nation's New Deal; and death sentences against eight of nine black teenagers—dubbed the Scotts-

boro Boys—accused of raping two white women in Alabama would rivet
and enrage supporters nationwide.

Hill, Marshall, and some three dozen first-year classmates encountered a
physical plant that was a far cry from the ivied edifices and stately columns
of Houston's alma mater, Harvard Law. The Howard University School
of Law occupied what had once been an unpretentious family dwelling.
A large room used for classes and a moot court filled one floor. The law
library and added class space consumed a second. Houston and other professors kept offices on the third. In a faculty memo, Houston acknowledged some of the drawbacks, as well as his toughening standards. "Full
cognizance is taken of the facts (1) that Professor Taylor and Mr. Ransom
are both using the same office and (2) that Professor Buscheck's and Mr.
Kallis' offices are without natural light. But it is expected that no teacher
will let two full days pass without spending some time at the school," he
admonished.[13] Despite cramped conditions, the location offered students
a real-life legal laboratory. "The law building is situated directly opposite
Judiciary Square, in front of the Supreme Court of the District of Columbia and the Court of Appeals," a 1930 circular told prospective scholars.
The city's police court, its municipal court, and Congress all were within
range. It would be up to individuals to make the most of such resources.[14]

Houston's opening lecture to the students set the bar for what was to
come. "Look to your left and look to your right. Next year one of you
won't be here," he warned. That dire prediction would prove prophetic.
From the starting bell, students knew what to expect from the hard-nosed
leader. "Charlie told us, 'We're going to make this a first-class law school.
The faculty's going to work and you're going to work with us,' and as a
consequence, after the first year, we got approved by both the Association
of American Law Schools and the American Bar Association," Hill recalled.
"We worked six days a week to accomplish it."[15]

Controversy shadowed change. Ousted nighttime professors protested
the loss of their jobs; some students grumbled about Houston's unswerv-
ing expectations. Nicknames such as "Ironpants" and "Cement Shoes"
captured their exasperation with Houston's perfectionism. But those who
survived the tempest came away with admiration for their leader, a grasp
of the potential of the law, and an education worth having. The crux of
Houston's philosophy was repeated over and over. "A lawyer's either a
social engineer or a parasite on society," he lectured. The lawyer's goal

should not be personal wealth or stature but serving as "the mouthpiece of the weak and a sentinel guarding against wrong." He trained his students for "innovative and ambitious intervention." And he created what has widely been called the nation's first public-interest law school, with a focus on black advancement.[16]

The linchpins of Houston's assault included a committed faculty and a plan to expand the horizons of students whose lack of worldly experience might seriously disadvantage them. The day program began with five full-time and six part-time instructors. Besides Houston, early faculty included William H. "Bill" Hastie, Houston's cousin and a polished, soft-spoken fellow Harvard Law standout; the firebrand Leon A. "Andy" Ransom, who had been valedictorian of his law class at Ohio State; William E. Taylor, a top graduate of the University of Iowa School of Law; George E. C. Hayes, a first-rate trial lawyer who finished Brown University undergrad and Howard Law with unusually high grades; and Alfred Buscheck, who held law degrees from the University of Wisconsin and Yale and was the only white in the group. The competence of that cast was beyond question.[17]

Attempting to educate students even more broadly, Houston supplemented the curriculum with guest appearances by renowned attorneys and speakers. The civil libertarian Clarence Darrow, of John Scopes's "Monkey Trial" fame, delivered a series of lectures at the school in 1931. Hill and Marshall had the opportunity to hear, among others, Dean Pound of Harvard Law; Arthur Garfield Hays, chief counsel of the American Civil Liberties Union; William H. Lewis, the nation's first black federal prosecutor; and Edward H. Morris, a wealthy black railroad attorney from Chicago. Houston "was so well-respected; he had no difficulty getting the greatest lawyers in the country to come and lecture to us," said Hill.[18] Simultaneously, students were expanding their horizons with field trips to the Federal Bureau of Investigation and local police headquarters, St. Elizabeth's (psychiatric) Hospital, DC court buildings, prosecutors' and coroners' offices, and various law firms. "Most of us in the class, including me, all of us really, had very little outside experience in these sorts of things. He recognized that," Hill said.[19]

Despite its rigor, Howard Law did not erase Hill's penchant for fun. Hastie, who was destined to become governor of the Virgin Islands and the first African American on the federal bench, was also a fraternity brother of Hill's. Less than three years separated them in age, and it was not unusual for Hill and his suave, David Niven–lookalike professor to wind up at the same parties. One night, they were together at an affair that Hastie's biographer described as "a night to remember—foxy women, handsome men, music, drink, laughter." When the party broke up, Hill went home to study, then made his bleary-eyed way to Hastie's early morning class. "Well, I know our good friend is well prepared this morning," Hastie teased, tossing out a question that Hill fortunately was able to answer. Crossing his arms in satisfaction, the student leaned back in his chair—too far back. The next thing Hill knew, "the daggone chair had tumbled all the way back, and I landed on the damned floor."[20]

Hastie was not Hill's only faculty friend. Much as Hill admired and was in turn befriended by Houston, the vice-dean was not the sort to let down his hair at day's end. Andy Ransom, lively and down to earth, described socially by Hill as an unpretentious, "old-shoe" sort, was another story. Ransom and his gregarious wife, nicknamed "Bill," made up a regular Sunday-afternoon bridge quartet with Oliver and his now steady girl-friend, Beresenia "Bernie" Walker.[21]

Tall, long-haired, smart, and gracious, the future teacher had emerged early in Hill's law-school days as the favorite in a long trail of girlfriends. Oliver and Bernie first crossed paths when he was a Howard undergrad-uate and she was attending the nearby Miner Normal School, which had a respected teacher-training program. More sheltered than many girls her age, she nonetheless showed a spark of confidence that intrigued her older suitor. They began seriously dating sometime after Hill entered law school.[22]

Four years younger than Hill, Bernie had been born in Richmond, where her father, Andrew Walker, and his brother, Armistead, ran a successful bricklaying business. When Armistead—who was married to the enter-prising Maggie Walker—was killed in a tragic accident, the grieving An-drew decided to leave the city. He and his wife, Yetta, moved their five children to Youngstown, Ohio, where Andrew worked in the steel mills. Both of the Walker girls, Bernie and her older sister Evalyn, who would play an important role in Hill's future work, were academic standouts at their Youngstown high school. Later, Andrew and Yetta decided to move east, in part to allow Bernie to pursue her teaching dream at Miner.[23]

Bernie, who had grown up in a straitlaced household with church-oriented parents, quickly became enamored with her intelligent and high-spirited suitor. Her mother was another matter. The relationship got off to a rocky start when Oliver brought Bernie home from one of their first dates well past midnight. The disapproving Mrs. Walker was up waiting. And when Bill Ransom let slip that the couples had been playing bridge on Sundays, Bernie's mother—already skeptical about the urbane young man passing time with her daughter—seethed.[24]

An active social life did not squelch Hill's more serious ambitions. His professional goals remained paramount. During their long afternoons studying in the Howard Law library, Marshall and Hill had become protégés of Houston's. Both envisioned careers that buttressed their mentor's grand design for black advancement. "I came under the tutelage of a brilliant scholar, a wonderful lawyer, and an all-around excellent person," Hill said, describing the relationship. Houston provided the model to which Hill aspired.[25]

The budding attorney's first taste of Houston-style civil rights advocacy resulted from a bid by Thomas Hocutt, a student at the North Carolina College for Negroes, to desegregate the pharmacy school at the University of North Carolina in Chapel Hill. Conrad Odell Pearson, one class ahead of Hill at Howard Law, conceived the challenge to North Carolina's segregated higher-education system while a student. After graduating in 1932, and during Hill's final year at Howard Law, Pearson, along with the Durham attorney Cecil McCoy, initiated action on Hocutt's behalf. Hill intimated that he and other Howard Law students provided support for Pearson and Bill Hastie, who would argue the case in court. "Some of us tried to move the case to integrate the University of North Carolina," Hill said, "but the president of North Carolina College didn't want any part of it." The bid ultimately failed on a technicality, but the effort fired a warning signal that an aggressive, new breed of black lawyer intended to target the exclusion of blacks from public professional schools in the South.[26]

Soon it was Hill's and Marshall's turn to test their wings. The rigor of the course load and the economic challenges of the times had taken a heavy toll on the class of 1933. Once some three dozen strong, its roster had dwindled by more than two-thirds, fulfilling Houston's prophecy. An archivist's list at Howard Law names eleven graduates that year. The *Afro-American* newspaper, reporting on the class commencement, said nine new lawyers received degrees. Hill recalled the number of actual graduates as only six. Whatever the accurate count, it was far below the number matriculating into Howard Law three years earlier. So uncertain were most students of graduating that only three—Hill, Marshall, and one other—walked in the baccalaureate line the Sunday before graduation.[27]

Hill completed his final exam at about three o'clock on a Thursday afternoon. By prior arrangement, he and Marshall celebrated deep into the evening. "In the lingo of that day, we went to a 'nip joint' and 'booted up a few,'" Hill said. The next day, they joined a crowd of about two thousand at Howard's football stadium in sweltering, one-hundred-degree heat to receive their degrees. Hill was twenty-six years old, and Marshall was twenty-five. Their friendship would last until Marshall's death, sixty years later.[28]

Others also were readying for the struggle. Another Virginian who would become crucial to the civil rights movement and the future work of Robinson and Hill came away from Howard's 1933 commencement with diploma in hand. At only nineteen, Sam Tucker had just completed an undergraduate liberal arts degree. The usual path for someone with an eye on civil rights activism would have been to go straight to Howard Law. But the impatient young Alexandria native—known in his youth by his middle name, Wilbert—had never had time for frivolity or convention. He could read before he started school, owing in part to the attentions of his teacher mother. At ten or eleven, he began devouring legal cases in books belonging to his father's business partner and office mate, Tom Watson. By thirteen or fourteen Tucker already could write a deed; soon after that, he learned to draw up divorce papers.[29]

Tucker's father, a real-estate agent and a founding member of the Alexandria NAACP, and his educated mother had imbued their children with an awareness of racial injustice. Sam was just fourteen when he, two brothers, and a friend had the opportunity to test those lessons. Returning to Alexandria from Washington, the boys had arranged a reversible seat on a streetcar so that they could face one another. Once the trolley passed into Virginia, a white passenger, Lottie May Jernigan, insisted that the seat now facing backwards be switched to accommodate whites. The boys refused to move, and Jernigan swore out a warrant charging them with disorderly conduct, assault, and abusive language. A police-court judge fined Sam Tucker five dollars and his older brother, George, fifty dollars. Their younger brother, Otto, was deemed too young, at eleven, to be held responsible. Remarkably for the times, an all-white jury of seven men reversed those judgments on appeal, finding that the youths had not committed a crime.[30] For Sam Tucker, the acquittal proved a powerful tutorial in the potential of the law.

A few months after graduation, Tucker and Hill ran across each other on a street corner in downtown Washington. The two had met a few years earlier in a Latin class at Howard and were friendly. The inevitable question came up: "What are you doing these days?" Hill reported that he was working at O'Donnell's, a popular seafood restaurant, while studying to take the Virginia bar exam the following December. "How about you, Tucker?" Surprisingly, the younger man also had his eye set on the December test. After years of working and studying with the lawyer Tom Watson, Tucker believed he could skip law school and go straight to practicing. At least he intended to try. Why not study together? the men decided.

For the next several months, on Thursday afternoons, his one free afternoon each week, Hill hopped a streetcar to Alexandria and hunkered down with Tucker. They studied Watson's 1924 copy of the Virginia Code—then almost a decade old—and a set of exemplary bar-preparation notes prepared by a renowned William and Mary law professor, Dudley Warner Woodbridge. Hill usually caught the midnight streetcar, the last run of the day, back to the District.[31]

When the big day arrived, the friends traveled to Richmond separately. Hill went down the night before the exam and checked into Slaughter's Hotel in Jackson Ward, one of the few accommodations for blacks in the segregated city. He asked the clerk for a seven o'clock wake-up call and went to bed. Rising early in the dim light of a rainy day, Hill steadied himself by reviewing various notes. After a while, he sensed that too much time was passing. A check of his watch threw him into a panic.[32] It was already half past eight, and the test was due to begin in thirty minutes. Racing downstairs, Hill rushed to Broad Street, grabbed a taxi, and ordered the driver to the Capitol. "Which side? Where do you enter?" the driver wanted to know. Hill had no idea. "Hell, I don't know where the Capitol is, much less how to get into it," he barked.

After considerable confusion, Hill located the right chamber. Hurrying in, he saw only one vacant seat, far down in front. He took it, realizing too late that all the other black applicants were seated in the back row. Never mind, he told himself. He could not worry then about Virginia's segregationist protocol. As Hill opened the test, he felt his heart drop for the second time that morning. The first question addressed federal procedure, a topic that had not been covered in the Howard Law curriculum. Trying desperately to focus, Hill skipped the question and went on to the next.

At a break later that day, he approached Stuart Campbell, an examiner from Wytheville, and cautiously asked, was it possible to do poorly on the first section of the test and still pass? Not typically, Campbell replied. Chagrined, Hill completed that day's queries and breezed his way through the next day's sections. With low spirits, he boarded a bus back to Washington. Thurgood Marshall already was practicing law in Baltimore. Hill did not like the idea of falling further behind his friend and competitor. But for the time being, there was nothing to do but keep serving tables and wait for the test results.

Hill was at a dance in early February, in his own words "high as a Georgia pine," when the answer arrived from an unexpected source. An acquaintance stopped him: "Congratulations, counselor." "Congratulations for what?" Hill asked, to which the acquaintance replied, "You don't pass a bar exam every day, do you?"

Ecstatic, Hill sobered up immediately. The next morning, when the Library of Congress opened, he was at the door. An old issue of the Roanoke newspaper confirmed the report. Sure enough, Oliver White Hill had passed the Virginia bar. Sam Tucker had passed as well (although he would have to wait until he turned twenty-one in June to be allowed to practice). Later, Hill pieced together what had occurred. Notice of his achievement had been mailed to Mrs. Pentecost in Roanoke. The bar had asked for copies of his poll-tax receipts for the past three years, a final requirement to practice law in Virginia. Mrs. Pentecost had handed the request over to a local lawyer, who had put the paper aside. Hill's surrogate mother had planned to call him with the news, but—in an era when telephone calls were a luxury—had not yet done so.[33] He wondered how long it might have taken him to get the results, save for a chance encounter at a dance.

Elated that his dream was finally becoming reality, Hill shared the good news with Houston and others at Howard Law. He intended to move back to Roanoke in the fall, he announced. There, Hill would see what he could do to mine the mountains for greater justice for black citizens. In August, Houston escorted Marshall and Hill to their first meeting of the National

Bar Association, the black equivalent of the American Bar Association. On a hot summer day in Baltimore, they sat outside the building where J. Thomas Newsome, a gifted newspaper editor and lawyer from Newport News, Virginia, was speaking. Listening through an open window, Hill thrilled to the power of Newsome's delivery. Later, he rubbed shoulders with Raymond Pace Alexander of Philadelphia and other well-known black attorneys whose brotherhood he now joined. He observed their adoption of a slew of resolutions, calling for appointment of black federal judges, inclusion of lawyers in President Roosevelt's group of black advisers, and elimination of segregation and discrimination toward black schoolchildren. It was a heady moment for a young man ready to launch out into the world.[34]

Hill had one more step to take before leaving Washington. Two years earlier, while en route to a dance, he had pulled out an engagement ring and asked Bernie Walker to become his wife. Like many other young couples struggling through the Depression, Oliver and Bernie had agreed to an engagement of indeterminate length. Both had educations to complete. Now, Oliver was a lawyer, and Bernie, as one of Miner Normal's top graduates, had secured a teaching post with the District's public schools. If they were going to be living apart, Oliver thought, it was best to make the arrangement official. On September 5 the couple married at her parents' home at 1909 Second Street NW. Within days, they kissed good-bye, and Hill set off for western Virginia in pursuit of his future.[35]

In Richmond that autumn, Spot Robinson's focus also had shifted from academics to the real world. Ready to enter his third year at Virginia Union, he had been confronted by a maturing experience. His father had unexpectedly become ill, and only one person knew enough about the real-estate business to take over running the firm. Young Spot dropped out of school to support the family. At eighteen he was being forced to become a man.

THREE

A Gamble on Roanoke

Oliver and Bernie Hill took a calculated risk when they launched their union in separate locations. The newlyweds preferred to be together. But in the midst of the Depression, both knew the danger of Bernie's giving up a secure teaching job without assurance that Oliver could generate income as a lawyer. The Roanoke destination made sense, given Hill's familiarity with the city. He could count on warm friendship and inexpensive lodgings with Lelia and Bradford Pentecost. Meanwhile, Bernie could continue to board with her parents. While she sometime chaffed at the Walkers' strict propriety, their embrace of a now-married daughter allowed for gradually relaxing standards. "Mom even let us serve cocktails. Now ain't that something," Bernie reported after a party featuring the broadcast of a boxing match between Joe Louis and Max Baer.[1]

Hill staked his fortunes on a gritty, vibrant city of seventy thousand—about one-sixth black—where schools and hospitals were strictly segregated, visiting African American luminaries, including Marian Anderson and Duke Ellington, were barred from the finer hotels, and black lawyers were only slightly more plentiful than palm trees or Eskimos. The scarcity offered a fine opportunity to test Charles Houston's plan to spread African American legal talent across the South. By the calculation of Hill's mentor, there were far fewer black lawyers practicing south of the Mason-Dixon Line than the 487 listed in the 1930 census. Houston put the number of active, full-time black attorneys in the South at 100 or fewer. As for Virginia, the census listed 57; Houston believed the real number was closer to 15.[2] Whatever the count, soon there would be one more.

When Hill arrived in Roanoke, the city was joining the rest of the nation in jettisoning the shackles of Prohibition and struggling to escape the drag of an economic undertow. The presence of the Norfolk and Western Railway remained a godsend, offering steady employment for both blacks and whites. Still, declining coal prices and economic malaise were taking a toll. City leaders across Virginia urged Governor George Peery to spend $5 million on relief "because a revolution was feared," wrote Raymond Barnes in a history of the city. "People were breaking store windows for many had not enough to eat to serve human needs."[3]

Hill planned to set up shop with J. Henry Claytor, an older attorney of middling ability whose training had consisted of correspondence courses through Chicago's LaSalle Extension University. Their office would be located near Henry Street, the center of black commercial life. A drugstore occupied the ground floor at 40 High Street; upstairs were professional offices with space for two dentists, two physicians, and Claytor and Hill.[4] A month into his association with Claytor, Hill was still sanguine about its prospects. "Mr. Claytor appears to be a very congenial fellow to work with," he reported to Bernie in an early October letter. There were glimmers of trouble, however. With office space at a premium, Hill's desk and chair occupied a spot in the reception room. Only on the rare occasions when a client visited was Hill allowed the privacy of Claytor's office. When the firm's new stationery arrived, the young attorney voiced dismay. Expecting "Claytor & Hill" to appear in bold letters at the top of the page, he instead saw his name in tiny print in the left-hand margin.[5]

Even so, Hill's natural confidence and optimism dominated his early days in the city. He greeted with bravado the court-ordered assignment of his first client in hustings court, an indigent black girl facing one to ten years in prison on a malicious-wounding charge. "But of course she hasn't got anything to worry about," he cheekily proclaimed. Five days later, he described the outcome with equal bluster: "The big case came up today and when the Commonwealth's Attorney saw Who & What he was up against why he just threw up his hands and surrendered." An elated Bernie telephoned Hill's mother with the news. "All day Monday I was hoping so that you had won," she told her husband.[6]

If Roanoke and the Depression presented challenges for Hill, the timing of his arrival in southwestern Virginia proved a boon in at least one way: his sojourn coincided with turning points in civil rights activism locally and nationally. The Roanoke NAACP, dormant for several years, was stirring, thanks to the energy of its president, J. A. Reynolds. In February 1934 Reynolds wrote to Walter F. White, executive secretary of the national NAACP, asking for a list of Virginia branch presidents. "I want to call all of them together and see if we can do better business in the future then we have in the [past]," he wrote. A response listed eight Virginia chapters, in Alexandria, Hampton, Norfolk, Petersburg, Portsmouth, Richmond, and Roanoke, along with a Virginia Union college chapter. By May, Reynolds was urging a visit from White and the organization's newly named part-time special counsel, Charles Houston. "I would like to make a drive against Jim-Crowism in the state if the time is ripe enough for it," Reynolds wrote.[7]

When Hill left Washington, he had not yet joined the national group. Even for advocates of racial justice, affiliation was less automatic than it would soon become. Within months of setting foot in Roanoke, he was contemplating the step. "Last night I attended the N.A.A.C.P. meeting[.] I think I am going to connect myself with them," he informed Bernie in December 1934. She approved: "I do think it is a fine organization and it would be fine for you to be connected with it."[8] A February 27, 1935, Roanoke branch report to the national office lists three enrollees, including attorney Hill. A month earlier in Richmond, the group's first statewide board meeting had resulted in a decision to unite.[9]

Even more fortunate for Hill, he began law practice just as Houston's drive to spread racial justice was entering an important new phase: a focused assault on educational inequality. During Hill and Marshall's three years at Howard Law, Houston had been tending to more than legal education. The vice-dean also had been helping devise NAACP strategy for attacking segregation. In 1930 the American Fund for Public Service, a left-wing foundation also known as the Garland Fund, had allotted about one hundred thousand dollars for the civil rights group to attack Jim Crow segregation in the South. Following Houston's advice, the fund hired Nathan Margold, a white scholar and Harvard Law graduate, to devise a plan for spending the money.[10]

By the time Margold's blueprint for a multipronged attack on segregation was complete in 1931, the value of the Garland Fund gift had plummeted. In response, Houston and others advised narrowing the focus to education, specifically graduate and professional programs in public colleges that excluded blacks and unequal salaries for black and white teachers in elementary and secondary schools. Margold advocated a full-bore attack on public-school segregation as unconstitutional, but Houston argued that a push for immediate integration would be legal suicide. Better to first demonstrate the impossibility of trying to make black and white schools truly equal. Costs of dual systems would prove prohibitive, leading to integration, he believed. Houston's view would prevail.[11]

In May 1934, as Hill was planning his move to Roanoke, Houston joined the NAACP as its part-time first special counsel, charged with implementing the legal plan he had helped devise. In the summer of 1935 he bade Howard Law farewell and moved to New York to make the job full time. The school-equalization campaign would take the former vice-dean to Virginia regularly over the next several years.[12] En route to investigating complaints of inadequate and occasionally nonexistent education for rural blacks in southwestern Virginia, Houston sometimes stopped off in Roanoke to visit his former student. Soon he began steering NAACP questions and concerns in the region to Hill.

Hill's emergence as the organization's point man in southwestern Virginia was still a year away, however, when he hung his law shingle and began describing his new life to his bride far away. From the start, the couple's correspondence revealed similarities in interests and differences in temperament. Far more emotional than Oliver, prone to occasional melancholy (the contemporary term for depression), Bernie soon let it be known that she expected regular and affectionate communication. If she was intimidated by her husband's superior education and more worldly experiences, she gave no hint. "Your letter was greatly appreciated *when* it did get here," Bernie admonished three weeks into their marriage. "I have to admit I was a little disappointed in both the lateness of its arrival and its practicability. . . . Please try next time to put a little warmth into your letters." Oliver needed to understand that "I miss you terribly."[13]

Governed by logic and rationality, Oliver saw the merit in the request and adjusted quickly. Five days later, he wrote: "I had a wonderful dream about you last night, it seemed that, you were all 'gowned down' looking too gorgeous for any earthly good, and you were officiating at some social function or the other, and I was sitting off gazing at you in mute admiration." From then on, Hill's letters rarely lacked a sentimental or even florid tribute. "To The Sweetest Little Girl In All The World, My Wife, Dearest

Darling," he wrote. Or, after Bernie's first postwedding visit to Roanoke in November 1934: "Even the Angels missed you today for last Sunday when you were here the air was balmy—the sun shone splendidly and nature was decked in all its grandeur—while [today] there was a melancholy haze covering the sky. . . . Such is the difference in the life of this poor mortal when you are present and when you are not present."[14]

Oliver developed a signature sign-off, "S.A.S.A.Y.A.," based on the 1934 hit song "Stay As Sweet As You Are." In return, Bernie composed a poem with a compliment attached to each letter of his name. The Hills made a handsome couple. Oliver paid a teasing tribute to his wife with the title of a bawdy song, "It takes a long, tall, brown-skin gal to make a preacher lay his Bible down." Bernie was his long, tall gal, not classically gorgeous but eye-catching because of her poise, graciousness, and wide, expressive smile. Oliver also stood out in a crowd, literally. He towered above most of his associates, and a frequent cigar or a slight tilt of his hat added a jaunty exclamation point to his usual suited formality.

Oliver could be detached, practical, sensible, lawyerly, sometimes maddeningly so for a wife who acknowledged her own impulsive, demonstrative nature. "Cultivate and develop the habit of weighing matters before acting. . . . It is something that you will have to acquire by continuous and persistent effort," he instructed. Bernie countered with advice of her own. "I've come to the conclusion that tears are really very good things," she counseled. "See you can't cry so your feelings and emotions are all closed inside of you. Mine are washed out."[15] But when it came to sociability, a talent for leadership, and genuine commitment to each other's success, the Hills were natural soul mates. Bernie in Washington and Oliver in Roanoke assumed leading roles in fraternal groups and enjoyed a wide circle of friends. Both excelled at games. As contract-bridge partners, they sometimes wrote out a description of an entire hand's play when apart.

Socially and politically, Hill thrived in Roanoke. Finances were another matter. Locals had not yet embraced Houston's vision of the black lawyer as an agent of revolutionary change. Many citizens appeared reluctant to hire a fellow black for even mundane legal tasks; the Depression further dampened willingness to do so. In Hill's early months in the city, he reported handling a contested will, a few lawsuits, and occasional court-appointed criminal cases. The work did little to build a bank account. In mid-October 1934 he described a "strenuous week" helping Claytor gather evidence and copy court records. The effort earned him "the magnificent sum of $3." He was not desperate enough to accept a client asking him to draw up a fake marriage license, however. "I told him that I didn't do that kind of business."[16]

Determined to be productive while awaiting clients, Hill reported that he had begun rising at 6:30 a.m. "in an effort to help develop my strength of character." He planned to improve his memory through a series of exercises. "While I am not busy otherwise I am going to try and acquire all the little essentials that [go] to make up the polished and well rounded lawyer." He studied a book of modern essays and read the speeches of the abolitionist Frederick Douglass. "Those old brothers were wizards at the masterful use of the English language," he wrote to Bernie. Back in Washington, Bernie filled the void with night classes toward an undergraduate degree from Howard. She uncomplainingly supplemented her husband's meager income and urged him not to despair. "I really think Roanoke is your place. . . . Keep your chin up and always know that I believe in you," she wrote.[17]

Meanwhile, opportunities abounded for Hill to immerse himself in Roanoke's lively black society. Outgoing and popular, he seldom lacked for invitations. The young lawyer also juggled a growing list of engagements to speak before various church and voter groups. After his first sermon, delivered at a country church outside Roanoke, he joked: "Oh it was a masterpiece—a beautiful gem. . . . The sisters shouted and all the old deacons cried 'preach it Brother.'" Churches were at the heart of Roanoke's black social life. The robust directory of churches offered more than a half dozen choices, including the well-established First Baptist, which found Hill sporadically in its pews.[18]

A lifelong distaste for the emotionalism associated with many black ministers and churches surfaced in Hill's letters. "Guess what? I went to church this morning, did you?" he wrote in January 1935. "No—my, my how sinful. The preacher got off on the holy ghost and all the old sisters and brothers got happy and commenced to holler and clap their hands. It was wonderful to them and disgusting to me." On another occasion, he described a visiting minister's address as splendid but added: "I still don't believe in all that baloney they hand the people and all that playing upon the emotions of the people." Even when he joined First Baptist during his second year in town, his irreverent report to Bernie hinted at a touch of insincerity. "Well your husband started a new life today—I went up this morning and joined the church on my Christian experience (ha ha you did not know I had any did you)."[19]

If the socializing boosted Hill's spirits and rooted him in the community, it also produced his first serious marital fight with Bernie. The incident, pitting Bernie's propriety against Oliver's free-spirited nature, began innocuously enough. Oliver's regular Sunday night letter in mid-February 1935 described a weekend dinner party as a "partial success (your presence would have made it a complete one)," including conversation, games, and dancing. "At the request of one of the dear brothers," he noted, "I accompanied his girlfriend. . . . I had tried to get Mrs. Pente[cost] to go but she turned me down Friday."[20]

Oliver's letter reached Bernie the next day. Word of the dinner had preceded its arrival. "Some of the Roanoke people just sent the news on that you carried the lady to the dinner," observed Bernie's stony Monday-afternoon missive. "Also they sent word that you'd been to Washington only once and was perfectly happy there in Roanoke. This was relayed to the Bullocks who in turn spread the news during the lunch hour in front of everyone." She seethed: "I've tried and have succeeded in keeping all my actions so that no one could even think anything of them. Of course our ideas never coincided before we were married on those particular things." Accusing Oliver of "embarrassing me beyond words," Bernie concluded: "If this hurts you it won't hurt like the hurt you laid me open to today."

Oliver responded with equal fury. His ten-page letter quickly devolved into half lecture, half rant on the evils of gossip. "Either you believe in a person or you don't and if you have confidence in a person it wont be shaken by the idle prattle of some gossip monger who can't attend to their own business for attending to somebody elses," he began. "During the time I was courting you—I played fair and I showed you my self as I actually was and am. . . . I told you when you were my sweetheart and I repeat it now to my wife that I trust you and I will continue to trust you until I find that you are unworthy of trust." Eight pages followed.

The reason he had been to Washington only once since their marriage was purely economic, he said. During January 1935 he had made only ten dollars. "During no other month have I made over five and this month so far I have made $1.25 all in cash money—you can show this to *your* good friends since they are so vitally interested in my affairs." With his usual emphasis on dispassionate thinking, Hill wound up by prescribing a course of action. "Sit down and think the situation out—why must you live in fear of the opinion of those so-called friends—who are they any way and after all just what do [their] opinions amount to in the long run."

Over the next week the furor receded. He had been "quite angry," Hill said, because he had not allowed himself even to think about cavorting with another woman. He urged Bernie to do all in her power to temper her jealousy. She agreed that "starting today I'm beginning my campaine for temperance." The matter was put to rest with one last proviso: "I still dont think so much of you taking that lady to the dance, but I'll try to show myself wherein it was O.K." She concluded: "More Love than before, Bernie."

A ten-day visit by Bernie during the Easter holiday helped the couple regain their equilibrium. Afterward, as he often did, Oliver waxed philosophical: "Life owes no one anything—but everyone owes Life. Everyone should feel that he is indebted to life and that indebtedness can only be wiped out by some worth while accomplishment—the only thing that life owes any individual is an opportunity, a place in which to stand and perform. . . . What I really wanted to tell you was that I love you and that I miss you terribly."[21]

Bernie was dreaming of the future as well. After seeing William Powell with Ginger Rogers in *Star of Midnight,* Bernie reported that "the suave old lawyer . . . was so keen and clever that he made me think of you. One of these days we'll have everybody sitting up and taking notice of us. . . . Everybody will say There's Attorney Hill and his wife. I'll be satisfied to stay in the background because I'll be so proud of you."[22]

By autumn 1935 Hill's position in Roanoke seemed on a more solid footing. He wasn't earning much more money, but his growing reputation was bringing him more interesting cases and a deepening connection to the state's racial activists. Two legal cases stood out. In mid-September Hill's first capital defense resulted in an execution order that seemed to sear his soul. His client was a black transient accused of shooting to death another transient in a fight at a rooming house.[23] "It is a terrible feeling," he wrote, "to know that a man is guilty and that the evidence is of such a revolting nature that the odds are a hundred to one that he will get the electric chair. . . . I have been worried silly and right now I am a hollow eyed wreck."[24]

Hill elected to forgo a jury trial in hopes that Judge J. Lindsay Almond Jr., who recently had imposed a death sentence, would not want to order two executions in one week. Almond, who as Virginia's attorney general and governor would clash with Hill over segregated schools years later, was undeterred. Hill's gamble failed, and Ferguson was sentenced to die. Given Hill's own acknowledgment of his client's guilt, it seems unlikely that a jury trial would have had a different result.

In mid-September, Charles Houston tapped his former student to investigate a complaint from Wytheville. The case provided Hill's first assignment for the NAACP and his most consequential encounter yet with southern justice. Frank L. W. Clarke described the situation in a letter to the New York office: "I am writing to have you investigate a recent case in the above name Town of [Southwest], Va. of [young] man (Colored) who was intoxicated in the home of his wife—last Sunday Night, his wife's brother called an Officer of the law to arrest him, The Officer enter the home without a warrant, in an altercation—the Officer was shot in the arm and the man was shot by the Officer in the face. I with other citizen[s] feel that because of tense feeling of the (white race) the Colored man will not get a fair trial."[25]

Race relations merited concern in Wytheville, a county-seat town about halfway between Roanoke and Bristol. Memories lingered of the gruesome lynching of Raymond Bird there nine years earlier, in August 1926. Bird, a black farmhand, had been jailed after being accused by his white employer of raping the man's two oldest daughters and fondling a third. On the morning in question, a masked lynching party of about fifty men had broken into the jail, shot and bludgeoned Bird, tied him to a car, and dragged him through the town before hanging him from a tree. Later evidence suggested that Bird had been in consensual relationships with the two older girls and had been accused of rape only after one daughter gave birth to Bird's child.[26]

Houston contacted the Roanoke NAACP president, Reynolds, about the new complaint. "Will you please ask Atty. Hill to go over to Wytheville, if possible, and investigate the case," he wrote on September 20. The same day, Houston suggested to Clarke that Wytheville citizens begin raising twenty-five dollars to pay Hill's expenses.[27] The case of Harrison Little, who was tried on October 23 and 24 in Wytheville's stately, tan-brick courthouse, earned Hill regional notice. "Owing to the local prejudice of the people it is going to be an uphill battle," he confided to Bernie. "We will be quite a curiosity—for if there has ever been a colored lawyer who pleaded a case before the Bar of the Wytheville County Court it was beyond the memory of living man."[28]

On the opening morning, Hill encountered a procedural challenge that deeply impressed him. In the 1930s, Virginia required lawyers to be formally accepted to the bar of each individual court in which they appeared. Typically another lawyer spoke on behalf of the applicant, but Hill had no such advocate. For a black lawyer appearing in a court where he knew no one and where no black lawyer had appeared in years, if ever, the requirement was a daunting hurdle. Hill later described the moment: "When I walked into court, nobody in there but the commonwealth's attorney. . . . I went over, handed him my card, offered my card, and told him I was a lawyer from Roanoke and I was there that day to represent the defendant, and would he move my admission to the court? And he didn't take my card. He looked me in the eye and said, 'I don't know you.' And I said, 'You're just as right as you can be,' and put my card back in my pocket, went over and sat down."[29] In a courtroom filled with whites, Hill moved his own admission to the bar. His frequent mention of the episode in later years suggests that his racial isolation in the Wytheville courtroom, coupled with the possibility that he might have been barred from representing his client, created a harsh memory and a potent lesson in the so-called Virginia Way of race relations.

At trial, the major witnesses agreed on events leading up to the shooting. On the night of September 15, Little, an employee of the Wytheville Cleaners and Dyers, came home intoxicated to the house he shared with his mother-in-law, wife, and children.[30] When he threatened suicide, his brother-in-law summoned the police. By the time Officers C. J. "Jack" Williams and an Officer Myer arrived, Little had quieted and was upstairs in bed. From that point the stories diverged. According to Williams, he knocked on the bedroom door and ordered Little to come out. When there was no response, the officer pushed the door open and Little opened fire. According to Little, he had started to dress when Williams entered the room and, without warning, opened fire, striking him in the cheek. Little said he fired back in self-defense.

During the trial, Hill established that Williams had been dismissed from the state police force because of altercations, and he argued correctly that the officer had entered the house without a warrant. When an all-white jury found Little guilty of unlawful wounding and sentenced him to four years in the penitentiary in Richmond, some students of southern justice saw victory in defeat. "You must feel assured that you won the case in Wytheville, when the sentence was only four years for malicious wounding," wrote J. E. Anderson of Gary, West Virginia, a candidate for the Virginia bar exam.[31]

Convinced that his client had been wrongly convicted, Hill did not let the matter rest. In perhaps the earliest example of his legal tenacity, he sought and won a meeting with Governor George C. Peery the following spring to protest the punishment. Hill's pardon application included surprising letters of support from both C. J. Williams, the wounded police officer, and Judge Horace Sutherland, who had overseen the trial. Sutherland as much as said that Little had been railroaded. "It was my opinion that the defendant should have been acquitted. . . . I do not think he should have had any punishment at all," the judge wrote.[32] After initially rejecting Hill's petition, Peery relented on December 23, 1936. He attributed his pre-Christmas pardon to Little's good record while incarcerated, his previous good reputation, and the recommendations of Williams and Sutherland. But the man who assembled the statements of support and other documents—Hill—was the indispensable force behind the release.[33] Years later, Hill cited the Harrison Little case as an indictment of southern judges in the 1930s and 1940s. "The judge acted in typical fashion," Hill said. "Too many judges refused to set aside [jury] verdicts and free Negro defendants in situations where they had a different opinion and knew justice had been denied."[34]

In November 1935, not long after Little's conviction, Hill accepted a new assignment from the NAACP, one that foreshadowed his life's work. On November 20, Houston mailed Hill a check for ten dollars to cover expenses for investigating the condition of black schools near Roanoke.[35] A week later, the photographs Hill took formed a visual backdrop for his first address to a statewide group, at the inaugural meeting of the Virginia State Conference of Branches.

The newly formed organization planned its maiden convention for Saturday, November 30, in Roanoke at the close of the annual gathering of the Virginia Teachers Association. The momentous coupling of the two organizations foretold their historic, joint assault a few years later on racial disparities in teacher pay. In part by happenstance, because he was living in Roanoke in November 1935, Hill participated in the birth of the alliance. Hill offered the upcoming festivities as an enticement to Bernie, who planned to visit Roanoke for the Thanksgiving holiday. About five hundred teachers were expected, he wrote, and there would be a host of social events. "Of course none of them will be a social success unless you decide to grace them with your presence," he flattered her. A subsequent letter mentioned that Houston and Andy Ransom were expected in Roanoke for the Thanksgiving events. "Charlie is supposed to make his big speech Thanksgiving night," Hill wrote. "Now you have something to look forward to. Isn't that just to [sic] ducky."[36]

In its coverage of the weekend meetings, the *Roanoke Times* gave no hint of their overarching significance.[37] The public anonymity suited the NAACP hierarchy. Teachers rightly fearful of economic payback also had no interest in alerting white superiors that plans were afoot to align with the activist group. But those in attendance for Houston's speech, including the Hills, recognized that something significant had occurred. Luther P. Jackson, one of the state's premier black educators, later described Houston's keynote address, which challenged teachers to begin seeking legal answers to injustice: "This brilliant attorney succeeded for the moment in carrying the 500 teachers present up to the very verge of the promised land." Houston urged creation of a thousand-dollar scholarship fund to support any plaintiff willing to challenge unequal teacher salaries, a tacit recognition that such an individual would likely be fired. In response, the group agreed to turn over all reserve funds to the teacher-salary-equalization effort.[38]

Ransom compensated for the newspaper's failure to mention the maiden gathering of the NAACP Virginia State Conference of Branches by providing a six-page, single-spaced account to the national office. The report noted that Hill had briefed the group on his investigation of black schools in Roanoke County and that he had joined in a strategy huddle aimed at electing a slate of officers sympathetic to Houston's goals. Ransom also updated the national office on the disgraceful disparity in black and white teacher salaries, writing that in seventy-four of one hundred Virginia counties and twelve of twenty-four cities the minimum salary for white teachers was higher than the maximum salary for black ones.[39]

Bernie's letters reveal that her husband narrowly missed playing a visible and perhaps historic role in yet another aspect of NAACP educational strategy: forcing integration in graduate and professional programs at state universities. The NAACP's first major breakthrough in the push to

integrate higher education had come in June 1935, when a state judge ordered the University of Maryland School of Law to admit Donald Gaines
Murray, a highly qualified Amherst graduate. Marshall, just gaining his
sea legs as a litigator, handled the case together with Houston.[40] Like Hill
in Roanoke, Marshall had struggled since leaving Howard to gain a toehold in Baltimore's legal community. The *Murray* victory afforded him a
much-welcomed taste of acclaim.[41]

With the Maryland case on appeal in state courts, Houston began searching for a plaintiff to bring a similar lawsuit in Virginia. Temporarily, he
believed he had found the ideal candidate in Alice C. Jackson. The daughter
of a Richmond pharmacist, Jackson had graduated from Virginia Union
in 1934 with an English degree. She spent a year doing graduate work at
Smith College in Massachusetts. Unable to continue for financial reasons,
she requested an application from the University of Virginia to pursue a
master's degree in French. On October 5, 1935, Fred W. Scott, the university rector, informed Jackson in writing that her application was denied:
"The admission of white and colored persons in the same schools is contrary to the long established and fixed policy of the Commonwealth of
Virginia."[42] As the autumn passed, Houston was dismayed to discover that
Jackson's academic record at Smith might be problematic. Publicly, the
prospect of a legal challenge in her behalf remained alive; privately, the
search for an alternative quickened. "As you can appreciate, we need a case
where there can be no possible objection except on the ground of color,"
Houston advised.[43]

Communication between Bernie and Oliver reveals that while the
NAACP national office had not yet settled on a Virginia plaintiff, it had
identified a lawyer worthy of handling the case—Hill. In a brief note on
January 21, 1936, as she awaited a social engagement with Andy and Bill
Ransom, a delighted Bernie passed along the good news. "Am waiting right
now for Bill and Andy to come by for me to go to play cards," she wrote.
"He told me I could tell you and I want you to know. He and Charlie will
be there some time soon. You have been selected to handle that university
case there in Virginia. That surely is swell. Did you know? Well this isn't
a letter. I'm already proud of you. Now maybe you will see that silver
lining."[44]

Hill's opportunity for early fame never materialized. Instead, the Virginia legislature did an end run around the insurgents. The Educational

Equality Act, approved in March 1936, provided scholarship assistance for qualified black students to pursue graduate studies out of state. There would be no court case against the university. In July, newspapers reported that about thirty black students, including one Alice Jackson, had qualified for the new aid program in its first year.[45] Still, the willingness of the national NAACP legal staff to cast Hill in such a pivotal role signaled that his abilities had gained notice and respect.

As 1936 progressed, mounting professional esteem did little to ease the couple's financial woes. Bernie's teaching salary remained their anchor; Oliver contemplated taking out a loan to keep himself afloat. In January Bernie urged Oliver to "by all means swing the loan. . . . I'll carry it all right. Summer will be the only difficulty but I guess I can manage." A few weeks later, she inquired about late payment for legal books: "How are your financial problems working out? . . . I think about you and hope for some solution every day, but until one presents itself let's keep our chins up and keep hoping." Oliver replied: "I paid the book company $20. That will pacify them for a month anyway."[46]

By May 1936 the cumulative effect of strained finances and long separations had grown too taxing. After struggling for almost two years, Oliver could no longer escape reality. He was broke. To all outward appearances, his experiment with launching a law practice had failed. Mr. Pentecost's death that spring added a somber tone to the household. "It is almost certain, however, that I will be leaving here within the next two weeks. So if you here [sic] of any kind of a job—notify me at once," Oliver wrote home. Bernie welcomed him with open arms. "A man and wife should be together to share alike the problems, failures and successes of each other," she answered. "After all what is success anyway. To me it means happiness however obtained."[47]

As Hill prepared to pack up his law books and return to Washington, where job prospects looked almost equally dim, the cocky optimism of his early days in the mountain-shadowed railroad town gave way to sober expressions. "I have always made it a practice not to make extravagant promises," Oliver wrote to the young wife who awaited him. "In all seriousness, I promise you that before this year of 1936 has folded and pasted into the great beyond I shall be on a definite paying basis and I am going to do it at the practice of the law."[48] "I'm pulling for you one hundred percent in this new resolve," Bernie replied. "I know you can do it. . . . Keep trying and think often of a wife who loves you dearly."[49] Neither of them knew then that it would be three years before Hill fulfilled his promise—or that the unwelcome retreat from Roanoke was a course correction necessary for the struggle and glory to come. The Depression had foiled hopes for monetary gain, but the Roanoke sojourn had produced intangible rewards. Hill had confronted the injustices of southern courtrooms without flinching. He had strengthened professional connections that would serve him for many years. He had distinguished himself to a greater extent than might have been expected in so remote a setting. And he and Bernie had secured a marriage that would sustain them for their lifetimes.

In June 1936, what Bernie provided were suitcases sent by train for packing for the trip back to Washington, news of several job prospects, and a suggestion that her husband contact the office of Representative Clifton A. Woodrum of Roanoke for a letter of recommendation.[50] Oliver liked the idea, so much so that when he returned to Roanoke for a few days in late July he decided to seek a letter from Senator Carter Glass of Lynchburg as well. Glass's well-known segregationist views were no deterrent to the ambitious and determined lawyer, still a year shy of his thirtieth birthday. "If I can get the support of Woodrum and I think I can, then I will stop off in Lynchburg and try and see Carter Glass and get a letter from him also." He signed off from Roanoke one final time. "Sasaya, loads of love and kisses, Oliver."[51]

Hill's request of Woodrum apparently succeeded. His papers include an unsigned letter dated July 23, 1936, from the congressman to James A. Farley, chairman of the Democratic National Committee. "I am very glad to endorse the application of Oliver W. Hill, colored, 40 High Street, Roanoke, Virginia" for a suitable position, Woodrum wrote. "The applicant has been very active in party affairs and is thoroughly reliable and responsible." The recommendation places Hill solidly within Democratic ranks at a time when the Republican Party's pivotal role in emancipation still bred loyalty from many black Americans. An even greater coup—an ironic one, given the enmity that would later emerge between the two men—lay in a handwritten note scrawled at the bottom of the page: "I concur. Harry F. Byrd, U. S. Senate."[52]

FOUR

"The Best Student I Ever Taught"

The fall of 1936 brought Oliver Hill and Spottswood Robinson into geographic proximity for the first time. As yet, neither was aware of the other.

Back in Washington, Oliver set up housekeeping with Bernie at 1322 Q Street NW, scrambled to find work—*any* work—and resolved to rise above his wounded pride. His mother's words of advice offered the same sort of practical, unsentimental reasoning that would anchor Hill's own outlook through perilous shoals in the decades ahead. "Of course I am sorry things didn't come up to your expectations," she wrote as he was leaving Roanoke. "You are still young and your chances will be better than ever, for the experience you've already had, so as you say the sensible thing to do now is to try and find something to do and get some money ahead and begin right for nothing helps prosperity like looking prosperous." She also took note of a prime handicap saddling black lawyers in the era: "You know the white man has always been prefered [*sic*] in your work even among the older [black] men."[1]

Spot Robinson was absorbing some parental advice as well. At his father's prodding, the earnest twenty-year-old agreed to ignore personal misgivings and embark on a career in the law. That meant heading north. Because of segregation, "no law school in Virginia would admit me," he recalled. "I made an application at the University of Virginia, and I just couldn't get in." The Howard School of Law offered the closest alternative. Elevating his father's counsel and pressure above his own doubts, Robinson arrived on campus in September 1936.[2] An exemplary record in his major course of study at Virginia Union supported Robinson's acceptance to Howard Law; a bachelor's degree did not. The young scholar's undergraduate plans had been derailed when his father suffered a serious gallbladder attack at the start of Robinson's junior year. Just eighteen, Robinson had taken over management of the real-estate firm. "Nobody else in the family knew about the business," he said. "I ran the thing until he got back on his feet." The next September, Robinson had returned to Union for a third and final year.[3]

Determined that his son not fall behind, Robinson Jr. urged Spot to forgo a Union diploma and get on with the next phase of his life, law school. Howard Law's admissions policy required only two years of undergraduate work. A career in the law held minimal allure for a young man whose secret passion was sketching architectural plans or imagining some intricate invention. Even selling real estate seemed livelier. "I thought that law involved a lot of close work inside an office, a lot of lonely evenings," he said. Still, parental respect and coercion trumped. "As I've always said, my father always had more sense than I did, so I became a lawyer," Robinson said.[4]

As Spot was winding up his final year at Virginia Union, the elder Robinson played a critical role in another area of his son's life. Spot and his sweetheart, Marian Bernice Wilkerson, also from Richmond, married at St. Vincent de Paul Catholic Church in Washington, DC, on May 5, 1936. She had barely turned nineteen when they wed; he was still a couple months shy of his twentieth birthday. In an interview late in life, Robinson described the marriage as an elopement. If so, it was a runaway wedding with parental approval. "Consent of boy's father filed," noted the marriage certificate for the underage couple. It was a match of opposites. Cheerful and earthy, the wholesome, freckle-faced bride provided a counterpoint to Robinson's meticulous nature. He was a scholar; her education ended with business courses at the Catholic-run Van deVyver Institute at First and DuVal Streets in Jackson Ward. Over the years, her spontaneity offset his perfectionism; her common sense balanced his drift toward stuffy bookishness. "Marian grounded Spot," his son-in-law Oswald "Ozzie" Govan said of the relationship. "She did all the things he wished he could do—just being spontaneous and natural."[5] Marian soon provided additional incentive for Spot Robinson to get about the business of adulthood. By the next year, the arrival of Spottswood William "Billy" Robinson IV had turned the couple into a threesome. With Marian settled into the Robinsons' family home in Richmond, Spot moved into a dorm on the Howard University campus. He began a periodic commute between the capital and his hometown that would continue for the next decade.

Soon, Robinson encountered the first serious academic crisis of his life. An epiphany about the law balanced that setback. Robinson had grown accustomed to academic success with modest effort. To his surprise, he initially found himself overwhelmed by the pace and demands of law school. His first real absence from Richmond and his young wife complicated the situation. "I am really sweating it out for my first few weeks in law school because I didn't know how to study," he recalled. "I managed to get through high school and college without really giving my fulltime attention and devotion to what was going on."[6] A lackadaisical attitude did not pass muster at Charles Houston's law school. The venerable administrator had resigned at Howard and moved to New York a year earlier to head NAACP legal operations, but the stamp of his drive and rigid expectations remained. Only five students had completed the requirements for graduation the spring before Robinson arrived. Now, under the interim dean William Taylor, Howard hoped to further strengthen its faculty and student body.[7] The changes would occur in a new location. Amid some alumni disgruntlement, the law school had moved the previous winter from the downtown judicial complex to the undergraduate campus further north in the city. What students lost in easy access to the Capitol and the courts, they gained in proximity to campus activism and intelligentsia in a city still strictly segregated by race.[8]

Rattled by what he perceived to have been a poor academic start, Robinson applied himself to his studies with single-minded ferocity as the autumn of 1936 passed. Meanwhile, the Houston-inspired teachings of the faculty began to work a quiet magic on Robinson's negative perceptions of a legal career. What had appeared to be a stiflingly boring pursuit suddenly emerged as an exciting, even heroic endeavor. The aim was not paper shuffling but the very real prospect of forcing America to live up to the promise of the Constitution. A combination of exactitude and hard work, both of which Robinson exemplified, could culminate in the stuff of dreams. "The turning point in my life was the day I set foot there," Robinson said of Howard Law. Before his first year was over, the bleak beginning had blossomed into a panorama of vibrant possibility.[9]

Three factors figured in the transformation. First was the message, from opening day, that attendance at Howard Law was a great privilege. The beneficiary was not to be the student alone. No one would begrudge a graduate respect or a stable financial future, but the end aim was larger than self-aggrandizement. "You are to work not simply for yourself to make money, but to make this a better society for all of us. That is an obligation you have," Robinson recalled the instruction. Second was the radicalized view of lawyers as instruments of change. Robinson and his classmates had grown up in a society characterized by separateness and inequality, but they could lead in righting the imbalances. "That was a very new insight," he said. And third was the repeated admonition not to settle for second best. Each student had an obligation to perform to his or her highest potential, not just in some areas but in all areas, all the time. Robinson took the message deeply to heart.[10]

No one preached the last point more forcefully than James M. Nabrit Jr., a porcelain-faced civil rights attorney imported from Houston, Texas, to help bolster the faculty. Nabrit's arrival in 1936 serendipitously coincided with Robinson's. A Georgia minister's son and an honors graduate of Northwestern University, Nabrit taught Robinson's first class on opening day, contract law. His admonitions stayed with the idealistic young student throughout his career. Standing at the front of the classroom, Nabrit pounded away. "Maybe you are doing a good job, and that job would be acceptable, but you could do it better. You never settle for second best," he lectured. "No matter what the problem is, if you work on it long enough and hard enough, you'll get it solved." In later years, Robinson teased his former professor about overstating the case. "Jim, that's not quite accurate. Some things are impossible." Replying in a gruff, southern dialect, Nabrit acknowledged the hyperbole: "Yeah, I know that some things are impossible, but you got to try. You always got to try. And if you try, you will find out that many things that you thought you couldn't do, you can do." "And Jim was as right about that as he could be," said Robinson, describing a philosophy that became a personal cornerstone. "There almost is no situation, if you follow that prescription, that you can't make things better. You might have a case where there's no way in the world that you can win. But you can certainly make progress. I know. I won cases that looked pretty hopeless to me."[11]

Fortified by rigor bordering on obsession, Robinson turned into an exemplary law student whose performance would set academic records and inspire admiring anecdotes. William B. Bryant, a classmate who later became a federal district judge, recalled often seeing a light burning in Robinson's room in Miner Hall long after midnight. "I honestly don't think I saw many more sunrises than Spottswood saw during that time," said Bryant, who worked the graveyard shift, midnight to eight, in a nearby switchboard room. Robinson himself laughingly recalled breaking the rules in the nineteenth-century building, a former women's dormitory where his mother had lived as a Howard undergraduate. He kept a hot plate and a percolator active during his late-night sessions, a combination that saved money but sometimes blew fuses in the ancient wiring system.[12]

Robinson's law-school social calendar was a far cry from that of his future law partner. There were no fraternity galas or late-night soirees. He spent his free time studying or commuting to Richmond to visit Marian, Billy, and his parents. The only time Bryant recalled seeing Robinson at leisure was on the tennis court. His frequent tennis opponents later came to include the political scientist and future Nobel Prize winner Ralph J. Bunche and Bill Hastie, who served in the Department of the Interior and then as a federal judge for the Virgin Islands during Robinson's student years. Even on the tennis court, Robinson's steady, methodical style proved more purposeful than playful. "He was from the beginning a very proper person and one who approached everything with the same seriousness of purpose," Bryant said.[13]

Two pivotal events foreshadowed Robinson's future during the 1938–39 academic year, his last as a Howard Law student. First, the school initiated a course in civil rights law, taught by Nabrit. Later recognized as the first such course in an American law school, the curriculum familiarized students with issues involving the civil and political rights of African Americans. The class reviewed a variety of problem areas, including police brutality, restrictive covenants, voting, educational disparities, and discrimination in state and federal employment. Nabrit expected each student to pick a topic, exhaustively research it for two semesters, and produce a paper of doctoral quality addressing the steps necessary to secure and preserve rights in the affected area. Robinson chose restrictive covenants, the clauses in real-estate deeds barring sales to racial, ethnic, or religious minorities. The paper he produced would stamp his ticket into the inner sanctum of NAACP strategists. "Spot was the best student of the law I ever taught. . . . He was always reading, always thinking, and worked harder than anyone I have ever known," said Nabrit, who would go on to his own stellar career as dean of the law school and president of Howard University.[14]

Second, Charles Houston—back in Washington as of mid-1938—elected to make Howard Law faculty and students a central part of his preparation for an assault on segregated education. On November 8, 1938, the day before he argued *Missouri ex rel. Gaines v. Canada* before the Supreme Court, Houston made a trial run at Howard Law. Listeners included Robinson, as did the audience for oral arguments before the high court the next day. The hearing was the future attorney's introduction to the august arena that would prove so pivotal in his life.[15] Houston's presentation involved the NAACP's bid to gain admittance for Lloyd L. Gaines to the all-white University of Missouri Law School. Gaines, a Mississippi native who had grown up in St. Louis and received an undergraduate degree at Lincoln University in Jefferson City, Missouri, had been denied admission to the state law school because he was black. Missouri offered him an out-of-state scholarship instead. State courts upheld the exclusion. But Houston would argue, as he and Marshall had in Maryland's *Murray* case, that no out-of-state legal education could substitute for a law-school teaching Missouri law.[16]

A month after Robinson listened to Houston's argument, the Supreme Court agreed. The 6-2 ruling held that states providing a legal education for whites must provide similar, in-state training for blacks. "The payment of tuition fees in another State does not remove the discrimination," the opinion said. States must either integrate professional schools or provide separate, comparable schools for blacks. By the time Missouri had readied a black law school at Lincoln University, Gaines had disappeared, a never-solved mystery. But Houston's victory in the Supreme Court was seen by many as the "first major breach in the wall of segregated education," a pivotal moment on the way to undoing *Plessy v. Ferguson*.[17]

For Robinson, the episode held double import. First, Houston's rehearsal was Robinson's introduction to the broad possibilities of linking the NAACP and the Howard University School of Law. Over time, as Robinson rose to the fore of the desegregation movement, that interplay with students and, more importantly, with a small group of faculty would become a critical force in honing strategies and arguments for the assault on Jim Crow. After Houston presented his case in *Gaines*, students were allowed to join in the critique. When one of the questions raised by a student was repeated by an associate justice the next day in court, the moment acquired legendary status. Second, with the court's decision, Robinson now had firsthand proof of the heady potential of the law. "For the first time, you know, we were making a real contribution to something that was really important and very alive," Robinson said years later in an interview with the journalist Juan Williams.[18]

Robert Carter, a future NAACP luminary and federal judge, a year behind Robinson at Howard, also sat in the audience that day. For students, the lasting impression Houston conveyed was that "they, too, could someday appear before the Supreme Court if they challenged themselves, despite the racial discrimination that they were forced to endure," Carter said.[19] Both Robinson and Carter heeded the call.

Meanwhile, a few miles away, Oliver Hill was preparing himself to resume legal practice as quickly as possible. Hill's priority since leaving Roanoke in the summer of 1936 had been to build a bank account sufficient to allow him to return to southwestern Virginia and start afresh. "I . . . got myself a job doing something I knew what I was doing—waiting tables," he recalled years later with a laugh. A handwritten list of Hill's jobs in the years 1936–39 includes temporary waiter on a Potomac riverboat (he did not recall the name), temporary waiter on the Atlantic Coast Line Railroad and the Seaboard Air Line Railway, and full-time waiter at the popular Harvey's Restaurant. For a man with two higher-education degrees and a plan to help revolutionize America, the period was a sojourn in the valley of humility.[20] Bernie continued to provide a stable income through teaching while also working at night toward an undergraduate degree at Howard.[21]

Hill was not the only struggling Howard Law graduate, a small consolation. Marshall also was feeling an economic weight despite successes in the University of Maryland Law School case and several others. "Things are getting worse and worse," Marshall wrote to Charles Houston in May 1936, urging his mentor to hire him. That autumn, the NAACP offered Marshall a six-month contract. He moved to New York, launching a quarter-century affiliation.[22] Many years later, Hill speculated about why he had not pursued a similar legal collaboration with Houston rather than focusing his energies on Roanoke. "I was kicking myself because if I really hadn't been so naïve and all about a lot of things, I probably would have gone on down and worked for Charlie," Hill said.[23]

Hill's higher-level skills did not go entirely untapped during the period. Shortly before Marshall left Maryland, he enlisted Hill's help with a Baltimore County education case on behalf of a thirteen-year-old plaintiff seeking admission to the all-white Catonsville High School. With his knowledge of Virginia law, Hill also earned a few dollars in a loose collaboration with J. Byron Hopkins Jr., a Howard Law graduate who had become the principal NAACP contact in Richmond and central Virginia. An August 1938 accounting reports that Hill received seventy-five dollars from Hopkins for his assistance in a Virginia case.[24]

Meanwhile, Hill joined William T. Whitehead, a former Dunbar High and Howard undergrad classmate, in a labor-organizing venture. Operating out of Whitehead's small restaurant on Georgia Avenue, the pair tried to rally the city's black waiters, cooks, and bellmen to form a united front. They hoped to affiliate with the Congress of Industrial Organizations (CIO), then battling with the older American Federation of Labor for the hearts and minds of the nation's workers. Hill's handwritten notes reveal that the group's early gatherings seesawed between trivialities and high purpose. The first formal meeting of the Waiter's, Cook's and Bellman's Club, on May 16, 1938, did not get under way until eleven o'clock at night, Hill recorded. After that, "it looks like this meeting is going to peter out before it gets started." Then, he added, "It finally did get started after all."[25] Ultimately, the unionization effort failed. The local CIO had other designs and "wouldn't take us in," Hill said. The union did offer Hill and Whitehead organizing positions on the railroad, but Hill had spent enough time riding the rails. Bernie, who struggled for more than a decade after their marriage with miscarriages and related health problems, was not entirely well. He declined.[26]

The winter of 1939 found Hill restless to return to the practice of law. Finally, the break he had been awaiting arrived in the form of a visit to Professor Ransom by Hopkins and another Richmond attorney, J. Thomas Hewin Jr., a successful, second-generation lawyer whose talents were offset by unpredictability because of drinking. The pair wanted to consult on a Virginia murder case, and Ransom invited Hill to the meeting.[27] Winding up the session, Hopkins asked Hill about his plans. He intended to return to Roanoke as soon as possible, Hill replied. Why not Richmond instead?

Hopkins asked, floating the idea of a three-H law firm, Hopkins, Hewin, & Hill. Intrigued by the prospect, Hill agreed to visit the city.

On Easter Sunday, April 9, 1939, Hill made the fateful journey that would rejuvenate his languishing career. Back in Washington, that day the contralto Marian Anderson made history as she solemnly and defiantly trilled "My country 'tis of thee, sweet land of liberty" from the steps of the Lincoln Memorial. Denied permission by the Daughters of the American Revolution to perform before an integrated audience in Constitution Hall, Anderson triumphed with an elegant performance broadcast to millions.[28] Meanwhile, in Richmond, anticipating his own resurgence, Hill shook hands on a plan to set up a law firm with Hopkins and Hewin. The pair would look for office space. Hill would return May 1 to launch the partnership.

Spot Robinson was approaching a new phase of life as well. In June he graduated with what was widely reputed to be the highest grade-point average in the history of the Howard School of Law. His 93.5 average qualified him for magna cum laude honors. Robinson joined twenty other law students in earning a degree, and the NAACP secretary, Walter White, received an honorary law degree during the evening exercises on campus.[29]

Back in Richmond that summer, helping out at his father's real-estate firm while contemplating next steps, Robinson was surprised and delighted to receive a letter from Hastie. The federal district judge had recently resigned to become dean of Howard Law. Now, the renowned litigator was offering Robinson a teaching fellowship on the faculty of the school he had just left. It was previously unheard of for a new graduate to move directly to the faculty. In fact, by offering part-time lectureships to both Robinson and James A. Washington Jr., another magna cum laude graduate from the class of 1939, Hastie was tacitly acknowledging the law school's cash-strapped condition. The hiring drew some criticism within Howard Law circles owing to the inexperience of the two young men.[30] Bernie Hill, intimately familiar through her husband with the rarefied world of Howard Law, joined those voicing displeasure. "Say[,] what about Spottswood and another last year graduate being added to the faculty of the law school," she asked in a letter to her husband. "Now I do call that sumpin'. No experience at all yet put there to teach other students. I think that's terrible."[31]

Still, for Hastie the price was right, and over time Robinson and Washington proved their mettle. Each later served as dean of the law school. Bernie's reference to "Spottwood" verifies that the two Richmond natives, her husband and his future law partner, were by then on a first-name basis. In the summer of 1939 Robinson was thrilled to accept Hastie's offer, in part because the job allowed him almost immediately to begin repaying his father for financing his law-school education. Spot had borrowed about one thousand dollars a year for three years. That money would be repaid within two years, a point of pride for the younger Robinson.[32]

Settling into his first semester, Robinson received a phone call one day that would alter the trajectory of his life. "Hello, this is Charlie Houston. I have a little something I'd like to talk to you about. When would you have a little bit of time?" Robinson had completed Howard Law without ever having a class with Houston. Even so, like most undergraduates, he knew all about the great man and had admired him from afar. But Robinson had no idea that Houston knew anything about him. Surprised, Robinson mentioned that his classes were over for the day. When would Houston like to get together? "I'll see you in twenty minutes." Click.[33]

Shortly, Robinson heard brakes squeal as a car came to a fast halt in the parking lot outside his office. Houston, bundled against the autumn chill, appeared at the door a moment later. He carried a pile of file folders under one arm. There was no briefcase, no container of any kind, just a mountain of folders, which he deposited on Robinson's desk. "I have so much to do. I need some help. These are all restrictive covenant cases. I'm hoping you can give me some help on these cases. . . . This one is going to trial. This one right here you may want to look into first, because it's in the court of appeals. We've got to get the brief to them," he said. Houston never sat down, never took off his hat. He wheeled around and started out of the office. "Mr. Houston?" Robinson interjected. "Charlie," Houston replied. From then on, the pair were on a first-name basis. "Charlie, I have a question. What in the world gives you the idea that I can do work that's going to be suitable?" "Aw, forget that. You're going to do fine. You start on this case first. And what we need, we need a draft of a brief. And when you get it ready, give me a call." A shocked Robinson got to work. Later, he learned from A. Mercer Daniels, the longtime librarian at Howard Law, that someone, probably Jim Nabrit, had informed Houston of Robinson's stellar work on restrictive covenants in Nabrit's civil rights course. The paper was on file in the library; Houston had taken it home to read.[34]

The episode was Robinson's initiation into the small brotherhood of lawyers, formed first around Houston and then around Thurgood Marshall, that emerged as the brain trust of the legal assault on Jim Crow separatism. "The group wasn't a country club, but we didn't want anybody in that group who wasn't going to make a contribution," Robinson said. That Robinson belonged was never in doubt after Houston's overture. Working closely over the next decade, the pair "became very good friends, as good as Thurgood and I were to become."[35]

As 1939 unfolded, the separate orbits of Spot Robinson and Oliver Hill were moving slowly into alignment. Each traveled frequently between Richmond and Washington. Each nourished deepening connection, through Howard Law, to the emerging core of the legal assault on Jim Crow. The serious work of reforming America was poised to begin.

INCUBATION, 1939–1950

You just got the fever. Here are guys who're spending as much time
as they could muster, all knowing that something had to be done.
—Spottswood W. Robinson III

FIVE

Breakthrough in Norfolk

Oliver Hill arrived in Richmond on the first day of May 1939, his thirty-second birthday. Global events dominated the morning headlines. A nervous world winced as Adolph Hitler demanded that Poland relinquish a fifteen-mile-wide swath of land connecting Germany and East Prussia. Meanwhile, a day earlier in New York City's Flushing Meadows Park President Franklin Roosevelt had ignored Hitler's saber rattling to launch the much-anticipated World's Fair extravaganza. In a speech broadcast nationwide and overseas, Roosevelt hitched the nation to a "star of goodwill, a star of progress for mankind, a star of greater happiness and less hardship, a star of international goodwill, and, above all, a star of peace." Closer to home, on the pages of the *Richmond Times-Dispatch* that Monday morning, the Liggett and Myers Tobacco Company boasted that its Chesterfield cigarettes were showing millions "the way to more smoking pleasure." The popular, everyman's (at least, every white man's) downtown department store Thalhimers advertised hand-embroidered toddler dresses for 59¢ and chenille bedspreads for $2.39. The editor, Virginius Dabney, urged adoption of James Bland's "Carry Me Back to Old Virginny" as the official state song. The tune, replete with nostalgic references to "massa" and "this old darkey's heart," was "universally sung, hummed, whistled, and strummed," he noted.

On a more troubling note, Richmonders did not need to look to Europe to observe violent intimidation that May Day. Some nine hundred miles to the south in Miami, a band of hooded Ku Klux Klan members advanced menacingly through a black neighborhood to warn against voting in the next day's citywide primary. With license plates shrouded, more than fifty automobiles joined the procession. An effigy twisting on a pole warned, "This Nigger Voted." In a sign of strengthening black resolve, the scare tactics backfired: black voting increased substantially in the city's May 2 primary.[1]

Happy to be back in the city of his early childhood and impatient to start carving a professional name for himself, Hill scrambled to find temporary housing and begin introducing himself to the movers and shakers of black Richmond. "I am still meeting people and impressing them favorably, I hope," Hill wrote soon after his arrival. Tall, prematurely balding, frequently sporting a cigar, the newcomer appeared both distinguished and approachable. He could chat easily with almost anyone, and his level-headedness inspired confidence. Meanwhile, Hill had a surprise to digest: while Byron Hopkins had signed off on the idea of a new law firm that included Hill, Tom Hewin, it developed, had not. Hewin, who shared an office with his attorney father in the St. Luke Bank Building, apparently wanted to continue that arrangement. Besides, he was nowhere to be found.[2] A week after arriving in the city, Hill described Hewin's odd behavior to Bernie: "Tom Hewin has been absent for about ten days. This morning we learned he is in New York. Whether that is the jive or not, I do not know. He goes on [drinking] sprees every now and then I have been told." Bernie counseled: "Where in the world does he go—you all should make him see how serious it is."[3]

Adjusting to changed circumstances, Hill located office space at 117 East Leigh Street in Jackson Ward. For a weekly rent of five dollars, he acquired use of a back room and a bathroom and shared reception space in a house where a friend had set up a medical practice. To save money, Hill began sleeping there as well. Bernie, awarded an undergraduate degree at Howard's June commencement, remained in Washington. Her teaching salary once again balanced the vagaries of her husband's fledgling law practice. While she would make many weekend visits and even spend parts of summers in Richmond, Bernie did not take up residence with her husband until after World War II.[4]

Despite the collapse of plans for an official firm, both Hopkins and Hewin proved eager to involve the assertive new member of Richmond's black bar in their cases. Soon, Hill was joining one or the other as they traveled the region, tending to criminal and general law matters. Before the summer was out, he would be helping with NAACP antidiscrimination work as well. He relished the challenge. "I'm very proud of my attorney husband who travels over the state in various cases," wrote Bernie to him in early June. And a month later, "You all certainly seem to be getting around the [country]. Did Hop go with you? I surely am glad you're so interested in what you're doing. . . .How do you like living in the office? Is the bed soft?"[5]

Hill's letters contain no mention of another Richmond lawyer, Spottswood Robinson Jr., but it seems certain that the newcomer would have crossed paths with his future law partner's father. The ranks of black professionals were too small and too dependent on mutual support to think otherwise. When Spottswood III returned to Richmond in mid-June, after completing his law degree, he and Hill surely interacted as well. The nine-year age gap put the pair in different social circles, but each had developed a reputation that would have intrigued and attracted the other.

The summer of 1939, as it evolved, proved to be a watershed for black activism in Virginia. Years of NAACP grassroots instruction and preparation coalesced in demands from the western Alleghany Highlands to the eastern Tidewater, from the North Carolina border to the outskirts of Washington, for greater fairness in voting, access to public facilities, and improved educational amenities. The surge led Lutrelle F. Palmer, a prominent black educator and longtime editor of the *Virginia Teachers Bulletin*, to contend that historians would likely choose 1939 "as the turning point in what seemed to be a futile and hopeless struggle." Both Hill and Robinson were well positioned to ride that wave.[6]

The increased activism occurred against a backdrop of rising NAACP visibility and expectation nationally and statewide. Under the tutelage of President J. M. Tinsley, a compact and fastidious Richmond dentist who was deeply committed to the cause, the Virginia State Conference of Branches had emerged as one of the advocacy group's most successful state organizations. A graduate of the dental school at Meharry Medical College in Nashville, Tinsley was a native Virginian whose courtliness did not entirely mask a blunt edge and a steely core. He had been chairman of the Richmond NAACP branch since 1931 and state president most years since the merger into a statewide organization in 1935. By 1941 the Virginia conference would boast more local branches than any other state NAACP group. Reflecting that success, Marshall in 1940 cited the Virginia and Oklahoma conferences as the only two "worth a dime." That same year, Andy Ransom referred to the Virginia conference as "the strongest unit of its kind in the United States." The success was attributable in no small measure to the hardworking, exacting Tinsley.[7]

The national NAACP rewarded Virginia's diligence by selecting Richmond to host the group's national convention in the summer of 1939. Both Hill and Robinson likely attended a bold address to the conventioneers by Charles Houston, who rattled white Virginians by urging integrated classrooms at public universities. The future law partners would also have known of the galvanizing moment at the gathering when First Lady Eleanor Roosevelt presented Marian Anderson with the NAACP's Spingarn Medal, its highest award—one that Hill himself would receive sixty-six years later.[8]

Aline Elizabeth Black stood at the eye of the storm in Virginia that spring and summer. The accomplished chemistry teacher at Norfolk's Booker T. Washington High School had agreed to lend her name to a lawsuit challenging the shameful imbalance in pay for black and white teachers. For the genesis of Black's case, one needs to dial back four years to the first tandem meeting of the Virginia Teachers Association and the state NAACP in Roanoke, which Hill attended. Activists in the teachers' group had long wanted a more aggressive response to racial inequities in education. More conservative members held back, fearing reprisal. Following what the historian Earl Lewis called "a massive [NAACP] education program" on the merits of pursuing equality through the courts, a dramatic shift had come at the association's golden jubilee state convention at the Hampton Institute in November 1937.[9] After an address in which Thurgood Marshall reminded his audience of recent successes in Maryland courts in equalizing teacher pay, the executive committee offered a proposal for a similar campaign in Virginia. At that moment, the association changed from "a Reading Circle to an aggressive, fighting, teacher-and-child-representative organization," wrote Rupert Picott in a history of the group. "Not a dissenting voice was heard" as the teachers agreed to push for salaries equal to those of whites.[10]

Under the new plan, the NAACP and the teachers' association each named five members to a joint committee on equalizing black and white teachers' salaries. The teachers immediately invested one thousand dollars, and the two organizations committed to jointly raising another five thousand. Everyone understood that the fund guaranteed the salary of anyone courageous enough to mount a legal challenge. To minimize opportunity for white retribution, Tinsley agreed to serve as the public face of the Joint Committee for Equalization of Teachers' Salaries even though leadership was shared with the teachers' group.[11]

Finding a teacher willing to lend his or her name to a court challenge proved to be no easy task. Donating money was one thing; opening oneself up to firing, or worse, required tougher mettle. Ideally, NAACP strategists thought, the lawsuit should come in a populous and relatively progressive area of the state. As Virginia's largest city and a citadel of independent political views, Norfolk fit the description. Finally, in the fall of 1938, Black stepped forward. Highly skilled and proud of it, Black considered the city's pay scale to be an affront. The maximum pay for the port city's black high-school teachers ($1,105 for women and $1,235 for men) was only slightly higher than the minimum for whites ($970 for women and $1,200 for men). With an undergraduate degree from Virginia State College, a master's from the University of Pennsylvania, a dozen years' classroom experience, and certifications to teach English, Spanish, science, and chemistry, Black was an ideal candidate to insist on equal pay.[12] The Virginia Court of Appeals judge James Benton, a student of Black's two decades later, recalled the force of her personality and the quality of her teaching. "She was tough. She was very demanding." She was also "very bitter about her treatment by the courts and the school system," Benton said.[13]

As an NAACP legal team including Marshall, Ransom, and Hewin began preparing a lawsuit on Black's behalf, other Virginia communities also roiled with discontent. In March 1939 the Norfolk-based *Journal and Guide* reported that out of almost $350,000 allotted for new schools in Alleghany County, less than $34,000 was slated for a new black high school. Adding insult, the school was due to be built on a spot known locally as Slaughter Pen Hollow, reflecting its previous use. In February the *Richmond Afro-American* recounted a speech in which the state supervisor of black education, Fred M. Alexander, told of visiting a one-room school in which a single teacher served 118 black students. And throughout the year, a writer by the name, or pen name, of Nat Turner used official state data to inform *Afro-American* readers of widespread school discrimination. (Another Nat Turner had led a brutal slave uprising in Southampton County in 1831.) In Cumberland County, west of Richmond, for instance, black children made up 63 percent of the school population but received only 27 percent of educational funds. Similarly, in Essex County, northeast of Richmond, not a single high school served an almost two-thirds black majority. Comparable stories abounded across Virginia.[14]

Against that backdrop, Black and her lawyers appeared in state court on May 31, seeking an order compelling Norfolk officials to set a single salary scale for black and white teachers. Paying Black less solely because of her race violated the equal-protection and due-process clauses of the Fourteenth Amendment, they argued. City attorneys countered that Black had waived those rights when she voluntarily signed a contract to teach under the existing pay scale. Ruling from the bench, Judge Allan R. Hanckel displayed none of the enlightenment the NAACP had hoped for in picking Norfolk. He agreed with the city that Black's contract trumped. Her lawyers immediately filed a protest with the Virginia Supreme Court of Appeals.[15]

The action coincided with Hill's first weeks in Richmond. "Too bad about the Norfolk case or was it too bad?" Bernie asked in a letter a few days after Hanckel's decision. "Maybe you all will plan an appeal, eh?" The reference suggests that a month after his move to Virginia, Hill already was part of the circle weighing NAACP legal strategy.[16] Two weeks later, Black's appeal became moot when the Norfolk School Board brazenly denied her a contract for the next teaching year. Black had no job, and the NAACP had lost its plaintiff. In New York, the national legal staff issued a furious rebuke: "The attitude of the Norfolk, Va., school board in denying Miss Black reappointment and deducting $4.01 from her check for the day she lost [due to her court appearance] is utterly shameless."[17]

A few days later, an estimated twelve hundred black citizens jammed St. John's African Methodist Episcopal (AME) Church in downtown Norfolk to protest the action. Within range of the nation's largest naval base, a group of black schoolchildren led by a Boy Scout drum and bugle corps paraded down city streets brandishing banners proclaiming, "Dictators— Hitler, Mussolini, Norfolk School Board" and "Our School Board Has Vetoed the Bill of Rights." Louis Jaffe, the Pulitzer Prize–winning, racially liberal editor of the city's white-owned morning newspaper, the *Virginian-Pilot*, viewed the firings and their fallout with dismay. "This kind of thing does untold damage to the city's interracial relations," he wrote in urging Black's rehiring.[18] Outrage aside, the NAACP lawyers had no option other than to start afresh by seeking a new plaintiff. The Joint Committee assumed Black's salary of $1,105 for the coming year, as agreed. In the flurry, a similar result across the state went relatively unnoticed: three black teachers in Pulaski also lost contracts after they advocated improved school conditions for black children.[19]

While the NAACP launched its search for a new plaintiff, other civil rights activities in Virginia did not languish. Close to midnight one evening in early August, Tom Hewin dropped by Hill's office-home to enlist his help in a voting rights case in Greensville County. The Democratic primary was coming up the next week, and a group of black men known as the Hundred Men's Club wanted a court order guaranteeing their participation.[20] Virginia operated under a decade-old federal-court ruling qualifying blacks to vote in primary elections paid for by the state. James O. West, a black Richmonder who had met poll-tax and other voting requirements, had protested the refusal of election judges to give him a ballot in the April 1928 Democratic primary. A federal-district-court judge sided with West, and the Court of Appeals for the Fourth Circuit agreed. Fearing another loss, Democratic-primary officials elected not to take the case on to the US Supreme Court. So within the judicial circuit the ruling stood.[21]

Still, election officials did not always comply. Hewin and Hill agreed to make sure Greensville County's did. Working into the night, the pair drew up the necessary papers, and the next morning they set off on the sixty-mile trip to the county seat, Emporia. After hearing the arguments, the judge agreed that black voters should be allowed to participate in the primary. He was not going to assume that the election officials would act improperly, however. Hill and Hewin could monitor the next Tuesday's election. If problems arose, they should seek an immediate compliance order.

The follow-up to the judge's ruling produced what for Hill was the single most frightening episode of his civil rights work. Over the years, a cross would be burned in the Hills' yard and he would receive numerous threatening letters and phone calls, but no episode alarmed him more than what occurred as he and Hewin drove the lonely, leafy back roads of Greensville County that August primary day looking for possible election trouble. They did not doubt that word of the court action brought by two cheeky, big-city lawyers had preceded them. Nor did their imaginations need travel far to envision the sinister welcome party that might await them around any turn. Earlier in 1939, the jazz singer Billie Holiday had released her rendition of "Strange Fruit," with its chilling image of lynched bodies. Now it was moving up the Billboard charts. Moreover, the region was no stranger to racial violence. Fourteen years before Hill and Hewin's visit, a five-hundred-person mob in neighboring Sussex County had dragged from the county jail James Jordan, a twenty-two-year-old black man accused of attacking a white woman. The frenzied throng had hanged Jordan from a tree, riddled his body with bullets, and burned the remains to a crisp.[22] State officials claimed that there had been no lynchings in Virginia since 1928, when the state became the first to pass an antilynching law. Doubters believed that two state deaths ruled suicides—one each in 1932 and 1935—likely had resulted from mob violence, however. Meanwhile, federal antilynching legislation sat bottled up in Congress, blocked by southern senators. A decline in lynching since the fever-pitch days at the turn of the century did not mean that the noxious practice had been erased. Charred and mutilated bodies still swung from southern trees.[23]

As Hewin and Hill rounded a curve in Hewin's 1936 Ford, the road plunged down a steep hillside to a covered bridge over the Meherrin River. Suddenly, a swarm of white men holding rope, sticks, and long poles took shape. Alert to the danger, Hill scanned the roadway for an escape route. He saw none. The only option was to drive forward. As they slowly descended the hill, one of the men blurted out what both were thinking: "Looks like this is it." "Sure does," the other replied. Reaching the bridge, they slowly inched the car through the crowd. No one stopped them. About midway, Hill saw a gaping hole in one side of the bridge. Then, he recognized the object of the white men's concern: not two black lawyers but a car that had gone off the side of the bridge. The crowd was attempting to pull the car up with the poles and rope. "Looks like they're fishing—trying to fish that automobile out of the river," Hill joked, easing the tension. Exhaling, he regained his equilibrium. A short stretch down the road, Hewin pulled the car to a stop and offered the wheel to Hill. "'I'm too weak [to drive],'" Hill recalled Hewin saying. Both men had thought they were driving into a lynching—their own.[24]

Two weeks later, emerging resistance to Jim Crow segregation popped up in yet another Virginia jurisdiction, Alexandria. On the humid summer morning of August 21, 1939, the assistant librarian Alice Green was staffing the desk at the city's public library when a neatly attired, young African American man requested a lending card. When Green explained that the library was only for white citizens, he calmly walked to the shelves, pulled out a book, and sat down at a table to read. Moments later, a second black man entered the library and repeated the drill, then a third, a fourth, and a fifth. A library worker rushed to the home of the head librarian, Catharine Scoggin, with the news. She, in turn, hurried to city hall to discuss the matter with the city manager and the chief of police. By the time the group headed back to the library to confront the troublemakers, a crowd of several hundred observers, including newspaper reporters and photographers, had gathered. When the five insurgents calmly refused to move, the police arrested them and escorted them out. Employing a term then in vogue to describe a labor-organizing tactic, the *Washington Post* the next day called the episode a "sit-down" strike.

Nowhere to be seen, but monitoring from his nearby office at 901 Princess Street, the mastermind of the political action—Hill's former study mate, Sam Tucker—smiled as the events unfolded as planned. Over the next months, the twenty-six-year-old rebel would see his celebration sour. Tucker wanted an integrated public library. What he got instead was a well-constructed but inferior separate library for blacks. The Robert H. Robinson Library opened in April 1940. The charges against the young demonstrators quietly faded away, never resolved. The outcome satisfied some, but not Tucker. He adopted a stance that foretold decades of defiance to come. He applied for a library card at the main library. The attorney had no intention, he told Scoggin, of accepting second-class citizenship by frequenting the new library for blacks.[25]

The Alexandria action had not been planned by the NAACP. But as the charges moved through the courts, the sit-down drew the group's admiration. Houston, now back practicing law in Washington, offered advice and support to Tucker. As for Hill, a man still hoping to find a law partner, the episode served as a reminder that his old friend, home after a two-year stint with the Civilian Conservation Corps, was alive, well, and adept at needling Virginia's white power structure.

Back in Norfolk, in September a new plaintiff emerged to shoulder a pay-inequity lawsuit. A reluctant recruit, Melvin Alston, president of the Norfolk Teachers Association and a fifth-year veteran at Booker T. Washington High, agreed to lend his name to a second challenge. A cautious and somewhat nervous sort, Alston had no illusions about the likelihood of success. He wanted clear assurance that his salary would be covered if—or, more likely, when—he was fired.[26] At a September 15 meeting of the joint committee for salary equalization, Thurgood Marshall laid out the particulars of the revised NAACP strategy. Rather than seek a mandamus ordering equal salaries, as the lawyers had with Black, they would simplify matters in Alston's case by asking for an injunction to stop payment of unequal salaries. Even more significant, this time they planned to file in federal rather than state court.[27]

The strategy paralleled the NAACP's new approach in Maryland. Marshall and others had tired of the plodding, county-by-county, state-court effort to equalize teacher salaries. By switching to a federal arena, Marshall might gain a precedent that would carry broader weight nationally. A complaint by Walter Mills, a teacher and principal in Anne Arundel County, offered one such opportunity. Marshall filed Mills's lawsuit in the US District Court for the District of Maryland.[28]

The decision came as Marshall was acquiring added clout within the NAACP. In May 1939, with Houston's return to Washington, the charismatic, younger attorney officially acquired the group's top legal title, "special counsel." The next year, Marshall would land another credential, becoming director-counsel of the newly formed NAACP Legal Defense and Educational Fund, Inc. Over time, that group would most often be referred to as the Inc. Fund or simply the LDF. Creation of the Legal Defense Fund allowed the parent NAACP to separate its lobbying arm from its legal and education work for tax purposes. Major donors could make tax-exempt contributions to the Legal Defense Fund but not to the NAACP, which lobbied for antilynching and other legislation. An overlapping board coordinated the efforts of the two groups until the mid-1950s, when the oversight and legal functions also split. Marshall's assaults on Jim Crow during the 1940s and 1950s would be leveled under the Legal Defense Fund's banner.

As the New York and Washington lawyers readied for the Alston case, they welcomed a new team member. Tom Hewin still assisted, but now Oliver Hill also was named as a Virginia contact. The NAACP reimbursed the men a combined $28.80 for attending federal court in Baltimore in

October, presumably on the Mills case, as well as for conferences in the District of Columbia involving the Virginia teachers' salary case. In addition, the gifted Bill Hastie was back in circulation as dean of Howard Law School. When the formal petition for an injunction was filed on behalf of Alston and the Norfolk Teachers Association on November 2, the papers listed the plaintiffs' attorneys as Hewin and Hill of Richmond, Ransom and Hastie of Washington, and Marshall of New York.[29] Over the next several months, the unreliable Hewin faded, and Hill emerged as the primary Virginia lawyer in the case. Soon, correspondence from the national team was being directed to Hill's address. Irreverent greetings and joshing put-downs reveal the closeness of the group and the extent to which Hill already was an established peer. He often addressed Marshall familiarly as "Dear Nogood" and signed his letters with flair, "Blah, blah, Peanuts." Marshall usually greeted Hill by his old nickname, "Dear Peanuts." Once, after chiding Hill for writing a confusing letter—"Your letter of June 27 was almost as clear as mud"—Marshall wrapped up, "Love and kisses, Thurgood." Hill clarified the matter, then replied in kind: "I hope even you can understand this now darling. Blah, blah, Peanuts."[30]

Fearing a repeat of the Aline Black fiasco, Alston's legal team wanted to move the new challenge along as quickly as possible. If matters dragged into the summer, the NAACP might find itself outfoxed by the school board once again. Already the city appeared to be stalling. Since the school-board office was working overtime to prepare for a new school term, "we will not be able to give you access to various records you wish to examine next week," wrote C. Alfred Anderson, the city's principal lawyer, on January 13, 1940. Marshall's team had little option but to grit their teeth and wait.[31] Finally, on February 12, Alston and his attorneys—Marshall, Hastie, Ransom, and Hill—filed into Norfolk's massive art deco federal courthouse to debate the city's motion to dismiss the case. If the Alston team won, then the district-court judge, Luther B. Way, would schedule a trial, probably in March. A North Carolina native and graduate of the University of Virginia School of Law, Way had served as a special assistant US attorney before being appointed to the federal bench by President Herbert C. Hoover in 1931. A genial sort, the judge had been broadly endorsed for the judicial post.[32]

Alston's legal team planned for Marshall to introduce the case. Then Hill would take over for his debut performance in a federal courtroom.

That was not to be. When Way greeted Marshall with aggressive questioning, the team quickly recalibrated. It would be safer for Hastie, the more experienced of the two lawyers, to substitute for Hill. As it turned out, it hardly mattered who fielded the questions. After a half day of arguments, Way ruled from the bench in favor of the city. While he acknowledged the oddity of maintaining separate salary scales based solely on race, he said that the overriding factor was "the solemn obligations of a contract." Those who wished to challenge the constitutionality of a pay scale should do so before signing a contract. Never mind that they would have no income while the matter meandered through the courts.[33] A discouraged quartet noted an appeal and started the long slog back to Washington, via Richmond to drop off Hill. En route, a radio newscaster injected a ray of light into the gloom. Earlier that day, the report said, the Supreme Court had ruled for the NAACP in *Chambers v. Florida*, a death-penalty case involving brutally coerced confessions. In an eloquently written opinion, Justice Hugo Black—himself a former Ku Klux Klan member—decreed that state courts no less than federal ones must uphold due process of the law under the Fourteenth Amendment. The gratifying victory salved the attorneys' disappointment over the *Alston* setback.[34]

Over the next month, the lawyers worked feverishly to speed Fourth Circuit review of Way's ruling before the summer recess. Waiting until the court's mid-June term would be too late, they feared. Neither Alston nor his lawyers had any doubt that, given the chance, the Norfolk School Board would strip Alston of a contract for the next year, just as it had Black. "I hope you agree that we have all got to put everything into this brief and, if necessary, I will drop most of my other work," Marshall counseled members of the legal team.[35] Hill complained that Norfolk again was up to familiar tricks. "I talked with Anderson today on the telephone and he came up with a lame excuse. . . . I am positive he is purposely delaying drafting the final order," Hill wrote.[36]

Acknowledging Hill's growing role in the case, Marshall took time out to compliment his colleague: "If you will send also a bill for Fifty Dollars ($50.00) for services in case to date, I will see if I can get you a check for that amount some time in the future. I do not know just when we will be able to pay it but we certainly should pay something to you on your fine work."[37] A week later, he forwarded Hill's invoice to Roy Wilkins, assistant to Walter White, urging payment. "In the first place, I think he has actually earned much more than the $50 and in the second place, he is the only lawyer in Virginia whom we can rely upon 100 percent," Marshall wrote. In a separate note, he updated Hill with typical banter: "If our treasury continues to maintain its present balance you should get this Fifty Dollars some time within the next twenty years."[38]

As the April term approached, the lawyers pondered how to slip the case onto the court's docket. The Fourth Circuit's clerk advised that consent by opposing counsel would be helpful, if not essential. Hill contacted Anderson, urging his cooperation. To no one's surprise, the city attorney balked: "If conditions permitted I should be glad to accommodate you, but we will have to insist that the case take its regular course."[39] A disheartened Marshall resigned himself to the inevitable. "It seems to me that Anderson will not move from his position and we will have to wait for the case to go on the June Calendar," he wrote to Hill.[40]

With the court set to end its April term on Friday, April 12, the lawyers gathered at Howard University the prior weekend for a last-ditch review. Hill arrived from Richmond; Marshall took the train from New York. Ransom, as a faculty member, and Hastie, as dean, were already at the law school. For several hours, the team considered—and discarded—various ideas. Nothing seemed workable. Then, just as the group was about to disband, Hill tossed out a novel idea: what if one of them went before the Fourth Circuit panel, explained the stakes, and asked for *Alston* to be heard in a special session between April and June? Why not throw themselves on the court's mercy? With all other options foreclosed, Hastie looked Hill in the eye and asked, "Are you willing to do it?" "I'll do it," Hill replied with a confidence that had evaporated by the next day.[41]

Four days later, Hill entered the stately federal courtroom on the fourth floor of the United States Custom House and Post Office building on Main Street in downtown Richmond. A historic structure that had housed the office of the Confederate president, Jefferson Davis, during the Civil War and was one of only two major buildings in the city core that survived the burning of Richmond at the war's end, the building itself evoked awe in Hill. The eminent three-judge panel looming over the proceedings added a touch of trepidation. It did not help that the chief judge, John J. Parker, an imposing North Carolinian, had an unpleasant history with the NAACP. The organization had opposed his nomination by President Hoover to the Supreme Court in 1930 in part because of Parker's assertion during a gubernatorial bid a decade earlier that blacks in politics were "a source of evil and danger to both races." That opposition had contributed to Parker's rejection by the Senate.[42]

"May it please the court," Hill began his first speaking appearance in a federal courtroom. "Wait a minute," Parker interrupted. "You mean you want the United States government to go to the expense of bringing this court back here just for the purpose of hearing your case?" Yes, Hill replied. "And what's so important about your case?" asked Parker. In answer, Hill launched into the story of Aline Black. If the *Alston* case went unheard until June, the school year would end, and Norfolk might well deny a second plaintiff a contract. Once again, a case would be moot. Judge Morris A. Soper, a Maryland judge considered relatively open to NAACP persuasion, interrupted, "What you want is an injunction, isn't it?" Hill could scarcely contain his delight. "Yes, sir, it is."

At that moment Anderson, who had been calmly listening to the proceedings, leapt to his feet and hurried toward the bench. There would be no need for any such order, he told the judge. But were the facts of Hill's claim regarding Aline Black true? Anderson had to admit that they were. In that case, said Parker, the matter should proceed to a June hearing. He was not going to order a special session. However, no black teachers in Norfolk were to receive their contracts for the next year until the pay-parity question was resolved, and Anderson should understand one thing: if there was any attempt to fire Alston, Judge Parker wanted the principals back in his courtroom with an explanation. "We'll find a way to do something about it," Parker warned.[43]

Elated, Hill dashed off a special-delivery bulletin to Hastie, Ransom, and Marshall. The news was better than anyone had dared hope. From New York a delighted Marshall wired praise: "Congratulations on Splendid Job. Suggest you send press story to Journal and Guide and Afro."[44] The heady victory signaled Hill's coming of age to his former law professors and the NAACP legal staff. From that moment forward, if there had been any doubt, the Virginian was a full-fledged member of the inner circle. Within hours of notification of Parker's action, Marshall forwarded Hill's note to the joint committee for salary equalization. He applauded the Virginian's central role. "We left the matter entirely in the hands of Hill," he said. The special counsel could not offer his law-school buddy much in the way of financial remuneration, but he could buff Hill's reputation. Meanwhile, he prodded Wilkins regarding the fifty-dollar check. "We have had a tremendous amount of difficulty with local lawyers in Va. and at last we have one whom we can work with. . . . FIFTY DOLLARS does not begin to pay Hill for his services but it will be a good gesture." Two days later Wilkins authorized the payment.[45]

As the Asheville hearing on the Norfolk pay case approached, Hill had to quiet the fears of Melvin Alston and other black teachers who were confused by the court's order delaying the renewal of their teaching contracts. "This has the local group very much upset," Alston telegraphed Marshall, who instructed Hill to set them straight. He complied, writing Alston an understated note: "I am surprised to hear that some of the teachers are perturbed over what to me seemed to be very heartening news." Hill explained that the blanket delay of contracts protected against anyone being fired for challenging the pay system. It also indicated that the court was taking the case seriously. The letter appeared to satisfy Alston, but the episode signaled a level of distrust between at least some Norfolk teachers and the national NAACP. That skepticism would surface again on both sides, fraying nerves, before the teacher-pay issue finally was resolved.[46]

Just back from Texas, where he was trying to develop yet another case challenging all-white Democratic primaries, an overextended Marshall cemented plans for the Fourth Circuit hearing in Asheville. He arranged hotel rooms in the scenic mountain town for June 11 through June 13, and he proposed driving to North Carolina in a single car. "It would be cheaper if we drive down in my car and this trip can be made easily with three drivers, namely, Hastie, Hill and TM," he wrote. In a separate letter, Marshall urged the president of the Asheville branch of the NAACP to rally black teachers for a courtroom appearance: "The psychological effect of well-dressed, intelligent and interested colored people in the court room is a vitally important part of such procedure."[47]

On June 13, as dismayed Americans grappled with news of the fall of Paris to German troops, Marshall, Hastie, Ransom, and Hill entered the Asheville courtroom. They faced a formidable panel—the strong-minded Parker, Soper of Maryland, and Armistead M. Dobie, who the attorneys feared might sympathize with school officials. Dobie's father, after all, had once served as superintendent of Norfolk schools. The black lawyers reviewed the constitutional arguments against paying teachers different salaries solely on the basis of race. Norfolk's attorneys countered that school boards hold discretionary power to set salaries, independent of constitutional rights. A newspaper reporter covering the hearing ventured that action by the court was unlikely before the beginning of its next quarterly term in Richmond.[48] That proved to be a misreading. Five days later, in a unanimous opinion written by the one-time race-baiter Parker, the Fourth Circuit reversed Judge Way. "This is as clear a discrimination on the ground of race as could well be imagined," Parker wrote. Pay differentials based on race violated the Fourteenth Amendment. School authorities could decide whom to employ, but all employees were entitled to compensation "fixed without unconstitutional discrimination on account of race." Furthermore, the petition should be considered a class-action suit, applicable to all black teachers.[49] NAACP attorneys were recognizing an important truth: federal judges were friendlier to their arguments than many state and local jurists.

Once again, Hill had the happy task of conveying electrifying news northward. In a Western Union wire he informed Marshall: "Alston case reversed. [Court clerk] Dean will mail copy opinion as soon as printed."[50] Technically, Norfolk had a three-month window in which to appeal the decision to the Supreme Court, but the lawyers doubted that the city would waste time doing so. They expected the case to return to Judge Way for either a perfunctory trial or a quick settlement. Victory was within reach. This time the surprise was on them. Two days before the deadline, Hill notified his colleagues that the city indeed had filed a request for a high-court review. Marshall cautioned against discouragement. "We are in a better position than we have ever been before and the School Board is now on the defensive more than ever," he reassured the Norfolk Teachers Association. Ever mindful of the potential for mischief, he advised, "Just one word of caution: It is necessary that all of you do your very best teaching while this fight is going on so that there will be no casualties."[51]

Meanwhile, Marshall once again showed his gratitude to Hill, as well as his determination to imbed Hill at the helm of black lawyers in Virginia. In a private letter to Lutrelle Palmer, who served as executive secretary of the Norfolk Teachers Association in addition to editing its magazine, Marshall asked an important favor, one not to be publicized. "I am wondering if it will be possible to put Oliver W. Hill some place on the program" of the group's upcoming annual meeting, Marshall wrote. "He has worked hard throughout the case and he has given us better cooperation than any other local attorney we have ever had in any of our teachers' salary cases throughout the country." Placement on the program would help compensate for the very little the NAACP had been able to pay Hill, Marshall said. More importantly, it would help position Hill for a new role Marshall envisioned: "We hope that after the Alston case is finally completed we will be able to turn the balance of the cases in Virginia over to him in order to reduce expenses and to enable us to go into other States." The statement was an unequivocal vote of confidence. A week later, Palmer acquiesced. "I am very glad that you made this suggestion to me as I have long recognized the value of Mr. Hill's services to our cause," he replied.[52]

On October 28, the Supreme Court flushed Norfolk out of its last refuge with a one-word answer to the city's petition, "Denied." Writing in the next issue of the *Virginia Teachers Bulletin*, Palmer waxed euphoric. The combination of *Gaines* and *Alston* "form the Magna Charta for the education of Negroes in the segregated schools of the South," he wrote, adding that the latest decision "marks the beginning of the end of the shameful practices" denying black children equal education.[53]

Alston was not the first public-school pay-equalization order to emerge from a federal courtroom. That distinction had gone to the Walter Mills case filed by Marshall in Maryland in the fall of 1939. But the Maryland case had gone no further than the federal district court. In Virginia, a federal appellate court had upheld the principle that contracts did not trump the Constitution's guarantees of due process and equal protection regardless of race. And by refusing to reconsider that opinion, the Supreme Court had validated it. This was the precedent for which Marshall had yearned. The ruling should speed rebuke of unequal pay and substandard black schooling all across the segregated South.[54]

The *Alston* ruling would serve other, unintended consequences. The case also demonstrated the resolve of the white power structure in clinging to the status quo, and it exposed fissures in the African American community. Marshall had long worried about the mettle of Norfolk's black teachers. However, not only reluctant educators obstructed the NAACP's vision in the days ahead; stalwarts of Norfolk's black establishment, accustomed to negotiating every inch of progress, also would elevate cordial race relations above pay parity. The NAACP team knew exactly what the city's black teachers deserved as a result of the court case: an immediate equalization of salaries, estimated to cost about $129,000. As the case returned to Judge Way's courtroom, the NAACP lawyers were willing to grant the city a bit of leeway. To them, that meant delaying full implementation for a year, no more, with partial settlement beginning as soon as final orders in the case were signed. Others had a different vision.

Chief among them was P. B. Young, the noted publisher of the *Journal and Guide* newspaper. An up-by-the-bootstraps entrepreneur, the North Carolina native over three decades had made his Norfolk-based paper into the third largest circulating black weekly in the United States. Serious minded and often dour faced, Young had begun his career as a Booker T. Washington conservative, trumpeting the virtues of hard work, thrift, and compromise. "I am definitely opposed to frontal attack. I believe in nego-tiation, arbitration, conciliation and persuasion," he had said during the early years. As white America stalled and dissembled its way around pleas for antilynching legislation, open voting, and other nonnegotiable rights of citizenship, Young had gradually toughened his tone and his tactics. On the local level, however, he valued cordiality and dialogue.[55]

Over the next several months, Marshall and Young would spar angrily over the terms of the Norfolk settlement. Young saw in the Supreme Court's action a bargaining chip for addressing the needs of Norfolk's black community. Marshall, Hill, and the other Legal Defense Fund law-yers saw an unequivocal order for pay equalization and an opportunity to build the clout of the NAACP. Port-city officials stoked dissent with subtle threats of community retaliation if blacks insisted on confrontational tac-tics and a supposedly budget-busting settlement. On election night, as Roosevelt coasted to a third-term victory over the Republican business-man Wendell L. Wilkie, Norfolk's city council and school board approved a three-year settlement offer. The thirty-thousand-dollar minimum to be paid to teachers in the first year was less than the NAACP attorneys thought they were due.[56]

Two days later, with a vote by the teachers scheduled for that evening, Marshall and Ransom closeted themselves with Young in the editor's of-fice to hash out differences. Dripping sarcasm, the special counsel accused Young and his allies of acting as if the NAACP had lost the case, not won it. When Young replied that Norfolk's city manager had long wanted a settlement, Marshall mocked the notion. "I told him that it was mighty strange that the City Manager did not take any action toward compromise until after they had lost in every Court up to and including the Supreme Court." When the special counsel added that he planned to warn the teachers against Young-style accommodation, the editor—by Marshall's telling—became visibly enraged. "He became angrier and less coherent. He then said that he didn't care what I said and if we wanted to have this thing out, he was willing. I told him that we had no desire or idea of fighting anyone." Young urged Marshall to let the teachers make up their own minds, and Marshall consented.[57]

When the educators gathered that evening, Young put in an unexpected appearance. Invited to speak, he made an impassioned plea for conciliation. Seated in the audience, smoldering, Marshall remained silent, honoring what he believed was the agreement made earlier in the day. When the teachers voted to adopt the city's offer, however, Marshall was furious. "It is the joint opinion of Hastie, Ransom, Hill and myself that this is the most disgraceful termination of any cases involving Negroes in recent years," he wrapped up the situation in a memo. Unless the joint committee for salary equalization agreed at an upcoming meeting that nothing similar would happen again in Virginia, "we will be forced to resign as counsel on all of these cases," he seethed.[58]

Over the next two weeks matters quieted somewhat. The Virginia Teachers Association helped by approving a one-thousand-dollar contribution to the NAACP in appreciation of its work on *Alston.* Young wrote Marshall that "I am sorry about the misunderstanding." Marshall replied, "I personally would prefer to let the entire matter drop if it is agreeable to you."[59] Then, controversy erupted again, this time over the timetable for paying the teachers. When the teachers sided with the city on the matter, 87-6, Marshall made clear his repulsion. "I am sick about the whole thing," he reported in a letter to Hastie, Ransom, and Hill. Separately, in a fit of pique and hyperbole, he predicted that the effect of the willingness of Norfolk's black leaders to "accept whatever the City might see fit to offer . . . will be to set us back 75 years."[60] Even then, a final blowup loomed. The NAACP attorneys thought it essential to cement the new pay plan with more than a good-faith agreement. A consent decree, approved in court, should buttress the plan. Once again, Norfolk officials balked, insisting that such a document would "destroy the good we believe has been accomplished." Trusting in the city's upright intentions struck the NAACP attorneys as ludicrous, but Young weighed in on the side of accommodation once again.[61]

The matter came to a head on February 4 at a hastily called meeting of the Norfolk Teachers Association. Winston Douglas, the principal of Booker T. Washington High, and a small band of administrators who agreed with Young orchestrated the gathering by invoking a little-known rule in the bylaws. They intended to vote the consent decree up or down, catching the NAACP lawyers unaware. Alerted by Alston, Ransom and Hill sped to Norfolk to intervene.[62] The teachers, many of whom appeared upset by the strong-arm tactics, greeted the lawyers' unexpected entrance to the school auditorium with cheers. Escorted to the office to deposit their coats, the lawyers discovered, to their surprise, the city manager and city attorney waiting to speak to the group. After an exchange in which Ransom asserted that the teachers had already sacrificed their financial rights and were not going to fritter away their legal rights if the lawyers could help it, the red-faced city officials left the school. Returning to the auditorium, Ransom spoke first, explaining the importance of a formal, binding agreement. Principal Douglas countered, embracing the virtues of compromise and warning of possible reprisals if the teachers insisted on a formal court order. In a final rebuttal, Hill reminded the teachers of their rights and urged them to stand tall. The tally registered 132 votes for the NAACP's viewpoint, 34 for the city's. Finally, in the attorneys' view, they had salvaged a modicum of dignity.[63]

Two weeks later, on February 18, 1941, Hill informed his colleagues in Washington and New York that with the signing of the long-awaited consent decree, the final page had been written on the *Alston* case. The fight had taken longer and proved more contentious than the NAACP had hoped, but any future lawsuit anywhere in the United States demanding equal public-school salaries had been handed an important precedent to extol. And despite the turmoil in negotiating a final plan, the NAACP had delivered a pay bonanza to Norfolk's black schoolteachers. "*Alston* represented more than a legal victory," concluded the historian Patricia Sullivan. "It was a pivotal moment in the application of Charles Houston's approach to lawyering and organizing."[64]

Now, the harder fight—extending that victory to hundreds of communities throughout Virginia and indeed the South—could begin. At least in the Old Dominion, there was no question who would marshal the assault. Three months earlier, just days after the Supreme Court had rendered its verdict, the Joint Committee for Equalization of Teachers' Salaries had designated a commander for the legal wars. "It was agreed that Mr. Hill be given chief legal authority over future cases," the minutes of the meeting stated. There was also consensus that Hill should finally be paid a fair sum for his efforts. "He was instructed to present at the next meeting a proposal for his remuneration."[65] Eighteen months after returning to Virginia, Hill had cemented his role as the state's leading civil rights attorney. His and Bernie's years of sacrifice finally had earned their reward. Still, reality tempered elation. "We did not celebrate," Hill recalled. "It was too early in the fight."[66]

SIX

Storm Clouds Near and Far

As a new decade unfolded, Spot Robinson seemed destined to become a legend at the Howard University School of Law. Entering students heard of the youthful instructor's academic prowess. They measured their achievements by Robinson's top marks, a record that would stand for many years. That he had emerged as Charles Houston's protégé only burnished his reputation. Those who absorbed Robinson's lectures on real property, business units, and torts knew to expect encyclopedic knowledge and patient coaching from their instructor. In return, he demanded no less than their best.

Not yet twenty-five, Robinson already was a father of two. His daughter Nina had arrived in 1939. He was a rising faculty member at the nation's most esteemed training ground for black lawyers, and his voice was increasingly respected in the august circles slashing a legal path through the thickets of America's racial intolerance. Robinson was not, however, a licensed lawyer, credentialed to argue cases in court. That mystifying omission dated back to the year following his May 1939 graduation. Robinson initially expected to complete the bar exam in a timely fashion. The plan evaporated when he fell ill just before his first scheduled test. From then on, as the twice-annual offerings slipped by each June and December, he found himself psychologically blocked from taking the exam.[1] How could that be? How could the man who reputedly had achieved the highest grade-point average in the more than seventy-year history of Howard Law be crippled by anxiety at the thought of an exam on which he almost certainly would shine?

Robinson's personal standards of excellence likely proved his undoing. Even with the enhanced Howard Law curriculum, instructional gaps remained. Oliver Hill had discovered as much when he found himself unnerved by a bar-exam question on federal procedure in 1933. If Robinson expected to know every possible answer before taking the test, then even he would prove inadequate. Unquestionably, as the years passed, perfection seemed to be the standard to which he aspired. The Supreme Court associate justice Ruth Bader Ginsburg, who served with Robinson on the US Court of Appeals for the District of Columbia during the 1980s, recalled that quality. Admiring as she was of Robinson's uncomplaining, gentlemanly demeanor and herculean work ethic, Ginsburg acknowledged being exasperated at her colleague's unwillingness to release an opinion until every possible thread had been woven into the cloth. "He was meticulous. That was the biggest problem with him," she said. In fact, the court adopted a rule, known informally as the Robinson Rule, requiring that any judge with three opinions pending for ninety days or more could not sit on another case until he whittled down the backlog.[2]

Robinson's fondness for footnotes slowed his pace. At a memorial service in October 1998 Harry T. Edwards, a successor to Robinson as chief judge on the Washington, DC, Court of Appeals, said that as far as he could tell, Robinson held the record for the most footnotes ever in a federal appellate opinion. The astonishing number, 676, was unlikely to be surpassed anytime soon, an amused Edwards speculated. "His opinions, as research tools, they're wonderful because there isn't a case that's not cited," Ginsburg added. But at some point, if one is not careful, "justice delayed is justice denied."[3] What underlay that thoroughness, the desire for completeness almost to the point of compulsion? Certainly scrupulousness was embedded in Robinson's nature. Judicial colleagues recalled the precision of Robinson's routine as he left the courthouse each day. First, observed his longtime secretary LaVerne Williams, he made sure that the water was turned off in the bathroom. Then he checked every light so that none was left burning. He placed any papers that might be confidential out of harm's way. And he checked and rechecked doors to ensure that they were fastened. "He did that all the time, day or night, anytime we were all leaving the office," she said. "No cutting of corners."[4]

By Robinson's telling, the Howard Law training of Nabrit and others boosted his natural tendency toward perfectionism. Then, too, the necessity of crafting legal arguments that could withstand the crucible of hostile courtrooms no doubt reinforced his resolve to examine every pebble in the path. As a civil rights attorney in the segregated South, he enjoyed little to no margin for error. The Yale law professor and author Stephen L. Carter, who served as a law clerk to both Robinson and Marshall, offered an additional explanation for Robinson's measured pace: "He loved the law so much that he wanted to get into every detail of every case—just absolutely fascinated by it." Once Robinson had examined the facts, he had no trouble making up his mind. "He knew what he wanted to say. He just wanted to make sure there was no nuance he had overlooked."[5] Carter recalled an air-pollution case during his clerkship year in which the record ran to thousands of pages. "He *read* it," Carter said. While others asked for briefings from their law clerks, Robinson devoured the thousands of pages of testimony and exhibits on his own. He was determined "to know the stuff himself and to make sure that he understood it himself." He brought to the task not only a brilliant mind but a rare ability to "focus in for a very long time." During the 1940s and 1950s, as groups of lawyers convened to perfect legal arguments, that skill would set Robinson apart. Long after others had withdrawn to settle their minds with a game of poker, a shot of whiskey, or a few hours of sleep, Robinson would stay at the task, refreshing himself with catnaps before pressing forward alone.

While Oliver Hill was moving to the forefront of Virginia's civil rights movement with the *Alston* case in the early 1940s, Robinson continued his weekly commute by train between Richmond and Washington. At Howard Law, he advanced from teaching fellow in 1939 to instructor in 1941, assistant professor in 1943, and associate professor in 1946. Over time, he taught classes on bills and notes, business units, civil rights, constitutional law, real property, appellate practice, legal argumentation, and torts. Consistent with his father's profession and his personal immersion in the real-estate business from an early age, Robinson's specialty was property law. "To this day, if I have a question involving real property, I just have to think about what he said about the subject," said the Alexandria attorney Bobby B. Stafford, a student in one of the last classes Robinson taught at Howard before becoming a federal judge.[6]

The youthful professor looked the part of a well-groomed accountant. His slicked-back dark hair already was receding at the temples. Wire-rimmed glasses framed penetrating eyes. A long face, broad at the forehead, narrow at the chin, seemed slightly out of proportion to his thin frame. He spoke with a slow, formal cadence and the accent of a patrician, eastern Virginian. At home in Richmond, a multigenerational household supported Robinson's frequent absences. The 1940 census lists the residents of 1255 Dubois Avenue as parents Spottswood Jr. and Inez (both age 46), Spottswood III (23), wife Marian (22), Billy (3), Nina (1), and sisters Nancy (19) and Isadora (17). The future judge was described as an educator with an income of $525. When in Richmond, he continued to assist in his father's real-estate business. Nina Govan warmly recalled that setup, one that would continue into her teenage years. After her parents, her brother, and she moved into their own home in the 1950s, family dinners became a rarity. Working at a fevered pace, her father was rarely home before bedtime. "It was habitual," she said. In contrast, "my grandmother had all of us around the table." While Spot III and Marian were convivial, they operated largely within the family and a small circle of close friends. The future judge's primary hobbies of fishing and woodworking were largely solitary affairs, only occasionally involving others. "We were house people," Govan summed up the arrangement. "We didn't do anything, go anywhere."[7]

On the days when Robinson commuted to Howard, more than teaching occupied his time. The growing affiliation with Houston and others in the civil rights brain trust also consumed hours. After Robinson and Houston's somewhat chaotic introduction in the fall of 1939, their camaraderie grew, particularly around restrictive-covenant cases. Such bans on property sales to blacks, Jews, Chinese, or other minority groups became popular in the wake of an early-twentieth-century mass migration of blacks from the rural South to the industrialized North and Midwest. The covenants were rooted in a bogus belief in the biological inferiority of blacks. Initially, whites tried to restrain residential mixing through municipal and state ordinances. But in a 1917 decision, *Buchanan v. Warley*, the Supreme Court nullified those statutes citing Fourteenth Amendment prohibitions. Soon, neighborhoods began substituting private covenants that barred property sales to groups deemed undesirable. After the Supreme Court upheld restrictive covenants in *Corrigan v. Buckley* in 1926, the snowball became an avalanche. For the next two decades, almost every court to take up racially exclusionary housing cited *Corrigan* as governing authority. Consequently, "in every city that had a black population of any significance, racial minorities were confined to specific geographic districts," observed the law professor Leland Ware. As migration continued apace, the covenants bred wretched overcrowding and unsanitary living conditions in many cities, including Washington.[8]

Deciding to tackle that blight, Houston faced daunting obstacles. The Washington real-estate board had incorporated into its code of ethics a rule against selling houses to black buyers in the extensive areas designated for whites. Anyone who violated the code risked having his or her membership yanked. Dozens of community groups assisted the board in monitoring the lines.[9] Even so, some property owners were willing to test the limits by selling restricted property to black purchasers or to straw purchasers, whites who would quickly flip the property to a black buyer. Straw purchasers, typically motivated more by profit than by social justice, benefited when the changing demographics of a neighborhood resulted in housing turnover. Given the benefits to blacks, Houston was more than willing to defend such pass-through sellers when lawsuits ensued. The venerable attorney represented housing-covenant violators in numerous cases throughout the 1940s.

As Robinson learned early in the decade, Houston was anxious for assistance with the load. Not so desperate, however, but that he subjected the work of even the meticulous Robinson to strict scrutiny. The Houston biographer Genna Rae McNeil described the scene after Robinson submitted a brief to Houston in a restrictive-covenant case early in their association, probably in late 1939 or early 1940. Meeting Houston at his downtown law office at about two in the afternoon, Robinson settled in for what he expected to be a fairly cursory review. Instead, Houston donned a green eyeshade, gathered several crayon-style pencils, and began to dissect the document word by word, line by line. At dinner time, the men took a short break to eat takeout sandwiches. Then the work continued until after midnight, when Houston, still not finished, gave Robinson the option of continuing or recessing until the next morning. Consistent with his usual approach to work, Robinson elected to stay with the task. Finally, at about four in the morning, the job was finished. Houston was satisfied, and two souls had aligned. "Thoroughness was Charlie," observed Robinson approvingly four decades later.[10]

Thoroughness also was Robinson. When L. Douglas Wilder began an informal law partnership with Robinson in Richmond in 1960, the senior attorney's practices mirrored Houston's. "He was a task master, made me a little upset when I first started working for him," laughed Wilder, who in 1990 became the nation's first elected black governor. "He'd say, very good, Doug, but let's see if we can get another word for 'notwithstanding.' By the time he had finished, he almost rewrote the thing. It would take, maybe, a couple of hours before you would finish with it. I was ready to strangle him." But Wilder knew the rare value of a man who personally built his law-office bookcases to such exact height that dust could not filter onto the tops of the books. "He was that way in everything he did," Wilder said. Not only did Wilder consider Robinson brilliant, but "he was a precise guy, and he didn't tolerate nonsense."[11] A perhaps apocryphal story circulated that the demanding Robinson failed eight out of fifteen students in one class at Howard Law in the 1940s. Irate, the eight appealed to then dean Hastie for review. He honored the unprecedented request, turning the matter over to Andy Ransom, a notoriously easy grader, for reexamination and regrading. After all was said and done, only one additional student passed. The story was meant to show that Robinson, while tough and exacting, was also fair.[12]

The combination anchored Robinson's reputation as he began establishing himself with Houston and others. "I started off by being the youngster around there that they would tolerate," Robinson said self-deprecatingly. "Commencing in the late '30s and gathering momentum in almost geometric proportion from then on," Howard Law was at the hub of civil rights activity, he said. When a strategy huddle was required, "Thurgood would hop The Congressional [train] from New York down to Washington." Bill Hastie, Andy Ransom, Jim Nabrit, and George Hayes were already at the law school as part of the faculty, as was Robinson. "Oliver would come up from Richmond, and maybe somebody would come from someplace else. You'd have a little gathering. This went on constantly, starting with a group of not quite as many as a dozen, not necessarily the same people all the time, and finally growing into a group that never got more than about twenty-five, maybe thirty. After I shed a little of my greenness, I became a full-fledged member of the fraternity. You just got the fever. Here are guys who're spending as much time as they could muster, all knowing that something had to be done, feeling that unless they tried to do it, it wasn't going to get done. Nobody getting paid for any of this. Nobody expected to get paid for it. Nobody gave a damn about being paid for it. It was simply a matter of dedication, and the reward being just feeling when you got through, you'd given it your best try."[13]

Correspondence from the era confirms the growing appreciation at NAACP headquarters in New York for Robinson's expertise in property law, especially restrictive covenants. "I am referring your letter to Attorney Spottswood W. Robinson, III, at Howard Law School who has done a tremendous amount of work on the question of restrictive covenants," wrote Marshall in 1942, answering a Virginia State College employee dismayed by a public auction at which house lots were marketed only to whites. When the president of the Denver branch of the NAACP asked Walter White for assistance in planning a restrictive-covenant lawsuit, the executive secretary forwarded the matter to Robinson. In a third instance, a Washington, DC, homeowner, Mary Gibson Hundley, complained to White that the NAACP had not done enough to finance her lawsuit against enforcement of a restrictive covenant. Despite her complaint, she acknowledged that "the services of our attorney, Dr. Charles H. Houston, and his assistant, Mr. Robinson, on our brief have been a substantial contribution."[14] Mrs. Hundley may have been better satisfied after the US Court of Appeals for the District of Columbia (where Robinson would serve many years later) overturned a district-court ruling against her. The rare victory in *Hundley v. Gorewitz* reflected extensive research and a sophisticated argument by the duo involving changing neighborhood housing patterns.[15] A few years out of law school, Spot Robinson already had proven himself to be an invaluable legal scholar, researcher, and writer. All he lacked as a member of the Jim Crow demolition team was a license to practice law.

Despite Marshall's mercurial reaction to the *Alston* teacher-pay settlement, the decision proved to be the wedge that the NAACP legal office had been seeking. Newly minted as the organization's chief legal officer for Virginia, Oliver Hill was more than ready to lead the masses through the opening it created. Over the next two years, before answering Uncle Sam's summons to serve in World War II, he and Dr. Tinsley traveled countless miles, taking stock of abysmal conditions in one-room schools and talking at length with parents and elders about their dreams for future generations. Everywhere, the pair confronted evidence of second-class citizenship. White

Virginians prided themselves on being a cut above more vitriolic racists to the south, but there was nothing color-blind about the inferior education offered black children, nothing equal about a justice system that too often railroaded black men accused of serious crimes, nothing visionary in the way Virginia's politically dominant Byrd Organization conspired through voting restrictions to keep blacks in a subservient place. No white families faced the quandary of a Sussex County farmer who told Hill that he had to choose between sending his daughter or his son to school. He could not afford transportation for both. Only whites enjoyed free school buses.[16]

All across Virginia, similar constraints curbed the education of black children. Statistically, black Virginians might have less to fear when it came to random violence than their brethren to the south; official violence was another matter. From 1900 to 1935, among southern and border states only Georgia and Texas surpassed Virginia in the number of executions, with African Americans making up a disproportionate number of those put to death. Incidences of police brutality against blacks were recorded in multiple Virginia cities. And as Hill himself knew from driving the back roads of the rural Southside, favorable statistics did not erase all terror. Nor did the numbers eliminate lynchings of a more symbolic sort. From Pulaski in western Virginia to Tidewater's Norfolk County (site of present-day Chesapeake), to Fredericksburg, south of Washington, black teachers and principals sacrificed their livelihoods in the late 1930s and early 1940s to protest unequal pay scales for black and white teachers.[17] Virginia's political elite rarely tolerated crushed bodies, but they excelled at breaking spirits. "They were not going to accept any violence, but they were just as mean and white supremacist as any Bilbo [Mississippi senator Theodore G. Bilbo] anywhere in their actual feelings," said A. Linwood Holton Jr., describing the state's political and financial elite. A racial progressive and the state's first Republican governor of the twentieth century, Holton clashed with those forces while building a political base during the 1960s and serving as governor from 1970 to 1974.[18]

The conservative, apple-cheeked Harry F. Byrd, a Winchester orchardist and newspaperman, dominated politics in his home state more thoroughly and for longer than perhaps any other American politician ever. Taking over the chairmanship of the state Democratic Party in 1922 as a youthful state senator, he went on to a consequential term as governor and more than three decades as a small-government, antitax, anti–New Deal irritant to national Democrats from his post in the US Senate. The political organization Byrd built was so pervasive that the historian V. O. Key, writing in 1948, famously described Virginia as the American state that "can lay claim to the most thorough control by an oligarchy." For many years, voter participation was so curtailed that it was not unusual for the Byrd Organization to nominate its candidate for governor in the Democratic primary—tantamount to election—with support from a mere 5–7 percent of the adult population.[19]

A direct descendant of one of Virginia's most esteemed colonial families, Byrd railed against the evils of a strong, centralized federal government, while, ironically, concentrating power at the state level in a politburo of intimate friends. He and his predecessors undercut the potential influence of perceived riffraff, white or black, through a series of undemocratic tactics. Prime obstacles to voting included the $1.50 annual poll tax, a voluntary fee that had to be paid three years running, with interest for missed years, before a citizen could vote; a blank registration form, which obliged applicants to supply information from memory, without the prompt of a printed form; and a requirement that a citizen, upon first registering, answer voter-related questions to the satisfaction of the local registrar. Malicious registrars were known to weed out unwanted applicants by asking questions such as, How many men signed the Declaration of Independence? or What are the names of the counties in the Twenty-Seventh Judicial District? The Byrd Organization further reduced voting by staggering state and federal elections and reducing the number of officials elected statewide to three.[20] The Organization, as it was often referred to in Virginia, benefited from a reputation for honest government, and indeed the state was for the most part free of political scandal. However, paying the poll taxes of friendly voters and crafting legislation to serve the interests of a well-connected, moneyed elite did not count as corruption. "Harry Byrd and his political allies did worse than steal money," observed the historian Brent Tarter. "They stole democracy."[21]

Limited as white voting was, participation was even lower among the quarter or so of the population that was black. Luther Jackson, a renowned chair of the history department at the Virginia State College for Negroes, later Virginia State University, tracked voting habits by Virginia's black citizens for many years. In 1941 he reported that in an adult black population of 329,000, only 25,000 had paid the poll tax for three successive years. Of those, only 15,000 had registered to vote. And out of that sub-set, fewer than 12,000 (less than 4 percent of black adults) actually voted. Blacks themselves bore some blame for that poor showing, but hostile white registrars, the poll tax, and a dearth of candidates with appeal to working-class blacks or whites curbed any incentive to participate.[22]

There were dual standards in criminal justice as well. "When the clients were Negroes and the alleged victims white, the defendants' guilt seemed presumed and their punishment was severe," Hill recalled. In the months after his return to the Old Dominion, Hill had multiple opportunities to watch Virginia justice in action, in part through his growing association with Martin Martin. As NAACP activists and solo practitioners, the pair formed an informal working partnership despite the 150 miles between Richmond and Danville, where Martin practiced law and served as the NAACP president in a thriving black community. His prominent father had helped found the black-owned and operated First State Bank in Dan-ville, and an older brother, M. Conrad Martin, would serve as its president for many years.[23]

Martin Armstrong Martin, born in 1910, acquired his dual name when his parents, both educators, decided to bequeath their surnames to their fraternal-twin sons. Bright and witty, young Martin had risen from the black schools of Pittsylvania County to study at Ohio State University and Howard Law. In addition to mental quickness, he exhibited a confident, fun-loving nature. His nieces, half sisters Edwina Martin and Paula Martin Smith, recalled him as being an exuberant ladies' man and very smart, with a hearty laugh. "It is pretty nice here but no girls. What few there are are as ugly as sin," Martin complained with typical irreverence in a letter to the Hill law firm after a partnership formed in the mid-1940s.[24] Such playfulness coexisted with a driven will. After graduating from Howard in 1938, Martin had quickly established himself as a force in the Danville community, pushing for a high school for black students in the southern part of neighboring Pittsylvania County and contemplating a challenge to teacher pay scales. In response to a query from Martin about NAACP strategy in *Alston*, Thurgood Marshall urged him to coordinate with Hill. A visit by Hill to Martin's thriving Danville office in the autumn of 1939 apparently triggered a hint of envy. "Yes, Martin has all that set-up which is really lovely and I wish you could have started out like that," Bernie counseled in reply. "But you know, the harder the journey the more you'll appreciate the success in the end."[25]

In the first of many joint ventures, Hill joined Martin for the retrial of Willie Bradshaw, a black man convicted of shooting a white deputy sheriff and sentenced to die. Bradshaw had been represented at his first trial by two white lawyers, but after the Virginia Supreme Court of Appeals set aside Bradshaw's death sentence and ordered a new trial, an all-black team that included Martin and Hill took charge. The *Richmond Afro-American* described the appearance of the black attorneys as "something revolutionary for Halifax County," calling it "an inspirational tonic." When the retrial also resulted in an execution order, Hill joined the team that appealed to Governor Price for commutation to life in prison. The effort failed. Bradshaw was executed the same day Hill appeared before the Court of Appeals for the Fourth Circuit in *Alston*.[26] In yet another case, the Brunswick County branch of the NAACP secured the pair to defend a young black man charged with killing a white man in a row about wages. The NAACP's national magazine, the *Crisis*, described the resulting thirty-year sentence as the "first time that a Negro in Virginia had received less than death or life for killing a white man."[27]

Hill had only a minimal role in the most sensational race-murder trial to hit Virginia in the early 1940s, that of Odell Waller, a black sharecropper convicted of killing his white landlord in Pittsylvania County over a disputed crop share. However, Martin provided important service to the defense. The case gained national notoriety because of the considerable disagreement over various particulars of the shooting. Waller was convicted in September 1940 and sentenced to die. In preparation for his appeal, his defense team hired Martin to analyze the jury pool. The study revealed that every member of the petit jury at Waller's trial had paid his poll taxes for 1938, 1939, and 1940, and all but one of the members of the grand jury that indicted Waller had a similar record of payment. In effect, no one on the jury was Waller's true economic or social peer. The innovative analysis gave Waller's attorneys some hope, but ultimately the Virginia Supreme Court of Appeals rejected the argument and Governor Colgate W. Darden Jr. denied clemency. Waller was executed on July 2, 1942.[28]

Hill rightly worried that he himself had supplied an inadequate defense in another troublesome death-penalty case. Joseph Mickens, a fifteen-year-old black youth with a fourth-grade education, was arrested in Novem-

ber 1940 for the rape of a white woman living in Waynesboro. While returning home from a movie, Mrs. Clarice Pye was attacked, dragged to
a vacant lot, and raped. Mickens, who had had a few minor skirmishes
with the law, was detained after he asked why police were combing the
crime site. Mrs. Pye proved unable to identify Mickens, but that was immaterial because Mickens confessed. The confession, by multiple accounts,
followed a lengthy, nighttime interrogation by ten police officers who at
one point placed a noose on the table to suggest what fate might await an
uncooperative young man. The state NAACP dispatched Hill to investigate. After learning the facts, he agreed to represent Mickens. The pre-
Christmas trial was only a few weeks away. Several days before the court
convened, ptomaine poisoning further limited Hill's preparation. "Looking
back on the situation, I should have insisted on not going to trial because
the defendant's life was on the line, and I was sick," Hill said, ruing his
performance many years later.[29] Regardless, Judge Floridus Crosby found
Mickens guilty and sentenced him to die on February 21, 1941. Mickens's
distraught mother requested that a white attorney replace Hill in handling
her son's appeals, a raw rebuke. A year later, with Mickens's execution date
looming, Governor Price commuted Mickens's sentence to life in prison.
Price attributed his leniency to Mickens's young age.[30]

That might have been the end of the story, except that two decades
later another governor, Lindsay Almond, decided that Mickens had served
enough time. A week before leaving office in 1962, Almond freed the prisoner. Almond cited Mickens's good institutional record and the lack of opposition from key Augusta County officials. A parole board report issued
before the decision noted somewhat disapprovingly that the prisoner still
maintained his innocence. But more positively, he had accepted his sentence
and had shown a "hopeful and constructive" attitude. In what the parole
board apparently considered to be a favorable comment, it added: "No connection with NAACP." Almond's only stipulation was that Mickens leave
Virginia and not return.[31] Given 1940s justice, Mickens's confession likely
would have doomed him no matter how good a defense Hill mounted.
Even so, Hill knew and regretted that it had not been his finest hour.

As 1941 began, Oliver Hill's life sped into the fast lane. Given the semi-
lost years in Roanoke and Washington, he had no time to waste. Bernie
remained in Washington by necessity, not choice. Her paycheck secured

the couple's finances. Occasional appearances on the society pages of the *Richmond Afro-American* confirmed that attorney Hill had an attractive wife who was very much a presence in his life. A newspaper photograph in September 1940 showed Bernie with braided hair gathered at the nape of her neck and jeweled earrings. "Mrs. Oliver W. Hill, who has returned to Washington after spending the summer with her husband, an attorney, in Richmond," read the caption. The following May, photographs showing the couple at an Omega Psi Phi dance, attired glamorously in tuxedo and evening gown, appeared in the newspaper.[32] From Oliver's first days back in Virginia, Bernie made it clear, as she had in Roanoke, that her husband was the most important person in her life and that she expected to play a similar role in his. "The years are unimportant except that each one makes you that much dearer to me," she telegraphed for his thirty-second birthday. And when Oliver seemed more preoccupied with his law practice than with her on a visit a few months later, she confronted the matter head-on: "I love you but at times you're as cold and aloof as a stranger." Moments later, she reconsidered. "Already, Oliver, I see how silly this must sound— but you know I'm subject to these spells of melancholy. Forget it. . . . I believe in you and I hope you will always believe in me."[33]

As his work pace accelerated, Oliver began looking for reinforcements. With no law license and a busy teaching schedule, Robinson was not an option. Hill's sights turned to Alexandria. Since Sam Tucker's orchestration of the city-library sit-down in the summer of 1939, he and Hill had been in touch sporadically. Each saw the other as a potential law partner; their intellects and passion for justice were on par. Tucker had promised to come to Richmond on the third Monday of January 1941 to solidify the alliance. He envisioned working part time in each city before eventually moving to Richmond. At home, "I'm still little Wilbert Tucker, you see," the twenty-seven-year-old Tucker later explained. "I had decided I was going to practice elsewhere."[34] On the appointed morning, however, a letter from the War Department interrupted plans. It instructed First Lieutenant Samuel W. Tucker to report for active duty. Tucker had spent two years after graduation from Howard University in a government program designed to demonstrate that black officers could execute command responsibility. Now Uncle Sam wanted him back. "I telephoned Oliver," he said. "We knew the war was going to come."[35]

It was hard to assess the news from Europe and think otherwise. The past year had witnessed the advance across western Europe of a ruthless Nazi juggernaut, as well as the collapse of states trapped between the Russians and the Germans to the east. Norway, Denmark, the Netherlands, Luxembourg, and northern France, among others, lay flattened beneath the Nazi boot. London reeled under a blistering bombing assault. In Poland, hundreds of thousands of Jews were being herded into the Warsaw ghetto. And the Tripartite Pact, recently signed by Germany, Italy, and Japan, warned of devastation to come. The bleak reports triggered rising nationalism among both whites and blacks in the United States. But for African Americans, patriotism came with an asterisk. American democracy, for all its virtues, meted out rewards with an uneven hand. From jobs to housing to education, rank discrimination against blacks mocked the Constitution's promise of equal treatment. The shadows abroad added new urgency to the NAACP's effort to spread democracy at home.

Even before the final details of the Norfolk settlement in the *Alston* case were resolved, Hill and the Joint Committee for Equalization of Teachers' Salaries pressed forward with similar cases elsewhere. Within weeks the *Richmond Afro-American* reported that teachers in Portsmouth, Richmond, Roanoke, Lynchburg, Danville, and Chesterfield County were initiating plans to push for teacher-pay parity. Lutrelle Palmer, writing in the *Virginia Teachers Bulletin*, suggested even more widespread activity: "It is gratifying to know that our teachers have filed petitions for equal salaries in nearly every city and county in the state."[36] As the focus expanded to include attacks on substandard school buildings and nonexistent transportation, Hill perfected two bold maneuvers: He did not hesitate to flag down white school buses and try to get black children aboard. And he marched groups of black children living many miles from school into the principal's office at the nearest white school and demanded access. What gave Hill the courage to act so brazenly? The indomitable spirits of Lelia Pentecost and Charles Houston helped guide him. So did the camaraderie of the Howard Law brotherhood. A sense of higher purpose fueled his boldness. Beyond that, he seems to have possessed an innate fortitude, the sort of ineffable spark that destines some men for greatness. "I think he was born with it," former governor Holton has speculated. "He was smart; he had a great brain. He understood both what the Constitution said and what it meant and what it ought to mean."[37]

Hill waged his first major bid for free bus transportation for black children in Greensville County, the hardscrabble, tobacco-growing community on the North Carolina border where he had worked with Hewin on voter issues. A county history undertaken by the local Riparian Women's Club in the 1960s captured the myopic mind-set of prominent white citizens toward black residents and their forebears. "The slave might fear stern discipline; the master's fear was deeper, that of savage revenge," the book asserted. "It was a major miracle that life on the plantations was as peaceful as it was. Rebellion would have been widespread had it not been for the innate justice of the slave owners." The writer acknowledged the modern abhorrence for slavery but insisted that slaves were fundamentally content. "The fact that one was owned and one was free was a blurred line."[38] There was nothing blurred about the lines between black and white education in the county in 1941. Whites rode to school on fifteen public school buses; blacks walked, hitched rides, paid someone to deposit them at the schoolhouse door, or stayed home. Ollie May Branch, a high-school freshman, became the plaintiff in a court case protesting the inequity. In a complaint filed March 11, 1941, in the US District Court for Eastern Virginia, Hill noted that Branch lived ten miles from the black training school. Even though school buses went back and forth in front of her house daily, drivers refused to pick her up. Three days later Marshall directed Roy Wilkins to prepare a press release describing the case as the "opening gun in the campaign to secure equal bus transportation for Negro students in the South." Greensville would serve as the test case for equal transportation services, much as *Alston* had for pay parity. Hill would be the lead attorney.[39] Recognizing the indefensibility of the gap in services, the Greensville School Board agreed quickly to settle the matter out of court.[40]

In another instance, after the summary dismissals in June 1941 of three black principals in Norfolk County, Hill's gaze returned to Tidewater Virginia. School officials said a new administrative plan made the posts obsolete, but black leaders felt sure it was no accident that the dismissed principals had all been active in the pay-equalization movement. At a public hearing, Hill charged that handing supervision of the black schools over to white administrators was "degrading" and a clear attempt "to intimidate the [black] citizens of Norfolk County." Even so, the board stood firm; the principals would not be rehired.[41] The case highlighted the NAACP's limited hand in protecting black teachers and administrators. Hill pledged to resolve the matter to the satisfaction of local blacks, but in truth he had slim grounds for challenging the dismissals. Failure to mount a lawsuit in Norfolk County disappointed some black residents and led to grumbling. White officials might view the NAACP as a radical group, but for some black citizens the group was not aggressive enough. In January, two local lawyers—Thomas H. Reid, who was black, and Robert F. McMurran, who was white—took matters into their own hands, filing a lawsuit on behalf of the dismissed principals. Privately, Hill disparaged Reid and McMurran's legal work. Sending Marshall and Ransom a copy of their bill of complaint, he noted, "Now you can see why I was not anxious to join up with these babies." The eventual outcome bore out the wisdom of Hill's caution. In October 1943 in chancery court, Judge A. B. Carney threw out the case as "insufficient in law."[42]

In yet another case, in Sussex County, a quiet expanse of farmland and pine forests south of Richmond, Hill attended a nighttime meeting just before the opening of a new school year in September 1942. There, he heard the dilemma of the black farmer who could not afford to transport both his son and daughter to school. The story infuriated Hill, who also had a lawsuit regarding pay equity for teachers pending in the county. There were more than twice as many black children as white in Sussex County schools, but because of the long distance to the only black high school, the training school in Waverly, many black students ended their education with the seventh grade.[43] "Don't the white folks have a bus?" he asked at the community meeting. "Yes," the farmer replied. "Well, let's challenge it then," Hill said.

Early on the first day of school, after a bus driver refused to pick up several black students, Hill loaded them into a truck and drove to the nearest white high school, at Stony Creek. "I carried the kids into the school and told the principal I wanted to enroll them," Hill recalled. "He was a new principal, and he didn't know what it was all about. So he calls the superintendent. And I heard [the superintendent]. He yelled over the telephone, 'Well, hell, no.'" Expecting that result, Hill had already prepared papers asking the federal court in Richmond for an injunction halting unequal bus service. Filed on September 14, the lawsuit complained that white students attended consolidated schools of "modern construction, attractively designed, fully staffed and well equipped," while black children were relegated to "small, antiquated schools . . . poorly equipped, poorly heated, badly ventilated." The five plaintiffs traveled between thirty-one and forty-five miles to school in Waverly, even though white schools were within a few miles of their homes.[44] The school board replied that it had attempted to purchase additional school buses the previous spring, but the Office of Defense Transportation, which was monitoring such vehicles in wartime, had turned them down. Now, local officials were consulting with the governor on alternatives. The board also had considered building a high school for blacks near Stony Creek, but it had been dissuaded by "general economic conditions, together with the inability to secure construction materials."[45]

When Hill arrived at the federal courthouse in Richmond for a hearing a few days later, he was surprised to be directed by a marshal to the chambers of Judge Robert N. Pollard, who was handling the case.[46] Entering the judge's quarters, he found members of the Sussex County School Board and their attorney waiting. After some back and forth about whether it was proper for the case to be heard in federal district court (it was) and whether the county had been given adequate notice (it had), Judge Pollard barked: "You all know what the law is. You go out there and settle this." As he regularly did, Hill telephoned Martin for reinforcement. The pair met Sussex County officials in Petersburg on a Saturday. Before the negotiations ended, as Hill remembered them, he and the superintendent nearly came to blows across the conference table. "They grabbed him on his side, and Martin grabbed me on my side."[47] The young hothead who had once flung a stiletto knife at an adversary had not entirely vanished. Nonetheless, progress followed. By November, three buses had begun transporting black children to school, leading sixty more students to enroll at the Waverly training school. Two teachers had been added ,and "additional sewing machines and other equipment" had been ordered.[48] The outcome bolstered the NAACP's contention that lack of transportation hindered school attendance by black children across Virginia. Less positively, the focus on sewing machines suggested that school officials still viewed vocational training, not academics, as the primary educational goal for black children. Similar school-equalization work crowded Hill's post-*Alston* docket.

As the school cases continued, Virginia's growing coterie of black lawyers contemplated forging a more formal bond. Their desire for a professional organization reflected a mounting need for mutual support and coordination as attacks on Jim Crow segregation accelerated. Despite some evidence that courts were more color-blind than many parts of society, the white-dominated legal profession too often remained hostile to their aims.[49] An episode in December 1940 in the law library of the Virginia Supreme Court of Appeals demonstrated the problem.

Frederic Charles Carter, of Richmond, a black attorney, was preparing a brief when an assistant librarian waved him to an isolated alcove in the southeast corner of the room. A new policy required segregated seating, he was told. Unflappable, Carter refused to move. The head librarian then summoned him to his office.[50] "Fred Carter, I want to speak to you in here." "My reply: 'I do not choose to come now,'" Carter recalled. Next, a police officer appeared and ordered Carter to "get going. Mr. Richards [the librarian] wants to speak to you in his office." Carter replied, "I am a member of the Bar and don't have to talk to anyone unless I choose to do so. If I am under arrest I would like to know that." The policeman and the librarian disappeared. When Carter finished his work about forty-five minutes later, the pair had not reappeared. Returning to his office, Carter recorded the events in a letter of complaint to Chief Justice Preston W. Campbell, of Abingdon.

Several months later, having heard nothing from Campbell, Carter contacted Robert H. Cooley Jr., of Petersburg, another of Charles Houston's acolytes, suggesting a meeting of the state's black lawyers. They needed to be able to speak in unison when such matters arose. In response, Cooley contacted attorneys in Portsmouth, Norfolk, Newport News, and the Howard School of Law to weigh interest in forming a bar association. Informal discussions continued over the next year, and in March 1942 Hill sent formal notice of an organizational meeting to be held in Richmond on April 12. A preregistration fee of one dollar would cover both expenses and dinner at Miller's Hotel, at Second and Leigh Streets.[51] Twenty-five lawyers attended the first meeting. Calling itself the Old Dominion Bar Association, the group elected officers: Hill, president; Martin, vice-president; L. Marian Poe, of Newport News, the first black woman licensed to practice law in Virginia, secretary; and James M. Morris, of Staunton, treasurer. The association's active members over the next decades formed a communications and support network that bolstered, complemented, and enhanced the work of Hill and Robinson as they sought to penetrate the larger society.

Of the multiple teacher-pay cases consuming the attention of Old Dominion Bar lawyers during the early 1940s, none did more to unmask the ruthless tactics of some white powerbrokers than a case in Newport News. No one's house was burned, and no one's head was bashed during the pay fight in the blue-collar, shipbuilding city, but powerful whites did not hesitate to mangle the careers and fortunes of those who committed the sin of challenging the social order. The Newport News pay saga began like most others around the state: a group of black teachers petitioned the local school board for adjustments to the salary scale, the school board hemmed and hawed, and the teachers filed a lawsuit. Dorothy Roles, an elementary-school teacher for nine years, lent her name to the complaint. Judge Way, assigned to hear the case, proved to have learned a lesson from *Alston*. When the case was heard in court, city lawyers mounted a defense similar to that offered by lawyers for the Norfolk School Board two years earlier. This time Way had no stomach for delays. "They carried me up to the Court of Appeals, and I got spanked," Hill recalled Way saying. "I ain't gonna get spanked no more. We're going to try this case, starting today." In January 1943 Way issued a formal injunction against further pay discrimination.[52]

The matter did not rest there. Before Roles's lawsuit, blacks had regarded the school superintendent Joseph H. Saunders as racially progressive. In general, race relations in Newport News were better than in many southern cities. The attitude reflected the insistence on positive treatment of blacks by Collis P. Huntington, the founder of the Newport News Shipbuilding and Drydock Company. But white attitudes were more paternalistic than egalitarian. The lawsuit angered Saunders and others. He threatened to dismiss anyone who took things too far, and with the school board's help, he proved to be as good as his word. When contracts for the upcoming year were distributed in May, three school principals and three teachers who had been active in the equalization movement were not invited to return. Roles later would lose her job as well.[53]

Astonishingly, the list of discarded educators included Lutrelle Palmer, the principal of the city's sole black high school and a man whose name was synonymous with black education in Virginia. A tireless advocate for children, educated at Wilberforce University and the University of Michigan, the refined, bespectacled Palmer had been a driving force in the creation of the Virginia Teachers Association and served as its longtime executive secretary. Through the *Virginia Teachers Bulletin*, he spoke to the masses in a voice that combined passion with reason. The magazine's many articles had contributed mightily to the professional development of the state's black teachers. He had been president of the Association of Colleges and Secondary Schools for Negroes, and over the course of twenty-three years, as principal, he had shepherded Huntington High from a four-room, makeshift sham to an acclaimed institution. Moreover, Palmer was hardly a firebrand. In the dispute between Young and Marshall in the Norfolk teachers' case, Palmer had sided with Young. Just a few years earlier, Palmer had appeared on the *Richmond Times-Dispatch*'s honor roll of distinguished Virginians, as clear a signal as might be imagined of his acceptability to Virginia's white elite.[54] The subtext of the shocking firing could not have been more ominous: if Lutrelle Palmer was expendable, then not a single black principal or teacher in Virginia was safe.

Stunned, then outraged, the citizenry rallied to the defense of Palmer and his comrades in martyrdom, including T. Roger Thompson and Rupert Picott, two elementary-school principals with a combined service of thirty-two years. More than fifteen hundred people flocked to a rally in Newport News. Rumors flew of a student boycott. In Richmond, Hill joined a delegation pleading the case of the ousted sextet with Governor Darden. The high-level summitry acted to relieve the tension but produced little in the way of tangible results. Darden commended the group's plans to petition the school board for reconsideration but he gave no sign of being equally appalled.[55] Ultimately, efforts to reinstate the educators went nowhere. The school board refused to elaborate beyond an opaque claim that the dismissals had occurred "for the benefit of the school system." A lengthy court battle affirmed the board's right to hire and fire as it chose. Palmer quickly found employment at the Hampton Institute, but his son, Lutrelle F. Palmer Jr., who became a crusading Chicago journalist, said the episode had "deeply wounded" his father. "He once told me that losing Huntington was almost like losing one of his own children," the son wrote. The senior Palmer died unexpectedly seven years later at age sixty-two, and the son held Newport News officials responsible. His father, he said, died of a broken heart. "I am convinced that this was the act that killed our father."[56]

Impotent to correct the injustice, the plaintiffs won a slice of vindication in another courtroom. In May 1945 Judge Hutcheson held Superintendent Saunders and the Newport New school board in civil contempt for failure to obey Judge's Way 1943 pay-equalization order. Hutcheson directed them to pay 2.5 percent interest on all teacher pay that had been withheld in the last year and 6 percent interest on all future withholdings. Thirty-nine teachers received a total of twenty-two thousand dollars in back pay. The court ordered the teachers' attorneys to be paid as well. Writing in the *Virginia Teachers Bulletin*, Palmer praised the ruling as "the most difficult case for salary equalization yet fought in Virginia and perhaps in the entire South."[57] Ransom and Wendell Walker Jr. voluntarily split the three-thousand-dollar attorneys' fee in the *Roles* case in equal shares with Hill, even though he would be overseas in the army during the later contempt proceedings. Deeply moved, Hill called the gesture "a magnificent act." In November 1945, in an unusually formal letter among friends, he thanked the pair for easing his postwar return to civilian life: "You have provided me with material and valuable assistance in re-establishing myself in the practice of my profession. I assure you that your thoughtful and fine sense of loyalty will always be one of my cherished memories."[58]

World War II and Hill's civil rights work careened along a collision course. When he protested the Newport News firings in May 1943, his scheduled induction into the army was just weeks away. After the Japanese attack on Pearl Harbor on December 7, 1941, Hill had first thought to seek an officer's commission in the navy, a service branch in which most blacks were relegated to menial jobs. "The only apparent governmental response to my application for a naval commission was to hasten my being inducted into the military," he later quipped. Meanwhile, Hill had been questioned by an FBI agent in early 1942 in his law office. He had no idea what prompted the inquiry, but he feared that his application had somehow made him vulnerable to political whim.[59] Worried that he might be called to active duty at any moment, disrupting his legal work, Hill reached an accommodation with the local draft board: he would voluntarily enlist in June 1943.[60]

With that reprieve, Hill's first item of business was to secure a partner to maintain the law practice during his absence. The most attractive candidate was the Richmond attorney who was making a name for himself teaching and planning civil rights legal strategy at the Howard School of Law, Spot Robinson. Owing to either a health or family issue, Robinson appeared to be exempt from wartime service. Some office space was coming available in the Consolidated Bank Building at First and Marshall Streets, where the senior Robinson maintained an office. The two older men hatched a plan. Hill would approach the son with an offer to form a legal partnership. When Hill entered the army, the father would handle any formal legal matters, with his son doing the background work until he passed the bar exam. If Robinson took the exam in June 1943, there should be a gap of no more than a few weeks between Hill's departure and Robinson's assuming control. Neither man doubted Robinson's ability to pass the test easily.[61] An October 1942 letter from Spot to Oliver confirmed that the arrangement already was being executed. "You undoubtedly noted the exquisite workmanship of yours truly in hanging the blinds," Robinson wrote, displaying a touch of humor along with his usual exactitude. "This was done on the same afternoon they were bought in order that the wallpaper could be protected from sunlight."[62]

As the June deadline for Hill's induction into the army approached, a whirlwind of activity enveloped him. He updated Dr. Tinsley on pending NAACP legal cases. "This is to advise you that we plan to continue to run this office while I am away in the army," he wrote. The only active equalization court case was in Newport News, although there was "strong sentiment" for cases elsewhere.[63] The joint committee for salary equalization also was preparing for Hill's departure. At an April meeting, the group added Robinson to the legal staff, pending his passing of the bar exam in June. The minutes noted that salaries had been equalized in eighteen Virginia school divisions, netting an estimated $1 million in additional pay for teachers.[64]

Martin also was preparing to leave Virginia. In Hill's last days in the city, he attended his friend's swearing in as the first black associate attorney in the trial section of the criminal division of the US Justice Department. Martin was heading for California, where he was to prosecute German prisoners. Meanwhile, Hill celebrated a parting gift in the form of the release from the state penitentiary of Samuel Legions, a twenty-three-year-old black man who had spent a year on death row for the alleged rape of a white Leesburg woman. Hill had assisted Houston in the defense. Now, the Virginia Supreme Court had taken an almost unheard-of step, overturning the conviction. The court had accepted the defense argument that the facts of the case were too bizarre to be believed. The woman's husband supposedly had sat by, rocking a crying baby, while Legions raped his wife.[65]

Two events clouded Hill's final days in Virginia. First, domestic warfare battered Detroit, horrifying the nation. In seemingly grim affirmation of Nazi claims that American democracy was sick at its core, the city erupted in three days of racial violence that left twenty-five blacks and nine whites dead, hundreds wounded, and an estimated $2 million in property damage. Underlying the anger were months of tension, exacerbated by the migration of southern blacks to the city to seek wartime jobs and a housing crisis that forced many of them into cramped, unsanitary lodgings.[66] On a more personal note, Hill mourned the death of Lelia Pentecost, the surrogate mother whose encouragement and example had broadened his horizons and anchored his young life. The army granted him a deferment to attend the Roanoke funeral, delaying his scheduled departure for basic training at Camp Claiborne, Louisiana, until late June.

Two months earlier, Hill had written to Mrs. Pentecost an unusually frank letter about his ambivalence in taking up arms in the American cause. His message revealed a level of bitterness that could only have been intensified by such matters as the still-to-come firing of Lutrelle Palmer and the havoc in Detroit. "The good white folks and I are still having a great time, but it looks like they are going to clip my wings for awhile," he wrote. "While I firmly believe that Negroes should accept every responsibility that affects citizens generally, our good white brothers are so contemptible and conditions are becoming so much worse for Negroes, there existed in my mind for a long time a serious doubt as to what attitude I should adopt towards my induction when it did come. I have debated this question in my own mind for about a month. I have finally concluded to go along and accept it gracefully and make the best of it while it lasts. This conclusion is based upon the idea that perhaps I will be in a better position to do more effective work in race relations after this holocaust is over than might be possible if I manifest a different attitude now."[67] In four years, Hill had built a local and state reputation. He had helped win a Supreme Court precedent being used not only in Virginia but across the South, to attack racial disparities in teacher pay. He had carted black children to white schools and fearlessly petitioned school boards and federal judges in their behalf. Still, the work that remained far exceeded what had been achieved. Hill's voice was about to be drowned out, possibly forever, by the bugles of war.

As Hill was attending Mrs. Pentecost's funeral, Robinson was also in Roanoke, taking the long-delayed bar exam. In early July, four years after his law-school graduation, he received formal notification that his albatross finally had flown. He was ready to be sworn in as a member of the Virginia State Bar. Dorothy Scott, Hill's secretary, informed Bernie of the happy news. The results had arrived within a few days of the exam, rather than the usual month, because there had been so few taking the test in wartime. "I can now breathe a sigh of relief and I know it is a burden off of him, as he stated yesterday that the suspense was too great for him not knowing what is what. I wonder what he would do if he had to wait a whole month for the marks or the results?"[68] Bernie wired orchids to Robinson in celebration. The time had come for Spot Robinson to move from the classroom to the courtroom. It was his turn to grab the baton and run.

SEVEN

Robinson at the Helm

For the workaholic Spottswood Robinson, the wartime summer of 1944 promised to be a manageable respite. Throughout the winter and spring, maintaining a private law practice in Richmond, teaching at the Howard School of Law, directing various civil rights activities, and supporting a young family placed more demands on his time than most men could handle. With Hill away in the army, Robinson was in sole charge of the law office in the Consolidated Bank Building at First and Marshall Streets. Now, at least for a few summer months he could put the weekly commutes to Howard on hold and focus on legal matters, including the work of the state and national NAACP.

Thurgood Marshall already had plans for Robinson's time. "Will you please let me know how much would make it worth your while to put in final form your brief on restrictive covenants?" Marshall pressed in a May 2 letter. He wanted a cost estimate for Robinson's completing a legal brief started two years earlier. Marshall expected that paper to serve as the foundation for the housing-discrimination test case he was anxious to launch. "It is one of the hottest issues we have today and we cannot be ready to start on any of these cases without your brief."[1] Robinson's reply was conscientious to a fault. "I never have much idea about how long it will take me to complete a particular task—I merely keep at it until I am satisfied that a good job has been done," he replied. If a tentative figure of $750 seemed too high or too low, Marshall should "make such change as you may feel is appropriate." In any event, whether or not the NAACP matched the quoted fee, "I will do the work for the Association if the need therefor is imperative."[2] Neither man could have predicted then that the next major test case to reach the Supreme Court bearing Spot Robinson's imprint would focus not on housing but on transportation.

As late spring and summer passed, Robinson found himself pulled in multiple directions. He and two other lawyers tried vainly to stop the execution of the Winchester convict Howard Walker, who was scheduled to die a mere fifty-two days after an alleged rape. Amid concerns over whether Walker had been forced into a confession and whether a rape had even occurred, the trio managed to obtain a gubernatorial reprieve for a month. When the local judge refused to reopen the case, the three took the excruciating step of witnessing Walker's electrocution at the Virginia State Penitentiary in Richmond.[3] Meanwhile, the Virginia NAACP legal staff, with Robinson now in charge, prepared to challenge the refusal of the state Democratic convention to seat seven black delegates in a presidential election year. The staff also contemplated next steps in the ongoing court battle over the firings of Lutrelle Palmer and others in Newport News. And as July merged into August, they announced possible plans to intervene in the case of a Mrs. Irene Morgan, who had been convicted recently under Virginia's Jim Crow transportation law after a visit to Gloucester County.[4]

Irene Morgan, composed, wronged, and resolute as a long-distance runner, was the plaintiff for whom Marshall and the NAACP Legal Defense Fund had been searching. Robinson knew intimately the organization's preferred legal strategy on transportation. He had, after all, helped conceive it. His almost weekly train rides to Washington while teaching at Howard had created plenty of opportunity for the seldom idle Robinson to contemplate Jim Crow seating. While first-class parlor-car tickets allowed him comfortable accommodations, most black passengers were less fortunate. Conscious of their plight, Robinson developed a memo suggesting a challenge based not on segregation per se but on the commercial perils of forcing passengers to change their seating, based on race, when they traveled between states. The Commerce Clause, housed in article 1, section 8, clause 3, of the Constitution, grounded the theory.[5]

An 1877 Supreme Court decision, *Hall v. DeCuir*, centered Robinson's argument. *Hall* focused on travel between states rather than within a state and on the Commerce Clause rather than the Fourteenth Amendment. In *Hall*, Josephine DeCuir, a wealthy Creole woman traveling from New Orleans to Vicksburg, Mississippi, had complained about the steamboat captain's policy of segregating races on his boat. The action violated an 1869 Louisiana civil rights act, she said. The steamship company replied that it was exempt from the Louisiana statute because under the Commerce Clause only Congress could regulate travel between states. The Supreme Court unanimously agreed.[6] Robinson and the NAACP legal staff believed the *Hall* ruling offered their best prospect for chipping away at Jim Crow seating. *Hall* applied only to travel between states, not within them, but if the segregated seating in interstate trips could be outlawed, the constitutional right to travel freely within a state might tumble next.

Already, the Commerce Clause had helped secure one of the few victories involving segregated common carriers during the era. That case had resulted from an incident involving the Illinois representative Arthur W. Mitchell, the first black man elected to Congress as a Democrat, when he traveled from Chicago to Hot Springs, Arkansas, in April 1937. When the train entered Arkansas, a conductor ordered Mitchell into a dirty, foul-smelling Jim Crow car even though he had purchased a first-class ticket. Even a seat in Congress could not inoculate a black traveler against humiliation. The outraged congressman claimed that his transfer to second-class accommodations solely because of his race violated both the Fourteenth Amendment and the Interstate Commerce Act, which stipulated that neither race should be disadvantaged by segregated seating. The Supreme Court's April 28, 1941, ruling favoring Mitchell dealt only with unequal accommodations for first-class passengers in interstate travel. Still, that signified progress. In the wake of the decision, many southern railroads quietly began a kind of "qualified desegregation" in first-class cars. They also began opening some dining cars to blacks, but on a limited, segregated basis.[7]

The NAACP Legal Defense Fund wanted more. What the organization needed was an upstanding plaintiff who could take the assault on Jim Crow transportation to a new level with a Commerce Clause challenge. Typically, southern sheriffs and police officers, wise to doubts about the constitutionality of Jim Crow seating laws, charged violators with secondary offenses such as disorderly conduct. As Robinson knew, the NAACP had envisioned a national test case a few years earlier when the future civil rights activist, feminist, and educator Pauli Murray was arrested while traveling by Greyhound through Virginia. The hopes had collapsed when a Petersburg judge shrewdly dropped a charge of violating the Jim Crow seating law and convicted Murray and a friend of disorderly conduct instead.[8]

So when a determined Irene Morgan walked into Robinson's Richmond office in the summer of 1944 and apprised him of the two charges against her—misdemeanor resisting arrest and misdemeanor violation of Section 4097dd of the Code of Virginia (the Jim Crow transportation statute)—the lawyer sprang to attention. "I couldn't believe my ears," he recalled. "I looked at the charge sheet, and there it was: violation of that ordinance."[9]

Almost simultaneously, as the NAACP readied for its annual convention in Chicago, the assistant secretary, Roy Wilkins, prodded Marshall about the upcoming program. "It was suggested that you speak to the conference Thursday night, July 13, on the subject of Jim Crow Transportation," Wilkins advised Marshall. "At first I had you down for your old stand-by subject, equality in education, but the staff thought that that was not lively enough material for an evening address, and that people are greatly stirred up over transportation. What do you think about this?"[10] The change in topic fit the membership's mood. For thousands of black soldiers and their families, the war had highlighted the responsibilities of American citizenship. It also had exposed a ruthless double standard when it came to rights. The to-and-fro of war had sent Americans of every stripe scurrying to trains and buses in record numbers. For blacks, increased mobility highlighted the downside of segregated public transit—filth, discomfort, inconvenience, and even danger. A 1939 Seaboard Railway timetable unapologetically advertised air-conditioned cars for whites and non-air-conditioned cars for "colored" travelers on such lines as the Wildwood-to-Miami "Southern States Special." Stifling heat was the least of the insults. Often, conductors shuttled black rail travelers into the car nearest the engine, increasing the likelihood of exposure to dust and noise, and a bumpy ride. White coaches came equipped with water coolers, carpeting, and upholstered seating; black coaches typically did not. Dining service for blacks was spotty at best, and those who boarded without provisions tucked away risked going hungry. Black passengers who purchased first-class or Pullman (sleeping-car) tickets might lessen the hassles, but there was no guarantee in the South that a higher fare would trump black skin. Meanwhile, black bus and streetcar patrons faced a host of annoyances and embarrassments, from being forced to sit or stand in the rear of the carrier to having to relocate for the convenience of whites.[11]

Such difficulties were small change compared with the beatings and even death that occasionally awaited those who challenged the system. Hugh Gloster, a distinguished English professor who later served as president of Atlanta's Morehouse College, was traveling from Atlanta to Memphis by train to visit his mother in August 1942 when he was dragged from the train at Tupelo, Mississippi, severely beaten by policemen, and jailed. His crime? He had urged conductors to move a couple of white passengers to make room for an overflow crowd of blacks. Horrified NAACP staff telegraphed condolences: "We are inexpressibly shocked at the flagrant assault on you on the train en route to Memphis. We offer you the entire machinery of the NAACP to bring your assailant to justice and to assist you to obtain redress."[12]

Almost daily headlines validated Wilkins's decision to substitute transportation for education as Marshall's convention topic. "Colored People Wait for Days on Trains in Dixie Stations," "Buses and Trains Admit Whites First," and "Colored Passengers Get Space left" blared a series of front-page headlines in the January 29, 1944, edition of the *Richmond Afro-American*. A week later, the Virginia League for the Repeal of Segregation Laws pleaded with the Virginia General Assembly to abandon Jim Crow in public carriers. Such laws bred "confusion and resentment" among nonsoutherners forced to travel through the South because of the war, the group urged. The *Times-Dispatch*'s Dabney had astonished many readers by advocating a similar course in a lead editorial less than three months earlier. Known as a southern moderate in the years before court-ordered school integration revealed the limits of that moderation, Dabney had written that segregated bus and train seating spawned unnecessary friction. Besides, he had added, expanded wartime travel made it difficult to monitor who sat where.[13] As if on cue, the experience of twenty-nine-year-old Roland Banks, of New York City, demonstrated the problem. After visiting his mother in Richmond before being inducted into the army, Banks boarded an Atlantic Coast Line coach car reserved for whites at the Broad Street Station. His decision to take a seat prompted a furor. Ordered out of the car by railroad officials and military policemen, "he expressed his resentment of having to offer his services for his country without being accorded decent citizenship rights," the *Richmond Afro-American* reported. The police-court judge Carlton Jewett, a frequent thorn in the side of black Richmonders, fined Banks twenty-five dollars and sentenced him to sixty days in jail. When Banks groused that he would not ride in a Jim Crow car, Jewett rewarded Banks's outburst with an extra thirty days behind bars.[14]

Oliver Hill could testify to the black soldiers' travel plight. A telling incident had occurred during a furlough as the attorney-turned-soldier wound up basic training in Louisiana in 1943 and prepared to ship out for Europe. Ahead of him lay twenty-two months in the British Isles, France, and the Philippines. First, he had to deal with travel in the South. For several years, back in Virginia, Hill had taken to sitting in sections reserved for whites anytime he traveled by public transportation, secretly hoping to be arrested.[15] Perhaps because of his stature and his assertive bearing, that impudence seldom raised a challenge. Not so when he traveled from New Orleans to Atlanta en route to Washington, DC, and a much-anticipated rendezvous with Bernie. Basic training at Camp Claiborne, near Alexandria, Louisiana, had already schooled Hill in the dangers of testing racial limits in the Deep South. His favorite nickname for the area in later years was "hell hole." "Every time that I went into Alexandria, I went with an open knife in my pocket. Made up my mind that the first S.O.B. that messed with me, both of us were going to hell together."[16] Hill's boyhood resolve to stop carrying a knife apparently met its limits in Louisiana.

As Hill prepared to head north, a mixup in train schedules presented him with an ugly choice: either ride in a Jim Crow car through Alabama and Georgia or miss a day of furlough with Bernie. "Hell, I don't want to sit around here for twenty-four hours," Hill recalled saying. "So I did something I hadn't done in years, I went in the Jim Crow car and stayed in the Jim Crow car." Late that evening, Hill made his way to a dining car occupied only by one white couple. As Hill sat down, a steward appeared and told him, "You can't eat in here." "What do you mean I can't eat in here," fumed Hill, who was wearing his enlisted-man's uniform. "You've had the third call for dinner, and I've always eaten after the third call." No matter, the steward said. Either Hill could leave or the steward would have him arrested. Quickly, the couple intervened. "If we're keeping that soldier from getting something to eat, we'll leave," they said. The couple started to rise. Just then, three black Air Force officers entered the dining car. One happened to be a Richmond physician whom Hill knew. The steward steered the officers to a sectioned-off table and suggested that Hill join them. Citing military protocols against enlisted men eating with officers, he refused. But when his Richmond friend intervened—"Come on, Oliver, come on and join us"—Hill acquiesced. The incident was defused.[17]

Thousands of such moments underscored the conclusion of the Swedish economist Gunnar Myrdal in his seismic, fifteen-hundred-page study of American race relations, *An American Dilemma,* which hit bookstores in early 1944. "It is a common observation," Myrdal reported, "that the Jim Crow car is resented more bitterly among Negroes than most other forms of segregation."[18] Seething dissatisfaction meant that the Legal Defense Fund was scrambling to find a test case worthy of a constitutional challenge. Moments after Morgan walked through Robinson's office door, he knew: they had found one in Virginia.

Irene Morgan's historic case began ordinarily enough. The twenty-seven-year-old mother of two, convalescing from surgery due to a difficult pregnancy, came South in the summer of 1944 to recover at her mother's humble home in Gloucester County. Heading back to Baltimore on July 16 for a doctor's appointment, Morgan walked the half mile to the Hayes Store, an all-purpose country store, where she boarded a Greyhound bus to Maryland, leaving her children in their grandmother's care. The particulars of what happened over the next hour or so, as the bus rumbled up Route 17 to Saluda, varied with the teller. The story took on added twists as the years passed. "Testimony introduced by the Commonwealth and the defendant, respectively, is in hopeless conflict," Robinson acknowledged as the case wound toward the Supreme Court. Even so, there was no doubt about the basic thrust: when the bus reached Saluda, reserved, quiet-spoken Irene Morgan refused to obey the bus driver's order to give up her seat to accommodate a white passenger. Her defiance predated that of Rosa Parks in her celebrated Montgomery, Alabama, protest by more than a decade. Arrested, Morgan was pronounced guilty of violating Virginia's Jim Crow law and fined by a lower-court official. Now she wanted to appeal.[19]

Virginia's motor-vehicle segregation law did not, as Morgan and many citizens believed, mandate that blacks sit in the back and whites in the front of buses and streetcars. Common practice and company policies dictated that arrangement. The law specified only that blacks and whites should be segregated by color and that the accommodations for each should be comparable. It required that drivers, empowered as "special policemen," enforce segregated seating by asking passengers to move as needed. Individuals who violated their commands, as Morgan did, risked a misdemeanor conviction.[20] Such laws had taken root a half century earlier with *Plessy v. Ferguson*. Midwife to the South's enforced racial caste system, *Plessy* upheld a Louisiana law requiring segregated seating in railway travel within the state. By a 7-1 vote, the Supreme Court had decreed that the state law did not violate the rights of Homer A. Plessy, a Creole traveler, so long as railroads provided equivalent accommodations for blacks and whites. Southern states soon leapt on the separate-but-equal ruling to legitimize racial apartheid in transportation, housing, and other public arenas. Four years later, in 1900, the Virginia General Assembly had approved the Jim Crow statute requiring segregated cars for blacks and whites on railroads. Other such laws followed. In practice, separate rarely, if ever, meant equal.[21]

Arriving at Middlesex County's picturesque brick courthouse on the morning of October 18, 1944, Robinson, the law associate Linwood Smith, and Irene Morgan crossed grounds guarded by towering oaks and the requisite Confederate memorial. Across the highway sat the sleepy Esso station where Morgan had been arrested earlier in the summer; the small jail where she was briefly incarcerated nestled behind the courthouse. In July, Morgan had gained her freedom by calling out to a stranger through the window of her cell and asking him to get word to her mother. Mrs. Ethel Amos had then urgently solicited relatives and Gloucester black leaders, who cobbled together the five-hundred-dollar bail.[22]

Upon entering the courthouse, the trio climbed a set of steps reserved for blacks and took segregated seats in the second-floor courtroom. On one wall, a marbled tablet paid homage to the Confederate women of Middlesex County, "who sent their sons to the distant battlefields of the South and defended their homes by their own invincible virtue." Nearby, Robert E. Lee and his generals hovered in portraiture over the proceedings. The bus driver, R. P. Kelly, led off for the prosecution, according to an official narrative of the trial. In his version of events, after the bus had arrived at Saluda and various riders had disembarked, six white passengers were left standing. All the blacks were seated. Seeing two vacant spots on the long, rear seat at the back of the bus, Kelly had ordered Morgan and a black seatmate who was holding an infant to move back to the vacant spots. The other woman had started to move, Kelly said, but Morgan "pulled her back down" and refused to switch. In response, Kelly had secured a warrant from a justice of the peace charging Morgan with violating the segregation law. When Sheriff Richard Beverley Segar had boarded to serve the warrant, Morgan's seatmate had moved, but the outraged defendant had refused. She "knocked the warrant out of the sheriff's hand," the driver testified. Sheriff Segar and Deputy C. M. Bristow had then removed Morgan from the bus, he said.[23] Robinson began his cross-examination by establishing a point central to his case, that Morgan had been engaged in interstate travel between Virginia and Maryland. Then, he raised an allegation. According to Morgan, Kelly had announced that "colored passengers would be seated only after all white passengers were seated." That blatant discrimination had fueled her ire. Had Kelly made such a statement? The driver denied the charge.

The next to take the stand was Deputy Bristow, who supplied new details of Morgan's behavior. When he had tried to arrest her, Bristow said, she had swung her arm to strike him but missed. Sheriff Segar had not been so fortunate. Three of Morgan's kicks had landed on his leg, the deputy said. Segar followed Bristow to the witness stand. Then past eighty years old and in his fourth decade as the head of Middlesex County law enforcement, the sheriff said that two of Morgan's kicks had hit home.[24] On cross-examination, Segar acknowledged that he did not know whether there had been any vacant spots on the rear seat when Morgan was asked to move. Both Bristow and Segar described Morgan as well behaved until pressed to relocate.

An attractive woman with large, doe eyes, a chiseled chin, and a serene smile, Morgan took the stand in her own defense. Her description of events differed markedly from those of the white witnesses. As the bus traveled between Hayes Store and Saluda, whites had occupied all but a handful of seats, Morgan said. She had sat uncomfortably on the long seat at the back. When the bus arrived at Saluda, a white woman and her child who had been sitting in the third row from the rear had disembarked. Morgan and Estelle Fields, a black woman carrying an infant, had quickly taken their places. A number of riders, both blacks and whites, had still been standing, Morgan said. Then the troubles had begun. After about five minutes, a white woman and man had boarded the bus, and the driver, Kelly, had ordered Morgan and her seatmate to "get up so that the white couple might sit down." According to Morgan and four later witnesses, there had been no vacant seats anywhere, not even on the long rear seat. "I'll move to another seat, but I will not stand," she had informed the driver. Had she snatched the warrant from Segar's hand? Robinson asked. She had not, Morgan replied. Had she kicked the sheriff or struck at the deputy sheriff or "attempt[ed] in any manner to inflict bodily harm or injury upon either"? No, again.

Many years later, Morgan acknowledged both grabbing the paper and kicking the sheriff. In fact, she added a graphic detail: her kicks had landed in the sheriff's groin, she told a reporter for the Norfolk *Virginian-Pilot* in 1992.[25] How are we to explain the discrepancy between Morgan's 1944 trial testimony and her recollections almost fifty years later? Perhaps her trial testimony was colored by fear. After all, kicking a sheriff was a dangerous thing for a black woman to do in 1944. She may have been confused about what had happened in a rapid encounter on the bus. Or perhaps in later years she embellished her actions to fit changed societal sensibilities. Morgan, who died in 2007 at age ninety, was never asked publicly about the inconsistency. Ultimately, the answer is unknowable.

Continuing in the witness box, Morgan reiterated that she had offered to exchange seats but had refused to be left standing. The law-enforcement officials had then roughly removed her from the bus, she said, and paraded her before a justice of the peace. She had spent six or so hours in jail before her mother posted bail. Two remaining witnesses testified to Morgan's good character, and four, including Fields, affirmed Morgan's testimony that there had been no vacant spots on the bus when the two black women were asked to give up their seats. As added proof, Fields said she had been left standing, holding her infant, after being evicted from her seat. After all the evidence had been presented, Robinson moved to strike the Jim Crow charge on the grounds that Morgan had been an interstate passenger, not governed constitutionally by Virginia's transit laws. The disorderly-conduct charge should be dismissed too, both on those grounds and because it was within Morgan's rights to protest an illegal arrest, he argued. Rejecting Robinson's plea, Circuit Court Judge J. Douglas Mitchell found Morgan guilty on both counts. He upheld her ten-dollar fine on the segregation-law violation and the one-hundred-dollar fine, plus costs, for resisting arrest. The next day, Clerk C. W. Eastman informed Mitchell that Morgan had paid the larger fine but not the lesser one. The ten-dollar Jim Crow conviction was en route to the Virginia Supreme Court of Appeals.[26]

By January 1945 the NAACP's national legal staff had recognized *Morgan's* potential as a national test case. Money confirmed the commitment. "I am sending herewith a statement of the expenses, accrued and to be incurred, in the case of Commonwealth v. Irene Morgan, our case testing the constitutionality of the Virginia bus jim-crow law," Robinson wrote to Marshall. Four days later, Marshall replied that he had requested $176.56, which included pay to Robinson for costs to date in the *Morgan* case and a one-hundred-dollar advance on future expenses. "On my next trip to Washington I would like to sit down with you, Andy, and Bill [Hastie] and map out procedure for these transportation cases so that we will have everything coordinated," he added.[27]

Amid intensifying war news from Europe and the Pacific, Robinson filed briefs and prepared for argument before the Virginia Supreme Court of Appeals. As planned, he focused on *Hall v. DeCuir* and the dominance of the Commerce Clause in regulating interstate travel. The Virginia attorney general, Abram P. Staples, countered that the police powers granted the states under the Tenth Amendment trumped interstate commerce in *Morgan's* case. In mid-April, as the nation mourned the death of President Roosevelt and Allied forces battled for control of Berlin, Robinson and Ransom went before the assembled justices of the Virginia Supreme Court of Appeals to present their case. "We do not have the slightest idea as to what the Court will do," Robinson informed Marshall afterwards, submitting a bill for $148.61. "No questions were asked either side during the argument." He speculated that the court might order a reargument since "frankly, some of the judges might have been left behind" in understanding the case. That assessment proved unduly optimistic. The court's June 6 opinion, released from Wytheville on a day of record-setting cold, interpreted the Virginia segregation law as "a reasonable police regulation" applying to both intrastate and interstate passengers. The judges unanimously affirmed the state's position.[28] Within days, Robinson and other lawyers from the Howard brotherhood gathered to assess the prospects for a Supreme Court challenge.[29]

Closer to home, skepticism surfaced. Martin Martin, disillusioned with the Justice Department after his stint in California, had returned to Virginia. In the fall of 1944 he joined ranks with Robinson to form a three-partner firm, Hill, Martin & Robinson. In a letter to Hill, Martin confided his doubts about their partner's handling of the *Morgan* case. "As I told you, 'Spot' got his Irene Morgan segregation case all messed up, and now he, 'Turkey' and 'Andy' are thinking of taking it to the U. S. Supreme Court. I am not entirely in favor of this as I am afraid that the Supreme Court might affirm it also."[30] As usual, Martin had begun his letter with a merry greeting, responding to a bawdy postcard sent earlier by Hill: "I received your card showing me your hang-out there in Rouen. I think I will send this card to Bernie, since you are intimating that I would dare visit such a place being the gentleman that I am." In a separate mailing, an amused Dorothy Scott also took note: "Martin laughed when he received the card from you. He said that it looked like the red light district to him. (smiles) . . . He says 'you don't know Peanuts, he is just as bad as I am when it comes to having a good time and liking the skirts.' I told him that I know better; that if you were like that it was only because you were being led on to do so by him while being in his company."[31] As for Martin's critique of Robinson's performance, NAACP correspondence suggests no such displeasure.

By late summer of 1945, any doubts aside, the association was preparing a high-court appeal. As Robinson filed the necessary papers, the NAACP heralded the moment. The only transportation cases to reach the Supreme Court since *Hall v. DeCuir*, in 1877, had dealt with segregated seating, Marshall noted. "The Irene Morgan case is the first case which clearly challenges the validity of segregation statutes as applied to passengers in interstate commerce and on interstate carriers."[32] The showdown in the high court would come the following spring.

Transportation was far from the only matter consuming Spot Robinson's days. In the summer of 1944, he had optimistically—too optimistically, it would turn out—agreed to Marshall's request for the elaborate brief analyzing court cases related to restrictive covenants and laying out strategies against them. Several NAACP branches were anxious to get cases started. They needed guidance, Marshall said. Robinson's three-page reply, setting out the parameters of a study, offered a window into both his expertise and his love of scholarship. Robinson proposed extending an already finished, 113-page manuscript to about 300 pages. He intended to discuss between seventy-five and one hundred state and federal decisions involving public ordinances and private agreements, plus other related rulings. "As I ordinarily incorporate about 200 cases in every important brief which I write, I would expect that case citation will be ample," he said.[33] He also intended to give full weight to what he saw as the legitimacy of various unfavorable court rulings. Robinson's penchant for impartial assessment, which later would serve him well as a judge, shone through. "Regardless of my individual belief and opinion concerning many of the cases, a good many of them are correctly decided, and although they are unfavorable, I think the ultimate solution will come in an appreciation and overcoming of the difficulties, logical or otherwise, rather than in thin-ice rantings against the injustice of the law," wrote the cautious revolutionary. Apparently discounting his numerous other commitments, Robinson estimated that he could complete a draft report in about three months. He planned to devote five hundred hours to the task, the equivalent of twelve forty-hour work weeks. Inexhaustible as he seemed, Robinson had set himself a near-impossible goal. By Christmas the promised document was nowhere to be seen. Marshall's holiday card noted the omission: "Where in the hell is it? Merry Christmas."[34]

As Marshall and Robinson strategized, day-to-day demands continued. On top of the Irene Morgan case and restrictive covenants, assorted criminal and civil rights cases crowded Robinson's calendar in late 1944 and early 1945. In one high-profile matter, Robinson joined Hopkins, Cooley, and Smith in appealing the death sentence of Silas Rogers, a North Carolina man whose bizarre conviction in the shooting death of a Petersburg police officer included disturbing evidence of police abuse. In what appeared to be a case of mistaken identity, Rogers had been arrested shortly after arriving in town as a stowaway aboard a Seaboard Railway train. During an interrogation, police had beat Rogers, who was black, with blackjacks and fists. They had knocked him to the floor and at one point poured four glasses of water up his nose.[35] So much for notions of Virginia as an island of racial civility. The ensuing confession had been a farce, Robinson and the others argued to the Supreme Court of Appeals. In a sixteen-page opinion, Chief Justice Preston W. Campbell castigated the Petersburg police department for "inhumane treatment." The officers' assault on the defendant had been "a cowardly one, uncalled for and beyond the realm of justification," he railed. Still, the execution sentence stood. Supposed eyewitness testimony, later discredited, superseded police misconduct.[36] Twice, at the lawyers' urging, Darden delayed Rogers's execution. As the months passed, Robinson and others searched diligently for evidence that might clear their client.

Robinson's hectic pace did not go unnoticed by his coworkers. Dorothy

Scott updated Hill while keeping the soldier abreast of office happenings. "'Spot' says he will write you when he gets a chance," she reported in September 1944. "He does keep rather busy. I am afraid he will have a nervous breakdown if he doesn't get some rest." She added a cheerful description of the law firm's redecorated offices: "You should see the offices now—they look really lovely. We had the walls Kem-toned blue (light blue) and woodwork painted the same color it was at first. . . . The only thing missing now is you."[37] A letter from Marian Robinson to Hill also hinted at Robinson's fatiguing pace. Spot expected to write soon "but gets home from the office so late he's fit for nothing but sleep," she said. Some months later, Bernie provided a humorous take on the foibles of her husband's two law partners. "Maria tells me that she is getting a divorce from Martin," Bernie wrote, referring to Martin's first wife, Maria Wright. "She claims she has already filed through Spot. But if Spot takes as long to get that for her as he did and is taking to get my money from the bus company then Martin has no worry. (Smiles.)" Bernie did not elaborate on the nature of her claim against the transport company. The Martins did divorce, and he later remarried.[38]

As Scott was describing Robinson's work habits, Hill was holed up with his engineering regiment in an apple orchard in Normandy, France. Like tens of thousands of black soldiers, Hill had been assigned to a noncombat unit tasked with constructing and maintaining roads and bridges, building field hospitals, and the like. He did administrative work for the Headquarters and Service Company of the 1310th Engineer General Service Regiment, gradually rising to the rank of staff sergeant. Hill recalled only three black officers among a sea of white ones in the unit. In contrast, the enlisted staff was all black. After sailing from New York on New Year's Day 1944, he and his comrades had landed in Scotland. They had traveled south by military transport train to Hereford, about sixteen miles from the Welsh border in western England, where they had spent several reasonably calm months. From there, the route had led to Wales and then, three weeks after the D-day invasion, to France.[39]

Landing on the Continent, Hill was separated from his unit for two days. He recalled a night sky, when he was stranded on a beach, that looked much like "a glorified Fourth of July celebration" as Allied antiaircraft guns blazed at German planes overhead. Reunited, the regiment spent six months in the Normandy countryside before being loaded onto French freight cars and transported toward the Battle of the Bulge, which was raging in the ridges and dense woodland of the Ardennes Forest. As Allied forces struggled to resist the surprise German offensive, some black soldiers were pressed into combat for the first time. Hill himself was issued a carbine. Nearing Paris, however, the regiment was redirected back to Camp Lucky Strike, the site of an abandoned German airstrip near the seaside city of Le Havre. There, for the rest of the European conflict, Hill and his regiment helped operate a way station for former American prisoners of war and others returning to the United States. He and a cousin, Charlie Pollard, also assigned to the 1310th Regiment, had received passes and happened to be in Paris on May 8, 1945, V-E Day. "We arrived the night before and had the good fortune to celebrate VE Day with the French people," Hill recalled.[40]

Amid the dangers of war, Hill suffered indignities stemming from a largely segregated military. More educated than most of his fellow soldiers, inclined by training and nature to be assertive, Hill twice intervened with his superiors to protest ill treatment and low morale among black soldiers. While in Hereford, Hill was particularly incensed by a policy known as "white nights, colored nights," by which white and black soldiers were allowed to go into town only on alternating evenings. His understanding, Hill said, was that white soldiers disliked seeing black men socializing with English women. Army commanders viewed the segregated passes as a way of keeping the peace, but the policy was a major irritant to black soldiers. Hill recalled that his angry protest prompted the captain with whom he was speaking to threaten him with court-marshal. "I told him he could do anything he wanted to," Hill wrote. "I was not the least bit intimidated."[41] The incident resulted in neither a reprimand nor a changed policy, but the captain himself seemed to become more congenial after the exchange, Hill said.

In a second incident, after the move to France, Hill confronted a white captain who he believed was far more interested in winning a promotion than in protecting his troops. By Hill's telling, they exchanged harsh words, with Hill informing the captain that he had best hope the troops never became armed, because they were likely to turn against superiors as uncaring as he was. In an interview many years later, Hill repeated the charge that some black soldiers would have killed white officers if given the chance. "Whole lot of our officers, if we could ever have gotten into combat, there would have been no hope of them ever coming back," he told an interviewer. While possibly true, Hill's claim may have been grounded more in outrage and machismo than in fact. There is no indication that the black troops who did participate in the Battle of the Bulge turned on white superiors, for instance. To the contrary, their competence is credited with helping pave the way for President Truman's long-overdue desegregation of the military three years later.[42]

In at least one respect, wartime racism may have worked to Hill's advantage. While his unit was preparing to move from England to Wales, a chaplain in an advance group reportedly warned local residents that the soon-to-arrive black soldiers would put local women in jeopardy of being raped. "That damn cracker preacher," as Hill referred to him, created such a morale problem that an inspector general showed up to investigate. The officer recommended an additional three weeks of orientation for the unit, a timetable that Hill believed saved them from being part of the bloody Normandy invasion on June 6, 1944. Except for that delay, he said, "I might have been over there in the bottom of the English Channel or buried on one of those beaches like Omaha or Utah."[43] Had that happened, much future work on the home front would have passed to others or been left undone.

As World War II intensified, the scarcity of housing for blacks in major American cities also deepened.[44] The shortage in the District of Columbia was particularly acute. As the city's black population swelled, more and more people crowded into the small slice of the city open to black renters or buyers. Higher density worsened social ills, from crime to disease. At the NAACP Legal Defense Fund offices in New York, the increasingly untenable situation heightened interest in a challenge to restrictive covenants. The plight of Clara I. Mays, a federal employee in Washington, personified the problem. When the house she rented with her sisters and nieces was sold, the family had to store its furniture and split up into several rented rooms. The Mays clan simply could not find an empty house for rent or sale to blacks. In early 1944 Mays temporarily solved the problem by purchasing a home at 2213 First Street NW. The seller, who had acquired the house specifically for transfer to Mays, ignored a 1925 covenant forbidding sale or rental to blacks for a period of twenty-one years. For Mays, the new residence was a godsend, that is, until a lawsuit by neighbors thrust the matter into court.[45]

The District Court for the District of Columbia, citing long-established policy, ruled in favor of the neighbors in enforcing the restrictive covenant, even though its expiration was only two years away. The court gave Mays and her family sixty days to relinquish the house. In January 1945 an appeals-court panel upheld that verdict by a 2-1 vote. For the Legal Defense Fund, the disappointing judgment contained a silver lining—a dissent written by Justice Henry W. Edgerton. Edgerton acknowledged and lamented the unfairness and "very great hardship" created by the forced move. "We cannot close our eyes to what is commonly known. The conditions in which many of the 187,000 Negroes in the District of Columbia have long been obliged to live are now worse than ever," he wrote.[46] For the NAACP lawyers, Edgerton's acceptance of the sociological argument and his willingness to raise constitutional doubts created a hairline crack in what had been a nearly impenetrable wall. The handful of prior positive rulings included the 1942 *Hundley v. Gorewitz* decision, in which Houston and Robinson had stressed the changed racial makeup of a Washington neighborhood, and *Hansberry v. Lee*, a 1940 Supreme Court decision that had spurred the writing of *A Raisin in the Sun*. The prize-winning play by Lorraine Hansberry, daughter of the plaintiffs, focused on the human impact of housing discrimination in Chicago. The *Hansberry* victory had turned on a technicality, however. While it had opened some twenty-seven blocks in Chicago to black ownership and occupancy, it had not advanced legal doctrine for overturning racial covenants.[47]

Others had handled the early stages of the *Mays* case. Now, Robinson and Marshall joined in crafting a petition for Supreme Court review. The petition probed every ground of complaint yet tested, reflecting Robinson's encyclopedic knowledge. It also added to the list of distractions from the still-uncompleted restrictive-covenant study. "The study on restrictive covenants has not as yet been completed because of the fact that the lawyer who is working on it is our only legal representative in Virginia. . . . It is impossible for him to get back to work on the study except part time," Marshall informed a correspondent in April 1945.[48] The power of Edgerton's dissent and the mounting hardship for black Americans seeking housing fueled optimism that the Supreme Court would review the *Mays* case. To the disappointment of Robinson and the LDF, the court denied the writ of certiorari on May 28. In a small consolation, two of the seven participating justices dissented. Finally, a few white elites had acknowledged the damage being done.[49]

Courtroom setbacks and uncompleted Robinson study or no, Marshall felt that he could wait no longer to devise a uniform strategy on restrictive covenants. Too many cases were dangling in state and federal courts. If a problematic case reached the Supreme Court first, the outcome might cement discriminatory housing covenants for years to come. From California alone, the prominent black attorney Loren Miller reported cases in the state's trial courts involving between 125 and 150 parcels of property. Several additional cases already were on appeal.[50] "The question of housing now and in the post war period is the foremost problem confronting Negroes today," Marshall asserted in a memo announcing a summit on the matter. He urged members of the NAACP national legal committee to block out time to attend a July 9–10 gathering in Chicago. The meeting that ensued became "arguably one of the most significant gatherings of civil rights legal talent to that point in the Association's history," wrote the historian Jeffrey D. Gonda.[51] Robinson booked a drawing-room car on a train from Washington to Chicago, scheduled to arrive at 7:25 a.m. on the day of the conclave. He planned a return trip through New York, where he intended to spend several days at Legal Defense Fund offices focusing largely on transportation. On a day when American B-29 bombers streaked over Tokyo and President Truman was under sail to Potsdam, Germany, for a conference on postwar order, thirty-three participants gathered at the offices of the American Council on Race Relations to plan domestic warfare. The list included attorneys who would carry the restrictive-covenant cases to their conclusion several years later: Marshall and Hastie, Houston and Robinson, Miller of Los Angeles, George L. Vaughn of Saint Louis, and Francis M. Dent and Willis M. Graves of Detroit.[52]

Robinson and Houston led an opening afternoon session on possible lines of attack. The Richmonder dazzled—or perhaps exhausted—the group with his command of legal minutiae. According to the minutes, he drew distinctions between court rulings focused on covenants encased in contracts and those laid out in deeds. He illuminated differences between property transferred by signers of a covenant and that conveyed by nonsigners. He discussed the variations in enforcement against owners or occupiers. Soberly, he noted the limited success of any current legal remedies, but he also reminded listeners that covenants, at bottom, reflected "the aggressiveness of the few." In most cases, he said, they were hastily drawn documents fueled by agitators within property owners' associations. The lawyers might find strength in the knowledge that "such agreements thus lack stability."[53] Houston followed. Robinson's partner in the District of Columbia cases outlined a series of bold and unconventional strategies aimed at diverting the courts' focus from a narrow discussion of property and contract law. "Start out denying that the plaintiffs are white," he advised, demonstrating the complexity of establishing racial identity. He also urged a detailed analysis of who lived in the neighborhood and how many of the original covenant signers remained. "You get down to whether a few old people are going to be allowed to disturb the orderly trend of development in a city," he said.[54] The attendees returned home without a clear game plan but assured that housing had risen to the fore of the NAACP's legal agenda.

Back in Virginia, Robinson's breakneck schedule continued apace. As autumn 1945 approached, strategy huddles and filing preparation for the Irene Morgan appeal to the Supreme Court competed with state and local matters. In September the pending execution of Silas Rogers returned to his agenda. For more than two hours, as rain beat against the hearing-room windows, Robinson pleaded with the Virginia State Pardon Board for clemency. Departing from his usually staid courtroom demeanor, Robinson delivered a dramatic and animated defense. He brought new information to the table, including a Burns Detective Agency report that Petersburg police had furnished one supposed eyewitness with a hotel room, food, laundry, and incidentals worth three hundred to four hundred dollars for his testimony.[55] A month later, in a letter to Robinson, Chairman William S. Meacham announced a reduction in Rogers's sentence from death to life in prison. The decision was Robinson's most significant victory thus far within the Virginia criminal justice system.[56]

Meanwhile, in New York and Richmond a tacit agreement seems to have emerged that Robinson's long-awaited restrictive-covenant study would never be finished. LDF attorneys shifted from telling inquirers about the upcoming report to directing them toward other recently published articles. Finally, in the spring of 1947, Marshall gave a final benediction: "We have been unable to make our proposed study because of other emergency matters involving pending cases, which have made it impossible for members of our research staff to get to it."[57] Spot Robinson had met his match. There were limits to what he could do, at least while meeting his own impeccable standards.

EIGHT

Rising Expectations

The first Western Union telegram sped east at 4:52 p.m. on October 25, 1945. "IN STATES SEE YOU SOON... LOVE OLIVER," read the message to Bernie Hill. A second telegram, directed to Oliver's law firm in Richmond, soon followed: "ROLL OUT THE BARREL THE WAR IS OVER FOR ME AM ON MY WAY HOME LOVE PEANUTS." Jubilation reigned. At the Hills' small apartment in Washington and at the law offices of Hill, Martin & Robinson in Richmond's Jackson Ward, World War II finally could be consigned to history. After two years, four months, and nineteen days in uniform, Hill relished thoughts of a return to civilian life and his personal calling.[1] Bernie had been planning the celebration for months. With her husband safe, her dreams reignited of a family and a life together. In July she had confessed that children were still very much on her mind. "By the way," she had written, "in preparation for your home coming—I sought advice as to whether or not I could still have children and was informed that I could. Now the only thing we need to do is get you home to plant a few seeds. Please come before it will be too late. . . . We'll have a genius I know."[2] After a month spiced with reunions and merriment, Hill was ready to pick up the pace. His magnetic presence injected the Richmond office with a burst of energy. "I got broke, so I came on down to Richmond last week and went to work," he quipped in an early December letter to a friend in his old army unit. "Tell all the fellows that I'm getting a great kick out of civilian life, and that I'm using all of my good influence towards their early return to the States. I haven't seen the President yet, but you never can tell."[3]

The Richmond that greeted Hill seemed ripe with possibility and laden with old weights. Glimpses of a less rigidly apartheid world emboldened returning black servicemen, even as poll taxes and segregated streetcars, housing, and public spaces stifled dreams of a more egalitarian world. A white newcomer to the city arriving at night by train a few months after Hill's return reported "a curious glamour about the place." Driving by cab down Monument Avenue, the city's elite residential address, the future civil rights leader Marvin Caplan described the scene: "I strove to grasp the grand scale of that boulevard of old mansions from the few details that went flashing by—a lighted window high up in a looming façade, a lamp-lit portico and a broad sweep of white balustrade, the tree-lined park down the center of it, interrupted at intervals by bright-lit clearings, each commanded by the statue of a Confederate hero."[4] Caplan found much to like in the city: its unhurried pace, the friendly faces of both blacks and whites, and the many amenities, from well-stocked department stores to ornate movie palaces to an inviting public library. A languid, cultured air blanketed the city's tearooms, sidewalks, and spacious parks. What he could never tolerate in his few years as a resident, however, was "the way law and custom forced us to live down there. For Richmond was a city riven by race." The separateness was apparent from the moment a traveler stepped off the train and confronted a dusty waiting room marked "Colored." At the Hotel Jefferson, the only blacks in the lobby and restaurant were waiters and busboys. Only whites occupied the reading tables at the city library. And when Caplan stopped by the elegant Miller and Rhoads department store, he encountered—"to my disgust"—his first segregated drinking fountains. Soon he learned that no black person could enter any midtown hotel by the front door, public restrooms were segregated by race, and in the major department stores blacks were forbidden to try on clothing or eat in the tearooms. Most whites simply accepted the arrangement as the natural order. Even those whites appalled by Klan raids and lynching "seldom saw that the everyday slights and injustices to blacks arose from the same arrogance as the atrocities," differing only by degree, Caplan wrote.[5] Such was the world to which Oliver Hill returned.

Hired to edit the *Southern Jewish Outlook* magazine, Caplan quickly found himself in the company of the city's handful of white progressives. They, in turn, introduced him to the principals in the city's leading black law firm. Caplan met Hill one night in the spring of 1946 at the home of Anne and Sam Gellman, an outspoken white social worker and her lawyer husband. Hill impressed Caplan as "powerfully built, with the shaven head and the bearing of a George Catlin Indian chief." That evening, the group launched what they believed to be one of the South's first racially integrated veterans groups, Richmond Chapter Number One of the American Veterans Committee, a liberal counterpoint to the American Legion and the Veterans of Foreign Wars.[6] While he admired Hill, the editor and his young wife became closer, over time, to Spot and Marian Robinson. Caplan found the junior attorney to have an "easygoing, offhand, unassuming manner" that masked a keen intellect and a zealous work ethic. After Robinson invited the couple to stop by his home, the two couples formed a regular foursome, sometimes gathering on Sunday afternoons to snack and chat and watch old movies on the Robinsons' still-novel television set. Caplan recalled Marian as warm, down to earth, and tart tongued in sizing up her husband's august calling. "Civil rights. You can't eat it. You can't wear it. You can't buy beans with it," she irreverently proclaimed. The Caplans also glimpsed Robinson's perfectionism. When Naomi Caplan, a psychologist, mentioned that she needed a new set of blocks for working with young children, Robinson insisted on putting his woodworking skills to use. The episode threatened to become a never-ending saga. On each visit, Robinson remained unsatisfied. One cube was a few millimeters off here, another was imperfect there. Finally, Mrs. Caplan "wrested them away from him one Sunday, refused to give them back, and assured him honestly, after she had used them for a while, that they suited her just fine."[7]

Hobbies took a backseat as the Virginia lawyers and others inaugurated a new era of intense focus on dismantling Jim Crow. In Hill's view, the global conflict and the segregated army had retarded the domestic push for civil rights. The time had come to reignite the flame. Education, housing, transportation, and voting all demanded attention—the sooner, the better.[8] With Irene Morgan's challenge to segregated bus seating already in the pipeline, transportation was poised to seize postwar headlines first. In February 1946, just weeks before the Supreme Court was scheduled to hear the *Morgan* case, a twenty-seven-year-old Army veteran erased any doubt about how dangerous public transit could still be for blacks in the South. Isaac Woodard Jr., a decorated sergeant who had served for more than three years, including fifteen months in a Pacific combat zone, was arrested at Batesburg, South Carolina, on the day of his discharge. After Woodard argued briefly with an Atlantic Greyhound bus driver, police administered a severe beating with night sticks. Ruptured eye sockets and irreparably damaged corneas resulted. By the time Woodard was grudgingly allowed medical attention, he was totally and permanently blind. A widely distributed photograph of his swollen, bruised face became a national rallying point against injustice.[9]

Ironically, the man who had recognized the potential in Irene Morgan's case and shepherded it to the threshold of the nation's highest court now was ineligible to close the deal. No matter that Robinson had filed the papers and perfected the legal theory of the case. Because of his earlier skittishness, less than three years had elapsed since his admission to the Virginia bar. That meant he was still shy of the prerequisite experience to practice before the Supreme Court when the justices took up *Morgan* on March 27, 1946. The presentation fell to Marshall and Hastie, then also awash in Senate controversy over his nomination by President Truman to be governor of the Virgin Islands. Robinson sat at the counsel table, passing notes to his colleagues and taking in every word but not allowed to speak. Before a packed courtroom, Marshall argued that the federal government alone could regulate travel between states. In reply, Virginia Attorney General Staples warned that courts meddling with race relations in the South did so at the nation's peril. "Laws cannot alter human nature or race antagonism," he insisted.[10] When Justice Wiley E. Rutledge tried to draw Hastie into a Fourteenth Amendment attack on segregated bus seating, Robinson "winced inwardly." He feared the court was not yet ready for a reversal of *Plessy*. Had Hastie switched to that line of reasoning, rather than the Commerce Clause, the case might have been doomed. Hastie did not take the bait, and Robinson relaxed. "We did not want to make bad law," he said.[11] A few weeks later, while awaiting the decision, the NAACP sent Hastie a $350 check for his role in preparing and arguing the Morgan case. Robinson netted $150 for research, preparation of briefs, and "assistance in argument" before the high court.[12]

On June 3, cheers rocked the NAACP headquarters in New York. In a decision written by Associate Justice Stanley F. Reed, a Kentucky moderate, the Supreme Court sided with Morgan. Only one associate justice dissented. Reed observed that under Virginia law an interstate passenger might have to repeatedly shift seats to meet segregation requirements. In light of such inconvenience, interstate motor travel required "a single, uniform rule to promote and protect national travel." Whites and blacks should be treated identically when traveling between states. For the first time in its history, the court had overturned a state law requiring Jim Crow seating in public transit.[13] In a gush of pride, the next edition of the *Richmond Afro-American* hailed the decision with six front-page articles. "Jim Crow on Southern buses is dead," celebrated the lead article. Morgan smiled out from the page, which also featured a solemn and immaculately groomed Spottswood Robinson. "Started Ball Rolling," lauded the cutline under Robinson's youthful photograph. Speaking from Columbia, Tennessee, where he was enmeshed in the defense of some two dozen black men charged in connection with a February race riot, Marshall praised the ruling as "one of the most momentous decisions in the history of the country." And in New York, the NAACP flooded Western Union with self-congratulatory telegrams to a list of sympathizers and donors, including the poet Langston Hughes; the singer and actress Lena Horne; the president of the University of North Carolina, Frank Graham; the recently retired New York mayor, Fiorello La Guardia; and the actor Paul Robeson.[14]

Within weeks, if not days, a more sober reality pierced the euphoria. Anyone paying attention to the 1946 session of the Virginia General Assembly might have predicted that Supreme Court ruling or no, white southerners would not surrender without a fight. One clue lay in an obscure piece of legislation approved on March 26, the day before the Supreme Court hearing on *Morgan*. With only one dissenting vote in the Senate and none in the House of Delegates, lawmakers approved a new code section dealing with "riotous or disorderly conduct" in certain public places, including trains and streetcars. Anyone causing an "unnecessary disturbance" by running through the public place, climbing through windows or on seats, or, notably, "failing to move to another seat when lawfully requested to so move by the operator" would be guilty of disorderly conduct, a misdemeanor. The bill's sponsor? None other than the delegate John Warren Cooke, a future Speaker of the Virginia House, the last son of a Confederate veteran to hold high public office in Virginia, and—assuredly, no accident—the delegate in 1946 from Middlesex County, where Irene Morgan had been tried.[15] If segregated seating could not be sustained in one way, it might be in another. Reluctantly, but rapidly, Robinson and the NAACP realized that *Morgan* was less than the unqualified victory they had hoped. Ordinary black men and women throughout the South might think they had been granted the right to travel unencumbered on bus rides between states; the experts soon saw otherwise. Yes, the ruling banned state laws mandating segregated interstate travel. However, as bus companies quickly ascertained, the justices put no restrictions on the private carriers themselves. Bus companies still were free to enforce their own segregation rules. At a minimum, proving otherwise would require another lengthy odyssey through the courts.[16]

Exhausted by the physical and emotional strains of his almost inhuman work pace, Marshall found himself hospitalized within a few weeks of the *Morgan* decision. He remained unable to work into the fall.[17] It fell to Robinson and others, including Marshall's deputy, Robert Carter, to sort through the fallout from the court decision. Referencing several conversations with Robinson, Carter advised Walter White on the urgent need after *Morgan* to find "some method of attacking the private rules and regulations of carriers." Devising a strategy would be "one of the first things on Thurgood's agenda, when he returns," Carter predicted correctly. That promised powwow convened November 16 and 17 in New York.[18] Over the next several years, no state conference in the nation did more than Virginia's, and no law firm in Virginia did more than Hill, Martin & Robinson to carry out the mandate that emerged from the New York gathering: to attack segregated, unequal seating in public transportation whenever and wherever it occurred.[19] The Virginians sifted through countless complaints and filed dozens of lawsuits, many seeking damages. Meanwhile, Robinson played an integral role in national NAACP efforts to challenge discrimination in interstate travel before the Interstate Commerce Commission. That included a long and ultimately unsuccessful effort to win relief for Morehouse College president Benjamin Mays, who had challenged his exclusion from the dining car on a train trip from Atlanta to New York. In May 1946 alone, Robinson and Carter reported pleading before the ICC "in about ten instances" involving discrimination in interstate travel.[20]

Some of the law firm's transportation cases resulted in modest victories. Some produced setbacks in which the only silver lining was having annoyed the transit companies. And some few helped in important ways to shorten the time until the inevitable moment when Jim Crow rode no more. Even a small sampling of the firm's caseload hints at its breadth. Relatively happy outcomes awaited Sam Tucker and Lottie Taylor, for instance. Back from the war, Tucker had set up a law practice in Emporia, south of Richmond, near the North Carolina border. Hill and Tucker still envisioned collaboration, but there was no space in the Richmond office for another attorney. For the time being, they would work together from a distance. After an October 1946 bus trip from Washington to Emporia, Tucker traded his defense-attorney stripes for those of a defendant. Heading into Virginia, Tucker occupied a seat in the fourth row from the front of the bus. In Richmond, he refused the bus operator's order to move further back. Charged with violating the state's recently minted law on "causing a disturbance," Tucker was convicted and fined five dollars in police court. With Martin and Hill handling his defense, Tucker appealed in hustings court. There, the heavyweight Richmond lawyer John J. Wicker Jr. insisted that Tucker's refusal to move constituted a "disturbance" under the new law. Even if the passenger "smiles and blows kisses" at the operator, Wicker argued, staying put constituted disorder. Judge John L. Ingram saw the *Morgan* decision as prohibitive of such tomfoolery, however. The new law was "doing indirectly what you couldn't do directly," he said, dismissing the charges.[21]

In a similar case with a broader impact, Mrs. Lottie E. Taylor protested her arrest and conviction in Fairfax County in September 1946 after refusing to change her seat while en route from Washington to Madison County, Virginia. The Hill law firm assisted attorney James Raby, who took the case to the Virginia Supreme Court of Appeals, winning a rare victory there. The court held that bus companies had a right to lay down "reasonable" rules of conduct in interstate travel, even including segregation by race, but riders could no longer be charged with disorderly conduct, jailed, or fined merely for refusing to change their seat. Rebuffing the General Assembly, the court said that the power of transit companies was limited to removing such riders from the bus. A state NAACP official later estimated that more than forty cases already in court were won because of the Taylor decision.[22]

Despite small gains, other verdicts among the Hill-Robinson caseload reinforced a sober reality: blacks and whites in the South continued to travel in two largely separate and unequal worlds. In one such case, Mrs. Ethel New, of Lynch, Kentucky, charged that she had suffered a miscarriage after being dragged by a police officer from a bus in Lynchburg. Ordered to move to the last seat on the bus, New had refused. The Virginia Supreme Court of Appeals in September 1947 affirmed a lower-court ruling denying her bid for ten thousand dollars in damages. Reinforcing the limits of the *Morgan* decision, the ruling erased any doubt that segregated seating on bus trips that began and ended inside Virginia, as did New's, was still permitted.[23]

Perhaps the most significant defeat suffered by the firm occurred in federal court in 1948 in the case of Mrs. Adeline A. Day, of Syracuse, New York. Then in her mid-sixties, Day sat in the second seat from the front as her bus left Richmond in January 1947 en route to Winter Haven, Florida. Ordered by the driver to move back, she refused. Day insisted that state segregation laws did not apply to interstate passengers and that she was being assigned unfairly to a less comfortable seat. At South Hill, according to a lawsuit filed by attorney Martin, Day was violently "pulled, dragged and ejected" from the bus. After police held her for three hours in the town jail, Mrs. Day sued the Atlantic Greyhound Bus Company for twenty-five thousand dollars. To the NAACP's dismay, both a federal-district-court jury and a three-man Fourth Circuit Appeals Court panel ruled against Mrs. Day. In an opinion written by Judge Soper of Maryland, the panel gave its seal of approval to bus-company policies mandating racial segregation in interstate travel so long as they had an aura of "reasonableness." Writing about the case several years later, Lester Banks, the executive secretary of the Virginia NAACP conference, called the ruling "the only important transportation case lost by your NAACP." The decision was not appealed, because the national staff was developing two other promising similar cases, one in Virginia.[24]

That Virginia case, *Chance v. Lambeth*, argued by Martin and Hill, with Robinson assisting on the brief, resulted in a substantial victory in January 1951. William Chance, a high-school principal in North Carolina, was on a return train trip from Philadelphia when he was ordered to move to a less comfortable, Jim Crow car at Richmond. He refused. In Emporia, police met the Atlantic Coast Line train, arrested Chance for disorderly conduct, and escorted him to jail. Charging grievous injury and humiliation, Chance sued for twenty-five thousand dollars. The Fourth Circuit ruling was again written by Judge Soper. This time, the three-judge panel found the train policy invalid. The Supreme Court refused to review the decision, in effect, invalidating railroad rules requiring white and black interstate passengers to occupy separate coaches. The cumulative weight of such actions was wearing on Jim Crow. Whatever its limitations, noted the historian Catherine Barnes, "*Chance* was the first legal inroad against the Jim Crow railway coach, and it supplied blacks with a favorable precedent which they quickly put to good use in other suits."[25] It would be more than a decade after *Chance*, and more than a decade and a half after *Morgan*, before Jim Crow transit sputtered to an end in the South. *Browder v. Gayle*, the 1956 Supreme Court decision evolving out of the Montgomery bus boycott, heralded a sea change by proclaiming segregated, in-state bus travel unconstitutional under the Fourteenth Amendment.[26] Still, even without legal sanction, enforced habits die hard.

Over time, the *Morgan* ruling proved to have been a crucial peak on the long path to transportation equality. It signaled an emerging interest by the Supreme Court in protecting minority rights, created a valuable precedent, and spawned an early instance of direct-action, nonviolent protest. In the spring of 1947, sixteen young men traveling in eight interracial pairs fanned out over the Upper South to test the results of the *Morgan* decision. After stopping off in Richmond to pay tribute to Robinson, the group headed south. There, they encountered widespread ignorance and defiance of the court ruling. Four of them, including the activist and pacifist Bayard Rustin, later served thirty-day sentences on road gangs in North Carolina for violating that state's Jim Crow bus law. The group, sponsored by two interracial pacifist groups, the Fellowship of Reconciliation and the Congress of Racial Equality, became the model for the more widely remembered Freedom Riders. Those hundreds of students and supporters encountered vicious hostility and mass jailing as they traveled on interstate buses through the segregated South beginning in 1961, testing court rulings in *Morgan* and the later *Boynton v. Virginia*. That decision, also attributable to the Hill law firm and the work of Martin Martin, in particular, established the principle that black citizens could not be denied access to dining facilities at rail and bus terminals. It too would be widely ignored for a time across Dixie.[27]

The many transportation cases handled by Hill, Martin & Robinson reveal a central truth about the long struggle to eliminate segregated transit. While icons such as Rosa Parks and, to a lesser degree, Irene Morgan give a national face to those efforts, hundreds of unknown black men and women made similar, heroic stands for justice, scores of them in Virginia. Their actions occurred against a backdrop of enormous risk. Decades after Irene Morgan's courageous stand, her niece Cleo Gregory Warren said her generation of the family was amazed in the early 1990s to learn of Morgan's defiance. It seemed "totally out of character for her. She was always quiet, gentle," Warren said. But Morgan's life story revealed a woman of strength. She went on to run both day-care and building-maintenance businesses, and she earned undergraduate and graduate degrees late in life. As for the court case, "she just explained to us that she did what she had to do," Warren said. "They were wrong. She had paid for her ticket."[28] For Robinson, the *Morgan* verdict brought a flurry of local attention and increased investment by him in the NAACP's transit work. In naming him to its honor roll for 1946, the *Richmond Afro-American* branded him the "people's counselor." He was being honored, the newspaper said, for efforts to "safeguard the rights of the most lowly of individuals, as well as those with power and influence." Asked to identify his greatest thrill in 1946, Robinson chose a more personal matter. The best memory, Robinson said, was of a day when he and Marian took an eleven-year-old girl on her first fishing trip and she caught twenty-five fish.[29]

No one knew better than Robinson how elusive victory remained. Had there been any doubt, it was erased by numerous letters of woe written to NAACP headquarters in New York, including one describing an event at the Richmond train station in July 1950. Vera Micheles Dean, a prominent editor and research director at the Foreign Policy Association in New York, wrote regarding "my very fine housekeeper." Mrs. Julia Johnson, who was expecting a baby, had boarded an Atlantic Coast Line Railroad train on July 13 to visit her family in South Carolina. The ticket seller had assured her that she would not have to change seats. Acting on that assurance, her husband had placed her heavy suitcase in the rack above her head. At Richmond on the morning of July 14, two or three white passengers had entered the coach and the black passengers, including Mrs. Johnson, were peremptorily told to move to another car. Having no one to help her, Mrs. John had lifted her suitcase off the rack. "Thereupon she had a miscarriage which, according to her doctor here, would not have occurred had she not been forced to lift a heavy weight," Mrs. Dean wrote. "I fear that you receive daily instances of this kind, but I am so shocked by the physical, as well as psychological damage this incident has caused one of the finest women I know that I cannot refrain from writing you."[30] For Spot Robinson and Richmond's black citizens, such treatment was not a shock. Four years after *Morgan* it was still a way of life.

As the NAACP Legal Defense Fund readied its postwar assaults on Jim Crow in the autumn of 1945, education remained at the forefront. It had been a half decade since the last major advances involving schools, the Supreme Court's 1938 *Gaines* decision and its 1940 refusal to reconsider the circuit-court pay-equalization ruling in *Alston*. Acting on *Gaines*, the state of Missouri had set up a separate and very unequal law school for black students. Lloyd Gaines's unresolved disappearance had thwarted plans to confront that inequality. Now the LDF was exploring other law-school challenges. Meanwhile, in Virginia and elsewhere in the South, gaps between black and white teacher pay were steadily eroding, thanks to *Alston*.[31] A deep chasm still separated black and white children when it came to school facilities, courses, and transportation, however.

Thurgood Marshall was anxious to probe those gaps. Prone to worry, he also foresaw a major hurdle. "We have the lawyers ready, but we do not have the cases," Marshall fretted to Walter White in October.[32] The Virginia State Conference of Branches saw the matter differently. Reinforced by Hill's return, the legal committee was eager to accelerate its school-parity efforts. After a meeting with Hill, Robinson, Victor J. Ashe of Norfolk, Wendell Walker of Newport News, and Robert Cooley of Petersburg, Robert Carter informed his boss that lack of plaintiffs was not an issue in Virginia. "That phase will undoubtedly be adequately worked out by Spottswood and Hill," he wrote.[33] Eager to sculpt a united front, Marshall convened a summit of southern lawyers working on education cases in Atlanta on April 27 and 28, 1946. He squeezed the event into the weeks between the Supreme Court arguments in *Morgan* and its anticipated early-June decision. Andy Ransom made arrangements for himself and the two Richmond attorneys to fly to Georgia from Washington. "Hill and Robinson assure me that they can not obtain their advances from the Virginia State Conference for their expenses until some later date," he wrote, requesting $180 for plane and taxi fares for the trio. Marshall had specifically warned attendees against expecting help with expenses, but he approved Ransom's request. The gesture underscored the critical role Marshall expected the Virginians to play in the summit. After all, no other local attorneys had spent more time planning and executing school-equalization lawsuits. The special counsel wanted them present.[34] More than a dozen lawyers from eight states and the District of Columbia gathered at the Butler Street YMCA, a stately Georgian Revival building later dubbed the "black city hall of Atlanta." Inspired by the pulsating rhythms of the Sweet Auburn neighborhood, the storied heart of black cultural and economic life in the South, the men took up the appalling lack of education for many black youth. They swapped stories of states that shut down black schools during harvest time and large districts that failed to operate any accredited schools for black youth.[35]

The questions tackled in Atlanta struck at the heart of the movement. Were the masses ready to push for true integration? How could the lawyers reconcile the NAACP's stated policy against segregation with its push to equalize black and white schools? Every time a black school improved, did the gain make it that much harder to insist, down the road, on abandoning a dual school system? The broader debates entwined with a targeted focus on strategic options. Was it better to pursue writs of mandamus (ordering a locality to provide equal facilities, for instance) or injunctions (ordering a locality to cease discriminating)? Were state or federal courts more welcoming? Should the lawyers try to encourage blacks to apply to white high schools? Would consolidated black schools become "monuments to segregation"? Hill waded confidently into the robust debate. His work in Virginia had led him to prefer seeking injunctive relief when educational opportunities were denied blacks, but he also thought that each case had to be weighed separately. He favored first petitioning white principals and school boards, or both, for admission of black students to white schools and then, when that inevitably failed, going to court to seek an injunction against discrimination. Dubbing the combination the "Hill plan," the group debated its merits.[36] Hill's preference for injunctions held a philosophical advantage that would become more apparent with time. Asking courts to correct the imbalance between black and white schools through a writ of mandamus demanding improvement in black schools implied an acceptance of segregated classrooms. But with an injunction the NAACP was not prescribing a fix; it was simply asking the court to halt the discrimination. Then, at least theoretically, all options, including integration, were on the table. That tactic was more consistent with the organization's commitment to end segregation.

Leaving Atlanta, the group broadly agreed to travel two tracks. At the graduate- and professional-school levels, where gains were less likely to fuel furor, the goal was integration—now. At the elementary- and high-school levels, where passions would be intense, the only viable short-term option in most communities would be protesting discrimination and pushing for parity. The lawyers took comfort in the belief that over the long term states would not be able to afford two completely equal systems. Ultimately, a push for equalization would spell the death of segregated schools. The group emerged with a broad outline of state-by-state strategy. At the university level, challenges involving law schools in Texas and Oklahoma would lead the way. At the elementary- and secondary-school level, several states, foremost Virginia and Louisiana, were poised to file court cases within three months or sooner, Marshall believed. An NAACP press release promised "a maximum number of cases at the same time in order to convince school authorities throughout the South that Negroes are determined to enforce the Fourteenth Amendment to the letter."[37] That assessment proved overly optimistic. At summer's end, no equalization cases had yet been filed in the lead state, Virginia. Pressure for action was fermenting, not only on high but at the grass roots. Hill, Martin & Robinson might be shouldering important strategic responsibilities for the national and state NAACP, but some local Virginia educators had run out of patience. They wanted attention—yesterday.

In Chesterfield County, a fast-growing suburb of Richmond, the local black teachers' association had been trying to eliminate salary inequality almost since the *Alston* ruling. The school board had adopted a single salary scale early in the decade, allegedly ending discrimination. However, the new system gave administrators great leeway to rate performance. In the 1945–46 school year, the county's highest-paid black elementary teachers still received no more pay than the lowest-paid whites. By September, when the Hill firm still had not filed a lawsuit, the local black teachers' group fired off a complaint to Rupert Picott, who had rebounded from his dismissal in Newport News by landing the head staff job at the Virginia Teachers Association. Detailing years of delays, including waiting for Hill to return from the army, the teacher representative Arthur M. Freeman concluded, "We feel that we have no other recourse than to ask you [for] a change of legal staff."[38] Forwarding Freeman's complaint to Hill, Martin & Robinson and others, Picott echoed the frustration. A local school superintendent had recently asked him if the teachers' association had any legal challenges pending. "It was with no little embarrassment that I had to frankly inform him that so far as I know no court action in these matters is actually pending," he wrote.[39]

Hill and Robinson assigned Martin the task of crafting a reply. He began diplomatically, agreeing that the Chesterfield group had "just cause for complaint." Then his tone toughened. "While we have been delinquent, we have not been derelict in these cases," he insisted. The law firm had to be "extremely careful in preparing and filing" lawsuits. Much depended on getting the facts and arguments right. "We must realize that the cases must necessarily be filed and tried in Virginia, a southern state, and that merely because a man is appointed or elected a Judge, he does not necessarily lose all of his natural or unnatural prejudices."[40] Too much was at stake, in other words, to risk a hasty or incomplete filing. All summer the lawyers had been traveling the state, interviewing potential plaintiffs and registering complaints with school boards about unequal conditions. Now the end was in sight. "We intend to file at least four or five suits in Court within the next six weeks," Martin promised. Finally, in mid-October the law firm was ready. The long-awaited opening salvo targeted King George County, a sparsely populated rural sanctuary nestled between the Potomac and Rappahannock Rivers east of Fredericksburg. The jut of land had garnered fame as the birthplace of James Madison, the nation's fourth president, and as part of the escape route for John Wilkes Booth as he fled the nation's capital after the assassination of Abraham Lincoln. While education for blacks had advanced mightily since those days, the county's black and white children still attended distinctly imbalanced public schools.[41] Nine black parents and nine black community leaders had signed on to a court case. By standing united, the elders hoped to lessen any retaliatory blows.[42]

Finally in motion, the Hill-Martin-Robinson express sped forward. On November 29 the law firm filed suit in federal district court against Chesterfield County, protesting blatant discrimination in the awarding of salaries. Three months later, the lawyers initiated action against educational disparities in the Tidewater's Gloucester County. The firm turned next to Pulaski County, in the mountainous terrain southwest of Roanoke. A May 15 filing in the federal district court for western Virginia protested that county's failure to maintain a public high school rather than bus students to an inferior regional academy in a neighboring county. Two months after that, Martin joined with the Hampton lawyers A. W. E. Bassette Jr. and W. Hale Thompson to file an equalization lawsuit against school officials in tiny Surry County, a ferry ride from Williamsburg. And on September 4, 1947, Hill, Martin & Robinson tackled its most populous and prosperous opponent yet, Arlington County, in the shadow of Washington. The die had been cast, and there would be no turning back. A full-fledged push for school equality had begun.

Nationally, as the postwar period progressed, ongoing injustice fueled anger among black citizens. The vicious beating of the veteran Isaac Woodard in South Carolina had not been the only act of violence shocking national sensibilities in 1946. Alarm at the shooting death of the newly discharged war veteran Maceo Snipes by a group of white men a day after he voted in Georgia's Democratic primary was quickly dwarfed by repulsion over the so-called Georgia massacre. The execution-style slayings of two young black couples accosted by a gang of whites near the Apalachee River occurred after one of the black males was released on bond in the alleged stabbing of a white man.[43] Late that fall, Marshall himself barely skirted harm outside Columbia, Tennessee, as he and three colleagues headed toward Nashville one night at the end of a trial. A group of white men that included a deputy sheriff and two highway patrolmen intercepted Marshall's car, accused him of driving drunk, whisked him into the backseat of their car, and ordered his associates to continue on toward Nashville. Ignoring that order, the Nashville lawyer Alexander Looby and the others trailed the three-car caravan of whites as it headed down a secluded dirt road toward the Duck River. Perhaps because of the unwanted audience, the whites turned abruptly and headed back into town, where they took the shaken Marshall before a local magistrate. The official promptly dismissed the charges after smelling Marshall's untarnished breath.[44]

Such outrages did not go unremarked in Harry Truman's White House. Nor did President Truman ignore the results in the 1946 midterm election, in which blacks, voting in greater than usual numbers, deserted the Democratic Party in some northern races and helped nudge results in a more progressive direction in a handful of southern contests. With the Cold War and anti-Communist sentiment intensifying, the president worried that ugly racial episodes were tarring America's image abroad. The combination of personal enlightenment and political calculation led him in December 1946 to appoint a fifteen-member Commission on Civil Rights, charged with developing a strategy to protect the rights of black Americans. No twentieth-century president—perhaps none ever—had shown such concern. Four months later, in yet another sign of changing times, Jackie Robinson jogged onto Ebbets Field for the Brooklyn Dodgers, becoming the first black man in the modern era to play for a major-league baseball team. Many whites fumed, but something fundamental in the American psyche was in flux. Capturing that spirit, stretching beyond his somewhat racist Missouri roots, Truman soon afterward agreed to address the annual NAACP convention, the first president to do so. His speech from the steps of the Lincoln Memorial on June 29, 1947, proved a watershed moment. Speaking to a throng of ten thousand lining the reflecting pool, plus a national radio audience, Truman said the nation had reached a turning point in its long struggle to guarantee equality to all citizens. "Many of our people still suffer the indignity of insult, the harrowing fear of intimidation, and, I regret to say, the threat of physical injury and mob violence," he intoned. "We cannot wait another decade or another generation to remedy those evils. We must work, as never before, to cure them now. . . . The way ahead is not easy. We shall need all the wisdom, imagination, and courage we can muster. We must and shall guarantee the civil rights of all our citizens."[45] White and Marshall themselves could scarcely have penned a more sympathetic and eloquent challenge to the nation.

The October release of *To Secure These Rights,* the Truman civil rights commission's manifesto for change, further eroded doubts about the president's commitment. The document riveted the nation, exposing inequities in almost every aspect of American life, from housing to health care, from education to voting. Truman lauded its blueprint for change as "an American charter of human freedom in our time." Three months later, in his 1948 State of the Union address, defying his party's southern wing, he proclaimed civil rights the most critical matter on his domestic agenda. An omnibus bill tackling lynching, discriminatory hiring practices, voting restrictions, and other barriers to full citizenship followed. Southern governors and lawmakers seethed. Even so, facing a withering 1948 reelection bid, Truman capped his efforts by signing two historic executive orders on July 26. One desegregated the armed forces; the other eliminated discrimination in the federal workforce. Truman might lose some southern whites as a result, but in a four-way race for president he already expected white defections to South Carolina Dixiecrat J. Strom Thurmond. The executive orders also might stem the loss of black voters to Thomas E. Dewey, the racially moderate Republican nominee, and liberal Henry A. Wallace's New Progressive Party.[46] For Robinson, Hill, and others who were making civil rights their life's work, the changes at the top echelons of government, in-cremental as they might be, seemed a godsend, affirming that their efforts were not in vain.

At the NAACP Legal Defense Fund headquarters in New York, legal challenges involving higher education and housing intensified in tandem with the altered political mood. On the heels of the 1946 Atlanta education conference, university desegregation cases had moved forward in Oklahoma and Texas. Ada Lois Sipuel, an honors graduate of Langston University in Langston, Oklahoma, had applied for admission to the University of Oklahoma Law School. Now she was challenging her rejection. After state courts dismissed her claim, Marshall turned to the Supreme Court. On January 12, 1948, four days after hearing the case—an unusually speedy turnaround—the court ruled unanimously that Oklahoma must provide Sipuel a legal education comparable to that offered students at the white law school. The ruling relied on the earlier *Gaines* decision. The court did not say that the plaintiff had to be admitted to the white school, however. Oklahomans quickly set about creating a three-room law school for blacks at the state capitol, staffed by three white attorneys. Citing the inherent inequality in that arrangement, Marshall petitioned the court for an order admitting Sipuel to the white law school. That was a step further than the justices were prepared to go. The court rejected the plea, telling Marshall to first air his complaint in state courts.[47]

As Sipuel was planning her next step, George W. McLaurin, a sixty-year-old black teacher, applied to pursue a doctorate in school administration at the University of Oklahoma. Meanwhile, a case that would join with McLaurin's to create a seminal moment in the push for integrated education was under way in Texas. The Texas applicant, a letter carrier named Heman Sweatt, a graduate of Wiley College, sued Texas officials shortly after the Atlanta education conference attended by Robinson and Hill. Earlier in 1946, he had been denied entrance to the University of Texas Law School. When the trial court ruled that the state must provide a law-school education for blacks substantially equal to that for whites, the legislature had set about creating the Texas State University for Ne-groes (now Texas Southern University) in Houston, which included a law school. In the meantime, Sweatt was to attend a three-room, makeshift law school in the basement of a state office building across from the capitol in Austin. He refused, and his historic legal challenge protesting the inequity of a substandard law school for blacks moved forward.[48]

Concurrent with the higher-education cases, the Legal Defense Fund pressed its fight against segregated housing. Nationwide, the housing problem for blacks had become a crisis. Loren Miller, the NAACP's West Coast expert on restrictive covenants, described the situation. Contractual exclusion of minorities "has become a fashion, almost a passion," he said. Even well-to-do blacks struggled to find housing. Virtually every black neighborhood in any sizable city in America was overcrowded. In Chicago's South Side there were seventy-five thousand persons to the square mile, seven times the density in the city as a whole. In Baltimore, blacks, who made up 20 percent of the total population, crowded into 5 percent of the residential area. Sociologists preached a uniform conclusion: such density bred juvenile delinquency, crime, disease, and family disintegration.[49] In January 1947 Marshall summoned his experts, including Spot Robinson, to Howard for another conclave on housing discrimination. Once again, the attorneys disbanded without reaching a firm conclusion about the best cases to take to the Supreme Court. A Michigan case, *Sipes v. McGhee*, held promise. State courts there had ruled that because of a restrictive covenant signed ten years earlier, Orsel and Minnie McGhee had no right to occupy their recently purchased Detroit home. But some lawyers questioned whether the particulars of the court record were ideal for raising important arguments.[50]

Within months, the idea of waiting for the perfect case became moot. George L. Vaughn, a veteran Missouri lawyer and political activist, the son of former slaves, let it be known that he intended to seek a writ of certiorari from the high court in a Saint Louis case, *Shelley v. Kraemer*. Ethel Lee and J. D. Shelley, who were black, had bought a two-apartment house for themselves and their six children. The seller was a white straw purchaser, who had held the property briefly in an obvious attempt to circumvent the previous owner's agreement to sell only to Caucasians. Within hours of the Shelleys' occupying their new home, a group of white neighbors had sued to enforce the covenant. A lower-court judge had rejected their bid, on the grounds that several blacks already owned property on the block, but the Missouri Supreme Court had reversed the decision. Now the Shelleys were in danger of losing their home.[51] Once Vaughn's intentions became clear, the NAACP lawyers could wait no longer. Vaughn was a competent attorney, but he had very little appellate experience. Nor was he grounded in the crucial body of new work linking restrictive covenants to grave sociological ills. Vaughn's interest in challenging covenants based on the Thirteenth Amendment, which eliminated slavery, struck the Legal Defense Fund crowd as risky. They could not afford to have the Supreme Court bestow its long-awaited consideration on an inferior or uncertain argument. Within days, the Legal Defense Fund petitioned the court to take up an appeal of Detroit's *Sipes v. McGhee,* now renamed *McGhee v. Sipes.* The court responded affirmatively, granting certiorari in both cases and setting up the high-profile showdown.[52]

That fall, the justices accepted two more cases combined as *Hurd v. Hodge,* both out of Charles Houston's Washington portfolio. Importantly, the lower-court records in those cases included extensive testimony about the dangers inherent in crowding minorities into racial ghettos. Throughout the fall of 1947, Spot Robinson involved himself deeply in the preparation of briefs in both *Sipes* and *Hurd.* As a property-law expert, he already had worked on both cases in earlier pleadings. In preparing for *Hurd,* Houston and Robinson focused on economic and sociological data. "More than 150 articles, reports, and books were cited, and charts and maps were interlaced in the brief that Houston carefully stitched together with help from the brainiest and most painstaking of the younger Howard law graduates, Spottswood Robinson," wrote Richard Kluger. Robinson's methodical imprint was apparent in the exhaustive product.[53] The Virginian also was among a half dozen or so attorneys intricately involved in preparation of the brief for *Sipes,* the only one of the three cases directly under control of the Legal Defense Fund. On September 11, Robinson submitted a bill for $33.37 for related travel. And in early October, Marian Wynn Perry, an assistant special counsel at the Legal Defense Fund, wrote that she and Robinson had carved out three days to work on the brief at the Howard Library. "If you can work with us then, that will be swell," she urged Houston.[54]

Robinson did not address the justices when the court took up the far-reaching cases in mid-January 1948. That task fell to others. But his conscientious contributions were long remembered. At a portrait presentation ceremony at the Washington federal appeals court four decades later, Judge Constance Baker Motley recalled her first encounters with Robinson. They had met in the days leading up to the Supreme Court hearing on restrictive covenants. "It was the time that I remember learning how Spot Robinson worked," said Motley, then a young LDF staff member. "When the rest of us would go out to lunch, Spot Robinson was back there working. When we went out to dinner, he wasn't hungry then either. He worked all the time. . . . If it had not been for the dedication of Spot Robinson and a few other lawyers that Thurgood had come to rely on, I don't think that we could have claimed victory in those cases."[55] Had Robinson not made a major personal decision, such involvement might have been impossible. Much as he loved the order and intellectual inquiry of the classroom, Robinson had decided that he could do the most good in the nitty-gritty world of real-life experience. At a June 9, 1947, meeting of the executive committee of the Legal Defense Fund board of directors, Marshall announced the shift resulting from Robinson's decision. Robinson had taken leave from the Howard cloisters to focus on the practice of law and the annihilation of Jim Crow. He planned not only to continue his affiliation with the LDF but to enhance it. "He still wants to remain with us," Marshall reported. The group approved.[56]

Already, Marshall was hatching an agenda for Robinson. In October, just as the Truman administration was releasing *To Secure These Rights*, the director-counsel unveiled a bold new education initiative. The program would begin with a "full-scale legal attack on the inequalities in education in the State of Virginia." Attorney Robinson would direct the project, with full cooperation of the Virginia State Conference of Branches and the national office of the Legal Defense Fund. In a series of letters in the fall of 1947, the two attorneys worked out details. Robinson would be paid forty-six hundred dollars for a one-year trial period in which he would devote "practically full time" to the cause. Disparity of any sort anywhere in the state was to be exposed and challenged. Virginia would create the model for similar efforts in Georgia, Alabama, Mississippi, and other southern states.[57] Braced by the goodwill of a sitting president and the swelling resolve of the masses, the drive to squelch separate but equal education had entered an end stage. In pushing for educational equality for black and white children, Robinson and others intended to prove that it could not happen within segregated schools.

NINE

"A Man among Men"

Six blocks and a cultural chasm separated the posh Hotel John Marshall from Jackson Ward's Second Street, the thriving nucleus of postwar black Richmond. When Thurgood Marshall or Andy Ransom passed through town for a federal-court appearance or an NAACP speech, reserving a room at the John Marshall, with its promise of "sun-filled" guest rooms and a well-heeled clientele, was out of the question. They bunked with friends or bedded at the modest Eggleston or Slaughter's hotels. There, Marshall and other out-of-towners might find themselves in lively, even famous company. Over the years, Count Basie, Louis Armstrong, Joe Louis, Jackie Robinson, and other elite black performers and athletes numbered among the guests. Such luminaries often drew white audiences when they performed in the capital, but when the lights dimmed, they were no better off than any other black citizen.[1] If they needed to eat or sleep, they headed toward Jackson Ward. So complete was the divide that merely walking through the front doors of the elegant, sixteen-story John Marshall carried the risk of humiliation for nonwhites. In a setting that catered to governors, senators, and even presidents, blacks might be directed to a side door or discreetly turned away from the front desk or the brightly lit coffee shop.

Threat of rebuff shadowed Oliver Hill and Marvin Caplan as they entered the hotel lobby by the front entrance on November 27, 1946. With Thanksgiving a day away, a festive holiday stir filled the air. Even so, "we steeled ourselves for trouble," Caplan recalled. The friends planned to meet Charles G. Bolte, the celebrated twenty-six-year-old chairman of the American Veterans Committee, who had arrived in Richmond earlier in the day. A war amputee and a future vice-president of the Carnegie Endowment for International Peace, Bolte was on a recruitment tour of the South, lining up members for the progressive, interracial veterans' movement that already had enlisted Caplan and Hill.[2] Striding across the John Marshall lobby, the pair assumed an authoritative air. Both stood taller than six feet, and their poise silenced any surprised desk clerks or skeptical elevator operators. An elderly black attendant allowed them inside the elevator and, without incident, took them to Bolte's floor. Hill had first tested the John Marshall's racial policy five years earlier. Then, he had scheduled a meeting in the hotel room of a visiting Washington lawyer. As Hill had approached the elevator, its operator had redirected him to the freight elevator, further back in the hotel, then hurriedly closed the elevator door. Nonplussed, Hill had stubbornly planted his finger on the button and held it there until the elevator returned. As soon as the doors opened, he had stepped inside. The operator could either create a scene or take Hill to the desired floor. "The operator hesitated but took me to the sixth floor," Hill recalled.[3]

Such boldness characterized Hill's interaction with whites. Genial, not intimidated by rules he regarded as senseless, Hill determined early on that he would behave in ways consistent with how he felt he ought to be treated. He also would recognize and, when possible, reward those whites who went out of their way to treat him and other black citizens with dignity. As he had told Mrs. Pentecost a few years earlier, some whites might be contemptible, but he was able to look at people as individuals. Over the years, that capacity would put him at odds with more radical blacks more than once. An early instance came in 1948, when many Virginia progressives, black and white, were lining up behind Henry Wallace's presidential campaign. Hill angered some of them by siding with Truman. While he thought Wallace would make a "wonderful president," Hill said, Truman's civil rights advocacy had earned Hill's loyalty. Truman had jeopardized his reelection chances by aggressively affirming the rights of blacks. "I was voting for Truman come hell or high water," he later wrote.[4] The attention to political quid pro quos fit with Hill's ambitions. If blacks ever expected to assume their rightful place in American society, they could not endlessly rely on the courts alone. They also needed to infiltrate the political arena. And who better in Richmond to challenge political blockades than a smart, attractive, dynamic personality such as Hill?

A youthful Oliver Hill with his mother, Olivia, and an unidentified child. (Oliver Hill Collection, Special Collections and University Archives, Johnston Memorial Library, Virginia State University)

Spot Robinson in tennis whites during his Virginia Union days. (Courtesy of Oswald and Nina Robinson Govan)

Oliver and Bernie Hill early in their marriage. (Oliver Hill Collection, Special Collections and University Archives, Johnston Memorial Library, Virginia State University)

Spot and Marian Robinson *(left)*, along with Robinson's parents, at a wedding celebration for the young couple. (Courtesy of Oswald and Nina Robinson Govan)

Hill's swearing-in as a new member of the Richmond City Council in 1948. (Oliver Hill Collection, Special Collections and University Archives, Johnston Memorial Library, Virginia State University)

Robinson as a member of the Howard University School of Law faculty. (Scurlock Studio Records, Archives Center, National Museum of American History, Smithsonian Institution)

Early gathering of the Old Dominion Bar Association, including Hill, *seated second row, fourth from right;* Robinson, *seated far left in same row;* and Sam Tucker, *standing behind Robinson.* (Oliver Hill Collection, Special Collections and University Archives, Johnston Memorial Library, Virginia State University)

Martin A. Martin, accomplished trial attorney and Robinson and Hill's law partner during the desegregation era. (Oliver Hill Collection, Special Collections and University Archives, Johnston Memorial Library, Virginia State University)

Granite Elementary School, Pulaski County, Virginia, about 1948. (From case files of *Corbin v. County School Board of Pulaski County*, National Archives at Philadelphia)

Tin can and other unsanitary drinking cups used by pupils of Bethel School, Gloucester County, Virginia, about 1946–47. (From case files of *Ashley v. School Board of Gloucester County*, National Archives at Philadelphia)

Brown v. Board of Education plaintiff attorneys with Oliver Hill and Spottswood Robinson flanking Thurgood Marshall *(fourth from left)*. (Courtesy of the NAACP Legal Defense and Educational Fund, Inc.)

Attorneys representing Prince Edward County and the state of Virginia in *Brown v. Board of Education* and its aftermath. *From left,* John W. Riely, Attorney General J. Lindsay Almond Jr., T. Justin Moore, Henry T. Wickham, and T. Justin Moore Jr. (Photo archives, *Richmond Times-Dispatch*)

Law Offices
Hill, Martin & Olphin
118 East Leigh Street
Richmond 19, Virginia

Oliver W Hill
Martin A. Martin
James R. Olphin

September Seventeenth
1 9 5 7

Telephone 2-8033
7-6441

MEMORANDUM

RE: Davis vs. School Board of Prince Edward County

SUBJECT: Financial statement of receipts, disbursements and
attorneys' fees collected and disbursed by Hill,
Martin & Robinson and/or Oliver W. Hill from 1951
to date.

RECEIPTS:

Virginia State Conference -------------------------------	$ 4,908.45
NAACP Legal Defense and Educational Fund ------------------	2,500.00
Walkley E. Johnson, Clerk, refund costs in Supreme Court -	2,975.19
Total Receipts -------------------------------	$ 10,383.64

DISBURSEMENTS:

Court costs, service fees, etc. -------------------------	$ 3,013.19
Reporting services, additional stenographic help, research, etc. -------------------------------	1,873.50
Travelling expenses of attorneys and witnesses, attendance fees, etc. -------------------------	1,137.06
Printing and photostating -------------------------	302.51
Telephone, rental of machines, and miscellaneous expenses	297.38
Total Expenses -------------------------------	$ 6,623.64
ATTORNEYS' FEES -------------------------------	3,760.00
Total Expenses and Attorneys' fees ------------------	$ 10,383.64

N.B. Under the partnership agreement of Hill, Martin & Robinson,
Oliver W. Hill received 1/3 of the total attorneys' fees, amounting
to $1,253.34, paid as follows: 1954 - $326.72; 1955 - $207.26;
1956 - $500.00; 1957 - $219.36.

Financial accounting (1957) in *Davis v. County School Board of Prince Edward County*. (Oliver Hill Collection, Special Collections and University Archives, Johnston Memorial Library, Virginia State University)

Cross burned on the lawn of Oliver and Bernie Hill in August 1955. (Oliver Hill Collection, Special Collections and University Archives, Johnston Memorial Library, Virginia State University)

Students George Leakes and Elaine Bowen with attorneys Robinson and Hill in West Point, Virginia, school-desegregation case, mid-1950s. (Photo archives, *Richmond Times-Dispatch*)

NAACP attorneys and representatives gather at the Virginia state capitol for February 1957 hearing before legislative investigators. *From left,* W. Lester Banks, Hill, unidentified man, Robinson, and Marshall. (Photo archives, *Richmond Times-Dispatch*)

Hill and Robinson entering the Alexandria, Virginia, courthouse in the Arlington school-desegregation case, 1958. (Reprinted with permission of the DC Public Library, Star Collection, © *Washington Post*)

Hill receiving Presidential Medal of Freedom from President Bill Clinton in August 1999. (Photo archives, *Richmond Times-Dispatch*)

Robinson sits, as chief judge, with the US Court of Appeals for the DC Circuit, 1982–83 term. The future Supreme Court associate justices Ruth Bader Ginsburg and Antonin Scalia are in the second row, far right. Robert H. Bork, nominated to the high court but not confirmed. is in the second row, far left. (Courtesy of the US Court of Appeals, DC Circuit)

Elaine Jones, former director-counsel of the NAACP Legal Defense and Educational Fund, Inc., greets Oliver Hill at the celebration of his 100th birthday in May 2007. (Photo by Jerome Reid/*Richmond Free Press*)

In postwar Virginia, the yoke of the Byrd oligarchy still constrained black voters. The organization's aim of tight control by an elite few had curtailed voter participation by everyone, black or white. Still, the overt racism behind the 1902 constitution, coupled with decades of ingrained powerlessness exacerbated by the poll tax and other restrictive tactics, had created a particularly acute black languor at election time.[5] By the mid-1940s, institutional barriers to black voting had eroded somewhat. James West's victory in *Bliley v. West* had opened primary voting to blacks within the state. In 1931 W. E. Davis, a southeastern Virginian, had defused mischief further when he successfully challenged his disqualification by an election judge. The Virginia Supreme Court ruled that two questions asked by the judge—when is poll-tax payment not required? and what are the requirements to register in Virginia?—served no legitimate purpose under the law. The decision put a chill on renegade registrars. Meanwhile, registrars in more urban settings were gradually switching from a blank to a printed registration form, although efforts to reinstate the blank sheet would surface in the late 1950s.[6]

In April 1944, when the Supreme Court weighed in with the landmark *Smith v. Allwright* decision, declaring the Texas Democratic primary to be "an integral feature" of the state's election machinery and therefore open to blacks, some Virginia elites responded smugly. "It's a little difficult to understand the tremendous amount of indignation and heat generated in the Deep South" since black Virginians had voted in Democratic primaries since the 1930s, chided a *Times-Dispatch* editorial. "The skies haven't fallen."[7] If they had not, that was likely because black voting posed no threat to white supremacy. Throughout the early 1940s, fewer than 10 percent of eligible Virginia blacks were registered to vote. Actual voting participation was even lower. By 1946, following a registration push, the number of black citizens who had paid the poll tax jumped to about 124,000, but fewer than 50,000 of those had paid for three years running. In a tough but telling assessment, the historian Luther Jackson, of the Virginia Voters League concluded that much of the remaining disenfranchisement of black Virginians by the mid-1940s was self-imposed, through either apathy or nonpayment of the detested poll tax.[8] A history of subjugation fostered and abetted the indifference. Still, increasingly it was within the power of black citizens to change course if they chose.

Hill and a number of returning black servicemen shared that view. If black voter registration and turnout could be maximized, and if black candidates could earn a modest level of white support, then they could be elected to political office, especially in major cities. Clearly, that would take work. The handful of black candidates for local Virginia offices in recent years had been soundly rebuffed. Dr. Harry Penn, a prominent Roanoke dentist and fraternity brother of Hill's, had garnered only 424 votes when he ran for the city council there in 1942. Two years later he had upped his total to just 537. In 1944, the attorney Wendell Walker had run for the city council in Newport News to protest the firings of the six black educators, placing sixth in a field of nine. And black candidates for the House of Delegates from Chesterfield County and Portsmouth had done poorly in 1945.[9] Aggressive young black leaders returning from the war were undeterred. Black city-council candidates in Norfolk, Charlottesville, Danville, and Lynchburg suffered defeat in 1946, but the total black vote increased noticeably as a result of increased registration. In the best showing, the Norfolk lawyer Victor Ashe polled more than 3,100 votes, equivalent to a respectable two-thirds of blacks registered in the city, though still far behind the winners.[10]

As 1947 began, two developments outside Hill's legal practice commanded his attention. First, almost eight years after his arrival in Richmond, he and Bernie ended their long-distance marriage. She moved south. Their first-floor apartment at 512 East Leigh Street in Jackson Ward came with a one-year lease, effective February 1, and an annual rent of $540. Second, he announced his candidacy in the August Democratic primary for one of seven seats in a Richmond-area district in the Virginia House of Delegates. In a heavily Democratic region, nomination in the primary typically proved tantamount to election.[11]

In Richmond, Bernie immersed herself in the role for which she had longed, that of the loyal, loving partner of one of the community's most accomplished and constructive black citizens. She secured a job as an elementary-school teacher, commuted by train to Howard while completing a master's degree, launched her own social and community commitments, and turned attention to her lifetime dream of becoming a mother. Plagued by miscarriages, including two in the years immediately after the war, she and Oliver contemplated adoption. She also learned firsthand the negative consequences of her husband's growing prominence.[12] One night during the 1947 campaign when Oliver was out of town, Bernie endured a series of events that clearly, in retrospect, were designed to unnerve her. First, the police knocked on her door with the alarming news that her husband had been reported killed. Moments later, the fire department arrived, responding to the erroneous report of a fire at the Hills' apartment building. And not long after that a mortician showed up, answering a request to pick up a body at the site. "This was purely part of a plan of racial harassment," wrote Oliver. It also was an early episode in a pattern of anonymous threats that would plague and annoy the couple for years to come.[13]

Bernie's emotionalism and Oliver's more aloof, analytical mind sometimes put them at odds, but overall theirs was a united partnership. "Although in some respects my wife and I were partially opposites and partially compatible, as far as my civil rights and political activities were concerned, she was totally devoted," Oliver observed late in life. Commuting to Washington each Monday morning for a period in the late 1940s in order to confer with her Howard adviser, Bernie acquiesced to her husband's request that she sit in a coach car designated for whites. "I would take her down to the station, carry her bag into the white coach, and she'd sit in it. She didn't want to do it, but she did," he recalled. No one ever challenged the classy, well-dressed, and well-behaved matron.[14]

In Hill's election playbook, the same coolness that allowed him to expect service at the Hotel John Marshall also steeled him for running a biracial campaign in a segregated city. He would stress a progressive agenda that went well beyond matters of race, and he would campaign citywide, showing up at every forum and candidates' night that he could identify, invitation or no. Attired in well-pressed suits and boldly patterned ties, frequently sporting a pipe or cigar, Hill moved easily in mixed circles. He already knew the legal community, and white attorneys could serve as a bridge to the rest of an audience. Appearing unexpectedly at the all-white West End Democratic Club one night, Hill encountered a typical scenario. Asked about his purpose, he explained that he hoped to solicit the group's support as a candidate for the state legislature. In speaking, he stressed his platform: hour and wage legislation, a minimum salary of twenty-four hundred dollars for teachers, increased funding for hospitals and public health, revision of the child labor act, creation of a state department for race relations, and abolition of the poll tax. After the speeches, Hill hung around for the socializing. The audience included a couple of white lawyers whom he knew. At their invitation, he joined a group in the clubhouse's covered garden. Before the evening ended, "I sat there and drank beer with the other candidates and white voters," he said.[15] Hill's refusal to accept that he did not belong was perhaps even more groundbreaking than his candidacy.

In preparation for the 1947 elections, the Richmond Civic Council, a consortium of about one hundred black religious, civic, business, labor, and fraternal groups, joined the NAACP and the Virginia Voters League in an intensive drive for poll-tax payment and voter registration. At its end, estimates of the number of black Richmonders eligible to vote ranged from five thousand to just over six thousand. Later, the *Richmond Afro-American* raised its estimate to eight thousand, including veterans and others exempt from the poll tax.[16] As the August 5 primary approached, political observers weighed in on whether black voters would cast a single-shot ballot for Hill rather than vote for a full seven-man slate. Five incumbents and thirteen newcomers, counting Hill, were vying for the seven legislative seats. "Much speculation is abroad regarding whether the unusually large number of Negro voters will 'solid shot' Oliver Hill,'" reported the *News Leader*.[17] What the newspaper did not report—or know—was that Hill and W. H. C. Murray, a typographer and president of the Central Trades and Labor Council, had formed a secret, eleventh-hour alliance. Each planned to urge his backers to support the other. Hill could not expect to win in a majority white city without a solid bloc of white support. In turn, Murray, as a white liberal, needed an extra source of backing in a voting pool dominated by conservatives.

Early election-day accounts suggested a strong turnout. One reporter speculated that the early swell "may be due to heavy voting among Negroes seeking to nominate Oliver Hill." By late afternoon it appeared that participation in black precincts had well surpassed that in recent elections. Whether it would be enough to nominate and later elect the first black member of the Virginia legislature since the 1880s remained to be seen. As the ballot counting and the evening wore on, fate took an unexpected turn. Six of the seven seats seemed certain to go to five incumbents and one newcomer, all white, but the seventh seat remained up for grabs. The tally had narrowed to a nip-and-tuck race between the two liberal allies, Murray and Hill.[18] Many Richmonders went to bed with the outcome unsettled. Not until Wednesday morning did they learn that the seventh seat had gone to Murray. In a photo finish Hill had been defeated by about

190 votes. In an election in which each voter had had the opportunity to support seven candidates, the results showed that many blacks had voted solely for Hill, while many others had honored the Hill-Murray pact, voting only for the two. For instance, at First Lee, a heavily black downtown precinct, Hill had received 691 votes; Murray, 401; and the next closest candidate, 143. Unofficial returns put Murray's vote total at 6,500 and Hill's at 6,310.[19]

Recriminations broke out immediately. The *Afro-American* reported "bitter denunciations" toward the Murray campaign from Hill's campaign manager, Washington W. Owens. He blamed Hill's defeat on an alleged double cross by the out-of-towner Henry Lee Moon. A journalist and activist who would go on to a long career with the NAACP, Moon had represented the political action committee of the CIO in forging an alliance with the Richmond Civic Council to back Murray and Hill. The CIO had failed to deliver on its promise to swing white votes to Hill, Owens alleged. Moon denied the charge, expressing "deep regrets" at the outcome.[20] The episode offered a defining moment for Hill. He could join his manager in excoriating the Murray camp or he could side with Dr. Tinsley in arguing that blacks themselves needed to do more. "We must face squarely the fact that although we are now certain of progress, we just haven't succeeded yet in stimulating and registering enough voters to give us a clean cut majority," Tinsley said.[21] Hill elected to echo Tinsley. While it was impossible to say definitively how many of his votes had come from white unionists, Hill accepted that the number was substantial. As he would do many times in future years, he treated Murray with the deference he would have expected had the situation been reversed. As the November general election approached, he urged solid black backing for Murray. The only hope for black political advancement in the near future was to develop "a strong liberal element within the Democratic Party," Hill said. That meant cooperating with like-minded whites while "seeing to it that far more of our own people become voters."[22]

Whatever else he had accomplished, Hill had attracted a citywide audience. His intelligence and his cooperative spirit had cast him in a positive light. His name was now a household word in white circles as well as black. Virginius Dabney widened the mantle of respectability by calling the defeated candidate "qualified by character and training" for public office. In an editorial, he shushed angst over the near election of a black man to the

Assembly, while unintentionally revealing the limits of white elites in tolerating black advances. Citing the election results, Dabney predicted that the days of lily-white representation in the General Assembly were numbered. "The prospect of a Negro sitting in the General Assembly as a spokesman for his people does not carry with it implications of racial intermarriage or of undue racial intermingling," he counseled. "It is certain that the vast majority of lawmakers will always be white, so it is difficult to see why the coming of a Negro or two among them should cause anything remotely resembling consternation."[23] Election of a black candidate or two was acceptable, in other words, since there was not the slightest possibility that the social or political order would be upended. Even such a lukewarm endorsement tagged Dabney as more progressive than many of his peers.

When the 1948 Virginia General Assembly convened the following winter, the champion of progressive goals would be none other than W. H. C. Murray. Hill's graciousness in defeat had proved justified. The thirty-seven-year-old printer introduced five bills aimed at eliminating Jim Crow in transportation, movie theaters, and restaurants. The unconventional action made him a pariah within his own union, which dropped him from its delegation to the Central Labor Council. Undeterred, Murray lined up speakers for a public hearing before the House Courts of Justice Committee. Addressing an overflow crowd, he urged: "If we are to make of democracy the real and meaningful ideology that is to challenge the 'isms' of the world, we will have to begin here at home."[24] The *Afro-American* hardly could contain its glee at the reception. "Not One Person Protests Bills" read a headline in its next edition. If the black newspaper editors thought politeness translated into receptivity, however, they were sadly naive about Virginia protocols. Events would soon bear out a harsher reality.[25]

After the outpouring of support for Murray's bills, the committee scheduled a second hearing for February 26. Again the crowd overflowed a small committee room and poured into the hallway. This time, Hill joined a dozen or so speakers favoring the bills. But the real news of the day—an address to the General Assembly by Governor Tuck regarding the Truman civil rights agenda—diverted attention from the antisegregation bills and revealed the true feelings in Virginia's seat of power toward racially discriminatory practices. A crowd feverish with anticipation flooded the House chamber and gallery for the speech. Tuck orated for seventeen minutes against federal encroachment on states' rights. He proposed amending ballots in the fall presidential election to include slates of electors identified only by party. No candidates' names would appear. Under the scheme, state party officials could instruct electors to withhold their vote from the national party nominee if they chose. If enough southern states followed suit, the dissidents might even throw the election outcome into the House of Representatives.[26]

In Washington, Senator Byrd promptly read his ally's speech into the Senate record. He endorsed Tuck's plan "without reservation" and urged southern governors to join the revolt. "Virginia again is a leader. I think other Southern states undoubtedly will follow," he said. Tuck and Byrd framed the strategy as a blow for states' rights. But at bottom, the high principle for which they fought was Virginia's right to oppose legislation curtailing lynching, poll taxes, and discriminatory hiring practices. Five days later, the House Courts of Justice Committee unceremoniously disposed of the five Murray bills. The lawmakers failed even to take a recorded vote. Shortly afterward, the full House made clear its colors. Members overwhelmingly approved a resolution urging that southern states "be permitted to improve the relations between the races in their own way." White legislators were not antiblack, the critics maintained. They merely detested Truman's intrusion into the southern way of life.[27]

The contours of the Virginia Way and its racial overtones received added definition a few weeks later in Richmond. The previous fall's election had been about more than legislative seats; it had included a referendum on a new charter for city government. The proposal would replace an unwieldy, thirty-two-person bicameral council, elected from four wards, with a nine-member unicameral body, elected citywide. A ceremonial mayor and a strong city manager would lead the city. And for the first time elections would be nonpartisan, ending the stranglehold of the Democratic primary.[28] Crafted by a commission led by the future Supreme Court associate justice Lewis F. Powell Jr., then a rising lawyer, the proposal had garnered support from a coalition that included the League of Women Voters, the Chamber of Commerce, labor unions, and various other civic entities. Its chief sponsor had been the city's foremost white political organization, the Richmond Citizens' Association. Hill, who had first met Powell during the campaign, had been an early supporter of the charter change. He had vocally encouraged black backing for the plan, which had passed by a margin of almost three to one.[29] The large margin of victory precluded any claim that blacks had determined the outcome. Still, precinct results confirmed strong black backing for the reforms. Hopes soared that the heavyweight Citizens' Association, in a spirit of cooperation and enlightenment, would include a black person on a slate of endorsed candidates for the nine new city-council seats. That was not to be.[30]

On March 25, a banner headline on the front page of the *Times-Dispatch* announced the slate approved by the executive board at a marathon session. Given the association's clout, the endorsees acquired instant frontrunner status in the upcoming election. The list included two lawyers, the president of a coal company, the general manager of a major clothier, the president of a department store, and several others. There were no Republicans, no women, and no blacks.[31] Republicans exploded in anger at their exclusion from the list. "The spirit, if not the letter, of the nonpartisan charter was broken," charged the state GOP leader. Speaking for the NAACP, Tinsley took a more diplomatic tone. "It just goes to show that the Negro has got to do his own job," Tinsley said. "If anything is to be accomplished, he cannot depend solely upon others."[32] Hill was ready to accept that challenge. Already, he had announced his candidacy for a council seat. He believed himself equal to the task. In his autobiography Hill recalled that black leaders had expected Booker T. Bradshaw, the well-known president of the Virginia Mutual Benefit Life Insurance Company, to be named to the slate. When he was not, Hill said, Tinsley and Bradshaw approached Hill about running. Although he preferred another bid for the legislature, he bowed to their request. That memory was either incorrect or incomplete. According to a newspaper account, Hill had announced his candidacy four days before the Citizens' Association decided its endorsements. Possibly, someone had warned Bradshaw, Tinsley, and Hill in advance of the probable outcome. Otherwise, Hill decided to run irrespective of the Citizens' Association endorsements.[33]

Once again, Hill campaigned throughout the city, addressing white audiences as well as black whenever possible. This time, however, he aggressively confronted the white establishment, arguing that wholesale adoption of the slate of the Richmond Citizens' Association would turn the city over to a group of powerbrokers. The failure to diversify its endorsements affirmed the insular nature of the group, he charged. Also, this time there would be no behind-closed-doors alliances with any of the twenty-eight other candidates. This time he intended to go it alone.[34] If Hill did not outright urge black supporters to vote only for him, many of his chief allies did. "We advised everyone, black and white, who wanted to see him elected, to 'single-shot': to vote for Oliver only, and not for any of the other candidates," Caplan wrote. The *Afro-American* came close to echoing that call in its endorsement editorial. Given the failure of the Richmond Citizens' Association to recognize the efforts of blacks in supporting the charter changes, "we take the liberty to urge our people to vote only for their known friends," the newspaper said. It tacitly acknowledged that black votes would not suffice for Hill's election; whites also must join the cause. "If there is any democracy and Christianity among white citizens here," that would occur, the editorial concluded.[35]

As the election approached, Hill and other candidates scheduled radio speeches and bought newspaper ad space to extend last-minute appeals. The Citizens' Association urged backing for its entire slate as a way to ensure success of the new governmental structure. Hill and other independents countered that concentrating control in the hands of few was a sure path to bossism. Taking his challenge to mainstream Richmond, Hill urged his victory in a quarter-page ad in the *Times-Dispatch* on the Sunday before the June 8 election. "Through the years Oliver W. Hill has demonstrated his willingness and capacity to serve all of the people," it read.[36] On Monday evening, with polling less than twelve hours away, Hill boldly reiterated his case over radio. He reasoned with WMBG listeners: "The presence of a Negro on the city council would be an affirmation, rather than a refutation of citywide voting." Blacks made up 30 percent of the city's population. "If you held thirty percent of the stock in a corporation, wouldn't you want a voice on its policy-making board?"[37]

As Election Day dawned, Hill's headquarters pulsated with activity. Student volunteers, Omega Psi Phi fraternity brothers, members of the Richmond Civic Council, and others fanned out across the city, ready to distribute leaflets and cart would-be voters to the polls. The Citizens' Association also was taking no chances, even lining up babysitters for young mothers who wanted to vote. Radio broadcasts detailed a carnival-like array of evening festivities, open to all, at the midtown city stadium. Sally Foster and the Westernaires, the Sabbath Glee Club, Miss Julia Mildred Harper's dancers, and the bands of two white high schools would entertain the crowd, interspersed with announcements of election results every fifteen minutes. Those wearing a gold feather as a sign of having voted would be eligible for prizes, including a three-day, all-expenses-paid trip to New York, a deep-freeze unit, and several electric irons.[38] As the sun set on what Dabney and others labeled one of the most important city elections of the century, most white candidates headed for the city stadium. Hill monitored results from his headquarters. Early returns reflected single-shot voting in mostly black precincts, giving Hill a startling and commanding lead. When news that Hill was running first in a twenty-nine-man field was announced at the stadium, cheers and whistles erupted from a section of the stands occupied exclusively by whites. A newspaper account suggested that the shouts reflected genuine delight, not boisterous behavior. Across town at Hill headquarters, the reaction was more guarded, at least among those in the know. Hill could not possibly maintain his huge early lead once white precincts weighed in. Soon enough, the erosion began. After the first twelve precincts had reported, Hill led the next highest candidate by almost three to one. At the quarter-way mark, Hill's margin over the second-place candidate had dwindled to a few hundred votes. Quickly, even that small lead evaporated. As results poured in from white enclaves, one candidate after another from the Citizens' Association slate overtook Hill.[39]

At 11:15 p.m., with only two precincts unreported, members of the Citizens' Association slate occupied the top eight slots. Hill was ninth, a mere 414 votes ahead of T. E. DuCuennois, a labor leader included on the Citizens' Association slate. Once again, the final spot on the winners list was coming down to a head-to-head contest between blacks and labor. And once again, white observers expected labor to squeak through because the larger of the two missing precincts, Westhampton Number 40, represented one of the city's most affluent white areas. "It looks like the entire slate has won," celebrated a Richmond Citizens' Association member over the radio.[40] But he spoke too soon. When returns from the two tardy precincts were reported, "the boys lost for a time their power of speech and didn't fully recover it before the election program went off the air," the *Richmond Afro-American* later gloated. Number 40 had given DuCuennois 474 votes and Hill, 388. A black man had fared better than seventeen white candidates in the overwhelmingly white precinct. Hill's citywide lead over DuCuennois had diminished slightly, but in effect one of the wealthiest, toniest corners of Richmond had fired Hill's final sprint to victory. By

263 votes, the forty-one-year-old had bested DuCuennois to become the first black elected to the city council since the 1890s and the second elected to public office anywhere in Virginia since the early twentieth century. Hill tallied 9,097 votes out of 28,143 ballots cast.[41]

Surrounded by exuberant well-wishers, sobered and elated by victory, Hill issued a message of racial inclusion. He expressed gratitude to Richmond's black citizens for "their faith in me as indicated by putting me forth as their representative" and proclaimed himself "fully cognizant of the fact that I have been elected by vote of the citizens of Richmond as a whole." His gratitude extended to "my friends of both races."[42] Telegrams flooded in from around the state and the nation. "Congratulations on your election will expect you to make history," rejoiced Robert Carter from NAACP headquarters in New York. "Heartiest congratulations from the office and our families," telegraphed Charles Houston's law firm. William B. Thalhimer Jr., scion of the prominent department-store family, sent "sincere congratulations, along with those of my father." The *New York Times* and the *New York Herald Tribune* notified readers of the historic event in the former Confederate capital. The National Broadcasting Corporation's "News of the World" radio report detailed the breakthrough.[43] A combination of blacks who voted only for Hill and middle- to upper-income whites who approved his cross-racial appeal had elected the new councilman. Ninety-year-old Edward R. Carter, stooped and bespectacled, the only living former black councilman, typified thousands of blacks in defiantly casting a single-shot vote for Hill. In a typical black precinct, Number 59, Hill received 700 votes out of 719 ballots cast. The closest white opponent in that precinct received only 38 votes. Meanwhile, estimates differed on how many whites had backed Hill, but the consensus was that they had numbered in the low thousands, not hundreds.[44]

The eye-catching victory elevated the Virginian into a new realm, setting him apart from even such illustrious lawyers as Marshall and Hastie. Now national politicians looking for access to black voters sought Hill's counsel. Congressman William L. Dawson of Chicago, who was spearheading Truman's appeal to blacks, urged Hill to travel to New York City to campaign for the Democratic ticket. He did. Boarding a flatbed truck, Hill and others traversed the city, pausing wherever a crowd assembled. Typically, Hill was introduced as a man who had proven that blacks could win anywhere, given the right combination of effort and talent. Later, the publicity division of the Democratic National Committee issued a statement in Hill's name urging support for Truman over Dewey: "No President in the history of our country—including the illustrious Franklin D. Roosevelt—has made the frontal attack on racial and religious discrimination as that made by Mr. Truman!"[45]

Color magazine, a national publication aimed at a black audience, featured Hill as the prototype of an emerging new southern black—"no longer handkerchief-headed or an educated Uncle Tom." The article described his enjoyment of radio dramas, his participation with Bernie in two book clubs (leaning toward history and biographies), his preference as a social drinker for straight rye, and his habit of retiring at midnight. One photo pictured Hill, improbably attired in a suit and flowered tie, a pipe in his mouth, playing gin rummy with Bernie "in the privacy of their apartment." Another showed him in shirtsleeves and tie, conversing with Sterling King, chairman of the new Richmond council. This "tall, slender, spare man" represented a new wave of black men, "not asking but legally demanding his rights as a man among men. . . . Slim, educated Oliver White Hill is the first Negro to emerge as a true leader in the new pattern," the article concluded.[46]

Life allowed little time for pause or reflection. Events were progressing on too many fronts and at too fast a pace. In late March, just as Hill's campaign was getting under way, Judge Hutcheson had ruled that the lack of equal school facilities in Surry County violated the Constitution and the law. Within days, he had punctuated the dramatic decision by denouncing racial discrimination in Chesterfield, Gloucester, and King George Counties. Now the lawyers were awaiting a court order on how the judge expected the communities to proceed. The Supreme Court had not been silent either. As Hill was politicking, the high court handed down historic decisions involving voting and housing. The South Carolina legislature had sought to escape the 1944 *Smith v. Allwright* ruling opening party primaries to blacks by repealing all primary laws. If such gatherings were conducted privately, without state sanction, then they could not violate the Constitution by remaining all white. Or so South Carolina lawmakers hoped. In mid-April 1948 the court nailed shut that escape hatch, refusing to review a Fourth Circuit opinion nixing the idea of a private primary. Poll taxes, voter apathy, intimidation, and prejudiced registrars might still curtail voting in the South, but all-white primaries no longer bedeviled the equation.[47]

One other set of rulings had caused even greater jubilation in the offices of Hill, Martin & Robinson. On May 3 the Supreme Court had decreed in *Shelley v. Kraemer* and *McGhee v. Sipes* that enforcement of restrictive housing covenants by state courts violated the Fourteenth Amendment. A companion decision in *Hurd v. Hodge* extended the ban to federal courts, barring such enforcement as contrary to federal law and public policy.[48] It was not an unqualified victory, but in the realm of civil rights few, if any, were. "Live Anywhere You Can Buy," summed up the *Pittsburgh Courier* with both delight and a hint of irony. Homeowners could still refuse to sell to blacks or other minorities if they chose. But those who elected to sell could no longer be stopped by antiquated agreements or government intervention. As a half measure, it was one worth winning.[49]

In just over a month, both Robinson and Hill had tasted delicious triumph. The younger partner's decade-long quest to dismantle discriminatory housing covenants had been vindicated. The passion birthed during James Nabrit's pioneering civil rights course at Howard Law finally had borne fruit. Meanwhile, Hill had joined the elite circle of black southerners elected to public office. That his triumph had come in the one-time capital of the Confederacy made it all the more sweet. The nation had taken note. Hard challenges lay ahead, yet the two men would face future trials seasoned not only by struggle and setback but also by success.

TEN

Farewell to Separate but Equal

In the winter of 1948, as the Virginia legislature was giving a cursory glance to bills dismantling Jim Crow and as Oliver Hill was contemplating a run for a seat on the city council, a stalwart duo set out to crisscross Virginia. Spot Robinson and Lester Banks loaded files and law books into the back of Banks's Chevrolet and embarked on a noble mission. The law professor, temporarily retired from teaching, and the recently installed executive secretary of the Virginia NAACP planned to make a thorough study of conditions in black schools. They also intended to assess the urgency among black parents, educators, and community leaders to confront inequities. Where appropriate, Robinson would launch legal challenges. Thurgood Marshall had ordered the investigation and tapped Robinson to lead it. The NAACP's Virginia Conference of Branches, one of the strongest, if not *the* strongest, in the nation, lent its considerable weight, including the newly hired Banks.[1]

As the pair navigated coastal marshlands and Southside cotton fields, Piedmont foothills and Blue Ridge hollows, logging an estimated thirty thousand miles in a single year, they encountered a swelling tide of frustrations and expectations. They were not tilling unplowed ground. Already, the joint committee for salary equalization of the Virginia Teachers Association and the state NAACP had reaped a considerable harvest. By the state's accounting, salaries had been equalized in all but thirty counties and five cities. Moreover, per capita state spending on black students, while still trailing spending on white students, had more than tripled in the decade ending with the 1946–47 school year. In addition, six high-profile cases attacking discrimination in Gloucester, King George, Surry, Chesterfield, Pulaski, and Arlington Counties were moving steadily through opening rounds in federal district courtrooms.[2]

Still, extreme imbalances in the overall educational programs for black and white children remained. Fairfax County, in northern Virginia, told the tale. Eighty-five hundred children, 89 percent of them white, attended school in the county. Ten of the eleven schoolhouses serving black children were wooden; none had running water and all had outside pit toilets. In contrast, all twenty-three schoolhouses for white children were brick and had indoor toilets and running water. Unlike white youth, many black children of elementary-school age walked four to six miles per day to school. The county ran four high schools for whites and none for blacks. The only school buses for black youth were those used to transport high-school students outside the county to a regional school in Manassas. Some children traveled up to fifty miles per day.[3]

Robinson's travel companion for his new assignment was more workhorse than show horse. The witty, chain-smoking Banks knew the school situation from the ground up. A native of Lunenburg County, in Southside Virginia, he had spent much of his childhood in West Virginia, just across the Virginia state line. After graduating from Bluefield State College, he had returned east to teach in Halifax and Charles City Counties, where his assignments ranged from teacher in a one-room school to principal of a small high school. Energetic and organized, he had caught the eye of NAACP leaders, who needed an overseer for the Virginia conference's ever-expanding programs. In April 1947 he had become the national organization's first full-time, paid state director.[4]

If Robinson and Banks grew hungry as they traveled, Jim Crow conventions forced them to order from the back doors of restaurants or seek out black-owned country stores. "That was what you'd have to do a lot—takeout crackers and cheese because they wouldn't serve colored," Banks recalled. He refused to use segregated restrooms at service stations even though "you could get a hurt bladder waiting to get back home." Banks usually bought gas at Esso stations, which typically had more liberal policies on restrooms. Once, however, when traveling on the Eastern Shore of Virginia, the executive secretary already had allowed the attendant at an Esso station to start pumping gas when he saw Jim Crow signage: "White Ladies / Colored Women." "I told the attendant to stop," he said. The bill was thirty-eight cents. "So the owner comes out and asks, 'What's the matter?' The attendant says that I don't like the seg [segregated] toilets. And the owner says, 'You're on the Eastern Shore,' as if that makes it okay." In 1961 Banks would be arrested for refusing to leave a whites-only restaurant in a Lynchburg train station. Another time, he was assaulted by a white sawmill worker after sitting in the white section of a Charlotte County restaurant. His courage as he crisscrossed the state in the late 1940s, with Robinson or alone, fearlessly displaying an NAACP sign in the rear window of his car, qualified him as an unsung hero of the movement.[5]

As they traveled, Spot Robinson often worked late into the night preparing filings to leave with school boards or boards of supervisors the next day. "He'd sit up 'til three or four in the morning to search out a point of law he needed. . . . He's the most thorough man in the world," Banks later told an interviewer.[6] Robinson's formal manner contrasted with Banks's easy approachability. The attorney's exhaustive explanations and patrician accent—in which *time* became *tah-yme* and *out* became *ah-yout*—further separated him from the masses of tobacco farmers, domestic workers, and day laborers. Jack Gravely, who in 1977 followed Banks as executive secretary of the state conference, recalled his first impression of Robinson: "He was quiet, reserved, almost standoffish, tall and thin, fair-skinned. He seemed very particular and a clean man—his fingernails were clean." But those who penetrated the facade quickly recognized other qualities. Robinson also was unpretentious, and while he was not given to emotional displays, he showed genuine interest in the people he met. The combination of intelligence and attentiveness earned respect and affection from a range of acquaintances. "He was the kind of person you could talk to," said LaVerne Williams, recalling her boss's interactions as a federal judge. "He didn't know class. The cleaning people, they loved him to death, because he just had an innate way of treating everybody decently."[7]

As a mark of that generosity, throughout his career Robinson nurtured and encouraged promising young people. He deduced, for instance, that Williams's daughter, Reeda Butler, had the intellectual capacity to attend law school, and he encouraged her to do so. She recalled the day Robinson summoned her to his judicial chambers to reveal his plan. As usual, he was maintaining his exhaustive work schedule with a catnap. "He was stretched out on the sofa. I said, 'How you gonna talk to me in your sleep.' He said, 'I'm doing my best thinking.'" Then a schoolteacher, Butler accepted Robinson's advice. She earned a law degree while raising her daughter and studying at night. "I trusted him and I would never disappoint him. He was real down-to-earth," said Butler, who became an administrator in the Washington school system.[8] Similarly, Lucy Thornton Edwards followed Robinson's urging and earned a degree from Howard Law. She had first met the attorney in 1952 as a thirteen-year-old student protesting the refusal of a white school board to maintain a high school for black students in West Point, Virginia. Some years later, as a campus activist and senior at the Hampton Institute, she reencountered Robinson. He remembered her immediately, telling an acquaintance, "She's my client." Later, after she enrolled at Howard Law, where Robinson then served as dean, his shepherding continued. When she and a fellow student played a prank by pretending to have gotten married, Robinson was not amused. Hearing the news, he rushed from his office to convey a message. "Any foolish young woman from West Point, Virginia, who thinks she could up and get married has no regard for her scholarship," he admonished. "He saw himself as a protective figure. There was to be no horsing around," Edwards said.[9]

Marshall's selection of Virginia as the site for an intensive investigation of school equity was no fluke. If any state conference had the capacity to underwrite such a probe, it was Virginia's. Tinsley's meticulous and tireless oversight had boosted membership and programs to record heights. By 1946 state enrollment had grown to almost twenty-five thousand in ninety-one branches. The legal staff, headed by Hill, had expanded from six to eleven attorneys, covering every region of the state. The national organization's decision to award the Virginia conference its top prize for outstanding achievement in the summer of 1947 reflected the progress. Tinsley did not hesitate to tout the importance of the Virginia work. In letters to the national office in September 1947 and May 1948, he described the state as carrying "a surprisingly vast share of the total national aggregate legal load."[10] Unquestionably, it did. In appreciation, the New York hierarchy often showed deference to the sometimes demanding Tinsley. Shortly after the Irene Morgan decision, Walter White wrote to a member of the administrative staff, describing the need to salve the Virginian's ego: "I talked with Dr. Tinsley the other day when he was here for the Board meeting and in mentioning the Irene Morgan case he stated that he had really been the instigator of pushing that case from the beginning. . . . You know and I know that Dr. Tinsley likes a bit of kudosing every now and then. I think it would be well if we seriously considered some kind of honorable mention for him at the Conference. Do you agree?"[11]

As Robinson's investigation of school facilities began, Marshall once again found himself explaining where the national organization stood on school integration. Clarifying the matter was a tricky business. An internal debate had raged within the organization since the mid-1930s as W. E. B. Du Bois famously argued for building up separate black schools. A decade later, overall the NAACP favored working toward integration. Yet Marshall and other key strategists, including Robinson and Hill, feared that moving too quickly to ask the Supreme Court to dismantle segregated schools risked a devastating setback. The first step was to await the outcomes of the Texas and Oklahoma university cases. Then they would decide when and how to launch a full-bore assault on elementary- and secondary-school segregation.[12] In the meantime, they did not want to create either the perception or the reality of fostering separate schools. By one interpretation, the equalization lawsuits implied that localities could avoid integration by balancing school facilities and programs. Indeed, as pressure toward integration mounted in the 1950s, many localities would make a mad scramble to improve conditions in black schools as a defense against race mixing. Marshall wanted to be clear, from a policy standpoint, that the NAACP had no intention of settling for segregated schools. But while awaiting a clearer signal that the Supreme Court might entertain an end to separate classrooms, he was forced to walk a tightrope between those pushing for more action and those preferring less.[13]

In a September 1947 speech to the Texas State Conference of Branches, a frustrated Marshall took a swipe at Carter W. Wesley, a prominent black attorney and publisher who favored school equalization over integration. "The only solution to our problem is that of breaking down segregation in public schools," Marshall admonished. That could not be accomplished by improving segregated schools to the point of "'Jim Crow DeLuxe,'" he said.[14] Even as he spoke, however, Marshall himself was temporizing on when to start a direct attack on segregation in elementary and secondary schools. In his mind, the time clearly was not ripe. For now, the best the NAACP could do was take the two-pronged approach outlined a year earlier in Atlanta. At the college level, the NAACP would seek admission of blacks to white schools. But at the high-school and elementary levels, in most cases the lawyers would merely urge judges to order school officials to stop discriminating.[15] By failing to prescribe or even suggest a remedy to that discrimination, the Legal Defense Fund could say with a clear conscience that it had not condoned segregation, even if the remedies later consisted solely in improving segregated black schools. That sidestep was the strategy honed in Hill, Martin & Robinson's Virginia lawsuits. And it would be the basis for a host of new actions to be initiated by Robinson as he and Banks set out across Virginia.

Robinson was only a few months into his new assignment when Sterling Hutcheson handed him and his colleagues a splendid new cudgel: an order for Surry County school officials to stop discriminating. On the morning of March 30, 1948, a flock of lawyers crowded into the federal district judge's Richmond chambers to hash out the details of an improvement plan. Filed the previous summer by Martin and the Hampton attorneys Bassette and Thompson, the lawsuit described an array of problems in the small county that was home to piney woods, succulent hams, and vast peanut fields. Black children outnumbered white children in the county almost two to one. Even so, black children received a far inferior education. Not only was the Surry County Training School unaccredited and its course offerings limited, but its physical plant was deplorable. Cracks in the floors and walls made winter heating nearly impossible. The lavatory facilities were "so unsanitary as to constitute a nuisance and health menace."[16]

The county made a bold effort to refute those claims, but photographs and other evidence mocked the attempt. An honest jurist, which Hutcheson prided himself on being, could reach only one conclusion: the public schools of Surry County were decidedly unequal, and the differences were attributable to race. As a few hundred black citizens milled about in the hallways of the federal courts building, a cluster of attorneys, including Hill and Robinson, conferred with Hutcheson over the details of a consent agreement aimed at remedying the imbalance without a trial. In midafternoon, a drained-looking Hutcheson announced the results. There was no mistaking his intentions. The practice of sending black schoolchildren to an unaccredited high school and white children to an accredited one "violates the Constitution and laws of the United States, and is void," he began. Similarly, the Constitution prohibited unequal facilities, bus transportation, teacher salaries, and course offerings. Beginning with the new school year, starting on September 1, Surry school officials were "enjoined and restrained" from discriminating on account of race or color in any of these matters.[17]

The order was the logical extension of the *Alston* equal-pay decision eight years earlier, but there had been no guarantee that a federal judge reared in the South would issue so clear a mandate. It was the ruling that Robinson, Hill, and Martin coveted, and it was reinforced a week later by a memorandum from Hutcheson concluding that school officials in Gloucester, King George, and Chesterfield Counties also had discriminated. In one fell swoop, a federal judge had validated the NAACP position in four of the six major Virginia cases pending in federal court.[18] Sober observers recognized the far-reaching implications. School boards might offer excuses, but the disparity between black and white schools in Virginia and elsewhere across the South was obvious. "For generations we have insisted upon 'separate but equal' facilities as the basis of our social pattern," Dabney warned readers. "We have seen to it that there was separateness, but we have not seen to it that there is equality."[19] Now a federal court had exposed the duplicity. White Virginians—and by extension white southerners—could take action or face the consequences.

The spring and summer of 1948 proved a heady time for NAACP attorneys in Virginia. Augmenting the success in Hutcheson's courtroom, the Supreme Court handed down major victories in voting-rights and restrictive-covenant cases. Richmond voters elected Hill to the city's governing council. And Marshall tapped Robinson to be a star witness on education strategy at a national gathering of lawyers preceding the NAACP's annual convention in Kansas City. The special counsel urged Tinsley and the Virginia conference to foot Robinson's travel expenses, as his presence was "absolutely imperative."[20] A few days before leaving for Missouri, Robinson provided Virginia's joint committee for salary equalization a preview of his upcoming report. He was overseeing some sixty school cases, although only about two dozen of them might wind up in court, he reported. In some localities, local blacks and school officials appeared likely to work out compromises. In others, black leaders trusted white officials to make good on promised improvements. And in still others, legal action was the prescribed remedy.[21]

As the 1948–49 school year opened, the lawyers prepared for the next phase of their work in Gloucester and King George Counties. Hutcheson had followed up his April order with explicit directions: separate schools must be equal, and discrimination must end. Now began the long slog of turning a judicial dictate into reality. The opening salvo came as Robinson and Hill accompanied twenty-nine black students to Botetourt High School in Gloucester County to seek admission on the first day of the new school year. Simultaneously, Martin and Banks led a dozen or so boys and girls to the threshold of the King George High School, where they were invited into the office of the principal, William Smith Jr. The school superintendent, T. Benton Gayle, joined them. "What is the purpose of your visit?" demanded Gayle. "To get equal school facilities for my clients, as ordered by the federal district court," replied Martin, no longer a jovial sidekick. The tableau played out as expected. With Martin's point made and no one enrolled, the attorney led his charges back to the King George Training School.[22]

On October 22, Martin, Hill, and Robinson returned to Hutcheson's courtroom to argue that officials in both counties should be held in contempt. Martin laid out the case against King George. Despite Hutcheson's order, no substantial improvements had been made in the county's black schools. The defendants had failed to provide an equal—or, for that matter, any—auditorium or gymnasium for the black children. Laboratory facilities consisted of a two-burner hot plate and an unusable water fountain. Some fifteen hundred to two thousand books had been dumped on the floor of the principal's office in an effort to equalize libraries. And so on.[23] The school board attorney Horace T. Morrison acknowledged that equalization was a work in progress, but he questioned the significance of the disparities. "Brick and mortar do not make a school, and neither can you get brains from a book," he argued.[24] His questioning led Picott to describe this scene in the principal's office:

PICOTT: These books all appeared as if they had been carted there in a hurry and dropped on the floor—they were not sorted. . . .
MARTIN: In what part of the principal's office were they?
PICOTT: On the floor, most of them. . . .
MARTIN: Did you see any evidence that those books had been catalogued or classified?

PICOTT: No. I reached down in the pile and picked out a number of books. I picked out one book called Loves of A Worldly Woman. I wondered what good that would do in a high school, but it was there.

On cross-examination, Martin probed further:

MARTIN: I ask if you recall seeing on that day the Report of the Librarian of Congress of 1905?
PICOTT: Yes, I saw that book. I saw another one, Bell Telephone System Mechanical Report of 18-something or 1901. . . .
MARTIN: I will ask you if you saw two volumes named Kladderada[t]sch?
PICOTT: Yes. That was the German book that I tried to read. There were several of them entirely in German.

And after a few more questions:

MARTIN: Are any of these [German] books valuable for a high school that does not teach German?
PICOTT: No.[25]

Over the next year, the King George and Gloucester cases followed different trajectories. Despite dustups—including an aborted plan to drop chemistry, physics, biology, and geometry at the white high school as a way to equalize courses—the citizens of King George narrowly passed a bond referendum to improve black schools. Once new construction was complete, Hutcheson removed the matter from his docket.[26]

A more difficult progression awaited Gloucester County. In January 1949, after a fractious December hearing, Hutcheson held Gloucester officials in contempt of his July equalization order. Hopes of righting the situation before the judge imposed penalties imploded when citizens rejected a bond issue for black schools. A disgusted Hutcheson responded by fining four Gloucester school officials $250 each and threatening further penalties if white officials continued to balk.[27] Black leaders rejoiced at the rarity of a white jurist firmly rejecting the status quo. Even so, the punishment equated more to a sharp slap than to a whipping. A sentencing on the same day in another courtroom lent perspective. Three University of Virginia students convicted of shooting out three city traffic signals and five streetlights received heavier penalties than the school officials. Each of the student culprits was fined $650, with $300 suspended. Resigned to

Hutcheson's ruling, Gloucester officials set about completing the design of a new school for blacks.[28] In late 1948, Marshall advised that the Virginia team had "worked out a technique which has the best possibility of winning" similar lawsuits throughout the South. He urged Robinson to write out their system "in understandable English" for regional distribution. With the Gloucester case resolved, Robinson complied. His fifteen-page memorandum, describing how other southern states could piggyback onto the Virginia experience, went into the mail in mid-June.[29]

If any doubt existed that Sterling Hutcheson was ahead of his peers, two other Virginia jurists—the federal district judges Alfred D. Barksdale and Albert V. Bryan—erased it. Barksdale presided over Hill, Martin & Robinson's Pulaski lawsuit; Bryan ruled in the Arlington case. In the same week that Hutcheson was handing out the Gloucester fines, Barksdale was wrapping up a two-year school-equalization odyssey on the other side of the state; the Arlington case dragged on many months longer.

The primary issue in the Pulaski case was the lack of a black high school anywhere in the craggy, scenic county. Only whites were allowed to attend Pulaski's three secondary schools. Black students were bused to the Christiansburg Industrial Institute, located in neighboring Montgomery County. For some Pulaski children, the commute entailed round-trip travel of up to sixty or more miles per day. Hours that might have been spent on studies or extracurricular activities were squandered on travel.[30] Percy Casino Corbin, a native Texan and Pulaski's leading black citizen, took affront at the racial slight. As a physician and successful entrepreneur, he enjoyed a more refined lifestyle than many of his white neighbors. A dapper figure, Corbin sometimes rode a white stallion, and he accented his stylish wardrobe with a pince-nez. He had a biracial clientele, but because of his race, he did not enjoy privileges at the white hospital. Nor could his five children get the education he wanted for them in southwestern Virginia. His youngest son, Mahatma, named for India's Mahatma Gandhi, became a lead plaintiff, along with Dr. Corbin, in the lawsuit filed by Hill, Martin & Robinson in May 1947. By the time the case reached Barksdale's courtroom, Mahatma had left Virginia to finish high school and begin college in Detroit, Michigan. "The facilities at Christiansburg weren't adequate to give him the type of training that I wanted him to have," Corbin explained from the witness stand.[31]

The two-day trial in October 1949 exposed the same imbalances in facilities, courses, and teacher salaries evident in the eastern Virginia counties, plus the additional slight of having to travel out of the county to attend a black high school. But when Barksdale finally released his opinion in May 1949, the outcome proved markedly different from those ordered by Hutcheson. A Virginia Military Institute graduate, decorated World War I soldier, former state senator, and Byrd Organization sympathizer, Barksdale was not of a mind to second-guess education officials. In general, he said, any hardships experienced by black students attending the Christiansburg Institute were mirrored or even exceeded at the county's two smaller high schools for whites. "Public free schools cannot be brought to every man's door; they must be located where they will do the greatest good for the greatest number," Barksdale insisted. As for quality, "no two schools are ever precisely equal."[32] In a smartly crafted NAACP brief, Robinson had argued that the limitations on white students could be corrected by relocation, while black students had no such option. "The significant consideration is that while some white high school pupils may, all Negro high school pupils must, be subjected to such hardships and inconveniences," he wrote. Barksdale dismissed the point. If he were to order that every Pulaski County child be educated within county lines, "it would be the death knell of consolidated high schools for two or more counties or cities," he said, dismissing the discrimination charge and ordered the plaintiffs to pick up the court costs.[33]

His was not to be the final word. Six months later, on November 14, 1949, a three-judge panel of the Court of Appeals for the Fourth Circuit reversed Barksdale on the high-school discrimination claim and ordered him to reconsider the elementary-school situation in Pulaski County. The opinion cited the "real and severe" hardship that long bus rides caused black children and parents. It noted "manifest inequalities" in science labs and other facilities. And it concluded that in a host of matters, from summer-school offerings to library holdings, "a very significant inequality is quite apparent." It could hardly be denied that "this discrimination is due to race and color."[34] The judgment stunned leading white Virginians. The Fourth Circuit "may have wreaked havoc in public education in the South," warned the editorialist Douglas Southall Freeman, of the *Richmond News Leader*. Freeman acknowledged that forty-four Virginia counties and cities did not have an accredited black high school, while twenty-four counties and five cities had no black high school at all. Since many of those localities had small black populations, however, he was not alarmed. Travel to another county struck him as perfectly appropriate. He italicized his next message for emphasis: *"Virginia is not about to abandon segregation in its public school system."* Friends of blacks, among whom Freeman counted himself, should keep working for "reasonably equal" black schools.[35] Proclaiming themselves shocked at the Fourth Circuit ruling, Pulaski leaders mirrored Freeman's defiance. Fearful of the outcome, they elected not to appeal to the Supreme Court, but they also took no steps to create a black high school. Like every other court mandate growing out the Virginia school-equalization campaign, the Fourth Circuit ruling would prove easier to issue than to enforce.[36]

Arlington County offered added proof. The school-discrimination lawsuits in Pulaski and Arlington Counties had been filed just four months apart in mid-1947. But Judge Barksdale's Pulaski ruling already would be on appeal before *Carter v. School Board of Arlington County* meandered its way to trial. By then the original plaintiff, Constance Carter, had married and withdrawn from school. Hill, Martin, Robinson, and Ransom all sat at the plaintiff's table in the Alexandria federal district court when the foot-dragging finally ended on September 6, 1949. The local attorney Lawrence W. Douglas represented the Arlington schools. Judge Bryan, a former Alexandria city attorney and loyal Byrd man, nominated to the federal bench two years earlier by President Truman, presided.

Despite a few differences, including the relative superiority of both white and black schools in the prosperous county just outside Washington, the proceedings followed the basic blueprint established in the earlier equalization cases. Washington-Lee High School, for whites, and Hoffman-Boston High School, for blacks, differed substantially in their physical plants and course offerings, the NAACP lawyers contended. Black students could not avail themselves of an education comparable to that of whites purely because of race.[37] School officials attributed the differences to a wide enrollment gap. As a combined junior and senior high, Washington-Lee had nearly 2,500 students. Hoffman-Boston, which spanned elementary to senior high, had just 270 students. Middle- and upper-class black families contributed to the enrollment mismatch by often sending their children to Washington's elite black schools. It was neither practical nor possible to duplicate Washington-Lee's physical plant or its course offerings for so small a clientele, officials said.[38] The explanations satisfied Judge Bryan. Under the Fourteenth Amendment, all citizens must receive the protection and benefits of the state in equal measure, he said. "But neither the same nor similar treatment is commanded by the Amendment. Equal in its eye means equivalent." Certainly, he said, improvements were needed at Hoffman-Boston. Already, a $250,000 bond issue had been approved. "But these, and similar inadequacies, are deficiencies rather than discriminations." He dismissed the complaint.[39]

Once again the Fourth Circuit reversed the decision. The same three-judge panel that had sat in *Corbin*—circuit judges Parker, Soper, and Dobie—evaluated *Carter*. Robinson and Martin represented the appellants in court; Hill and Ransom contributed to the brief. As in the earlier case, the panel ruled that the differences between the two schools were not mere variations flowing from size or location. They were "unlawful discriminations against pupils of the colored race." On May 31, 1950, the panel ordered Bryan to reconsider the imbalances.[40] Again the NAACP lawyers had scored a significant victory, yet Arlington's children saw no immediate improvement. The matter returned to the district court. Another seemingly endless grind crept forward. Hill, Robinson, Martin, and their NAACP allies had invested hundreds, even thousands of hours in proving in court what anyone could see with their own eyes: the education available to black children in Virginia in no way equaled that available to whites. Even when judges agreed, however, discrimination did not end.

As Hill, Martin & Robinson awaited the Fourth Circuit's ruling on the Arlington case in the spring of 1950, stunning developments gripped the larger civil rights world. By eight o'clock a.m. on April 4, a crowd had begun to gather on the wide plaza leading to the imposing marble temple that houses the United States Supreme Court. The doors would not open until eleven, and the upcoming hearings on the university-desegregation cases of the Texan Heman M. Sweatt and the Oklahoman George McLaurin were not scheduled until the afternoon. But a long-anticipated juncture had arrived. Finally, the court was about to hear arguments challenging the racial-separation doctrine enshrined in *Plessy v. Ferguson*. At issue in the Texas case was whether the state, by forcing blacks into a separate law school, deprived them of the intangible benefits of the larger white law school and thereby violated their equal-protection rights. The Oklahoma case asked whether it was permissible for the state to seat McLaurin separately from whites in the library and cafeteria and also to position his desk outside regular classrooms, so that he had to peer in through an open doorway, as he pursued a doctorate in school administration.[41] Among the prominent persons awaiting entrance to the court that morning, the *Afro-American* reported, were Mr. and Mrs. Spottswood Robinson III, Mr. and Mrs. Martin Martin, and Oliver Hill, all of Richmond. Early in the day, Robinson moved that Hill and Martin be admitted to practice before the court, thereby guaranteeing their seating. Men who had spent their adult lives working toward this moment wanted to be within sight of the action.[42]

A few weeks later, as the NAACP nervously awaited the court's decision, death delivered a devastating blow to the community. Just as Charles Houston appeared poised to realize his greatest dream, the visionary leader suffered a heart attack. He died on April 22 at age fifty-four in a Washington hospital. Houston had been battling heart disease for several years, but his death came as a shock. Stunned admirers, including the trio of Richmond lawyers, saw an unmistakable parallel in his demise to that of the biblical Moses. "He lived to see us close to the Promised Land," eulogized Bill Hastie during a funeral attended by five Supreme Court justices. Someone else would lead the final steps across the divide.[43]

On June 5 the Supreme Court rendered its verdicts in the two university cases and in a transportation challenge, *Henderson v. United States.* The justices did not, as the NAACP had hoped, directly address the constitutionality of *Plessy,* but they came within a hair's breadth of doing so. Arthur B. Krock, an influential Washington correspondent for the *New York Times,* concluded that the rulings had left *Plessy* "a mass of tatters." The education opinions, written by Chief Justice Fred M. Vinson, of Kentucky, concluded that Texas and Oklahoma were not offering Sweatt and McLaurin instruction "substantially equivalent" to that afforded whites. Consequently, the universities did not meet the *Plessy* test. Significantly, in the Texas case, Vinson moved beyond comparing numbers to addressing intangibles—the reputation of the faculty, the experience of the administration, and the influence of the alumni. The unstated but implicit corollary was that a segregated law school for blacks could never be the equivalent of the highly regarded University of Texas Law School.[44] If

188 | INCUBATION, 1939–1950

that was so, it could never achieve the *Plessy* standard. In *McLaurin*, Vinson slapped down the Oklahoma strategy of segregating a black student within a white university. Such restrictions impaired his ability "to study, to engage in discussions and exchange views with other students, and, in general, to learn his profession." Oklahoma officials had argued that McLaurin would have been ostracized no matter what, given societal norms. The court found the argument irrelevant. Voluntary refusal to co-mingle did not have the same constitutional implications as a state ban, the opinion stated.[45] The court's third decision, *Henderson*, capped the NAACP's triumph. The ruling held that the Southern Railway Company had violated the nondiscrimination clause of the Interstate Commerce Act when it cordoned off a tiny area of a dining car for blacks and denied service to the traveler Elmer Henderson, while offering extensive service to whites. A railroad engaged in interstate commerce could not subject travelers to "undue or unreasonable prejudice in any respect whatsoever." *Henderson* was another nail in the coffin of Jim Crow.[46]

The trio of rulings brought Marshall and the NAACP to a crossroads. Had the time arrived to discard all pretense of willingness to accept separate but equal? Were the Supreme Court justices inviting an opportunity to thrust a dagger into the heart of *Plessy*, or had the court just said, in effect, "we will bend this far and no further?" Were the masses of black parents and educators ready to forsake years spent improving black schools and to demand, once and for all, nothing less than an end to segregation? Was this the moment for change?

Scholars differ on Marshall's readiness in June 1950 to make the leap. To the Harvard law professor Mark Tushnet, who chronicled the NAACP's assault on segregated education from 1925 to 1950, Marshall was primed to act. In a letter one week after *Sweatt* and *McLaurin*, he wrote: "All three of the decisions are replete with road markings telling us where to go next." Marshall had long preferred the direct attack. Now both NAACP internal politics and the external legal and political environment pointed to challenging segregation per se. As a leader whose strength lay in his "superb judgments about life and law," Marshall instinctively knew where the future lay and what course to take, Tushnet wrote.[47] The journalist and social historian Richard Kluger detected greater ambivalence. Although "no trace of such irresoluteness was to be found in Marshall's public remarks," the lawyer's "head was less certain than his heart," Kluger wrote in *Simple Justice,* his panoramic study of *Brown v. Board.* One concern was that it was far from clear how Chief Justice Vinson would come down on an assault to segregation in primary and secondary schools. A kindly and commonsensical public servant, Vinson as a congressman had pushed for passage of such egalitarian measures as the Social Security Act and the Fair Labor Standards Act. But he was not an avid defender of civil rights; nor was he adept at melding the court's fractious members into a united whole. Could he contemplate or manage a challenge to the social fabric of the South? Marshall knew the risk implicit in answering yes. Switching to a more confrontational course might set back progress.[48]

Whatever Marshall's leanings, Robinson had reached clarity in the wake of the court decisions: "From the minute *Sweatt* and *McLaurin* came down, I said, 'This thing has now arrived.'" He had spent two and a half years pressing the equalization campaign in Virginia. No American had devoted more time to making segregated primary and secondary schools truly equal. For both practical and philosophical reasons, he had concluded that it could not be done. School boards hemmed, hawed, and lied. Officials had to be dragged, kicking and screaming, toward every major advance. The strategy simply consumed too much time, money, and effort with too little result. The initiative was driving the Virginia NAACP into debt and exhausting him and his law partners. Moreover, Robinson had come to believe that the mere act of segregating black students constituted discrimination. It deprived them of the benefits of mainstream society and diminished their self-worth. "We won legal victories without measurably increasing the Negro student's share in the educational wealth," Robinson later wrote of the equalization campaign. "We refined the judicial concept of the equal protection laws but in practice it was not applied." Plus, "we were nailing the lid on our own coffin by the production of newer and costlier monuments to segregation."[49] The Virginian had understood the importance of waiting for the court to rule in *Sweatt* and *McLaurin.* Now the court had acted, and it had weakened *Plessy* without abandoning it. Even so, Robinson was ready to wash his hands of equalization. He made a promise to himself: "I just took the position that I wasn't going to get involved in any more equalization cases; it was going to be segregation head on."[50]

The matter came to a head shortly after the court rulings. By Robinson's telling, Marshall had scheduled one of his periodic two-day seminars in which lawyers from across the nation gathered to debate strategy on a topic of critical concern. Education was foremost on the agenda when the group convened in New York. The task of moderating the opening session fell to Robinson, George Hayes of Washington, and U. Simpson Tate, the southwestern regional counsel for the NAACP. Meeting with Hayes and Tate prior to their presentation, Robinson informed his colleagues that his position on equalization had changed: "I walk out of the courthouse after winning one of these damn things, and I just say, 'This is not it.' I don't like the inner feeling that I have." Having vowed to take no more such cases, Robinson could not in good conscience now counsel the assembled lawyers on "how you compare libraries and faculty and student-faculty ratios," he said. He recommended that the trio start out by telling the lawyers that "we have to think about taking the next step," an all-out assault on segregation. "George and Tate agreed wholeheartedly. So, we go out to make the presentation. I did not mention this to Thurgood [in advance]. I don't remember whether it was accidental or intentional. I think it was intentional because I didn't want roadblocks." The recommendation proved to be "a bombshell, and it set off all kinds of commotion. . . . Nobody was prepared" for the debate, Robinson recalled. He remembered Marshall doing more listening than talking, as was typical in such settings. "Thurgood always gets cautious in the beginning of any of these [strategy debates], no matter how good they might look," Robinson said. "Thurgood certainly did not make any opposition to this." Nor, however, did he recall the special counsel endorsing the idea. On a preliminary vote, Robinson's view prevailed, "but there was a hell of a lot of dissension." The group agreed to reconsider the matter a few weeks later.[51]

Back home, Robinson's law partners were among those harboring doubts about a changed strategy. Hill had long thought that the first front in the integration battle should be housing. He did not see how neighborhood schools could ever become integrated unless blacks and whites lived in proximity. "If we had licked housing, I thought the school problem would fall," he later explained. But recent efforts to integrate a white neighborhood in Chicago had met with shocking violence. "So based on that experience, it was decided that it would probably be better to go with the schools." As for Martin, he had little enthusiasm for attacking segregation per se in public schools. "He was something of a separatist," believing that black children developed best within a cohesive black community, Hill said.[52] Ironically, the law partner who had once quaked at the rigors of a bar exam and whose natural bent was to study any issue to the point of exhaustion became the first to be done with vacillating. The NAACP could do as it wanted, but if what it wanted was to continue settling for improvements in black schools, it would do so without Robinson.

At the end of June, Marshall convened a conference of forty-three lawyers and fourteen branch and state conference presidents in New York to resolve the education question. Robinson attended; Hill and Martin, who were occupied with a school case in Durham, North Carolina, did not. By this time opinions had settled. Some opposition remained, but it was less vocal. If Marshall had lingering doubts, none were evident. "We are going to insist on non-segregation in American public education from top to bottom—from law school to kindergarten," Marshall said, laying out his plan. Going forward, the Legal Defense Fund intended to aim for nonsegregated education. "No relief other than that will be accepted." The assembled group, including Robinson, agreed. In a meeting that fall, the NAACP board of directors stamped its approval.[53] The most profound redirection yet in the path to integrated public schools had arrived.

Robinson, Hill, and Martin would continue to shoulder the remnants of the equalization campaign for several years, as cases in Pulaski, Arlington, Surry, and other Virginia localities wound to a slow finish. Their reputations as experts led Hill and Martin to ongoing involvement in similar cases in Durham, Atlanta, and elsewhere. But for all intents and purposes, the fight to improve segregated schools was over. The exhaustive effort spearheaded by Robinson, as well as his courtroom work with Hill and Martin, had served several purposes. Most superficially, it had provided a focus as the Legal Defense Fund awaited an outcome in the Texas and Oklahoma university cases. More significantly, the results provided a clear, convincing rebuttal to anyone inclined to believe that equality could be broadly achieved without integration. The strategy was simply too costly, too time consuming, and too riddled with escape hatches to make it practical on a large scale. The efforts had impacted scores of localities. Yet even when cases were won, years often went by with little in the way of tangible progress. Most important, the lawyers believed, continued segregation psychologically damaged black children. It was one thing to speculate that separate but equal entailed such shortcomings, another to know it. With the massive Virginia equalization campaign, Robinson, Hill, Martin, and their associates had provided the knowing.

The drama surrounding *Sweatt* and *McLaurin* overshadowed a startling election result: Hill's defeat by forty-four votes in his bid for reelection to the city council in 1950. In early June the *Richmond Afro-American* had labeled him a shoo-in for a second term. "Richmond's colored councilman is virtually certain to be re-elected on June 13," the newspaper asserted confidently. The writer cited a recent newspaper survey in which Hill had been ranked the second most effective member of the council. Moreover, the Richmond Citizens' Association and the city's two major daily newspapers had endorsed his candidacy this time around. Such white organizational support for a black candidate was unique.[54]

Debate over a prospective downtown expressway dominated the campaign. Many business leaders supported the idea as a way to move traffic into and out of the city center, but others correctly foresaw the decimation of downtown neighborhoods, including Jackson Ward. Despite sizable black opposition to the project, Hill had expressed mild support for the so-called Segoe Plan, developed by the noted Ohio planner Ladislas Segoe. The proposal "was much less destructive than other plans under consideration," Hill argued, choosing political pragmatism over racial identity. However, in a nod to critics, he and another councilman had pushed successfully for a voter referendum, to be held on the same day as the council vote.[55] Hill's support for the expressway, however tentative, likely cost him. When the ballots were counted, voters in forty-seven of the city's fifty-five precincts rejected the highway. Hill's simultaneous defeat by fewer than four dozen votes led supporters to urge him to seek a recount; he declined, modeling the reasonableness he had shown as a councilman.[56]

In the aftermath, a *Richmond Afro-American* editorial called it "indisputable" that more single-shot voting for Hill by blacks could have reelected him. But the newspaper also noted that the candidate had won about as many white votes as black, a remarkable achievement. Meanwhile, a *Times-Dispatch* editorial observed that "any Richmonder who had studied Mr. Hill's council record or who had watched him at work in that body should have been convinced that he deserved re-election."[57] Condolences poured in from across the city. "I write with a heavy heart for I have not fully recovered from the shock of the election yesterday," Mayor King wrote. "Frankly, I feel that the results are tragic, for in my opinion you have been one of our most constructive Councilmen and I have relied upon your judgment in many instances." A host of white businessmen picked up the lament. "You have rendered fine service to Richmond and its people, and you deserved better at their hands than to be defeated in your bid for re-election," wrote T. Coleman Andrews, who six years later would become an independent, states'-rights candidate for president. And C. Merle Luck, president of a construction company, added: "You have done more for the City and its citizens while in office than any other councilman."[58] Such esteem did not translate into the council's offering Hill an appointment when a vacancy occurred less than a year later. As 1950 progressed, the goodwill engendered during Hill's two years on council began to fray. By the time he made his next and last political bid, a 1955 race for the Democratic nomination to the House of Delegates, white backing had all but evaporated. By then the NAACP's push for school desegregation had stripped away the veneer of civility, and in Hill's own assessment, "I couldn't have been elected dog catcher."[59]

A private joy—a nine-month-old son at home—softened the blow of the council defeat. After a series of risky and troubled pregnancies, Bernie had given birth to twins in September 1949. The dual births came as a surprise. Thinking that she was gaining weight far too rapidly, doctors had put the thirty-eight-year-old mother-to-be on a strict diet. Whether or not that was the determining factor, one of the twins was still-born. But the other was a healthy boy, whom the couple named Oliver White Hill Jr. "At present Papa Hill is suffering an acute case of 'diaper-amnesia,'" joked Banks in a memo inviting the larger NACCP community to join the celebration. Turning serious, Banks applauded the new father for "each step taken and each blow landed against the walls of segregation and discrimination." He urged the group to contribute ten dollars each toward a life membership in the NAACP for the new arrival.[60] Choosing a godfather, the couple picked a friend they knew would prove an admirable role model for the son they had awaited for fifteen years, Spot Robinson.[61]

Two newsworthy events in the summer and fall of 1950 tested the amity of white Virginians. First, a federal panel acting in the wake of the Texas and Oklahoma decisions ordered the University of Virginia School of Law

to admit a black student. Gregory Swanson, a Howard Law graduate practicing in Martinsville, had applied the previous fall to become a graduate
student in law. At a closed-door meeting on July 14, the Board of Visitors
rejected Swanson's application, citing Virginia's ban on coeducation for
blacks and whites. Attorney General Almond, who could read the *Sweatt*
and *McLaurin* decisions as well as anyone, had advised against that action.
Resistance was pointless, Almond warned. Proving him correct, a special,
three-judge tribunal took barely thirty minutes to command Swanson's
admission. Their order copied almost exactly that suggested by the plaintiff's chief counsel, Robinson. On September 15, Swanson reported to the
campus to register for classes.[62] His tenure at the university proved star
crossed. Shaken by campus hostility, Swanson withdrew from the law
school after one year. But other blacks soon followed, and the case settled
doubts about the future of integrated higher education in Virginia.[63]

Second, as the year progressed, the case of the Martinsville Seven divided public opinion, largely though not entirely along racial lines. Martin
had accepted a lead role in the appeals of seven men sentenced to die for
the shocking, January 8, 1949, gang rape of Ruby Stroud Floyd in Martinsville, a textile town near the North Carolina border. Few doubted the com-
plicity of the seven, who attacked the deeply religious, thirty-two-year-old
white housewife as she walked home through a black section of town after
completing an errand. There was doubt, however, about whether all seven
had sexually violated Mrs. Floyd. And there was raging controversy about
whether justice was served in a case that would spawn the largest mass
execution for rape in American history. In the course of brief trials conducted over eleven days, six all-white juries convicted and sentenced the
men to death.[64]

Over the next twenty-one months, Martin led the high-profile appeals,
assisted primarily by Sam Tucker and Roland Ealey. Hill and Robinson
played peripheral roles. Some initial sparring over control of the case between the NAACP and the Civil Rights Congress, a competing organization with Communist Party links, revealed Martin's fervent distaste for
radical ideologies. The NAACP retained the upper hand in the dispute
after Martin announced that neither the NAACP nor the law firm of Hill,
Martin & Robinson would associate with any organization that had been
declared subversive by Attorney General Tom C. Clark. The Civil Rights
Congress fit the description.[65] Martin's selection to oversee the appeals

came as no surprise. While Robinson and Hill more often stood in the spotlight in the 1940s and 1950s, Martin made exceptional contributions to the NAACP's efforts during the period. He was especially adept at trial work, and in many transportation and school cases his courtroom contributions equaled those of his law partners. If Martin failed to achieve the historical stature of his officemates, that may reflect both his early death less than fifteen years later and the fact that his demeanor outside the courtroom was more fun-loving and brash than theirs.

Initially, Martin, Tucker, and Ealey mounted a traditional defense focused on due process and errors of law. But when the Virginia Supreme Court of Appeals rejected those arguments, Martin saw only one approach that might save the men: a direct assault on the constitutionality of the death penalty as administered in Virginia. An unexpected discovery bolstered their case.[66] Assigned the task of securing a complete list of Virginia death-row prisoners convicted of rape, Ealey and Tucker were stunned to discover that since 1908, when the state assumed responsibility for executing convicted prisoners, every single one of the forty-five men electrocuted for the crime of rape had been black. Considerable evidence suggested that the record stretched back even farther. Just as NAACP strategy in housing and education had shifted into more abstract phases, so Martin and his associates began deconstructing the underpinnings of a criminal-justice system in which a particularly gruesome punishment was reserved for one racial group.[67]

As the case wound through a succession of courtrooms, jurists at every turn rebuffed the unfair-trial, equal-protection argument. As January 1951 passed, Martin and his colleagues launched a final sprint to persuade some judge, court, or politician to prevent the now-imminent executions. On the evening of February 1, as Martin and Tucker rushed to Washington to appeal for Supreme Court intervention, Hill and Robinson met with Governor Battle to plead for mercy. After their departure, the governor announced that he would sanction no further delays. Hours later, just after midnight, Martin, Tucker, and the NAACP attorney Frank D. Reeves were ushered into the Washington hotel room of Chief Justice Vinson, where they pleaded for ninety minutes. Already, Vinson observed, his court had twice refused to review the case. He would not now circumvent those decisions. His was to be the final word. At eight o'clock that morning, February 2, 1951, Joe Henry Hampton, who had been the first of the Martinsville men to approach Floyd, was led to the death chamber. The executioner administered twenty-eight hundred volts of electricity, and Hampton was pronounced dead at 8:12 a.m. Over the next several days, six other men would walk the same path.[68]

Many years later, Nina Robinson Govan still recalled the day the executions began. At the scheduled time, "we were in the house somewhere. Everything stopped, and dad said, 'We'll have a moment of silence.' The case wasn't about whether those men were guilty. It was a dual standard," she said. "Dad was really hurt by that case."[69] Robinson had dealt with families evicted from their homes because of their race. He had talked with teenagers deprived of upper-level courses and forced to spend hours on a school bus because they were black. He had seen youngsters educated in drafty, substandard classrooms and grandmothers jailed for refusing to surrender a bus seat, all because of their color. But he had never seen seven lives snuffed out in one fell swoop for a crime in which they had participated unequally and for an offense that netted white men only prison terms, if that. The NAACP lawyers had experienced unprecedented success in recent Supreme Court rulings. They might be on the verge of even more momentous triumph. Yet rarely had the consequences of being born black in America appeared so stark.

CRUCIBLE, 1950–1963

One remarkable thing about our country—if you're right,
you stand a fairly good chance of changing minds.
—Spottswood W. Robinson III

ELEVEN

Child Crusade in Prince Edward County

The letter launching the most consequential case of Robinson's and Hill's careers arrived at the law office on April 24, 1951, a day after it was signed, stamped, and posted by Barbara Johns and Carrie Stokes.[1]

> Gentlemen:
>
> We hate to impose as we are doing, but under the circumstances that we are facing, we have to ask for your help.
>
> Due to the fact that the facilities and building in the name of Robert R. Moton High School, are inadequate, we understand that your help is available to us. This morning, April 23, 1951 the students refused to attend classes under the circumstances. You know that this is a very serious matter because we are out of school, there are seniors to be graduated and it can't be done by staying at home. Please we beg you to come down at the first of this week. If possible Wednesday, April 25 between 9:00 a.m. and 3 p.m.
>
> We will provide a place for you to stay.
>
> We will go into detail when you arrive.

Robinson and Hill sympathized with the plight outlined in the girls' letter. The rebellious spirit of the young people impressed them. They needed no tutorial in the long and futile history of efforts to improve the Robert Russa Moton High School. Hill had witnessed the shortcomings firsthand during visits to the county. The men were familiar also with the myopic mind-set of white officials in southern Virginia regarding race and education. With straight faces, white school officials insisted they were doing all in their power to correct the sorry state of many black schools, even when such efforts dragged on for years without notable result. Still, the Moton students were angling for a better black school, and the attorneys had washed their hands of separate but equal.

Prince Edward County, a rolling stretch of small-acreage tobacco farms, pine-scented woodlands, and a few low-wage industries, could have served as a poster child for the region's disregard of black education. Moton had been overcrowded almost from the day it opened in 1939. Now conditions that once posed an inconvenience had evolved into a crisis. Just over 450 students crowded daily into a facility intended for 180. The school had no cafeteria, no science laboratory, no gymnasium, and no industrial-arts or woodworking shop. County officials had dawdled for years over plans to construct a new black school. So far, their only tangible advance had been the erection of three temporary wood-frame outbuildings wrapped in smelly tar paper and bearing an unsettling resemblance to chicken coops. In inclement weather, students dashed through slush and mud to classrooms where, depending on the proximity of their desks to an oil-drum heating stove, they either shivered or sweltered. Occasionally, a hot coal popped onto the floor through a crack in one of those stoves.[2]

Despite Moton's obvious shortcomings, Hill and Robinson's sights were set elsewhere. Almost ten months had passed since the NAACP Legal Defense Fund had charted its new course on school desegregation. The group had vowed to take no new school cases unless they demanded full integration—although that particular word was not yet in vogue, *desegregation* being the preferred term. Already cases challenging the *Plessy* doctrine were advancing in several states and the District of Columbia. The Virginia lawyers envisioned joining that cavalcade shortly with a new assault in Pulaski County or perhaps one of the state's major cities. Despite the Fourth Circuit's clear ruling that Pulaski's consolidated black high school flunked *Plessy*, the fortunes of black students in the western Virginia county had stalled. On the day Barbara and Carrie's letter appeared in the office mail, the lawyers were busy drafting legal papers asking the court to enroll black youth in Pulaski County's white schools.

Convincing ordinary, black Virginians that their primary goal should be racially mixed schools had not been a snap. The previous fall, not long after the NAACP unveiled its new strategy, the Virginia Teachers Association had battled for hours over whether to endorse the call for desegregation.

Finally, the exhausted educators, many of whom feared for their jobs if integration became the new order, had adopted a resolution condemning segregation as "the antithesis of American democracy." They had stopped short of embracing full desegregation.[3] Spot Robinson had lost patience with such thinking. In an education forum at Virginia Union in January he scolded doubters. If the NAACP had waited patiently for segregation laws to be repealed, Robinson advised the crowd, Heman Sweatt would not have been enrolled at the University of Texas Law School or Gregory Swanson at the University of Virginia's. The organization was going forward on the assumption that "segregation laws are unconstitutional, null and void."[4]

At a regional NAACP conference on April 22 in Sussex County, Virginia, Robinson again sought converts. Recently named the NAACP's regional counsel for the Southeast, he elaborated on hopes that a federal court would bar segregation in at least one southern school system before the year was out. The most likely candidate, he noted, was Clarendon County, South Carolina, where a case was scheduled for trial in late May. Robinson was not an orator, but his intellect and calm inspired confidence. The delegates embraced the push for full integration "without qualification," the *Afro-American* reported.[5] As he spoke, Robinson had no clue that over the next twenty-four hours, a few counties away, events would unfold to trump all his years of preparation for an attack on *Plessy*. On that pleasant spring afternoon, Barbara Johns was quietly preparing to execute the covert operation she had conceived the previous autumn. She and a handful of coconspirators met at the home of Carrie Stokes and her brother, John, for a final review. "We checked the weather report," recalled John Stokes. "We wanted to be certain that the weather was going to be good the next day. Next, we reviewed everyone's responsibilities to make sure that each person understood what he or she was supposed to do. At last, we were ready."[6] The best-laid plans of lawyers, educators, and politicians were about to take a backseat to those of a handful of children—especially the bravest among them, Barbara Rose Johns.

For all its similarity to dozens of other small counties in the loamy Black Belt region, which stretches from southern Virginia to eastern Texas, Prince Edward County at midcentury differed from the others in at least two important ways. It was home to two small, respected institutions of higher learning—Hampden-Sydney, a private college for men whose charter predated the Declaration of Independence, and Longwood College, the state's first public college for women. Those establishments, while hardly bastions of progressive thought, did breed an uncommon appetite for education and, over time, a few white voices willing to challenge prevailing social norms. Also, Prince Edward was the birthplace and occasional home of the Reverend Vernon Johns, a brilliant, polarizing black minister whose passion and fearsome intellect helped mold the two most memorable protagonists in the long drama that opened in the county in 1951: the Reverend Leslie Francis Griffin and Barbara Johns.

Born and reared in the rural Darlington Heights section of the county, Vernon Johns from boyhood displayed an inquisitive, outsized personality that the honeysuckled back roads of his native region could not contain. With his mastery of Greek and Hebrew, his reputed ability to quote the entire biblical book of Romans from memory, and his facility for persuasion and debate, he blustered and dazzled his way into an increasingly impressive list of schools and pastorates. By middle age he had emerged as one of the most renowned black scholar-ministers in America. At the Dexter Avenue Baptist Church in Montgomery, Alabama, whose pastorate he assumed in 1948 and where he preceded the Reverend Martin Luther King Jr., Johns thrilled and annoyed his congregation with a mix of erudition and eccentricity. His soaring sermons drew packed audiences, but he also might embarrass the deacons by showing up in muddy or unlaced shoes or by hawking watermelons from the back of a pickup truck in the off hours.[7]

Pastor Johns's restlessness regularly brought him and his accomplished pianist wife, Altona Trent Johns, back to the family home place in Prince Edward County. During those sojourns, his intellect and magnetic personality entranced, among others, Francis Griffin, the son of one of his local ministerial friends, and Barbara Johns, the daughter of Vernon's much younger brother, Robert. The two admirers came from separate generations. They were not even affiliated with the same church. But inspired by Johns, their ambitions for their race merged in the student walkout that enflamed Moton High School in April 1951. Francis Griffin arrived in Prince Edward County in 1927 at age ten. His father, Charles, had left a large church in Norfolk to assume a quieter, small-town pastorate. His new charge, the First Baptist Church (colored), sat as a stolid brick sentinel at the gateway to the busy main shopping street in the county seat of

Farmville. Within eyeshot, across the road and slightly to the left, lay the Longwood campus, a leafy repository of learning for young ladies (white). True to its name, First Baptist was the wealthiest and most established of Prince Edward's several black churches, affording its first family an instant cache. It was only natural that the Reverends Griffin and Johns would become friends. They were leading spiritual voices in the community, well-read, and aware of a larger world. So when young Francis finished the limited public education then available to black children in the county, he wound up from time to time in the Johnses' home, delving into a library more extensive and diverse than any other available to him. He respected his father, but his ideas tilted toward Johns's vision of a religion grounded in the here and now rather than in heavenly portals.[8]

Francis did not go straight to the ministry. A lively and headstrong youth, he served apprenticeships in the secular world, hitchhiking his way to California and back, earning passage on Florida fishing boats, and supporting himself with odd jobs in New York and North Carolina. World War II halted the meandering. The strapping young man enlisted in the army, eventually reaching Europe with the 758th Tank Battalion, a unit of black soldiers serving under General George S. Patton. Somewhere amid the carnage of war, Griffin resolved to follow in his father's footsteps if he was so fortunate as to survive. Returning to civilian life, he quickly completed a high-school degree and enrolled in Shaw University, in Raleigh, North Carolina. Soon he had a wife, a young son, and a rendezvous with destiny.[9] Griffin returned to Prince Edward County for good in the fall of 1949. When Charles Griffin died soon afterwards, the First Baptist congregation tapped Francis to fill his father's shoes. Quickly, the thick-set young preacher with a booming voice and friendly manner emerged not only as a spiritual leader but as a political one as well. "My dad was a great preacher," Leslie "Skip" Griffin Jr. has recalled. "But mostly he was a natural organizer. He could tell you who was with him and who was against him. Every encounter was an organizing opportunity; everything was purposeful."[10]

The members of the all-white county school board most assuredly were not with Griffin in the months leading up to the Moton High student strike. As head of both the local NAACP and the building committee of the Moton Parent Teachers Association, Griffin had become a fixture at school-board meetings, pushing and prodding for a new school. He drew inspiration from the iconoclasm and temerity of Vernon Johns, who continued to be a regular presence in Prince Edward even as his reputation in Montgomery grew. In December 1950 Griffin learned that the school board had identified a likely spot for a new high school. Two months later county supervisors authorized eight thousand dollars for a possible purchase. But during a meeting in early April the school superintendent reported that the land negotiations had failed. With potentially lengthy condemnations proceedings looming, the board advised Griffin that he need not return anytime soon. "After two years, they told me not to come back any more," Griffin recalled. "They would let me know when it was time to build a school. Before the PTA could decide what to do next, the kids went out on strike."[11]

The mastermind of that bold action was a sixteen-year-old junior, a fresh-faced beauty with wide cheeks, almond-shaped eyes, and a radiant smile. Barbara Johns's poise and determination belied her young age; in retrospect, even she seemed surprised by the serenity with which she had asserted herself during the two weeks of the strike. In later years, after she became a minister's wife, she took to explaining her actions as providential. Barbara's classmates described her as "quiet," a label her family found odd; there was nothing hushed about the Barbara they knew. She was introverted and studious, yes, but as with her revered Uncle Vernon and her paternal grandmother, the indomitable Sallie Price Johns, there was "a lot of spirit about her, no-nonsense," recalled Barbara's younger sister, Joan Johns Cobbs. Within the family, "she was strong-willed, outspoken."[12]

Prince Edward's student strike was not the first of the era, and it may be that Barbara found inspiration in hearing of others. The sociologist Christopher Bonastia identified fourteen school-related, student boycotts between 1943 and 1951, including two in North Carolina. At Moton, the music teacher Inez Davenport told her students—including Barbara—about a student strike in Massachusetts in support of higher teacher salaries. That planted an idea with the observant pupil, who later asked Davenport whether she thought such an action could succeed in Prince Edward County.[13] "Why not? You think about it," replied Davenport, who would soon find herself in the thick of the controversy as the bride of Moton's popular and outspoken principal, M. Boyd Jones. Barbara did think on the matter, and in the fall of 1950 her thoughts turned to action. She summoned Carrie and John Stokes and two other students to a private huddle on the concrete bleachers of the athletic field. There, she unveiled her idea for a walkout. Twins, Carrie and John were student leaders whose family occupied a position of respect within the community. Over the next several months, the fledgling group slowly expanded the list of conspirators, taking care to include only reliable students who could be trusted with the secret. By April 1951 the list had grown to twenty. According to John Stokes, the young upstarts dubbed their scheme the Manhattan Project, a nod to America's covert plan to develop an atomic weapon during World War II.[14]

The operation went into action shortly before eleven o'clock the morning of Monday, April 23. The opening ploy involved an anonymous telephone call to Principal Jones falsely informing him that a couple of Moton students were in trouble at the Greyhound bus station. Jones quickly left the school to investigate. The planners moved on to step two, distributing a note directing teachers to bring their students to the auditorium for a special assembly. Barbara Johns signed the directive with her initials, conveniently identical to those of Principal Boyd Jones. As the students packed into Moton's central auditorium, a deep purple curtain shielded the stage from view. When it opened, Joan Johns, then an eighth grader, gasped. There sat her sister, Barbara, and a few other students. The group first asked the teachers to leave, explaining that the adults should not be blamed for what the students were about to do. Most exited voluntarily, although one male teacher had to be escorted out. Then Barbara calmly explained that she and others were proposing a student walkout. Moton's shortcomings—the science "lab," where students crowded around a single microscope; the "lunch" program, whose sole offering was either plain or chocolate milk; the makeshift "classrooms" in a corner of the auditorium and even on a school bus—needed no elaboration. All of them knew that efforts toward improvement had languished for years. Now, Johns insisted, the students must vow not to return to class until the officials who ran the county gave them a timetable for fixing the mess.[15]

"We thought it was just going to be a regular assembly," said Joy Cabarrus Speakes, recalling the morning. Years later, Speakes would rise to a position of corporate responsibility in New York City, but in 1951 she was a mere twelve-year-old, amazed at what was unfolding before her eyes. "The curtains opened, and there were Barbara and John and Carrie Stokes. Barbara started to give a speech about why we should not accept second-hand books. Her sister Joan was three seats ahead of me." Embarrassed, Joan was sliding down in her seat. "Barbara didn't seem the type of person to do this, although she had it in her genes." Later, Speakes came to believe that a force greater than any individual student had propelled the events. "It was the time. Barbara was the catalyst to carry it out. She said, 'Just follow me,' and she walked out the back door." For the rest of the day, some students tramped the Moton grounds, lofting premade signs with messages such as "Down With the Tar Paper Shacks." Others returned to their classrooms but refused to do any schoolwork. The organizing committee unsuccessfully attempted to present their demands to the school superintendent Thomas J. McIlwaine at the school board offices downtown. Francis Griffin proved more accessible. In future years, the minister would join Principal Jones and other black leaders in steadfastly denying any preknowledge of the students' plans, but Griffin quickly came to their defense. Meeting by request with Johns and others, he advised contacting the NAACP's lawyers in Richmond, Robinson and Hill. Together, Barbara and Carrie composed their "We-hate-to-impose" letter. They posted it that day.[16]

If the students had expected next-day coverage in the state's major newspapers, they were disappointed. National and regional news dwarfed the grievances of a few hundred black students in an out-of-the-way hamlet. On the Korean Peninsula, a long-awaited Chinese Spring Offensive was pressing south toward Seoul. Two days earlier in New York, an estimated 7.5 million people had turned out to cheer a defiant General Douglas MacArthur, newly relieved of his Korean command by an increasingly unpopular President Truman. And across the South, a three-week-old strike by textile workers had turned ugly. The commonwealth's attorney in Danville soon would threaten to seek the death penalty for anyone convicted of throwing explosives into homes.[17]

The first account of the Prince Edward strike ran in the Richmond newspapers on the morning of Wednesday, April 25. As fate would have it, publication coincided with Robinson and Hill's planned trip to Pulaski, where they intended to pursue their ongoing court case. The morning paper confirmed that 455 Moton High pupils had walked out to protest inadequate facilities and were still on strike. The walkout had followed an assembly described as "so overcrowded that breathing was difficult." School officials appeared "slightly dismayed" by the action since they were planning a new, eight-hundred-thousand-dollar black high school. The officials acknowledged that the county had not yet applied for release of the state funds, however. How long that would take or when work might begin, no one could say.[18]

After receiving the students' letter, the lawyers informed the young rebels that they would be driving to Pulaski on Wednesday. They promised to stop by Griffin's church on the way, and they urged the students to come accompanied by their parents.[19] The group setting out from Richmond included Dean Thomas Henderson, of Virginia Union, who regularly testified in NAACP school lawsuits. The stopover in Farmville seemed almost an afterthought. "Tom Henderson said we thought so little of that case that—we were pulling out of Richmond, and I said, 'Oh Tom, I forgot to tell you, on our way to Pulaski we've got to stop for about a half an hour or so and take care of a little matter up in Farmville,'" Robinson recalled years later. "Our idea was to talk to the kids up there. Just what we were going to do depended on a whole lot that we didn't know." Both Hill and Robinson expected to inform the students of the NAACP's push for school integration in South Carolina and then urge the students to return to school while waiting for the momentous case to wend its way through the courts.[20]

Arriving in Farmville, the travelers stretched their legs and entered the community room at First Baptist. Empty, the gray room could seem chilly and unwelcoming. But a buzz of young voices and teenage energy lightened the air. There were fewer adults present than the attorneys had hoped. With eyes on their watches, they pressed forward. After hearing the students' complaints and plans, Robinson decided to test their mettle. What did they intend to do, he asked, if the county refused to meet their demands? The strike would continue, someone replied. They were not going to quit without reaching their goal. Did the students understand that they were violating school-attendance laws, possibly subjecting themselves or their parents to jail? They had thought that through, came the reply. There simply was not enough jail space in Prince Edward County to contain them all. How about seniors? Did they realize that the seniors might not be able to graduate if the strike continued? They were prepared to accept that consequence, the students said.

The NAACP lawyers were continually trying to ignite the passions of black citizens. Now here stood a group of students who were prepared to put themselves and their futures on the line for justice. How could the elders say no? "I turned to Oliver. I said, 'Getting these kids back in school ain't going to be the simple matter I thought it was,'" recalled Robinson. "On top of that, I'm not going to break their spirit. Let's go on up to Pulaski, come back, sit down and talk about it, see if we can't come up with something." Hill agreed, settling the matter. "So, I told them if their parents—that we weren't thinking in terms now of better facilities, but of eliminating segregation—that if their parents were willing to support them in that, we would take over the case," said Hill.[21] In a 1971 interview, Barbara Johns Powell recalled the seismic shift in thinking brought on by the lawyers' visit. When the strike began, "we weren't after integration then, just equality," she said. When Hill and Robinson explained that they wanted to sue for desegregation, "it seemed like reaching for the moon." But there was something about the two men that inspired confidence. "They believed that they could win." Of the leaders she had known, only her Uncle Vernon had seemed comparable—"assertive and confident."[22]

Over the next ten days, as the strike continued, two meetings cemented the deal. The next evening, Thursday, April 26, Lester Banks drove from Richmond to speak at a gathering of the Moton Parent Teachers Association at the high school. Hundreds attended. Banks repeated that the NAACP would take the case only if the adults were willing to push for a desegregated school system. A new black school would not guarantee equality, he said. To the contrary, "if it were built brick for brick, cement for cement, the prestige could not equal that of a white school because of discrimination." After Banks spoke, the parents voted to ask the NAACP to intervene. The *Afro-American* reported that only one speaker challenged the shift in strategy.[23] The clarity of that report counters later claims that the parents who joined the NAACP lawsuit in Prince Edward County did not know that they were asking for integration over equalization. Anyone who did not understand had not been listening.

A second opportunity for awareness occurred a week later, on the night of Thursday, May 3. That morning, the Hill law firm had filed a petition with the Prince Edward County School Board on behalf of thirty-three students asking for an end to segregated schools in Farmville and Prince Edward County. The lawyers demanded a reply within five days. If none came, they intended to take the matter to court.[24] Three days earlier, on April 30, Robinson and Hill had done just that in Pulaski County, filing a motion in federal district court seeking desegregation of the county's white high schools. The evening meeting in Prince Edward would determine whether a second community was committed to similar action.[25] This time, organizers held the gathering in the sanctuary of First Baptist. And this time, more than enough parents attended to make the event a referendum on action.

An overflow crowd milled outside as robust strains of "My County 'Tis of Thee" quieted and Robinson spoke. He informed the audience of the school-board filing earlier in the day. Preparing for that action, the lawyers had confirmed that the total value of the Moton school plant was $120,700, while the combined value of the county's two white high schools was $592,500—this in a county where more than half the school population was black. Given such blatant discrimination, "there is no other solution than to eliminate the policy of racial segregation that brought about Moton as a colored school and the others as white schools," Robinson said.[26] Now, having won the action they sought, the students could return to school on the following Monday, he advised. "Some 1,000 cheering voices rocked the place. Stomping feet shook the floor. Some persons shouted, 'Amen.' Some cried," the *Afro-American* reported. As Robinson finished, a former Moton principal interrupted from the floor. All eyes turned toward Joseph B. Pervall. "I was under the impression that the pupils were striking for a new building," he said, casting a severe gaze on the previous speaker. "You are pulling a heavy load, Mr. Robinson, coming down here to a country town like Farmville and trying to take it over on a non-segregated basis." A few moments of confused silence followed. Then, Banks reminded the audience that just a few days earlier the Parent Teachers Association had voted for desegregation. Robinson echoed the defense. "I don't think we have brought something novel and of a radical manner to Prince Edward, for what you overlook is that this is something people had been ready for a long time ago," he said. "Are non-segregated schools what you want?" Robinson asked the audience in order to be sure. Loud applause signaled approval.[27]

In the night's most dramatic moment, the young heroine of the two-week saga then walked unbidden to the podium and hushed the crowd. As a thunderstorm threatened outside, a wave of human electricity swept the pews. Barbara Johns spoke quietly, forcefully, and without notes. "Don't let Mr. Charlie, Mr. Tommy or Mr. Pervall stop you from backing us," she urged. "We are depending on you." She reminded the audience of Moton's limitations—no showers, no gymnasium, only two drinking fountains that worked, only two working basins in the girls' restroom, the inadequate heating system, and so on. "Back the pupils up in getting a non-segregated school," she pleaded.[28]

Two other speakers made impassioned pleas before the lights dimmed. While American soldiers were making democracy safe in Korea, it was just as necessary to make democracy safe in America, Oliver Hill admonished. He prompted sustained applause and shouts of approval when he advised deposing Superintendent McIlwaine. "You ought to get rid of him just as quickly as you can," Hill said. Finally, Reverend Griffin closed out the evening with a message that left no doubt about his loyalties. While Pervall and others had a right to disagree, Griffin said, "anybody who would not back these children after they stepped out on a limb is not a man. Anybody who won't fight against racial prejudice is not a man."[29] When the applause faded, what remained was the image of a young girl daring adults to match her courage. "I was amazed, overwhelmed, and proud of Barbara," said Joy Cabarrus Speakes, who sat in the audience, rightly fearing what might come next. "I wondered what was going to be the result. Will my grandparents be hurt? Would their farm be taken away from them?" That night, "I was thinking how much my grandfather loved what he had. You wouldn't want what we did as students to hurt him."[30] Hers was not an idle worry.

Shortly, Governor John S. Battle issued an ominous and prescient warning to blacks intending to push for integrated schools. "This movement to abolish segregation in public schools is going to practically wreck the public school system if it succeeds," Battle said. "I believe that there are a lot of people in Virginia who just would not send their children to mixed schools." White parents would steer their children into private schools, a step most black parents could not afford, he predicted. "I think that the responsible colored leaders should think a long time on this thing."[31] Responsible black leaders had done all the thinking they intended to do. When the Prince Edward County School Board did not reply to the NAACP petition for an end to segregated schools, the attorneys took the promised next step. On Wednesday, May 23, Spot Robinson walked down Capitol Hill to the federal courthouse and filed *Davis v. County School Board of Prince Edward County* on behalf of 74 parents representing an astonishing 118 Moton students, a quarter of the student body. The three signatories to the historic document were Hill, Robinson, and Martin.[32] By happenstance, they put first on the lawsuit the name of Dorothy Davis, a shy ninth grader who had played no particular role in the strike. Listed much further down were Barbara and Joan Johns, Carrie and John Stokes, and Joy Cabarrus. One name that did not appear was that of Elwilda Allen, the eighth-grade representative for the planning committee. Elwilda's mother worked for the school board, and she could not afford to jeopardize her job by joining the litigation. No matter. As a consequence of the strike and her daughter's role in it, her contract was not renewed. She was forced to find work in another county. "I grew up without a mother during my teenage years," said Elwilda Allen Isaacs, recalling the price of her activism. "I'm sad about that. I only saw her from Fridays to Sundays."[33]

Some other parents were denied store credit or pressured for rent payments because of their children's involvement in the strike. Principal Jones also fell victim to white wrath. In July the school board refused to renew his contract. With a young wife and a baby on the way, he left Virginia for Montgomery, Alabama, where he landed a job teaching math and physics at the Alabama State College. The joint committee for salary equalization of the NAACP and the Virginia Teachers Association approved a $150 payment "to tide him over." Barbara Johns also escaped to Montgomery. Worried for her safety, Barbara's parents sent her to live with her Uncle Vernon and Aunt Altona for her senior year of high school. "It was a hard decision and very upsetting to us," recalled her younger sister, Joan Johns Cobbs, but security concerns outweighed disruption to the family.[34] As for Reverend Griffin, when rumblings surfaced of an ouster attempt by conservative members at First Baptist, he survived by seizing the initiative. On a Sunday morning in late July, he gambled on his future from the pulpit. Taking as his text Isaiah 40: 4–5 ("Every valley shall be exalted, and every mountain and hill shall be made low . . ."), Griffin poured his heart into a forty-five minute sermon about the devastation wrought by Jim Crow. "I'm willing to die rather than let these children down. No one's going to scare me from my convictions by threatening my job. All who want me to stay as the head of the church, raise your hands," he concluded.[35] In that moment he secured his job. Prince Edward had never been intended as a national battleground for desegregation. Its assent was an accident of history. Hill, Robinson, Griffin, and other elders arrived at the confrontation less as leaders than as followers led to the fray.

TWELVE

Segregation on Trial

Spot Robinson filed *Davis v. County School Board of Prince Edward County* at Richmond's federal courthouse around midday. By nighttime he was aboard a train slicing through the Carolinas toward Charleston's sultry clime and the mannered remains of its plantation caste system. His travel companions—Marshall, Carter, and a little-known psychologist named Kenneth B. Clark—had boarded the train in New York. The addition of Robinson in Richmond reflected Marshall's growing reliance on the brain power and scrupulousness of a man who at first blush did not seem a natural soul mate. The old friends Hill and Marshall shared a boisterous love of life blended with a seriousness of purpose. Robinson seemed cut from different cloth—inexhaustible, less social, and more exacting. Preparing for a case, Robinson rarely diverted his gaze from the grindstone. Once ready, however, he could assume an air of composure that calmed Marshall. "Thurgood's got his peculiarities like I have mine. In time I got to understand him," Robinson explained the relationship, one that deepened during the 1950s. "I am trying to get as close to absolute perfection as I can. Thurgood has always kidded me. He says, 'That's the biggest trouble you have. You're a perfectionist.'" In contrast, Marshall "makes himself appear from the outside very jovial, not exactly happy-go-lucky, but he takes everything in stride easily," Robinson said. Over time, he came to realize that appearances were deceptive. Underneath, "Thurgood is a very intense person. He could get himself all knotted up sometimes in cases, and I occasionally used to tell him, 'Look man. Loosen up. We're going to win this case, I think.' He's a worrier from way back."[1] In such moments,

Marshall relished having at his side a man he could trust to stay steady and give his all.

In many ways the trial that opened five days after the travelers arrived in Charleston proved to be a dress rehearsal for the one that followed nine months later in Virginia. Attorney General Almond acknowledged as much by sending his deputy, Henry T. Wickham Jr., to South Carolina to monitor the proceedings. Robinson's presence during the trial and his participation in the high-spirited preliminary strategy sessions also helped shape the Virginia effort.[2] *Briggs v. Elliott* had been four years in the making. Its genesis dated to 1947, when the Reverend Joseph A. DeLaine, of Clarendon County, attended an NAACP meeting in Columbia and came away incensed that white officials were so indifferent to his people. He resolved to seek a plaintiff to attack what he saw as the most blatant of the injustices, the failure to provide a single school bus for the county's black children. The lawsuit that ensued met an unfortunate demise when the property of the plaintiff turned out to straddle the line between two districts. Levi Pearson paid taxes in one, while his children went to school in the other. That was the end of that, except for the part of the story where Pearson lost his store credit and the bulk of his crops for 1948.[3]

In the spring of 1949 Marshall went to South Carolina to urge Clarendon County blacks to renew the attack on school inequity. Blacks in the sandy-soiled agricultural district southeast of Columbia earned their living mostly as sharecroppers and tenant farmers. Their dependence on white landowners made them vulnerable economically, but Marshall allowed that there might be safety in numbers. Local organizers recruited some twenty courageous souls who agreed to challenge generations of neglect. Harold Boulware, the NAACP's lead lawyer in the state, took charge of the case along with the New York office. Harry Briggs, a Navy veteran who worked on cars and manned the pumps at a gas station in Summerton, wound up first on a petition of complaint. In short order, both Briggs and his wife, Eliza, a motel maid, were fired from their jobs. Other protesters soon found themselves unemployed as well. Even so, the Briggses and some neighbors did not withdraw from the lawsuit, which was filed in May 1950.

A curious development occurred en route to the trial a year later. When Marshall and the others appeared before the federal district judge J. Waties Waring for a preliminary hearing in November 1950, the iconoclastic

liberal judge essentially told Marshall to stop being so cautious. A pedi-
greed member of the Charleston aristocracy, Waring already had burned
bridges by allowing blacks to vote in the state's Democratic primaries.
Now he suggested that Marshall refile the education case to more clearly
test the constitutionality of school segregation per se. Marshall complied,
and the revised challenge went to trial in May 1951 before a three-judge
federal panel. Such tribunals rule on the constitutionality of state laws.
Appeals speed straight to the Supreme Court. The trio in the *Briggs* case
included Waring, an almost certain vote for the NAACP; the district judge
George B. Timmerman, a known segregationist and an equally sure vote
for the status quo; and the Fourth Circuit judge John Parker, a tradition-
alist who had nonetheless sided with the NAACP in *Alston* and several
other cases. What little hope the NAACP had of prevailing shy of the
Supreme Court depended on Parker.

Two features distinguished the proceedings. First, just as the trial was
getting under way, the defense made the surprise admission that Clarendon County's black schools were inferior. They would not contest the
point. Rather, the defendants would argue that the state was doing all in
its power to right the wrongs. The tactic temporarily threw the NAACP
off guard, although Marshall and Robinson gamely proceeded with the
planned grilling of school officials. The team had assigned Robinson to
tackle the chairman of the local school board, Roderick W. Elliott, a sawmill
operator whose name appeared in the formal title of the case. Elliott proved
either so uncooperative or so obtuse that he disclosed almost nothing of
value, and the proceedings moved on.

The most memorable component of the South Carolina trial was the
unveiling of an NAACP strategy aimed at exposing the social and psychological cost of segregation. To attack separate but equal at its heart, the
organization had to do more than document physical inequalities or gaps
in educational success. The NAACP also needed to prove that the mere
fact of racial segregation bred a sense of inferiority in minority students,
no matter how good their schools. That required testimony from eminent
psychologists and sociologists. Carter, Marshall's right-hand man in the
New York office, had been assigned to identify such experts. He had poured
his heart into the job. Kenneth Clark, the man Carter had settled on as his
star witness, had not been his first choice. At thirty-six, Clark was an up-
and-coming assistant professor of psychology at the City College of New

York. Eventually, he would become the nation's preeminent black social scientist, joining B. F. Skinner as one of the first six recipients of the American Psychological Association's prestigious lifetime achievement award. But in 1951 Clark did not quite rise to the level of a dream witness. When hopes for someone with a glossier résumé evaporated, however, Clark met the first essential test: he was willing. He also brought some intriguing research to the table. Clark and his wife and former student, Mamie Clark, were gaining notice for a series of experiments using dolls to assess the attitudes of young children toward race. Presenting a child with four dolls that were identical except for skin tone, the Clarks asked the child to identify the nice doll, the bad doll, the doll he or she liked to play with, and the doll most like him or her. Black children disproportionately favored the white dolls, and the Clarks combined those findings with extensive examination of academic literature in psychology, sociology, and anthropology to conclude that segregation damaged black children from a young age.

Behind the scenes at the Legal Defense Fund, the dolls had stirred up controversy. Some feared ridicule in the courts. Arriving in South Carolina, Robinson himself expressed a bit of skepticism. Carter's certitude won out. Clark's findings about the poor self-image of black children in Clarendon County became a critical part of the trial record.[4] His conclusions were not so powerful, however, as to persuade Judge Parker to break with legal precedent. Three weeks later, in a 2-1 decision, Parker and Timmerman upheld segregation in Clarendon County schools. So long as facilities were made equal, segregation did not violate the Constitution, Parker wrote. "Overwhelming authority"—seventeen states with segregated schools, the Congress, and Supreme Court precedent—supported the conclusion. He could not disregard such consensus "on the basis of theories advanced by a few educators and sociologists."[5] In a passionate dissent, Waring differed: Segregation as practiced in South Carolina schools "must go and must go now. *Segregation is per se inequality.*" It would be Waring's last significant opinion. Shunned and threatened in his home state, he quit the judiciary in disgust the following year and moved to New York, where he resided until his death in 1968. Within days of the ruling, Carter, Marshall, and Robinson had filed an appeal with the Supreme Court.

Throughout the summer and fall, as various challenges to segregated schools navigated the federal courts and as Robinson and Hill prepared to argue *Davis v. County School Board of Prince Edward County,* other events vied for attention. A boycott against segregated seating at the Mosque, Richmond's largest public forum, led to a federal district court date in which Robinson, Hill, and Marshall urged a three-judge panel to strike down the state's Jim Crow law on public assemblage. "The Supreme Court should stop beating around the bush and dodging this issue," said an exasperated Robinson in court. The situation was not grave enough to invoke the court's power, the judges countered. If the lawyers wanted to engage the federal judiciary, they should get themselves arrested, fined, or otherwise criminally punished.[6] In early January, Hill's political acumen and his loyalty to Harry Truman in the 1948 presidential election earned him a turn in the national limelight. Concerned that contractors were discriminating in awarding government contracts, Truman had issued an executive order in early December setting up the Committee on Government Contract Compliance. At a January press conference, he announced six citizen members of the committee, including Hill. In an era when presidential appointments of blacks remained rare, Hill's selection was a coup. Any thoughts of another run for the city council died with it. The citizen post, combined with his law practice, precluded other public service, he said.[7]

The appointment was a bright spot at the end of a horrific holiday season. On Christmas night a bomb had gone off under the white-frame home of Harry Moore, Lester Banks's counterpart in the Florida NAACP. Moore had died before reaching a doctor; his wife had survived for only a week. The deaths had occurred amid outrage over a criminal case originating in Groveland, Florida. The previous April, the Supreme Court had overturned the death sentences of two black men beaten until they confessed to the alleged rape of a seventeen-year-old white woman there. There had been no physical evidence to prove that a rape had even occurred. In a scorching opinion, two associate justices had held that the convictions "do not meet any civilized conception of due process of law." Then, in early November, as the local sheriff was escorting the two men to a retrial, a shooting had occurred, leaving one of the prisoners dead and the other clinging to life. Sheriff Willis McCall had claimed that the two tried to escape. But the survivor said the sheriff had stopped his car on a lonely road, ordered them both out, and shot them in cold blood.[8]

Finally, in mid-February in the southern Illinois town of Cairo, plans to integrate public schools in accordance with state law spawned a wave of violence. Within one week the home of one black activist was bombed, three sticks of dynamite were tossed in front of a shop owned by a local NAACP official, and a shot was fired into the home of third.[9] In that climate of unease, Hill and Robinson prepared for the most important trial of their careers.

Davis v. County School Board of Prince Edward County opened in federal court in Richmond at ten o'clock on Monday, February 25. Of the five cases eventually combined into the historic assault on segregated schooling in America, the *Davis* case was the last to go to trial. Owing to the prowess of Robinson and Hill, local attorneys played a larger role in arguing it than in any of the other state cases. Their unparalleled experience in confronting the duplicity and delays stemming from school-equalization lawsuits in Pulaski, Arlington, and other localities made them uniquely attuned to false promises. They knew firsthand how fleeting even courtroom victories could be when it came to dismantling discrimination. That knowledge informed and toughened the plaintiffs' resolve. The defense team also showed uncommon sophistication, making the Virginia trial perhaps the premier showcase for the strongest and weakest arguments of both sides. Determined not to let the assertions of Kenneth Clark and like-minded academics pass unchallenged, Virginia's defenders produced recognized experts of their own. They also peppered plaintiff witnesses with barely disguised racist disdain. "I mean are you half-white, or half-colored, and half Panamanian, or what?" pressed T. Justin Moore, the savvy, hard-nosed lead attorney for the defendants, when he began his cross-examination of Clark on day three of the five-day trial.[10]

The ghosts of Virginia's past kept company with the bevy of lawyers, reporters, and Prince Edward citizens who crowded the benches and spilled into the jury box on the trial's opening morning. The grandeur of the historic building housing Richmond's federal courts added an air of consequence and layered history. Within these granite walls the Confederate president, Jefferson Davis, and his advisers had planned strategy during the Civil War. Here, too, amid the richly hued wainscoting, the cast-iron railings and newels, the polished floors of heart pine, Davis had prevailed in a May 1867 hearing, ending with dismissal of his indictment for treason.[11]

As *Davis* opened, nine principal actors took center stage—three attorneys for the plaintiffs, three for the defense, and three jurists. Robert Carter joined Robinson and Hill at the plaintiffs' table. Toughened by his childhood days in Newark and East Orange, New Jersey, the poor boy made good had persevered through Lincoln University, Howard Law, and Columbia University, where he earned a master's degree in law. He trusted his own gut, did not suffer fools, and was known in NAACP circles for his intellect and his stubborn streak. He was "very able . . . a different personality from Thurgood Marshall—a writer, a stylist, a deep thinker, but not a good mixer, particularly with those he considered his intellectual inferior," Hill told Kluger in a 1971 interview. Carter also was more of a risk-taker than his boss, and that trait compelled him to endeavor to unwind the psychological wrappings of segregation.[12]

Justin Moore, a crafty courtroom bulldog and partner in Richmond's premier silk-stocking law firm, Hunton, Williams, Anderson, Gay & Moore, headed the defense. The red-haired, hawk-nosed barrister, a native Louisianan, had arrived in Virginia at age sixteen to attend the University of Richmond. After later excelling at Harvard Law, he had returned to the Old Dominion to teach law, marry well, and carve his niche as a rough-and-tumble adopted son of a patrician state. He blended a dogged work ethic, not unlike Robinson's, with an inborn knack for business, and by the early 1950s he was one of the most sought after utilities lawyers in the nation. Aggressive in the courtroom, demanding in the office, and strait laced in the community, Moore drew corporate clients like ants to honey. Chief among them was the Virginia Electric & Power Company, which he helped shape into a regional force. Despite teaching a popular men's Bible class at the city's First Baptist Church for years, he inspired more trepidation than love. Governor Battle and Senator Byrd could think of no better advocate than the razor-tongued Moore to defend Virginia's honor against what they saw as the northern aggressors.[13] Moore was joined at the defense table by Archibald G. Robertson, a Hunton-Williams associate, and Attorney General Almond. Almond, the Roanoke native and former judge who had dealt even-handedly with Hill from the bench years earlier, had since cast his lot in accord with his political ambitions. Neither Almond nor Robertson intended to yield any quarter in defending Virginia's segregated schools.[14]

The men assigned to decide the case—the appeals-court judge Armistead Dobie and the district-court judges Hutcheson and Bryan—were no strangers to school-segregation issues. All had acknowledged that racially segregated schools must be substantially equal. Would they, like Judge Waring in South Carolina, leap further? None was known as a rebel; there was little reason to expect apostasy now. Though no radical, Dobie did bring a showman's flair to the bench that could amuse or irritate. A seventy-year-old bachelor who would marry for the first time several years later, Dobie wore flashy bow ties and enlivened court proceedings with references to favorite topics, including opera and theater. A former dean of the University of Virginia law school, he had been appointed to a district judgeship by President Roosevelt partly on the recommendation of one of Dobie's admiring law students, Franklin Jr. Less than a year later, Roosevelt elevated Dobie to the Court of Appeals for the Fourth Circuit, where his careful judgments rarely failed to withstand judicial scrutiny. Away from the court, he maintained a reputation as a bon vivant, stemming in part from memories of his joyous exhortations to the University of Virginia football team before homecoming games and in part from his flair for constructing clever drinking songs. "Let No Man seduce us, said Cautious Confucius, Yo Ho, Yo Ho, We'll roll the men down," went one such ditty.[15] By comparison, Hutcheson and Bryan were paragons of propriety. A lover of literature, Bryan occasionally quoted Charles Dickens or Anthony Trollope from the bench—his most flamboyant deviation. On constitutional matters, prior rulings marked him as a legal conservative and strict constructionist. Hutcheson had shown courage as a pioneer in ordering equalized facilities in the cases in Surry, Gloucester, and King George Counties. But there was nothing in the judge's cultural or legal background to suggest that he might set Virginia on a radical new path.[16]

Virginia's Old Guard arrived at the trial ready to defend the state's separation of black and white children as centuries-old wisdom. Segregation remained a morally defensible policy, particularly in light of steady improvements in black schools, the defense lawyers argued in pretrial filings. Moreover, they insisted, continued separation was the only way to guarantee funding of public education. Many whites simply would not pay taxes to send their children to school with black youth. In contrast, the NAACP lawyers and their witnesses came prepared to insist that black children were entitled by the Constitution to equal treatment—now, not at some elusive future date. The mere fact of state-sanctioned segregation buried minority children under a pall of inferiority, Carter, Robinson, and

Hill intended to claim. Robinson opened the much-anticipated trial with a brief, dry recitation of the plaintiffs' principal arguments: the white and black high schools of Prince Edward County were nowhere near equal, and as long as segregation continued, it would be impossible to make them so. Dispelling any doubt that the case marked a departure from past challenges, Robinson promised to "demonstrate by evidence the invalidity of segregation itself."[17]

Surprised by Robinson's brevity, Moore assured the court that he planned a longer preamble. "It is perfectly obvious that we have here a case of statewide importance," he began, prompting Dobie to interject the first of many asides. "I think you have understated it," the judge surmised genially. "I think you can say it is of national importance or even international importance." Taking a cue from the *Briggs* trial, Moore said the defendants—the county school board, the school superintendent, and the Commonwealth of Virginia—agreed that the buildings and equipment in Prince Edward's black and white schools were not equal. However, curriculum, teacher quality, and all else were on a par, he insisted. A replacement school for Moton would soon be under construction and "will be the best high school in that part of the country, white or colored." He reserved his greatest disdain for the idea that segregation per se bred inequality. "It is purely speculation without any proper foundation," bristled Moore. Now hear this, he concluded. If the real purpose of the proceeding was to let black children mix with white in a social way, in school or elsewhere, "the gentlemen are not going to get it—they are not going to get it." Virginia's battle cry had been sounded. The white children of the South would remain pure from the taint of the society's lowest caste.

The first day featured testimony from a series of plaintiffs' witnesses about the condition of Prince Edward schools. The evidence exposed as fraudulent Moore's claim that the Moton and Farmville high schools differed only in their physical plants. The county's white students could take eighteen courses not available to blacks, for instance. The lineup included academic courses such as trigonometry, physics, world history, geography, and Latin, plus assorted industrial-arts classes. The few Moton courses not available to whites were a less academic and less costly lot, such as free-hand drawing and consumer buying. When Dean Henderson compared the value of science equipment at the two schools ($825 at Moton versus $2,875 at Farmville), Judge Dobie could not resist injecting himself into the discourse. As a student at the University of Virginia in the late 1890s, he had taken a course under an esteemed scientist. "I never touched a test tube. We had no laboratory," he regaled the courtroom. Did Henderson not agree that society placed too much emphasis on buildings and equipment and too little "on the man behind the desk?" Henderson gamely concurred, but he suggested that Dobie might enjoy sampling a modern science class.

Day two of the trial belonged to Carter and his laboriously constructed lineup of psychologists and sociologists. Despite a snowfall the previous night, a contingent of Prince Edward's black parents and community leaders filled the courtroom. Their presence offered ballast to black lawyers pitted against a formidable white power structure, and it reminded the judges of the real lives behind the court case.[18] The fate of the claim that segregation in and of itself constituted discrimination rested on the shoulders of a handful of New York academicians. In the months since the *Briggs* trial, Carter had created a small stable of professionals glad to attack school segregation. True to promise, Moore bared lawyerly fangs in response. He aimed to undermine the reliability of the experts' scholarship, while subtly mocking them as racial, ethnic, and geographic outsiders.

John J. Brooks, director of New York City's experimental, interracial New Lincoln School, took the stand first. Carter had scarcely uttered his initial question about the impact of segregation on the citizenship of black students when Moore pounced. "This line of testimony is immaterial and irrelevant and has nothing to do with constitutional rights," he insisted. Dobie acknowledged his own skepticism, but in perhaps the most critical ruling of the trial, he agreed to let Carter go forward. Under a national spotlight, Dobie had no intention of abetting accusations of bias. Freed to continue, Brooks suggested that democracy itself was on trial in the Richmond courtroom. It must be "very confusing and very frustrating" to black students to be taught the tenets of American belief and then kept cordoned off from the bulk of society, he said. Brooks held his own against Moore's cross-examination. What if the black children were given fine school buildings, well-paid teachers, and excellent course offerings—would that not balance the slate? Moore asked. "These are fine things and I am proud Virginia is doing them, but the large teaching salaries, shining buses, fine brick buildings are poor compensation for the humiliation, lack of self-respect, and a restricted curriculum," Brooks replied. Momentarily rebuffed, Moore slyly turned the argument to a topic even more emotional than school mixing: interracial sex. If Brooks's view of segregation prevailed, should not the same principle be applied to intermarriage? "It seems to me this has no bearing on it," objected Carter. Dobie agreed. "I think when you enter the field of [miscegenation], that is a little far removed," he said. He left it up to Brooks whether to answer.

M. Brewster Smith, chairman of the psychology department at Vassar College, testified next. Carter hoped to use Smith to make two points: that old beliefs about intellectual differences based on race had been discredited and that segregation damaged black children emotionally. When individuals refer to the "Negro race," particularly in legal terms as used in the South, "we are using an entirely arbitrary way of categorizing people," Smith informed the court. Moreover, cutting black children off from the dominant white culture "is, in itself, bound to be impoverishing" for both blacks and whites. He viewed segregation as "a social and official insult." "Did it ever occur to you," Moore shot back, "that perhaps there might be a corresponding insult to people in Virginia and some of these other southern states if the southern system were done away with?" Smith refused to take the bait. Law-abiding southerners, reared on an American creed of integrity, would come around "once the hurdle is gotten over," he predicted. "Bless you all, you seem to know very little about the South and Virginia particularly," Moore scoffed in reply.

Isidor Chein, director of research at the Commission on Community Interrelations of the American Jewish Conference and a part-time faculty member at the Columbia University School of Social Work, continued the parade of social scientists. Chein described a poll in which 849 of his peers had been asked whether Jim Crow segregation had a detrimental effect on minorities even when facilities were equal. Of the 517 who replied, 90 percent had answered yes. Eighty-three percent thought the majority group also suffered. Chein enumerated the negative consequences: self-doubt, self-hatred, a sense of isolation, cynicism, loss of initiative, and in the worst cases antisocial behavior and a disturbed sense of reality. In a racially segregated system, could there be any circumstances under which black children and white children in Farmville received equal education? Carter asked. "There could be no equality under those conditions," Chein replied. A lunch recess offered a stark example of the indignities inherent in southern separatism. As accomplished attorneys, Robinson, Hill, and Carter traveled among the upper echelons of their race. That did not grant them access to a single lunch counter in the downtown business district. They had to walk twelve blocks to Jackson Ward to find a restaurant that would serve them. The previous day, they had barely made it back to court in time. Could Judge Dobie extend the lunch break to about ninety minutes? "We have a long way to go to get something to eat," Robinson said. Dobie complied.

Back in court that afternoon, Justin Moore trained his heavy artillery on Chein. He began by highlighting the professor's supposedly exotic ancestry.

MOORE: Dr. Chein, just how do you spell your last name?
CHEIN: C-H-E-I-N.
MOORE: What kind of a name is that? What sort of racial background does that indicate?
CHEIN: The name is a poor English version of Hebrew which designates charm.
MOORE: What is your racial background?
CHEIN: I could not give an honest answer to that because of the complexity of the concept. I think what you want to know is, am I Jewish?
MOORE: Are you one hundred percent Jewish?
CHEIN: How do I answer that?
MOORE: I do not know, you know.[19]

Moore turned next to the fact that integration was limited in northern classrooms even though it was allowed. What difference could it possibly make to a child, he asked, whether segregation was based on housing patterns or on a law? "The effect would be much less marked if there were no law," Chein insisted. Moore appeared incredulous, and Chein elaborated: "Yes, that is my opinion, that it is the official sanction which says to the child, 'It is not only a matter of I, John Doaks, don't like you,' but it says to the child that the government of the state of Virginia thinks that you are not fit to associate with white children." Well, then, should not the same logic apply to laws on intermarriage? Moore asked. After a long, elaborate answer, Chein concluded: "I see no reason why individuals should not be able to follow their own choice in terms of skin color."

Next, Hill debriefed Francis Griffin about his role in pushing for a new school. Then Kenneth Clark took the stand as the last witness of the day. By this time Clark had testified in school-desegregation cases in South

Carolina and Kansas, and he was becoming increasingly at ease in a court-room. "I have come to the conclusion that prejudice, discrimination, and segregation in general, each has a basic corroding and distorting effect upon the personality of the Negro child who is a victim of these," he said, after explaining his doll tests. A curious Judge Dobie pressed Clark to elaborate on how segregation impacted learning. Children reacted to racial separatism in several ways: by becoming submissive or rebellious, fighting back constructively, or hating either the perceived persecutors or fellow victims, Clark replied. "You can then see how any situation which constantly reminds the person of his racial inferiority would be a situation in which he could not generally profit."

Finally, Clark described his interviews with fourteen Moton students aged thirteen to eighteen, conducted at the offices of the Hill-Robinson law firm as the trial was getting under way. Clark had pursued four avenues, first asking students, "Tell me about your school" and "Tell me about the white school." After the children identified the white school as better, he asked, "Why is the white school better?" and then, "What can be done about the situation?" He had not done the classic doll tests, he said, because those were intended for younger children. "In every single case," Clark said, the Moton students responded negatively to the first question, about the condition of their school. As for the white high school, "not one negative thing was said or even thought." The youth had mixed explanations for the superiority of that white school. Two blamed the situation on segregation; two said whites wanted "to keep us inferior"; and one said black people were too apathetic. Most offered no opinion. Asked by Carter what conclusions he drew from those findings, Clark replied that the black youth interpreted almost everything in racial terms. The findings, combined with his earlier research and study, supported the conclusion that "probably the most detrimental consequence of segregation is the degree to which it obsesses everybody with race—white and Negro children and adults, churchmen, and laymen." With that, the court adjourned for the day.

Moore arrived for the third day of the trial primed to rip apart Clark's research. The defense attorney regarded it as ridiculous. But first, Moore engaged in the now-familiar tactic of airing Clark's nonsouthern, non–Anglo Saxon roots. The attorney's disdain for the black scholar seemed even more pronounced than his disregard for the white academicians. After establishing Clark's Panamanian birth, Moore pressed forward.[20]

MOORE: In view of your reference to Panama, I must inquire if you know— you appear to be of rather light color—what percentage, as near as you can tell us, are you white and what percentage some other?

CLARK: I haven't the slightest idea. What do you mean by "percentage"?

MOORE: I mean are you half white, or half colored, and half Panamanian, or what?

CLARK: I still can't understand you.

MOORE: You don't understand that question?

CLARK: No. My parents were not born in Panama. My mother and father are from the West Indies. My father was born in Jamaica and so was my mother. They met in Panama, and I was the result.

After a similarly hostile review of Clark's largely segregated education and his limited experience living in the South, Moore turned to the student interviews. Perhaps, Moore innocently suggested, Clark could demonstrate his interview methods by recreating one of the sessions. The social scientist agreed to do so, and a delighted Judge Dobie settled back for the small dramatization. "Make me a child again," the judge quipped.

CLARK: Your name, please.

MOORE: Justin Moore.

CLARK: How old are you, Justin?

MOORE: I will play like I'm 18.

CLARK: What grade are you in?

MOORE: I will be in the tenth grade; I have been a little slow.

CLARK: What school do you go to?

MOORE: I go to the Moton school.

CLARK: What does your mother do?

MOORE: She works. She works on the farm and works every day.

CLARK: What does your father do?

MOORE: He works on the farm too.

CLARK: I would just like to ask you some questions. Tell me about your school.

MOORE: Well, it is not much good.

CLARK: Will you tell me about it?

MOORE: Well, we don't have all the things that they have got over at the
  other school. That is what my parents say.
CLARK: I don't remember one of them saying that, by the way. Not one of
  them volunteered information. . . . What about the white school?
MOORE: I hear at home that it is fine. I have never been over there.
CLARK: You hear that it is fine?
MOORE: Yes, that is what I hear.
CLARK: Why is that?
MOORE: Well, they have got more money, I suppose, for it.

After a few more questions, a satisfied Moore called the exchange to
a halt. To his mind, Clark had more than confirmed the absurdity of the
exercise. "Do you seriously contend," Moore bored in, "that a little, three-
minute conversation like we have had, or if you stretch it out to five minutes, really means anything . . . except that they wanted to complain about
their school and they wanted to get another school?" He had never claimed
that the interview results were earthshaking, Clark defended himself, but
neither were they trivial. To truly understand the impact of segregation,
Moore and the court would have to have seen "the shock, the surprise, and
in some cases it even seemed to me like it could be interpreted as horror"
on the faces of the Moton students when asked to imagine the all-white
Farmville High School. The barriers were so profound that they could
barely conceive of an integrated world. "They learn this as if—well, it is
like breathing oxygen—that you don't think in terms of the white school,
you don't think in terms of having the same things which whites have."
Accepting Clark's nuanced argument required a sympathetic ear. Years
later, Archibald Robertson told an interviewer that the play-acting had
"brought the house down. Everyone there enjoyed it, except maybe the
other side." His cocounsel had "put on a moronic face and the accent of a
little darkey." Moore's point had been to make light of Clark's testimony,
not to be nasty, Robertson insisted.[21]

At least one person in the audience failed to see the mirth. When Moore,
moments later, pushed his luck by suggesting that the whole matter came
down to a ploy by the NAACP to "stir up and foment critical situations,"
Hill jumped to his feet. "I challenge Mr. Moore to state any place where
[the] NACCP has been reported as being its policy to foment anything,"

he seethed. "We unquestionably are trying to break up segregation, and everybody will admit that. But if he is going to ask the question, let him ask it fairly." For a moment, two angry raptors hissed at each other with virulent intent. Neither yielded ground. Dobie quickly interceded, and the encounter ended in a draw. Unrepentant, Moore lobbed a final, race-laced question to Clark. Why, he asked, did black people want to be "in the category of what I believe someone has described as a 'sun-tanned white man'"? Recouping from his earlier embarrassment, Clark rallied for the last word. "I do not think that is the desire . . . . I think it is the desire of a Negro to be a human being and to be treated as a human being without regard to skin color. He can only have pride in race and a healthy and mature pride in race when his own government does not constantly and continuously tell him, 'Have no pride in race,' by constantly segregating him, constantly relegating him to a second-class citizen." With that, the plaintiffs rested their case.

The defense team had bared a venal streak in its questioning of the plaintiffs' witnesses. The attorneys switched into a loftier mode as their own witnesses took the stand. Over the next two and a half days a lineup of thoughtful, accomplished citizens explained why in their estimation black children would be best served by continued separation in a new, state-of-the-art high school. There would be no Theodore Bilbos on the witness stand, only intelligent, earnest officials with a paternalistic sense of right. Colgate Darden served as the lodestar. A cultured former congressman and governor, married to an heir of the wealthy DuPont family, then serving as president of the University of Virginia, Darden qualified in many minds as a beacon of southern enlightenment. From the witness stand, he acknowledged that Jim Crow laws had been used as "a shield of oppression," but he insisted that separation and stigma need not go hand in hand. "I think the races separated, if given a fairly good opportunity, are better off," Darden said. That would not be so, however, "unless there is good faith and good purpose and honesty in the giving them that opportunity, black and white alike." Darden did not say how he proposed that past oppression be transformed into future good faith and purpose. In cross-examination, Hill tried to shake Darden's resolve. The former governor remained unruffled.[22]

HILL: Wouldn't Virginians prefer to save money by funding one set of schools rather than two?

DARDEN: I think the net result would be, if mixed schools were compelled, the starvation of them.

HILL: Do you not think it is time that we should give consideration to preparing people of different racial groups to live more harmoniously and to think better of each other?

DARDEN: Yes, I think that as an abstract principle.

HILL: Don't you think that can be better acquired in the laboratory of the public school than anywhere else?

DARDEN: I do not. I don't believe that the condition of knowing people better leads you to like them more. . . . You realize that this problem we are dealing with is a by-product, and a fearful by-product of human slavery. We are the inheritors of that system, and we are attempting to deal with it, both white and colored, in what we perceive to be the most likely fashion.

Finally, Hill gave up.

HILL: Of course, what you have expressed is just your personal opinion.

DARDEN: I said that at the beginning.

Testifying next, Dabney Lancaster, the president of Farmville's Longwood College and a former state superintendent of public instruction, prophesied that Virginia's roughly five thousand black teachers would have trouble earning a paycheck under a mixed-race school system. Many white parents would not tolerate having their children taught by black educators, he predicted. Lancaster said that as a Prince Edward County resident, he saw no evidence that the county's black children were any less happy than the white children. If anything, "the Negro groups are a little bit the happier from my casual observations. Maybe that is due to the fact that the Negro race has a very fine sense of humor. I have seen that throughout my life," he said. Robinson leapt at the stereotype, refusing to let it pass unchallenged. "Wouldn't you consider the fact that an expression outwardly of happiness is, perhaps, a consequence of an oppressed people?" he bore in on cross-examination. "I think that that is possible," Lancaster replied.

As the trial entered its fifth and final day, Dobie promised that the court would toil into the night, if necessary, to complete its work. Both sides still had witnesses to examine, and six attorneys—several prone to long-windedness—had to rehash their arguments through closing statements.[23] Opening the morning session, Leslie Stiles, dean of the University of Virginia's Department of Education, picked up where Colgate Darden had left off. Stiles argued for continuing segregated schools even as he lamented their necessity. He looked forward to the eventual end of the practice, but for now he favored "the administration of the antidote education in ever-increasing dosages, rather than surgery at a time when the patient may not yet have strength to survive the shock." Following Stiles to the witness stand, Dr. William H. Kelly, a child psychiatrist and director of Richmond's Memorial Guidance Clinic, questioned the efficacy of Clark's doll tests. The witness had spent much of his life outside the South, so he could not be dismissed as a chauvinistic defender of southern ways. He was not accusing Clark of wrongdoing, Kelly said, but Clark's interview results could be manipulated and were open to a variety of interpretations. Late in his cross-examination, Carter managed to recoup somewhat from Kelly's damning testimony by drawing an unexpectedly frank admission. Asked about the impact of racial segregation on personality development, Kelly replied bluntly, "I would have to say that it is adverse to the personality."

The defenders of Virginia sovereignty saved for last their most potent witness: Henry E. Garrett, chairman of Columbia University's psychology department and a recent president of the American Psychological Association. Over the next few decades, Garrett would reveal himself to be a strident racial separatist and a believer in the intellectual inferiority of blacks. "Black and white children do *not* have the same potential. They do *not* learn at the same rate," he wrote in 1973, the year of his death. But in 1952, in a Richmond courtroom, other traits stood out about the polished and slightly imperious professor: he had been born in Virginia, he had taught both Clark and Chein at Columbia, and at least on paper his credentials trumped theirs.[24]

Turning to the student interviews, Moore led the willing Garrett through his testimony as smoothly as a dance instructor choreographing a waltz. He began with a critique of Clark's testimony: "In your judgment, was there anything abnormal or particularly striking in the responses he got in this interview test?" asked Moore. "I think if you call in a group of children, who are members of a school that a year before struck for two weeks, if you do not get answers which say, 'We don't think our school is good,' 'we don't think we have been well treated,' and so on, you should be very much surprised," answered Garrett. Garrett's point was hard to argue. Attributing much significance to Clark's interviews with fourteen Moton students seemed dubious. After months of discussion about the limitations of Moton High, students were bound to regard their school as inferior. Moore concluded with the question he had asked almost every witness: if Prince Edward County followed through with its promises to build a superior black high school, if teachers were well trained, and if the curriculum was as good as or better than that at Farmville High, was there any reason to think that black children would not get as good an education there as at the white high school? Garrett gave Moore the answer he wanted—and more. Assuming comparable amenities, "it seems to me that in the state of Virginia today, taking into account the temper of its people, its mores, and its customs and background, that the Negro student at the high school level will get a better education in a separate school than he will in mixed schools," Garrett said. A segregated school would not be just equal, in other words; it would be superior.

It fell to Carter to try to undo the damage. Addressing the fear of mixed schools, he recalled that Attorney General Almond had predicted chaos and even violence if the Supreme Court ordered full integration of graduate and professional programs in Texas and Oklahoma. Now public universities across much of the South were peacefully enrolling black students, albeit still only a handful. Might doubters such as Garrett be just as wrong about the prospects for public schools? Garrett stuck to his beliefs. "The Negro would be much more likely to develop tensions, animosities, and hostilities in a mixed high school than in a separate school," he said. Carter tried again, this time with slightly better results. Did Garrett agree with Dr. Kelly that racial segregation as practiced in the United States and Virginia adversely affected the individual? "In general, whenever a person is cut off from the main body of society or a group, if he is put in a position that stigmatizes him and makes him feel inferior, I would say, yes, it is detrimental and deleterious to him," Garrett acknowledged. Hoping to press the new-found advantage, Carter asked Garrett if he could think of a single place where racial separation existed without stigmatism. The question unleashed a polemic. "I think, in the high schools of Virginia, if the Negro child had equal facilities, his own teachers, his own friends, and a good feeling, he would be more likely to develop pride in himself as a Negro, which I think we would all like to see him do," Garrett began. "The Negroes might develop their schools up to the levels where they would not mix, themselves, and I would like to see it happen. I think it would be poetic justice. They would develop their sense of dramatic art, and music, which they seem to have a talent for—athletics—and they would say, 'We prefer to remain as a Negro group.'" Carter had nothing more to ask. Garrett's answer satisfied Moore, and the defense rested.

Save for closing arguments, the intense sparring was at an end. Stripped of racism and stereotype, of which there had been plenty, the state's case did contain elements of truth. As the next decades would attest, sadly, many white parents would refuse to send their children to public schools attended by large numbers of black children. Many would resist placing their child with a black teacher. For a time, in some places, none more dramatically than Prince Edward County, funding for public schools would suffer as a result of desegregation orders. The plaintiffs also had made sound arguments, however, illuminating larger truths—that numerous localities continued to evade making black and white schools equal, even when courts ordered them to do so; that across continents and decades, critics had forecast doom wrongly and often whenever disadvantaged groups advanced; and most important, that the state simply could not segregate minority children without branding them as inferior. A parade of white officials had engaged in hand-wringing over the potential reactions of white citizens to any desegregation order. Their failure to give equal weight to the aspirations and desires of black citizens underscored once again the racial imbalance in southern culture. Oliver Hill made that case in a closing statement delivered in the final moments of the trial. Outrage caged during the trial's long hours of tedium, insult, and obfuscation unleashed in one of the most eloquent and impassioned pleadings of his career. A death-threat letter delivered to Hill's home three days after the trial began—"You will be taken care of in the near future"—may have spurred anger as well. Some four decades later, sitting for an interview in the same courtroom, he had not forgotten the fury that he felt at Garrett's condescending reference to "Negro pride" and his eclipse of the full humanity of black people.[25]

"Sure, I am proud of the fact that I am a Negro . . . just as I am proud of my college, as I am proud of my high school," Hill ended the *Davis* trial. "I have plenty of pride for myself and for my friends. But what has that got to do with the ordinary affairs of life? It is time for us to wake up and to think in terms of what we want to accomplish in terms of our ideals, in terms of our Constitution, and our religion, and to stop all of this old bunk about white pride and race, Negro pride and race. What was significant about Dr. Garrett's testimony? Dr. Garrett said, 'Yes, they can get equal educational opportunities in separate schools, and I would like to see them build up their schools and develop their talents in music, in rhythm, in athletics.' That is foremost in the minds of these people who want segregated schools. Let a Negro develop along certain lines. Athletics, that is all right. Music, fine—all Negroes are supposed to be able to sing. Rhythm, all Negroes are supposed to be able to dance. But we want an opportunity along with everybody else to develop in the technical fields. We want an opportunity to participate in the business and commerce of this nation. In other words, we want an opportunity to develop our talents, whatever they may be, in whatever fields of endeavor there are existing in this county."

Judges Dobie, Bryan, and Hutcheson had an opportunity to say to the nation that the South could lead from within to abandon a shameful history. They could trust, as did Hill, that law-abiding citizens would rise to the challenge. They could ignore legal precedent and legislative action and rule solely on an understanding of what was just and right under the Constitution. They could, if they would.

The tribunal took just seven days to reject those arguments. On March 7, in a unanimous opinion written by Bryan, the trio sided with Prince Edward County and the state of Virginia.[26] Bryan noted that eminent scholars had testified with equal passion that separation distorted the educational experience of children and that it did not. Meanwhile, evidence "indisputably" showed that racial separation in the schools rested "neither upon prejudice, nor caprice, nor upon any other measureless foundation." Rather, it reflected a way of life. "Separation of white and colored 'children' in the public schools of Virginia has for generations been a part of the mores of her people. To have separate schools has been their use and wont." Bryan singled out the testimony of former Governor Darden as particularly influential. "We believe him delicately sensible of the customs, the mind, and the temper of both races in Virginia," Bryan wrote. In sum, "we have found no hurt or harm to either race. This ends our inquiry."

No hurt or harm whatsoever? A twentieth-century Pontius Pilate had washed his hands of the affair. The state must proceed with "diligence and dispatch" to complete its building program and to equalize curricula and bus transportation in Prince Edward County. But school segregation remained alive and well. "It is not for us to adjudge the policy as right or wrong—that, the Commonwealth of Virginia 'shall determine for itself,'" Bryan dismissed the matter. Hill, Robinson, and Carter had expected little more, but so summary a rejection of their efforts could not help but sting. There would be no Waties Waring in Virginia. *Plessy v. Ferguson* remained intact. Relief, if it came through the courts, would come only from the highest in the land.

THIRTEEN

Face-Off at the Supreme Court

May 17, 1954, is embedded in the American psyche as the date the Supreme Court issued what is arguably the most sweeping decree in its history. Focusing on the single moment when the court ruled segregated schools unconstitutional, however, diminishes the scope of proceedings that spanned almost three years, from June 1952 to May 1955, and required three full-throttle hearings plus two seminal court orders merely to set in place a framework for progress. Even then, it would take many more years and rulings before any semblance of true school integration began to take hold in the South.

With the Fourth Circuit's rejection of a direct attack on segregated schools, *Davis v. County School Board of Prince Edward County* joined four other lawsuits approaching finality in the lower courts. In South Carolina, a three-judge panel, with Virginia's Dobie replacing the liberal Waring, denied further relief in the *Briggs* case just days after the *Davis* ruling. Robinson assisted Marshall and Carter on the losing side, and the trio later delighted in mocking Judge Dobie's three-word admonition after they injected the prospect of integrated schools into the hearing. "Let that alone," Dobie had barked.[1] Meanwhile, in Topeka, Kansas, a group of parents was challenging a state law that permitted localities to segregate children by race in elementary schools. Only a few localities did, but the capital of the agrarian state was among them. Topeka's four all-black elementary schools included the one attended by Linda Carol Brown, a chunky, sweet-faced ten-year-old whose father had tired of her forced trek through railroad switching yards to a bus stop where, he testified, she often had to wait "through the cold, the rain, and the snow" for a bus to show up. Somewhat by chance, Oliver Brown and his daughter had wound up as the first-named plaintiffs on an NAACP lawsuit. A three-judge federal panel had rebuffed them the previous August, despite making the damning admission that segregation harmed black children. Now, the plaintiffs were waiting to hear whether the Supreme Court would take up their challenge.[2]

Two other cases with slightly different legal twists also were travers- ing the courts in the spring of 1952. In Delaware, a few weeks after the *Davis* decree, a state-court judge boldly ordered black children admitted to white schools. Until black and white schools were made equal, plain- tiffs Ethel Louise Belton and Shirley Bulah and other black children de- served admission to white classrooms, said chancellor Collins J. Seitz. Once schools were equalized, however, the children would have to return to segregated classrooms under the *Plessy* doctrine. The state had appealed Seitz's ruling to the Delaware Supreme Court. Meanwhile, in Washington, DC, the teenager Spottswood Bolling Jr. and other students at the run- down, overcrowded Shaw Junior High were awaiting appellate review of a federal judge's dismissal of their bid for an integrated education. Because the Fourteenth Amendment focused on state actions, it did not apply in the nation's capital. The Washington challenge had been brought under the Fifth Amendment, also guaranteeing due process—or fair treatment— to citizens.

The high court had not yet agreed to hear any of those challenges, but optimists in the NAACP believed it was only a matter of time until it would. Meanwhile, the cautious Marshall remained troubled by dissen- sion within the ranks over the aggressive push for school integration. The twentieth anniversary of the publication of the *Journal of Negro Educa- tion* proved an opportune moment to confront lingering doubts. Under the leadership of its founder and editor Charles H. Thompson, in April 1952 the *Journal* convened a three-day conference at Howard University to ad- dress concerns. The symposium drew leading lawyers, social scientists, and community activists from twenty-seven states, including Robinson and Hill.[3] The Virginians' testimony, recorded in Thompson's *Journal*, opens a window to their thinking at the brink of a sea change in American life. Leading off a panel that included the NAACP executive secretary, Walter White, and others, Hill defended bold action in the courts. "We must of necessity go into the court to fight for the elimination of segregation *now*, for the simple reason that it is the only available method of achieving it in any reasonable length of time," the towering attorney insisted. Coming from an expert on the creeping pace of equalization lawsuits, the view carried weight. Then, characteristically, Hill tempered his stridency. While hammering at injustice through the courts, black citizens also ought to appeal to the best instincts of whites by holding small group discussions, he advised. "Let them express their version, give them the valid answers, reason with them and try to develop community sentiment." Delving deeper into his personal philosophy, Hill urged the group to envision the elimination of all racial distinctions, with the ultimate goal "being not just white or colored but just true and simple Americans."[4] In years to come, black militants would join white separatists in rejecting such overtures for a color-blind society. But in Hill's waning days, a half century later, his vision shared at Howard in April 1952 of a universal egalitarianism had not withered.

Robinson also provided the Howard conference with a vigorous defense of the NAACP's push for school integration. Introduced as "a brilliant lawyer," he insisted that the public had pulled the NAACP lawyers toward mixed schools, not the reverse. Robinson's premise was debatable, but he offered two solid pieces of evidence. First, he recalled a meeting in Dinwiddie County, Virginia, south of Richmond, some weeks after the NAACP's historic decision to hit segregation head-on. The Virginia lawyers had been in the early stages of a school-equalization lawsuit in the county, and—with some trepidation—Robinson wanted to explain why the NAACP's position had changed. "I did not know what the reaction might be," Robinson recalled. After a lengthy explanation, he recommended that the Dinwiddie crowd go home to think over the matter. A farmer in the back of the room, dressed in overalls from work in the fields, rose to respond. "I have one question to ask," Robinson recalled the man's saying. "As I understand the position of the NAACP, it is impossible for our children to get equality so long as we have segregation. Is that correct?" "And I said, 'Yes, sir.' He said to me, 'Well, we have in this county known that for a long time, and we have simply been waiting for you and the NAACP to find out the same thing.'" When the laughter subsided, Robinson offered his second argument: the children of Prince Edward County. He and his law partners had had no intention of filing a lawsuit in the racially tense county, but the young people had forced their hand, he said. The walkout had been "the most perfect organization of a movement of that type that I have ever had the pleasure of being associated with." Then, Robinson embraced the NAACP's altered strategy with uncharacteristic eloquence: "With those people who have the determination to go forward, who want these things and who will not wait unless they are given these things, I plan to go hand in hand with them in making this rendezvous with destiny."[5]

Robinson had not always been so sanguine about public support for the changed strategy. Shortly after the Dinwiddie incident, in the fall of 1950, he had advised Marshall confidentially that it probably would be hard to find plaintiffs for an integration lawsuit in Virginia. His worry reflected hints of class division within the Virginia NAACP over the altered strategy. Some grassroots support was shriveling as a result. In the summer of 1952 Dr. Tinsley appealed to the NAACP administrator, Roy Wilkins, for a financial bailout. The state conference was fourteen thousand dollars in the red, Tinsley said in a special-delivery letter. The shortfall reflected opposition among some of the rank and file to the school-desegregation push. "Hence, their support to our defense fund efforts has been materially reduced," he said of donors.[6] Clearly, the push for integrated schools that so inspired some black Americans worried others. But the resolve of neither Robinson nor Hill lessened as the Howard conference adjourned and the movement entered the most pivotal phase yet in the legal war on Jim Crow.

In early September 1952, Marshall summoned his brain trust to the Legal Defense Fund headquarters in New York City for a marathon work session. The nine-story brick-and-limestone structure at 20 West Fortieth Street had been designed by the architect of the Plaza Hotel as a social club for wealthy gentlemen. Acquired by Freedom House, a nonprofit group dedicated to strengthening free societies, the space by the 1950s housed a teeming beehive of progressive groups. Ringing telephones, mounds of paper, and a warren of desks had replaced the building's former quiet elegance.[7] As Marshall prepared for the long-awaited assault on segregated schools before the Supreme Court, the lawyers trekking to Freedom House included, among others, Robinson and Hill from Richmond, W. Robert "Bob" Ming from Chicago, Nabrit from Washington, Hastie and William "Bill" Coleman Jr. from Philadelphia, and Louis L. Redding of Wilmington, a Harvard Law graduate and the first black lawyer admitted to the Delaware bar. They and others joined a staff that included Carter, Marshall's deputy and the lead attorney in the Kansas case; Constance Baker Motley, the LDF's first female attorney; and Jack Greenberg, a bright, young white lawyer and future successor to Marshall, who was working on both the Kansas and Delaware cases.[8] Hill and Robinson contributed the perspective of southerners who had engaged personally in every incremental stage of the push for educational equality. They also brought a lifetime acquaintance with the tradition-steeped mind-set of southern segregationists.

The Supreme Court had set an October date to hear both *Briggs* and *Brown*. Hopes ran high that an appeal of Virginia's *Davis* decision would be combined with the South Carolina and Kansas reviews. Meanwhile, the Delaware Supreme Court had upheld Chancellor Seitz's ruling ordering the integration of unequal state schools. The attorneys in that case, Redding and Greenberg, were holding their breath, hoping that the state would appeal the ruling, thus allowing Supreme Court review. The NAACP attorneys arrived in New York in the midst of a presidential campaign between the military hero Dwight D. Eisenhower and the Illinois intellectual Adlai E. Stevenson II and against a global backdrop of Cold War tension. The battle between the forces of communism and capitalism had reached a seesawing stalemate on the Korean Peninsula. As anticolonial fever gripped Third World capitals and ideological enemies competed for hearts and minds, the mistreatment of black Americans provided rich fodder for Soviet propaganda. Nightmares of a nuclear cloud haunted American schoolrooms, and the dark forces unleashed by the Red-baiting of the Wisconsin Senator Joseph R. McCarthy contaminated the domestic political well.

Even amid such challenges, industrialization, northward migration, and postwar prosperity had strengthened the black political class. Black voter registration in the South, while still anemic, had risen from about 3 percent in 1940 to 20 percent in 1952. Court successes involving transportation and public facilities had relaxed rigid Jim Crow rules somewhat, and many southern communities had begun to accept that blatant inequality in black and white schools could not go on forever. South Carolina, for instance, had levied a 3 percent sales tax and floated a $75 million bond issue for educational improvements. A substantial portion of the money would go to African American schools.[9] Concessions ended when it came to racial mixing of children, however. Seventeen southern and border states, plus the District of Columbia, prohibited mixed-race public schools in 1952, while four other states—Arizona, Kansas, New Mexico, and Wyoming—permitted school segregation. Approximately two-thirds of the nation's black schoolchildren lived in the affected areas, and the prospect of wide-spread intermingling was more than many southern politicians could stomach. Governor James F. Byrnes of South Carolina spoke for many when he threw down a gauntlet at a meeting of the South Carolina Education Association in March 1951. If the high court tried to force integration, "we will abandon the public school system. To do that would be choosing the lesser of two great evils," he warned.[10]

The lawyers who gathered in Manhattan to prepare Supreme Court briefs involving *Brown* recalled smoky rooms, long hours, vigorous debate, and camaraderie born of perilous, high-stakes purpose. "I never had so much fun in my life," recalled Charles L. Black Jr., a Columbia professor who sometimes joined the mix, describing Marshall's magnetism and intellect as he navigated competing personalities and ideas. Late-night rounds of Scotch and bourbon or a few hands of poker often quieted minds and nerves before participants drifted away for a bit of sleep. Robinson remained the technician, the craftsman, carefully isolating weaknesses in language and argument. Hill's specific role is less clear, but he likely excelled at broad strategy as the group weighed critical decisions: how to address *Plessy*, how much to rely on social-science testimony that some found unconvincing, and how to reassure justices worried about volatile public reaction to a desegregation order.[11]

No transcripts of the Legal Defense Fund planning sessions remain, but the briefs the lawyers produced reveal their conclusions: *Plessy* should be treated as a transportation case, not an education one. More recent decisions such as *Sweatt* and *McLaurin*, which spoke to the inherent inequality and injury of an education grounded in mandatory segregation, trumped *Plessy*. Social-science research bolstered the commonsense understanding that forced segregation branded a minority group as inferior. Finally, those who warned of violence and social upheaval had sounded similar alarms before public universities were integrated, yet dozens, even hundreds of black students were peacefully attending those institutions. White southerners were not so lawless as to disobey the highest court in the land—or so the lawyers intended to claim. Robinson stayed behind for an extra week to refine and perfect the language in the briefs. The assignment underscored, once again, Marshall's trust in and reliance on the reserved Virginian.[12]

In mid-October, just before oral arguments were to begin in *Briggs* and *Brown*, the timetable and dimensions of the school-desegregation case changed. The justices added Virginia's *Davis* case to the roster and postponed the hearing until mid-December. They also asked Nabrit, the chief attorney in *Bolling*, to file a petition that would bring the District of Columbia's challenge directly to the Supreme Court. Then, in mid-November, the Delaware attorney general appealed Seitz's ruling, and the court added that case to its docket as well. Finally, the parameters were set. For three days, December 9 through 11, the Supreme Court would hear back-to-back arguments in five school-desegregation cases spanning a variety of settings and situations. After two decades of groundwork, the showdown envisioned by Charles Houston when he launched the transformation of the Howard University School of Law loomed.[13]

The line began forming around daybreak on December 9. Bundled in coats and armed with umbrellas against a chill, damp day, first dozens, then hundreds of people snaked toward the Supreme Court building. Eyes scanning the pediment above the row of massive columns that guard the west entrance glimpsed the promise inscribed there: "Equal Justice Under Law."[14] The words were about to be put to one of their thorniest tests.

Ten days earlier, Thurgood Marshall had relocated command central in the assault on segregated education from Manhattan to Washington's Statler Hotel, two blocks north of the White House. Usually the NAACP lawyers bunked at a black hotel, The Charles. The Statler had gradually relaxed its color bar, however, after admitting its first black guest—the Cleveland Indians center fielder Larry Doby—during a team visit a few years earlier. Marshall elected to take advantage. Robinson and Hill joined him there. The opposing counsel set up headquarters at the nearby Carlton Hotel, a posh establishment whose elite clientele included the business tycoon Howard R. Hughes Jr. and the former secretary of state Cordell Hull. The Carlton was also a favorite of John W. Davis, the 1924 Democratic presidential nominee and accomplished Wall Street lawyer hired to defend the South Carolina state apparatus in the *Briggs* case. Snowy haired and rosy cheeked, the eloquent seventy-nine-year-old West Virginia native had appeared before the Supreme Court more times than any other living advocate. His prowess, both as a former US solicitor general and as a constitutional authority, was legendary. The aging attorney believed firmly in states' rights and school segregation, and he felt confident that *Briggs* could be won by the state.[15]

Seven attorneys combined to carry the banner of school integration at the Supreme Court; the opposition fielded six. Carter, representing the Kansas schoolchildren, was slated to speak first. The Kansas case had been thrown into confusion when a revamped Topeka school board elected not to defend segregation. At the Supreme Court's request, tantamount to a demand, the state agreed to proceed. Officials tapped a reluctant assistant attorney general, Paul E. Wilson, to defend Kansas's permissive segregation law. Second on the docket was *Briggs*, to be debated by the titanic duo Marshall and Davis. In the Virginia case, third, Robinson would face the defenders of segregation, Moore and Almond. Next, the Delaware lineup pitted Greenberg and Redding against H. Albert Young, the state's attorney general. And finally, George Hayes and Nabrit would argue the Washington case—the only one not under the banner of the Legal Defense Fund. Opposing them would be Milton D. Korman, the District's assistant corporation counsel. The court slated ten hours for argument, five for each side. Truman's solicitor general filed an amicus brief stressing the negative impact of school segregation on America's image abroad, an important addition to the mix. The court denied his bid to give oral testimony.[16]

Shortly after 1:30 p.m. on Tuesday, December 9, Robert Carter walked to the lectern at the front of the court chamber and began to speak. He faced nine justices seated in high-backed leather chairs along a raised mahogany bench. A royal-red velvet curtain and a quartet of marble columns served as backdrop. The chamber's soaring, forty-four-foot ceiling, dwarfing human scale, added to the grandeur. Behind Carter, every seat was filled. The crowd, including Hill, hushed as months of preparation became reality. Speaking in a quiet, even tone, Carter laid out the pivotal claim in *Brown* and, by extension, the other NAACP cases. It was immaterial whether Kansas had created comparable schools for black and white children, he said. What mattered was that the act of segregation in and of itself denied black children the equal educational opportunities specified by the Fourteenth Amendment. "Here we abandon any claim, in pressing our attack on the unconstitutionality of this statute—we abandon any claim—of any constitutional inequality which comes from anything other than the act of segregation itself," Carter said.[17] Many had waited a lifetime to hear those words.

The highly anticipated matchup between Marshall and Davis commenced late in the afternoon and continued into the next day. Both men displayed an ease born of intellectual dexterity and familiarity with the court. Marshall's opening remarks seemed a bit less focused than Davis's, in part because of Associate Justice Felix Frankfurter's frequent interruptions, but the strength of Marshall's closing rebuttal evened the score. The principal arguments of the two men would foreshadow the subsequent performances of Robinson and Moore, reflecting the kinship of the South Carolina and Virginia cases. The appellants claimed that segregation by its very nature harmed black children and that since rights under the Constitution had been held by the court to be "personal and present," aggrieved children deserved immediate, or close to immediate, relief. Any suggestion that state legislatures had more authority than the justices in deciding constitutional prerogatives was "directly contrary to every opinion of this court," Marshall said.[18] Marshall's argument seemed to be directed largely at Frankfurter, who peppered the LDF attorney with some fifty questions during his hour at the lectern. Born a Vienna Jew, Frankfurter had immigrated as a child to the United States, where his outsized intellect had led him to the Harvard Law faculty and eventual nomination by Roosevelt to the Supreme Court. There, he combined an instinct for civil liberties with a proclivity for judicial restraint. Frankfurter worried when the court appeared to be getting too far ahead of public opinion, and his questions went straight to the problem of how an integration order would be received in the South.[19] "Do you really think it helps us not to recognize that behind this are certain facts of life," Frankfurter asked. "Can you escape facing those sociological facts, Mr. Marshall?" "No, I cannot escape it," Marshall replied. "But if I did fail to escape it, I would have to throw completely aside the personal and present rights of those individuals."[20]

When his turn came, Davis spoke incisively and with appealing flashes of self-deprecation. First, he said, the mandate to equalize South Carolina's black and white public schools had been fully met. Second, if the framers of the Fourteenth Amendment had intended it to prevent segregated schools, then why had the same Congress that sent the amendment to the states for ratification funded segregated classrooms in the District of Columbia? Third, advocates of integration were relying on dubious scientific tests from Clark and others. For instance, black schoolchildren in the North had favored white dolls more than those in the South in Clark's study. If low self-esteem existed, Clark's results suggested that some force other than school segregation caused it, Davis said. As for the social scientists, "They find usually, in my limited observation, what they go out to find."[21]

Marshall had saved some of his time for a rebuttal, in which he hit hard at the notion that public sentiment trumped the rights of individuals. If the eminent black political scientist Ralph Bunche, winner of the 1950 Nobel Peace Prize for his mediation work in Israel, lived in South Carolina, his children would be forced to attend a Jim Crow school, Marshall pointed out. "No matter how great anyone becomes, if he happens to have been born a Negro, regardless of his color, he is relegated to that school." He reminded the court that similar prediction of chaos after the *Sweatt* decision had come to naught, and he emphasized an alternate set of "facts of life" in the southern states. "You will see white and colored kids going down the road together to school. They separate and go to different schools, and they come out and they play together. I do not see why there would necessarily be any trouble if they went to school together."[22]

Marshall's time elapsed, and Robinson's turn began. Unlike Marshall and Davis, Robinson was making his maiden appearance before the high court. His selection over his *Davis* cocounsel Hill for the task likely had to do with Robinson's intimate knowledge of the NAACP briefs, his scholarly demeanor, and his skill at appellate work. Robinson was less likely than Hill to turn a memorable phrase, but few could match his patient, detailed grasp of legal nuance. When it came to points of law, some of his circuitous explanations might be confounding, but he was not one to be either intimidated or undone by august company or a hallowed setting.

Robinson began with a detailed review of the district court's action, including a more than fair recital of the state's arguments. Then he isolated his key point: that having found facilities and curricula unequal in Prince Edward County, the judges had erred when they ruled that "no harm resulted to the student from the fact of segregation." The Virginia situation contrasted with that in *Briggs*, in which black schools had been made substantially equal with white schools, Robinson observed. No one claimed that the Virginia schools were yet equal, only that the state hoped to make them so. Judicial acceptance of the inequality in Virginia was a denial of both due process and equal protection of the law as laid out in the

Fourteenth Amendment, Robinson said. From there, he went on to unveil a layered, step-by-step dismantling of the logic surrounding school segregation, starting with the plaintiffs' premise that earlier court decisions did not bind the justices. "No court has ever considered itself irrevocably bound into the future by its prior determinations," Robinson said. Once inequality was determined, as it had been in Prince Edward, then more recent court decisions such as *Gaines* and *Sweatt* pointed to immediate relief. And once integration had been set in motion, students could not simply be yanked back and forth. "I submit that at least we get to the point, it seems to me, where the basis of decision must be something more than a basis which would permit of a shuttling of pupils back and forth into segregated schools and into an unsegregated system, something which would have no assurance, and something which I cannot conduce will be helpful, either to the school authorities or to the pupils involved," Robinson said.[23]

Reduced to its essence, the wordy statement made perfect sense. School systems could not be integrated one year and resegregated the next. As Robinson noted, courts were not equipped to endlessly review the level of equality between black and white schools. He offered several additional points. The "reasonableness" of school segregation at the elementary and secondary levels had never been tested in the high court. The consequences of school inequality in Prince Edward County were harmful and obvious. For example, Prince Edward's white high school was accredited by the Southern Association of Colleges and Secondary Schools; Moton was not. As a result, Moton graduates applying to colleges often had to be admitted on a probationary basis. And despite the court's finding of "no harm or hurt," most of the opposition's experts had admitted that segregation was either harmful or possibly harmful to minority students. Robinson weathered a grilling by Frankfurter; then he deflected the apparent annoyance of a snappish Chief Justice Vinson, who seemed to be struggling with how a school-integration order would play out. "What you do is, you simply make all the facilities in the county available to all the pupils, without restriction or assignment to particular schools on the basis of race," Robinson ventured.[24]

For the NAACP, the defining quality in Moore's rebuttal turned out to be his pronunciation of the word *Negro* to sound like *nigger*. The organization took note of the gaffe in a press release: "Mr. Moore, who apparently had difficulty in pronouncing the word 'Negro,' told the court that separation of the races is 'the way of life' in Virginia and is 'based on real reason' rather than on prejudice or caprice."[25] Most likely, Moore slipped into a common pronunciation by white southerners of the era in which the supposedly polite term *Nigra* often sounded remarkably like *nigger*. Otherwise, Moore spoke clearly and conversationally as he un-apologetically defended the state's performance. Virginia had undertaken "an amazing program" of public-school improvement and stood "probably at the top among all these southern states." He acknowledged that black schools in Prince Edward were not yet on a par with white, but the problem soon would be fixed. Money had been allotted, he said, and the program would have been further along had it not been for negative fallout from the student-led strike. Inaccurately, Moore claimed that the walkout "was really inspired by outsiders." The reason the court could find that school segregation did not harm black students in Virginia, he said, was "the great array of very distinguished persons" who endorsed that view.[26]

Attorney General Almond followed with what one constitutional scholar aptly called "a political speech." The words of the firebrand orator seemed aimed more at Virginia voters than at the nine justices. Almond extolled the generosity of white Virginians, who, he said, were "irrevocably dedicated" to and "enthusiastically in support of" equal school facilities for black high-school students. Then he issued a warning that went straight to Frankfurter's concerns. If the justices elected to strike down segregation, "contrary to the customs, the traditions and the mores of what we might claim to be a great people, established through generations, who themselves are fiercely and irrevocably dedicated to the preservation of the white and colored races," then they should watch out, Almond said. Forced integration would "destroy the public school system of Virginia as we know it today."[27]

Robinson fought back in a brief rebuttal. The claim that Virginia was poised to equalize black and white schools was disingenuous, he said. The stepped-up spending program to which Moore and Almond referred would not truly balance schools. On the program's completion, Virginia would still be allotting black schools only seventy-nine cents for each dollar spent on white schools, according to NAACP calculations. Chief Justice Vinson ended Robinson's testimony with an exchange that hinted at a reluctance to order integration. Noting Robinson's willingness to give states time to adjust if the court ordered mixed schools, Vinson asked why the attorney was unwilling to allow a similar grace period for states to equalize black and white schools. It was a tricky question, and Robinson rose to the challenge. He repeated what he had just said—that Virginia's stepped-up building program was not going to equalize schools statewide anytime soon. Beyond that, the attorney drew a distinction between administrative delay and the delay of a constitutional right. Prior Supreme Court decisions had held that individuals deserved immediate relief when denied a constitutional right. In the case of school integration, "immediate" might encompass some amount of time—he could not say how much—to work out the mechanics. But that was not the same as the court's telling a black child, as a fundamental principle, that it would be "some time into the future before he can get what the Constitution entitled him to, and what his white counterparts are getting already."[28]

With that, Robinson's testimony ended. He had made several important points and acquitted himself ably. The Washington, DC, and Delaware cases followed. When the latter concluded on Thursday afternoon, the court adjourned, and the lawyers dispersed. "After the last day, we just scattered," Greenberg recalled. There were no postmortems. No one could predict the outcome, but the NAACP lawyers felt satisfied. "Our side had ranged across all the possible styles of advocacy, from Spotts's [sic] meticulous, dry, complete coverage of the issues to Thurgood's vivid imagery," he wrote. "Everyone presented our arguments well. . . . All we could do was wait."[29]

By happenstance, Oliver and Bernie Hill had a personal connection to Fred Vinson. What they knew of the cordial and conciliatory Kentuckian created confidence that he would lead the court in doing the right thing. Bernie's older brother, Armistead—named after their uncle Armistead Walker, the slain husband of the entrepreneur Maggie Walker—had worked as Vinson's chauffeur. When Vinson had moved from a position as Truman's treasury secretary to the court, he had taken Walker along to serve as a bailiff. As a result, the Hills had gotten to know the prominent jurist somewhat. The connection was sufficiently friendly that Vinson even allowed the Hills' young son, nicknamed Dukey, to sit in his chair on one visit to the court. So it came as a surprise to Hill to learn many years later that Vinson had been skeptical about integrating public schools and even thought that *Plessy* might have been correctly decided. The episode reminded Hill of how difficult it could be to gauge the sentiments of whites who were not ardent segregationists.[30]

The court held its first conference on the just-completed school hearings almost immediately after the lawyers went home. Sketchy notes from two associate justices, Harold H. Burton and Robert H. Jackson, and later writings of others leave a murky picture of where the court stood. William O. Douglas thought that the tentative count was 5-4 against overruling *Plessy*, but the notes of both Burton and Jackson suggest a majority for striking down segregated schools. Frankfurter apparently counted himself with that side. More importantly, during the conference he tossed out for the first time the prospect of another round of hearings. Behind the scenes, regard for that idea would grow as the winter and spring passed and the court weighed the consequences of radical action.[31]

In January, Eisenhower assumed the presidency with an inaugural speech that promised racial equality but offered few tangible plans. For many black leaders, the depth of the new president's support remained in doubt. Meanwhile, in Virginia and elsewhere, NAACP lawyers pushed speculation over the court's deliberations into the background as they tackled more immediate matters. The Hill-Robinson law firm boasted a full docket of education, transportation, criminal-justice, and general law cases. Bread-and-butter staples involving wills or minor claims, necessary to keep the law firm afloat financially, coexisted with matters of overarching national significance. Newly included in the mix was a case growing out of yet another student strike, this one in the port and paper-mill town of West Point, about an hour's drive east of Richmond on the York River. A group of twenty-nine black high-school students had refused to board a bus on the opening day of school, September 4, for travel to a new black high school about twenty miles away. Previously, West Point's black high-school students had attended the Beverly Allen School in town, but the high-school portion of the facility had just been closed due to declining enrollment. Barred from attending the white high school in West Point, the black students were expected to commute to the Hamilton-Holmes school in the adjoining county. School officials had even purchased a new bus to transport them.[32]

During the summer, students and parents had engaged in some minimal discussion of how to respond, recalled Lucy Thornton Edwards, who as a rising eighth grader was among those scheduled to attend Hamilton-

Holmes. But for the most part, she said, the decision to strike was a spontaneous one, not fully realized until the moment the children refused to board the bus. Later in the day, "we got together, made signs, and marched two blocks to the white school," she said. The refusal of the white principal to enroll the students launched a year-long school boycott. During the 1952–53 school year the West Point Twenty-Nine, as the students came to be called, would attend makeshift classes in a Masonic-lodge building, study at home, give up on schooling to pursue jobs, or—in the case of Edwards and some others—go to live with out-of-state relatives.[33]

On the Sunday following the launch of the strike, black leaders called a mass meeting. Rumors swirled that parents might be jailed if they allowed their children to ignore school-attendance laws. Hill and Banks drove over from Richmond. Addressing the group, Hill explained that the NAACP could get involved only if the parents agreed to fight for integrated schools. While he thought it unlikely that parents would be jailed, if they were, "it would be the best thing to happen in West Point because it would focus public attention on your problem," he added. The gathering voted 141-0 to hold fast for integration. In mid-October, a state court judge fined eight West Point parents two hundred dollars each. He offered to suspend the fines if their children returned to school within ten days. The youngsters snubbed the deadline, and the Hill-Robinson firm filed an appeal. At trial in a case that would drag on for several years, the lawyers argued that the defendants had not violated the compulsory-attendance laws because, in fact, it was they who had been mistreated. Forcing children to attend a distant school that was inferior to a much closer school violated Fourteenth Amendment rights, the lawyers said. Ignoring the argument, the trial judge imposed fifty-dollar fines and thirty-day jail sentences. The penalties were suspended during an appeal to Virginia's highest court. Not until January 1957, well after the *Brown* cases had been settled, did the Virginia Supreme Court of Appeals rule that "application of a criminal statute so that it results in inequality of treatment to the two races is not justified." West Point officials had indeed violated the Fourteenth Amendment.[34] Once again a group of schoolchildren had exposed injustice.

Finally, on June 8, the Supreme Court spoke. What the justices had to say came as a surprise. They sidestepped the central question—whether segregated schools violated constitutional rights. Instead, in a delay pleasing neither side, the justices ordered the lawyers to return to court later in the year for yet another round of hearings, this time addressing five specific questions. The first two probed the original intent of the framers of the Fourteenth Amendment, the Congress, and the ratifying states as it related to segregated schools. The third asked whether the court had the power to apply the amendment to schools even if the framers' intentions could not be divined. And the fourth and fifth addressed practical matters related to a possible integration order. If the court ruled in favor of integrated schools, should the order be carried out "forthwith," or might there be a "gradual adjustment"? And what mechanisms should the courts follow in issuing integration orders?[35] Questions 4 and 5 gave the Legal Defense Fund lawyers the greatest cause for optimism. Unless the justices were seriously considering knocking down *Plessy*, what would be the point of asking for detailed instructions on how to do it? The justices had bought time for white southerners reeling at the possibility of integrated schools. They also had created a crack in the foundation of segregated schools.

In the six months between that order and reassembly at the Supreme Court, Marshall and his team mounted one of the most remarkable collaborative efforts in the history of American jurisprudence. By one NAACP count, more than 130 people from dozens of states and multiple academic disciplines participated in researching, debating, and drafting a brief that in its final version exposed *Plessy* as a subversion of the Fourteenth Amendment. Others put the number of participants at more than 200. The final edit on the eloquent plea for an end to a crippling social order would fall, yet again, to the indispensable Spot Robinson.[36] Within days of the court's June 8 directive, Marshall had begun organizing the mammoth effort. As usual, he gathered the best available minds, probed their thinking, and fashioned a plan. In a mid-July letter to the NAACP board of directors, the special counsel outlined a strict timetable for collecting research and churning out briefs by mid-November. His own staff had given up vacations, and many others had volunteered to work through the summer to complete the task. "We have been fortunate enough in getting men and women who are absolutely tops in their respective fields to work with us," he wrote. Meanwhile, the National Newspaper Publishers Association, a group of black newspapers, and others committed to helping fund the campaign. The "Dollar or More to Open the Door" slogan became a regular fixture in black papers across the nation.[37]

Robinson and Hill joined the throngs attending two major Manhattan conferences aimed at converting the findings into persuasive arguments. Once again, the Virginians contributed unparalleled expertise on the futility of efforts to make racially separate schools truly equal. The group faced two overriding challenges: how to contend that the Fourteenth Amendment applied to education and how best to argue for an immediate end to segregated schools. At the second of the conferences, held September 25–28 at the Newspaper Guild Club of New York, Marshall divided the tasks into four seminars, with Robinson and Hill helping lead the session on court-ordered integration.[38]

Meanwhile, the defenders of states' rights engaged in an intense research effort of their own. Meeting at attorney Davis's law firm in New York, the group assigned tasks. The Davis firm would review the congressional record; the Virginians would tackle state action involving the Fourteenth Amendment. According to John Riely, a junior partner in Hunton & Williams, assigned to work with Moore and Archibald Robertson on the *Davis* case, "My colleagues and I spent more than two solid weeks in the New York Public Library looking at the state records. Thereafter I spent days in the library at Richmond—with decayed calfskin spoiling my clothes and hands—reviewing the Congressional Globe." In Riely's view, the answers to the questions about original intent seemed self-evident. "This was a silly question to ask for several reasons," he wrote more than three decades later. First, "everybody knew" that the Congress had supported segregated schools in the District of Columbia for years after passing the amendment, and second, all of the southern states that ratified the amendment preserved segregated schools for decades thereafter. But the farcical part of the probe, he concluded, was its ultimate irrelevance. "The words of a constitution are not to be interpreted today to have the same meaning that they had at the time of its adoption."[39]

That assessment was not so different from the one gaining currency at LDF headquarters. Despite obstacles, Marshall's forces intended to make a gallant attempt to prove that at least some nineteenth-century congressmen and state lawmakers had believed the Fourteenth Amendment forbade segregated schools. The lawyers felt on much more solid ground with their second line of persuasion, that education fell within the amendment's broad purpose, because the framers intended to strip states of the power, in any form, to treat blacks differently than they did whites. If little in the historical record spoke specifically to schools, that was because public education for the masses had not yet taken hold when the amendment took effect.[40] When all the streams of argument and thought finally congealed into a single document, and Robinson had stamped the 235-page product with his painstaking review, the question that the brief moved to the fore was not the first or second, with their who-said-what focus, but the third: if the historical record was inconclusive, was it within the judiciary's power, in interpreting the Fourteenth Amendment, to abolish segregation in public schools? The NAACP brief flipped the query. "The substantive question . . . is whether a state can, consistently with the Constitution, exclude children, solely on the ground that they are Negroes, from public schools which otherwise they would be qualified to attend," it read. All the history and legal theory that followed could be reduced to a single word. No.

Thurgood Marshall entered the Supreme Court building on December 7, 1953, flanked by Robinson, Hill, and George Hayes.[41] The panel of judges that convened that day differed in one marked way from the body that had adjourned a year earlier: Vinson no longer sat in the chief justice's chair. The congenial, foursquare former California governor Earl Warren now occupied the seat. Vinson's unexpected heart attack and death on September 8 had stunned the court. Honoring a commitment made in the heat of the Republican nominating convention a year earlier, Eisenhower had skipped over more obvious choices and named Warren to the prestigious spot. Not a lot was known about his positions on civil rights, and his unequivocal support of the internment of Japanese Americans during World War II did not bode well. Unlike Vinson, however, Warren was a strong and secure manager, and he was determined to herd the court's unruly flock of egos and philosophies into a more united front. The caustic Frankfurter, who had had his quarrels with Vinson's peripatetic leadership, is reputed to have said in the wake of the chief justice's death, "This is the first indication I have ever had that there is a God."[42] Later, some NAACP leaders might have been inclined to agree. While it is impossible to know how the court would have ruled had Vinson lived, it almost surely would not have spoken with the clarity that emerged, at least initially, under Warren's firm hand. As Robinson rose to commence the oral arguments and Hill settled in to watch, however, it was still anyone's guess where Warren would lead the justices.

The LDF had decided to combine the Virginia and South Carolina cases for purposes of the three-day rehearing. Robinson's penchant for detail suited him to tackle the historical record; he would speak first at the *Brown* rehearing. Then Marshall would plead the moral and legal case for a prompt end to segregated education, much as he had a year earlier. The NAACP lawyers were uncertain how much weight the justices intended to give the history, but Marshall and Robinson could take no chances. Undeniably, there had been widespread school segregation in the wake of the Fourteenth Amendment's adoption. The lawyers needed to show that such separation had grown out of societal norms, not a conscious decision to exclude education from the scope of the amendment, as John Davis and Justin Moore would have it.

Robinson, then thirty-seven, had put in even longer hours than usual in the weeks leading up to the hearing. The strain showed. His cheeks appear hollowed and his eyes shadowed in photographs of the *Brown* attorneys. Greenberg once gave a fitting description of his Virginia colleague as resembling a portrait by the Italian artist Amedeo Modigliani—a long, stretched face with slicked-back hair and narrow lips set atop a thin but sturdy frame. Robinson's apparent fatigue did not prevent a learned opening oration. "Our position is this," he began. First, the Fourteenth Amendment "had as its purpose and effect the complete legal equality of all persons, irrespective of race, and the prohibition of all State imposed caste and class systems based upon race." Second, "segregation in public schools, constituting as it does legislation of this type, is necessarily embraced within the prohibitions of the Amendment." Both the amendment and contemporaneous civil rights legislation had originated in opposition to the Black Codes, laws enacted throughout the South to keep former slaves in an inferior position, Robinson explained. Drawing from the thousands of hours of research completed over the past six months, he quoted chapter and verse to argue that the radical Republicans who pushed the amendment had intended it to bar all future attempts, of any sort, to impose governmental distinctions predicated upon race. Even if they had not specifically said so, that included schools.[43]

Forty minutes into the winding discourse, Frankfurter interrupted. How much weight should be given to the individual utterances of any particular senator or congressman? he demanded to know. "I grant you we solicited and elicited that. But I just wondered, now that we have got it, what are we going to get out of it?" Was Frankfurter suggesting that after all the effort to unearth the historical record, the answers did not matter very much? Astonishingly, it seemed so. Robinson gave a reasonable reply. Any individual statement, standing alone, mattered little, he said. But when a person made a statement and others either agreed or did not dispute it, then "I think we get assistance" in understanding original intent. Stretching credulity, Robinson argued briefly that the fact that the postwar state constitutions did not mention segregated schools should be taken as proof that southerners understood the Fourteenth Amendment to forbid them. That was a reach. He righted himself when he returned to the central point: the framers wanted to ensure that nothing like the Black Codes could ever again get in the way of equal treatment of blacks. While they did not enumerate all the many possible forms of bias, "it is very clear that the breadth of the Amendment is such that it necessarily encompasses school segregation."[44]

Following Robinson, Marshall got off to a wobbly start. He had planned to review recent court rulings as a response to the third question—whether the court could apply the Fourteenth Amendment to education even if the framers' intentions were unclear. Associate Justice Jackson cut him short. The court had no need to be educated "about its own cases," he admonished. Forced to regroup, Marshall seemed to lose focus. He rehashed parts of the historical record and wound up in an unsatisfactory back-and-forth with Frankfurter over the meaning of the *McLaurin* decision. All in all, "it was one of his least creditable performances before the court," Kluger concluded.[45]

John Davis, in contrast, appeared to be in top form—calm, clear, even marginally spellbinding as he wove his way through the cast of historical characters who had shaped the Fourteenth Amendment. No one disputed that the framers wanted black citizens to be treated equally, Davis said. The central point—in his view, one untouched by the NAACP arguments—was that "equal" did not preclude segregated education. He spouted a list of congressional actions after the amendment's adoption that suggested matter-of-fact recognition of the permissibility of school segregation.[46] Only in ending did Davis misstep. He began his wrap-up with a misty-eyed embrace of South Carolina virtues. "Let me say this for the State of South Carolina," he said, moved to a trace of tears by the emotion behind his own rhetoric. "It does not come here . . . in sack cloth and ashes. . . . It is confident of its good faith and intention to produce equality for all of its children of whatever race or color." Then Davis went too far. "I am reminded—and I hope it won't be treated as a reflection on anybody— of Aesop's fable of the dog and the meat," he said. In the fable, a dog crosses a bridge with a piece of meat in its mouth. Seeing its shadow in the water below, it lunges greedily to grab the extra meat, losing what it already has. "Here is equal education, not promised, not prophesied, but present. Shall it be thrown away on some fancied question of racial prestige?"[47]

That was the kind of opening the trial lawyer in Marshall coveted. Before he could leap on the claim that black children wanted nothing more than "racial prestige," however, the special counsel had to bide his time. Moore's and Almond's replies must come first. Moore cited additional evidence that the ratifying states had not connected the amendment to schools. New York, New Jersey, California, Illinois, Missouri, Ohio, and Pennsylvania all had segregated schools both before and after adoption of the amendment.[48] Once again, Almond wound up with a stem-winder more appropriate to a courthouse rally than to a hushed courtroom. "They are asking you to disturb the unfolding evolutionary process of education," he began indignantly, "where from the dark days of the depraved institution of slavery, with the help and the sympathy and the love and respect of the white people of the South, the colored man has risen under that educational process to a place of eminence and respect throughout this Nation. It has served him well." Almond appeared to be living in an alternate reality.

In his rebuttal, Marshall compensated for his early lackluster performance. Returning to Davis's claim that blacks were fixated misguidedly on prestige, he thundered: "Exactly correct." Since the Emancipation Proclamation, "the Negro has been trying to get . . . the same status as anybody else regardless of race. . . . I got the feeling on hearing the discussion yesterday that when you put a white child in a school with a whole lot of colored children, the child would fall apart or something. Everybody knows that is not true. Those same kids in Virginia and South Carolina— and I have seen them do it—they play in the streets together, they play on their farms together, they go down the road together, they separate to go to school, they come out of school and play ball together." Much as his opponents might pretend that segregation did not demean black citizens, it did, he insisted. The only way the court could rule in favor of the states would be to proclaim race a legitimate classification for separating individuals within public policy. And the only way to arrive at that conclusion would be "to find that for some reason Negroes are inferior to all other human beings."[49]

The moment proved the emotional high point of the second *Brown* hearing. Marshall had narrowed the debate to its essence. Say what the opponents would about the noble intentions of white southerners, decreeing that black children could not enter white classrooms branded them as inferior. The concept mocked American ideals. The proceedings continued for a day and a half. Then another long wait began. "Most of us assumed that we would win," Greenberg wrote of the Legal Defense Fund lawyers' internal postmortems. Only two of the lawyers, however, thought that the victory would be unanimous, he said. Robinson and Nabrit held that view, while others contemplated smaller majorities.[50]

Robinson was not just prescient; he also was exhausted. He had kept to his typical work pattern throughout the hearing preparations. For so conscientious a steward, refining a crucial 235-page brief on which so much depended would have been an all-consuming task. At home in Richmond, Robinson had moved his family out of his parents' home to a new address at 508 Fells Street the previous fall. His daughter, Nina Govan, recalled that by then family dinners were a thing of the past. "Dad came in for dinner at ten or eleven at night. It was habitual," she said. Working at the LDF headquarters in New York, Robinson's pattern was to rest when the other attorneys quit for the day and then press on. Once he awoke, even in the midst of noise, "if I have something I'm trying to get settled . . . , I have enough concentration that I can just completely shut it out of my mind every time." At least once, however, possibly during the *Brown* preparations, Robinson made an exception. He went to a separate hotel to work. "He told one person in the group where he was going, and he started writing," Govan recalled her father telling her.[51] Robinson was not one to complain about his personal condition, but the never-completed study on restrictive covenants had pushed the limits of his endurance. The preparations for the second *Brown* hearing did as well. A decade later, filling out a questionnaire for the federal judiciary, he revealed a fact little known at the time. To a question involving health, he replied: "For a period of several weeks in December, 1953, and January, 1954, I was resting at home in consequence of a chronic fatigue syndrome." Although he reported a complete recovery, "this condition has recurred occasionally for brief intervals, but only after long periods of extreme overwork."[52]

Robinson did not bother to say that "long periods of extreme overwork" defined his adult life. In the wake of the *Brown* oral arguments, grateful members of the Virginia NAACP collected $968 for a Robinson Vacation Fund. Only insiders knew that that the money was not for some celebratory holiday. Rather, it was intended to cover Robinson's bills during an essential, physician-ordered convalescence. "Because Attorney Spottswood W. Robinson has lived with the school segregation cases for the past year, he is now in a state of complete exhaustion. He is literally out on his feet," Banks wrote in a letter urging secrecy and stamped "Confidential-Confidential-Confidential." "All of us have been very worried about Spot's health," Marshall confided in an appeal to close associates. During the fall of 1953, Robinson "was under terrific pressure and he was in a horrible state in so far as his health was concerned." The situation was so bad "that we were afraid that he would collapse at any moment. . . . We cannot allow him to just kill himself," Marshall concluded.[53] Spot Robinson was far too valuable for that. It had been six years since he embarked on the examination of conditions in Virginia's black schools. That study had led to the legal campaign for school equalization, which, in turn, had culminated in the push for desegregation. Health, wealth, and family all had taken a backseat to the work. Alarmed and grateful colleagues insisted—almost decreed—that he had earned a rest.

"MEMORANDUM TO THE STAFF FROM MR. WHITE, March 15, 1954: Thurgood telephoned at 1:30 that the Court DID NOT hand down a decision today. The next decision day will be April 5, after the Court takes a four-week recess."[54] No one wanted to miss the historic moment. For weeks, beginning in March, the attorneys in the five *Brown* cases shadowed the Supreme Court. The justices typically delivered decisions on a Monday, so throughout the late spring Robinson and Hill managed to be in Washington as often as possible at the start of each workweek. The morning of Monday, May 17, proved an exception. Both men had obligations that kept them in Richmond. Others held vigil at the Supreme Court.

Hill was at Fourth and Leigh Streets, driving downtown with the radio on, when a news bulletin interrupted his thoughts. The high court had just ruled in *Brown*. Astonishingly, the justices had spoken with a single voice. "We conclude that in the field of public education the doctrine of 'separate but equal' has no place," wrote Chief Justice Warren, who had miraculously welded the court's disparate voices into a cohesive whole. "Separate educational facilities are inherently unequal." Whipping the car around, Hill rushed back to the office, parked, and sprinted inside. "Turn the radio on! Turn the radio on!" he shouted, as others gathered to digest the news. The decision, applying to the Kansas, South Carolina, Virginia, and Delaware cases, dismissed the much-debated historical record surrounding the Fourteenth Amendment as inconclusive. The court had no doubt, however, that "education is perhaps the most important function of state and local governments. . . . It is the very foundation of good citizenship." For that reason, to separate children in grade and high schools "solely because of their race generates a feeling of inferiority as to their status in the community that may affect their hearts and minds in a way unlikely ever to be undone." The finding of psychological damage "is amply supported by modern authority," the opinion concluded. It attributed the finding to two of the experts maligned in the *Davis* case, Clark and Chein, among others. A separate, similar ruling grounded in the Fifth Amendment struck down segregated schools in Washington.[55]

Amid "much hurrahing," the office of Hill, Martin & Robinson shut down work for the day. The principals in the firm would have no greater moment of vindication in their long careers. In countless ways they had helped craft and assemble the building blocks undergirding the decision. Much of their work had occurred in schoolrooms, courthouses, and strategy huddles far distant from the national media's glare. But from Hill's gamble before a Fourth Circuit panel in the *Alston* teacher-salary-equalization case to Robinson's dissection of the history of the Fourteenth Amendment before the Supreme Court, with much effort in between, they had helped devise and implement the strategies and actions leading to this end. That they had done so from the unique perspective of southern lawyers navigating between the movement's foot soldiers and its top commanders, helping interpret each to the other, only heightened their pride in the outcome. The *Brown* decision, said Hill, "gave me the greatest elation that I have ever experienced in my life."[56]

Awash in euphoria, many black Americans paid scant attention to the order's final paragraph—at least for that day. The court had settled the overriding question of equal protection, but the justices were not finished. Now they intended to turn their scrutiny to questions 4 and 5. The lawyers should prepare to return to court, once again. This time, Warren and his colleagues would consider the thorny matter of the timetable by which black children should receive the justice they were due. Wittingly or not, the court had given segregationists a full year to gather themselves and prepare for the Armageddon to come.

FOURTEEN

Rocky Road to a New Day

An estimated two thousand citizens thronged the Mosque auditorium in Richmond on November 15, 1954, for perhaps the largest and longest public hearing in Virginia legislative history. Passions ran high as the all-white, all-male Commission to Study Public Education labored from midmorning until almost midnight. More than one hundred speakers addressed the men assigned to craft Virginia's response to the *Brown* ruling. Opinions ranged from support for speedy compliance to forecasts of anarchy if the federal courts tried to ram a liberal agenda down southern throats. Unsurprisingly, segregationists dominated the session. A smaller contingent of black activists and white churchgoers risked contempt by advocating for integrated schools. The *Richmond News Leader* reported that most of the black speakers took the stance of Oliver Hill, who said: "We're fighting to give every Negro child a chance to become a decent and honorable citizen."[1]

Over the years, Hill's face had grown familiar to most politically active Virginians. It would become more so as the desegregation push intensified. "Hill is a rabid nigger and very stupid, with only a fraction of the intelligence of his colleague, Spottswood Robinson, and is going to come to grief before things are over," groused David J. Mays, a prominent white Richmond lawyer and Pulitzer Prize–winning author, in an unvarnished diary entry a few years after the education commission hearing.[2] By then, Hill's work advancing desegregation cases in Arlington, Charlottesville, and elsewhere had sharpened the disdain of critics. There was nothing frothing or unintelligent about Hill's appeal at the Mosque hearing, however. The underlying basis of segregated schools, he said, was a slavery-era belief in the inferiority of blacks. The practical approach in a world dominated by people of color was to do everything possible "to help strengthen the foundations underlying the American democratic concept of life." That meant elevating black children through educational opportunities available only in desegregated schools. Hill ended with an appeal to his opponents' better angels. "Gentlemen, face the dawn and not the setting sun," he urged, paraphrasing a line from his favorite poem, "When All is Done," by Paul Laurence Dunbar. "A new day is being born."[3] The birthing of that new era would not go smoothly, although realization that the Supreme Court had delayed desegregation for the 1954–55 school year calmed critics, at least temporarily.[4]

The initial response of prominent white Virginians to the May 17 decision had been muted, surprisingly so. Governor Thomas B. Stanley, a Byrd acolyte and a wealthy furniture manufacturer from southern Virginia, had urged "cool heads, calm study, and sound judgment." He promised to consult with leaders of both races. The biracial consultation Stanley had in mind apparently consisted in beckoning a half dozen or so black leaders, including Hill, to his office a week later and urging them to soft-pedal the ruling. Even the conciliatory P. B. Young found the idea bizarre. Benjamin Muse, an enlightened journalist from northern Virginia widely considered to be a liberal on racial matters, also at that moment revealed an astonishing myopia about black aspirations. "Dr. Tinsley and Hill, Martin and Robinson, in the opinion of this column, should relax now and reflect on the vast significance of their recent gains," Muse urged immediately after the Supreme Court ruling. "They should get back to their personal business—or go fishing." Muse later correctly wrote that many white Virginians "were unaware of any race problem in this state" prior to the May 17 ruling. His own initial response to *Brown* suggested just how deep the misconceptions ran.[5]

Within weeks, the official tone had toughened, altered most likely by the displeasure of Senator Byrd. In an initial statement, Virginia's political kingpin left little doubt of his scorn, although he was slightly more restrained than leading politicians further south. The decision was "the most serious blow that has yet been struck against the rights of the states in a matter vitally affecting their authority and welfare," Byrd admonished. He labeled the unfolding situation "a crisis of the first magnitude."

Soon, other prominent white Virginians adopted a similarly defiant pitch. "I shall use every legal means at my command to continue segregated schools in Virginia," swore Governor Stanley. Attorney General Almond vowed that no Virginia child would be compelled to attend a mixed school, and some twenty lawmakers from the Southside, meeting at a Petersburg firehouse, recorded their "unalterable opposition" to school integration.[6] In contrast, NAACP Legal Defense Fund lawyers made plain that they had no intention of letting southern segregationists off the hook. Five days after the *Brown* ruling, Robinson, Hill, Tinsley, and Banks joined representatives of seventeen southern and border states in a mass strategy huddle in Atlanta. Their subsequent position paper, labeled the "Atlanta Declaration," expressed "utmost confidence" in a color-blind American future and instructed all branches to petition local school boards "to abolish segregation without delay." Returning home, the Virginians called an emergency statewide meeting to spread the word. More than three hundred attendees at the Richmond gathering unanimously embraced the Atlanta resolves, although delegates also agreed to postpone formal action pending development of a statewide plan.[7]

Over the next ten months, as lawyers prepared to argue yet again before the Supreme Court, both sides laid groundwork for a rapid response to whatever timetable the court eventually embraced. In Virginia, Stanley commissioned the thirty-two-member education study group, popularly known as the Gray Commission, in a nod to its chairman, Senator Garland Gray. Heir to a thriving family lumber business, with holdings said to approach forty-thousand acres, the Sussex County politician epitomized Byrd Organization lieutenants—loyal, self-assured, conservative, and presumed to be inflexible on racial matters. In the fifteen-month life of the commission, he allowed only one public hearing, that attended by Hill in late 1954. The commission conducted the bulk of its work behind closed doors.[8]

Once again the NAACP Legal Defense Fund mounted an elaborate, coordinated effort to prepare for the Supreme Court oral arguments. Briefs filed in November urged an immediate—or "forthwith"—end to public-school segregation by the upcoming fall term. Opponents stressed the inadvisability of forcing southern states to dismantle an ingrained way of life. A familiar cast, now minus two stalwarts, gathered at the Supreme Court on April 11, 1955. Roy Wilkins joined the audience as the NAACP's new executive secretary, replacing Walter White, felled by a heart attack less than a month earlier. The leonine John Davis also was missing, having died just three days after White. This time, Kansas, Delaware, and the District of Columbia led off the four-day proceedings. Each had begun desegregating schools; for them, remaining questions centered on whether the mixing was proceeding quickly enough. Only Virginia and South Carolina had made no progress at all on desegregation.[9]

As they had earlier, Robinson and Marshall addressed the deficiency in tandem. Robinson spoke first. The Virginian resisted any claim that the court should delay implementation of its ruling in Prince Edward County. Washington's school system had already desegregated, and a system "far less complicated and far smaller in size than the District could desegregate in an equal space of time," he insisted. Surely, Associate Justice Stanley F. Reed interjected, Robinson was not suggesting that "every place in the country is just alike." Robinson refused to give ground. The court had determined in several cases that the right to an equal education was "personal and present." The phrase denoted grave consequence. "Every day that this illegal system of racial segregation continues, it would mean that we have not one child, but a multitude of children, who are really being seriously injured," Robinson said. If the rights of children had any meaning, "they must be satisfied while they are still children."[10]

Archibald Robertson and Attorney General Almond mounted a passionate response. It had taken the court almost sixty years to disavow *Plessy*, they argued, and justice required that Prince Edward County and Virginia "be afforded fair opportunity to adjust itself to this revolutionary decision." Much had been made about the "emotional and psychological effects of segregation upon Negro children," but what of white children? Were they to ignore terrible imbalances in IQ scores, health, and morality? Robertson asked. Tuberculosis was almost twice as prevalent among blacks, he said. They accounted for 78 percent of the state's syphilis cases and 83 percent of its gonorrhea cases. The lawyers could not promise that angry citizens would not defund public schools or repeal public-attendance laws. "In all candor and frankness," Almond concluded, Virginia's response to the May 17 order would not "in the lifetime of those of us hale and hearty here, be enforced integration of the races in the public schools" of Prince Edward County. Answering, Marshall ridiculed the health statistics as "completely immaterial" unless the state of Virginia had no functioning public health service in its schools. He dismissed the blame-the-victim claims of black intellectual inferiority. "There are geniuses in both groups and there are lower ones in both groups, and it has no bearing," he said. "No right of an individual can be conditioned as to any average of other people in his racial group or any other group." The entire argument of the state's defenders rested on the hope that the court would allow the southern states to persist in business as usual, Marshall concluded. Only "a strong, forthright degree" would stop them.[11]

There was to be no such firm ruling; the court blinked. The order that came down on May 31 reaffirmed the unconstitutionality of segregated schools, but it also allowed lower courts "a practical flexibility" in shaping timetables for implementation. The plaintiffs deserved admission to public schools as soon as practicable, but courts might also consider "the public interest" in shaping orders. Jurists should require localities to make "a prompt and reasonable start" on desegregation, after which matters were to move forward "with all deliberate speed." In other words, there would be no fixed deadline by which integration was to be a done deal. Instead, *Brown* II, as the ruling came to be known, provided a vague, ambiguous prescription—clear in endorsing an underlying principle, enigmatic in describing how it was to be achieved. Rival headlines in the *Richmond Times-Dispatch* and the *Richmond Afro-American* revealed the contrasting lenses through which each side wishfully interpreted the ruling. "School Integration Left Up to Local Authorities; High Court Sets No Deadline," summed up the white-owned paper. "High Court Orders Integration of Schools Begin at Early Date," concluded the black press.[12] One result was clear to both sides. NAACP Legal Defense Fund lawyers might have hoped that the May 17, 1954, ruling would spell the end of years of litigation aimed at integrating black children into the mainstream of American life. To the contrary, the legal work merely had entered a new phase—one likely to be nastier and more vengeful than anything they had yet faced.

Years later, prominent white Virginians soft-pedaled the anti-integration mania that swept portions of Virginia in the wake of *Brown* II by touting the scarcity of overt violence. In that rosy critique, the fact that four localities shut down public schools in whole or in part—one of them for five years—constituted unfortunate collateral damage. "The program adopted in the General Assembly of Virginia bought valuable time during which people were able to adjust for conditions that were inevitably to come," rationalized Mills E. Godwin Jr., an architect of Virginia's response who later served two terms as governor.[13] That revisionist apologia addressed the needs of whites as they transitioned to a more racially integrated world. But it ignored the sometimes fierce economic and social payback to black families bold enough to challenge the social order. And it made no allowance for the physical, mental, and monetary price paid by the lawyers and NAACP leaders (and their families) who courted community scorn by treading in toxic waters. By the twenty-first century, the NACCP was viewed largely as a mainstream advocacy group. But in the 1950s, as requests for equal treatment of blacks evolved into demands, many southern whites came to despise the organization as a radical, subversive group bent on destroying a cherished culture. "It is difficult to describe the intensity with which the NAACP was hated by white Virginians," wrote Muse. Thousands believed it to be a Communist front. Even among better-informed white Virginians, "the NAACP was regarded by many as something diabolical."[14]

To imagine that such contempt had no impact on the individuals at whom it was directed or on their families stretches credulity. Skip Griffin, whose father led the post-*Brown* movement in Prince Edward County and who himself became a youth plaintiff in a historic court case there, later observed that living through the era had been harder than nostalgic memories suggest. "On the other side, it's all glorious," he said, referring to celebrations of the civil rights era. "But the journey there was not a smooth journey." His mother, Adelaide Payne Griffin, for one, suffered serious depression as the family's finances dwindled and community ostracism grew in the mid-1950s. "The last time, she was pretty far down," he said, recalling her hospitalization at the overcrowded Central State Hospital in Petersburg. The facility, which served only African Americans, "was a hellhole," he said. An artist and musician who had grown up in Atlantic City, his mother was unprepared for the rejection of white acquaintances and the loss of black friends forced to move from Prince Edward during the school turmoil. Several young white women who were students at Longwood College had come regularly to the Griffin home to share their enjoyment of the arts. "One day, they didn't show up," he said. One of them later told his mother, "We can't come back because of what your husband stands for." Devastated, Adelaide Griffin never painted after that, he said. "That thing just hurt my mama to the core."[15]

Countless scores of black Virginians bore the scars of the era, whether from interrupted schooling, loss of employment, or psychological intimidation. In his diary, David Mays spelled out the hateful tactics that underlay the Old Dominion's veneer of civility. Since the Supreme Court's decision had been "a dishonest one, we shall resort to dishonesty ourselves in combating it," wrote Mays, who served as chief counsel to the Gray Commission, won his Pulitzer for a biography of the revolutionary-era lawyer and jurist Edmund Pendleton, and served as an intimate of Virginia's leading 1950s politicians, including Byrd. Mays's reputation as a racial moderate was not born of any sympathy toward blacks. Rather, it reflected his clear-eyed understanding that efforts to avoid integration at all costs would not stand constitutional muster. An urbanite, insulated from the demands of rural segregationists for strict apartheid, he preferred to give an inch on school desegregation in order later to gain a mile. "The Negroes could be let in and then chased out by setting high academic standards they could not maintain, by hazing if necessary, by economic pressure in some cases, etc.," Mays wrote. As in war, "no general worries about a few of the enemy troops penetrating his line if the attack's back is broken, in which case the soldiers who break through are in a hell of a fix." That the "soldiers" mentioned in the analogy would in real life be innocent schoolchildren seemed not to matter.[16]

Mays correctly perceived the vulnerability of NAACP lawyers, who would be under mounting strain as lawsuits escalated in the wake of *Brown* II. That decision foretold endless litigation as various district courts weighed implementation. In 1958 Mays noted with satisfaction that "the Negro lawyers seem to be physically exhausted by having to rush from one end of the state to the other to meet court engagements. The white lawyers are more numerous and have a wider distribution of the work."[17] Stalwart as they were, neither Robinson nor Hill was immune to the negative consequences of hard work and modest pay. The deaths of Charles Houston and Walter White at ages fifty-four and sixty-one, respectively, and of Andy Ransom of a stroke in August 1954 at age fifty-five were reminders of the mortality of men strained by enormous workloads. Robinson's health scare in the winter of 1954 could not be minimized, although it did not deter his returning to work as quickly as possible. Perplexed by Robinson's refusal to take what friends considered a proper rest, Robert Carter urged the Richmond attorney to forgo a regional NAACP conference in Savannah in February 1954: "Why in the devil don't you take advantage of what I hear Banks has gotten together and take a nice vacation?" Robinson dismissed the overture: "I am back in the office on a restricted basis since I had my choice between the vacation and starving."[18]

Financial concerns shadowed Hill and Robinson. While the attorneys maintained a middle-class lifestyle, they regularly operated hand to mouth. Their compensation was nowhere near that paid many of the white attorneys who faced them in court. They scrambled to supplement meager payments for the civil rights cases with fees from a full-service law practice. A few retainers, including one from a local cab company, helped keep them afloat. Still, the imbalance between time spent on the civil rights cases and money earned bred ongoing tension around finances. "Please bring check with you. Can't pay any more bills until I get it," Robinson urged Marshall in a handwritten note at the bottom of a June 1948 letter. "How about sending a check for the last quarter of my services for 1950 in the school matters? I am somewhat pressed," he observed in January 1951. At times, the attorneys were lucky to collect expense reimbursements from the national office; the state conference routinely owed them several thousands of dollars. A memo prepared by Hill, Martin & Robinson in September 1957 revealed shockingly low reimbursement for the hundreds of hours invested in the Prince Edward school case, for instance. Since launching the litigation in 1951, the firm had received a total of $10,384 (about $90,000 in 2016 dollars). Of that, about two-thirds had gone toward office and other expenses and about one-third had been divided three ways in attorneys' fees. Under the law firm's partnership agreement, each of the three lawyers received $327 in 1954, $207 in 1955, $500 in 1956, and $219 in 1957—a total of less than $11,000 each in 2016 dollars—for work in one of the most consequential cases in American history. In contrast, an article in the *Richmond News Leader* in May 1956 noted that up to that point the state had paid Justin Moore's law firm $60,000 in fees and almost $12,000 in expenses for its work in the case. The total equates to more than $600,000 in current dollars, more than six times the payments to the Hill law firm even before the state's tally was complete.[19]

Moore was far from alone in profiting from state efforts to keep black children out of white schools. He and other prominent white lawyers in private firms hired by the state and localities to defend against desegregation lawsuits were paid handsomely with tax dollars. Cases often dragged on for years, boosting receipts. The *News Leader* reported that by May 1956 David Mays and an associate had received the equivalent of almost $175,000 in today's dollars for legal advice to the Gray Commission as it worked to avoid desegregation. Meanwhile, post-*Brown* governors began inserting a line item for "Legal Assistance to Localities in Segregation Cases" in their budget recommendations. The requested amount for the 1958–60 budget equates to more than $1.15 million today. Such figures suggest that white attorneys were paid the equivalent of millions of tax dollars to keep Virginia safe from desegregation.[20] The Legal Defense Fund's decision in the fall of 1947 to hire Robinson for the equalization campaign had provided a welcome source of steady income for the law firm. A $4,600 retainer in the first year extended at a similar rate into a second and third. By agreement of the partners, the money went straight into the firm's coffer. When Robinson was made the NAACP's regional attorney for the Southeast in November 1950, he received a welcome boost in his annual retainer to $6,000, which also went into the firm pool.[21]

As the NAACP lawyers braced to begin a series of *Brown* II legal challenges across Virginia in the summer of 1955, the finances and structure of the law firm were in flux. The twelve-year partnership between Robinson and Hill dissolved as the younger attorney elected to go it alone. The Hill, Martin & Robinson trio would continue to work in concert in civil rights litigation, but on day-to-day operations they would act separately. Reasons for the split remain murky. Hill made no mention of it in his autobiography. In a 2002 interview, he noted that "we had a little misunderstanding," with the result that he and Martin moved to another location in Jackson Ward and took on a third partner, James R. Olphin. Hill did not elaborate. Former governor Wilder, who formed a loose working alliance with Robinson after graduating from Howard Law in 1959, said he believed there had been "no hard feelings" between Robinson and Hill, who remained amiable colleagues. Robinson simply wanted a different type of law practice, one that focused more on real-estate work and representation of major clients. That list came to include such black-owned institutions as the Consolidated Bank & Trust Company, the Southern Aid Life Insurance Company, and the Virginia Mutual Benefit Life Insurance Company. The death of Robinson's beloved father in January 1955 likely contributed to the shift. The elder Robinson had been a director and vice-president of the Consolidated Bank, as well as a trustee of Virginia Mutual. Unlike Hill, Robinson did not have the financial cushion of a separate income from his wife. For years, the Robinsons had reduced monthly expenses by living with his family, but they had moved out a few years earlier and were in the process of building a home. He may simply have needed to earn more money.[22]

Whatever the source of the misunderstanding referenced by Hill, the loss of revenue came at a difficult time. Not only had some of the firm's most dependable income stemmed from Robinson's work for the Legal Defense Fund and from his strong connections to the black business community, but Hill had been distracted from wage earning that spring by a failed bid for the House of Delegates. Correspondence confirmed the strain. "Enclosed herewith is the balance due on my account," Hill wrote to the Esso Standard Oil Company in April 1955. "I thank you for the consideration extended me during this very trying period." In October he apologized to the owner of the Whitehead Realty Company in Washington for late payment on two notes. "I knew that Bernie was unable to send the money in September, but we had anticipated paying both notes before the due date in October," wrote Hill, enclosing the payment. And in November he made a late payment of $725 on his 1954 income-tax bill. "I reasonably expect to pay the balance of this indebtedness within the next thirty days," he promised.[23]

Nor could the attorneys escape psychological strain as they entered the thick of the fight for desegregated schools. A decade later, white politicians might gloat that Virginia had avoided bloodletting, but in the mid- to late 1950s there was no guarantee of that outcome. Those leading the integration fight had ample reason to fear that they too might become targets. Daily headlines reminded them of the dangers. In the months just before and following the *Brown* II decision, the Reverend George Lee, a Mississippi minister and the first black person from his Delta county to register to vote in the twentieth century, died from shots fired from a passing car as he drove at night near Belzoni. A few months later, a cofounder with Lee of the local NAACP chapter was shot and wounded in his grocery store. And the August 1955 kidnapping, disfigurement, and drowning of Emmett Till, a fourteen-year-old Chicago boy accused of flirting with a white woman while visiting in Mississippi, set a new low for atrocity. Virginia was not Mississippi, but virulent racism did not know state boundaries. No one could predict if or when a trigger-happy segregationist in Prince Edward County or elsewhere might try to copy the Mississippi model.[24]

"I used to get mail every day threatening me . . . so many scurrilous calls it was awful," Hill once told an interviewer. Throughout the 1950s, he and Bernie regularly took the telephone earpiece off the hook at night and dropped it into a wastebasket so that they would not be awakened by a malicious caller. Both Nina Robinson Govan and Oliver Hill Jr. recalled not being allowed to answer the home telephone when they were young because of what they might hear. "The profanity was terrible," Bernie said in a 1992 interview. "I sat at the front door with a gun some nights after a particularly threatening call." Once, after Bernie fielded an ominous telephone threat to her husband, she drilled a hole in the kitchen wall and ran an extension cord across the back yard to the garage. There, she installed a light bulb to illuminate Oliver's return home late that night. He was fearless, Bernie said, but she was not.[25]

Just over two weeks before Emmett Till's disappearance, the Hills experienced an unsettling episode that underscored the potential for harm. Around one o'clock in the morning on August 10, Bernie was awakened by a thud outside the house at 107 Overbrook Road. Oliver was awake, reading in a back bedroom. Peering through the curtains, she saw a blazing four-foot cross wrapped in oil-soaked burlap and anchored in a cinder block. Her screams brought Oliver running. "The flames were shooting way up. We thought it was going to start the house on fire," he recalled. Hill's response was to call the fire department, not the police, and the news of his reaction burnished his reputation for unflappability. "I was not surprised to read that this attempt to intimidate you would not succeed," Irving Engel, a prominent New York lawyer, wrote approvingly a few days later. In a flippant reply, Hill attributed the incident to "our local nitwits." More soberly, he admitted: "We have been and still are being annoyed and harassed with anonymous telephone calls at all hours of the day and night and threatening letters."[26] The cross-burning confirmed the potential for bedlam. "There was always the possibility" of physical danger, Hill acknowledged many years later. "You were always subject to it." Mays also observed the thin line between restraint and mayhem. "A time will come when the public will permit the emergence of the roughnecks who will do ugly things and who sympathetic petit jurors will not convict," he predicted as school closings took hold in the fall of 1958.[27]

Hill and Robinson steadied themselves in part by snatching moments to pursue passions beyond civil rights work. The Hills maintained a lively social calendar, taking in occasional football games and other sporting events, traveling to Washington and elsewhere for nights on the town, and playing an active role in various fraternal and civic groups. Hill's 1954–55 correspondence mentions a trip to Sag Harbor, New York, to visit friends; attendance at a North Carolina A&T–Virginia Union football game; and participation in events such as an Omega Psi Phi conclave in Norfolk and a meeting of the Treble Clef and Book Lovers Club at Virginia Union. He reserved rooms for four couples at the Hotel Alexander in Charlotte, North Carolina, for a May 1956 meeting of The Moles, a social club for African American women. By then Bernie already was a national officer; a few years later she would assume the presidency, an ascent gleefully described in her farewell message to the group. She and Oliver were on their way to Baltimore in May 1959 for his acceptance of an NAACP award, she wrote. "As fate would have it, we had car trouble and had to stop for car repairs near the Iwo Jima Monument in Fredericksburg." Calling home, Bernie learned that she had been elected the fifth national president of The Moles. "Needless to say, we never reached Baltimore. We returned home immediately and drove to Roanoke [for the annual meeting]."[28]

Robert J. Grey Jr., a prominent Richmond lawyer and a boyhood friend of Oliver Hill Jr.'s, recalled the Hills' dynamism. Oliver was "an alpha male, gregarious, commanding, demanding, a big, big person in stature and in the space he takes up," said Grey, who served as president of the American Bar Association in 2004–5. "And Bernie was an alpha woman. They were the alpha couple. She was leading this, leading that, very powerful." A proud member of the Delta Sigma Theta sorority, Bernie participated in a variety of African American social clubs, including the Links, Incorporated; the Suavettes; the Bridgettes (a contract-bridge group); the Girl Friends; and the Jack & Jills. Oliver upheld a lifetime allegiance to the Omegas, while becoming increasingly active in the Sigma Pi Phi fraternity, a prestigious professional group. He remained a serious and competitive bridge player throughout his life.[29]

The Robinsons maintained a quieter social life, but they too enjoyed a circle of close friends. Marshall regularly stayed overnight with the Robinsons when he was in Richmond in the 1950s. His second wife, Cecilia "Cissy" Suyat, whom he married in December 1955, sometimes joined him at the Robinson home. She and Marian became fast friends, shopping and socializing while their husbands labored over legal briefs and strategies. During much of the 1950s, Marian worked as her husband's secretary. At home, her interests tilted to the domestic—sewing and gardening. Preferring solitary pursuits, Spot designed the modern, split-level home the couple moved into in 1957. His crowning achievement as a craftsman proved to be a sixteen-foot fishing boat, dubbed the "Nina Mae" for his wife and daughter. Fifteen hundred brass screws, rather than nails, secured its mitered planks.[30]

Community accolades also strengthened the NAACP attorneys. Local and state NAACP chapters and other community groups regularly feted them with receptions and resolutions commending their work. Robert Turpin, a Richmonder who grew up in the Robinsons' neighborhood in the fifties and sixties, recalled the high regard in which the civil rights attorneys were held. "All of us knew the kind of work he was doing and the sacrifices his family had to make," he said of Robinson. While the lawyers were not poor, their incomes were not on a par with those of businessmen, doctors, and other professionals, Turpin noted. Nor could applause erase fully the heavy burdens the lawyers carried, including growing awareness that many anonymous souls would suffer for their challenges to the established order. A handwritten letter from Norfolk preserved in NAACP files and signed only "Working Man," laid out the heartrending reality. "I am just a working man and I been going along with all the promises of equality and more job opportunity and when I thought my kids could go to school with the white kids I thought that was pretty good to," the correspondent began. Now the man had changed his mind. "What good is it going to do me if I don't have no job," he asked. Until recently he had worked at a garage, the man continued. "The work was hard and dirty but I made enough to pay my rent and take care of my family and this week Mr. Jacobs told me he didn't need me anymore. I went by there Monday hunting another job and a white boy was working the wash rack and grease rack. . . . I know some others who lost their jobs to. What are we supposed to do."[31]

David Mays was not the only white Virginian who understood the power of economic intimidation. A group of constituents calling themselves "Four of the Disgusted Ones" urged Governor Stanley to promote economics as a wedge against black upstarts: "The NAACP could not exist were it not for the continued contributions of working niggers, so you see the white man is working against himself here. The money he pays his nigger employees is being used against himself."[32] Despite economic and personal struggles, Hill, Robinson, and their colleagues in the top echelons of the NAACP likely would soldier through. Not everyone might be so fortunate. "Working Man" spoke for legions of hidden, sacrificial victims of the lawyers' determination to give black children a future worth having.

Any illusion that *Brown* II would clear the path to school integration evaporated quickly. Reality soon settled in. School desegregation would unfold with far more deliberation—and willful obstructionism—than speed. The first proof came in courtrooms in Columbia and Richmond. On July 15, 1955, after a three-day proceeding in which Marshall, local attorney Harold Boulware, Robinson, and Hill pressed for the rapid integration of black children into Clarendon County schools, a three-man panel headed by Judge Parker struck the first blow. There would be no integration that fall in Clarendon County. In what became known as the Parker Doctrine, the shrewd jurist opined that the Constitution "does not require integration. . . . It merely forbids the use of governmental power to enforce segregation." Separation of the races could still occur, in other words, as long as it came about voluntarily or from race-neutral policies.[33]

Three days later in Richmond, the focus turned to Prince Edward County. Once again Robinson, Hill, and Marshall squared off against Moore, Robertson, and Almond in a sweltering and packed courtroom. The plaintiffs pressed for an end to segregation when schools opened in two months; the defendants urged judicial restraint, certainly until the Gray Commission had worked out a statewide plan. Judge Dobie, sitting with Hutcheson and Bryan, injected the prospect of shuttered schools. Drawing on Parker's logic, he pressed: "We are not recommending it, of course, but if all through the South they would abolish the public schools, that would be a perfect compliance with the Supreme Court's decree, would it not?" "That is a very difficult interpretation," Robinson replied curtly. But if the options were no schools or segregated schools, which would the NAACP prefer? Dobie pressed. Was the group truly advocating "come hell or high water, come darkness or dawn, non-segregation or nothing"? He did not believe that would be the alternative, Robinson gamely replied. The court had ordered "a prompt and reasonable start" to integration, and it also had stipulated that mere disagreement with constitutional principles could not quash them. "That, as I understand it, is the difficulty encountered by the school authorities in Prince Edward County," Robinson replied. The primary obstacle was a lack of will.[34]

Almond's outrage spoke for a white establishment aghast at the brazenness of the NAACP demand. "They come here and say, 'We are willing to cooperate.' They are willing to cooperate if they dictate every procedure of the process to cooperate," he thundered. His words gave comfort to untold numbers of Virginians suspecting the NAACP of evil intent. An organization "drunk with power and hell-bent to present chaos, they place their own construction on the term 'deliberate speed' and they place that construction by abrogating its every synonym and adopting its antonyms of haste and capriciousness." What the NAACP asked, he concluded, "cannot be done." The Virginia judicial panel agreed, at least with the proposition that Prince Edward schools should not be forced to integrate by September. The edict, joining South Carolina's, meant in effect that involuntary desegregation of public schools would not occur anywhere in the eleven Confederate states during the 1955–56 school term. As schools opened, dozens of districts in Kentucky, West Virginia, Missouri, and other border states moved voluntarily toward integration, but opposition hardened in the Deep South. Six Virginia counties approved plans to drop public support for schools altogether if the courts ordered integration.[35] The cross that had burned on the Hills' lawn a few weeks earlier had illuminated mounting hostility and distrust.

Throughout the fall, Hill, Robinson, and the legal team of the Virginia NAACP petitioned school boards in key communities—Norfolk, Newport News, Alexandria, Charlottesville, Arlington, and Isle of Wight—for voluntary integration and vowed court action if communities refused. Over time they would make good on that promise. More school-integration lawsuits would be filed with LDF backing in Virginia than in any other state, reflecting once again the prowess of the legal network established by Hill and Robinson. "We had to go to court to get them to do anything and everything," Hill recalled.[36] Meanwhile, Virginia's white establishment first deferred to the Gray Commission's aim of holding desegregation to a minimum and then, by the following spring, slid into outright defiance of the Supreme Court edict. The formation of the Defenders of State Sovereignty and Individual Liberties gave shape to the resistance. The group fancied itself a more upright faction of the White Citizens' Councils popping up across the South. But its intellectual focus on states' rights could not obscure its primary aim: depriving black schoolchildren of equality under the law. By September 1955 the Defenders had a reported twenty-eight chapters and twelve thousand members statewide.[37] That organization and its allies made common cause in the fall of 1955 with Jack Kilpatrick, the fiery young editor of the *Richmond News Leader*. Kilpatrick dusted off an antiquated notion known as interposition, under which states theoretically could exert their will over that of the federal government in rare instances in which federal lawmakers had acted egregiously. In Kilpatrick's mind, the *Brown* ruling qualified, and he soon found a regional audience for the dubious rallying point. As Kilpatrick's writings became more strident, Hill counseled a friend to pay scant attention. "As to why you would blow a valve over the editorial by dear brother James is more than I can understand," he advised Harry Penn in Roanoke. "After knowing him all these years such a statement is about the best you should expect from him."[38]

Kilpatrick's editorial campaign dovetailed with the November release of the long-awaited Gray Commission report. The plan favored three principal ideas: give local school boards a free hand to assign individual students to a particular school for a host of reasons short of race; create publicly funded private-school tuition grants for parents unwilling to send their children to integrated schools; and specify that no student, black or white, would be forced to attend an integrated school. A bit of integration likely would occur under the plan, but it could be held to a minimum. Since the state constitution prohibited use of public funds to pay for private schooling, that document would have to be amended to allow for tuition grants.[39] In a six-page memorandum to Robert Carter, Robinson rebutted the report item by item, concluding, "It proposes to accomplish indirectly what the Supreme Court had held invalid when directly done. Purely and simply, it is a scheme to continue the state in an educational system segregated on a racial basis."[40]

On November 30, as Governor Stanley convened a four-day special session of the General Assembly aimed at setting the constitutional amending process in motion, Hill weighed in as well. Speaking at yet another marathon public hearing—this one the day before blacks in Montgomery, Alabama, launched a seminal, year-long bus boycott—Hill shook his fist and warned against the folly of "irresponsible talking and irrational action." Attempting to circumvent the Supreme Court in order to carry out "the bidding of the racial fanatics" was doomed to failure, he said. "We do not believe that the most powerful government ever to exist on the face of the earth . . . will find itself impotent to protect its citizens from the ravages of a handful of officeholders" who lacked moral courage.[41] Years later, the state senator Henry L. Marsh III, who became Richmond's first black mayor and who for many years served as the legislature's leading voice on minority affairs, recalled Hill's speech that day as a personal turning point. Marsh, then the student-body president at Virginia Union, attending the public hearing in order to speak, had found a lifetime calling in the presence of Hill's passion.[42]

Neither Hill nor Robinson could have predicted that within months the controversial Gray report would be rejected by leading white Virginians as too moderate. In the meantime, voters overwhelmingly approved a constitutional convention. That gathering disposed of the ban on public funding of private schools, clearing the way for tuition grants. And the legislature by a huge majority embraced interposition. Then, in late February 1956, Senator Byrd confirmed an altered strategy. Speaking in Washington, he laid out a case for outright defiance of the Supreme Court. "If we can organize the southern states for massive resistance to this order, I think that in time the rest of the country will realize that racial integration is not going to be accepted in the South," he said. Many white moderates had supported the January referendum on amending the state constitution as a step toward enactment of the Gray Plan. Now the idea of allowing limited, voluntary integration seemed all but dead. Byrd's active encouragement of what became known as the Southern Manifesto further confirmed his entrenchment against *Brown*. That document, signed by 101 southern congressmen and issued on March 12, denounced the *Brown* decision as a "clear abuse of judicial power." The signers pledged to fight the ruling "by all lawful means."[43]

Historians disagree on whether Byrd's embrace of massive resistance was motivated primarily by political considerations, devotion to states' rights, or a personal belief in white supremacy. Overall, the first two positions garner the most attention. At a time when a fast-growing urban population was jeopardizing his political hold, Byrd surely knew that he ignored his rural base at his peril. But Hill's recollections add credence to the argument that the senator also shared the racist views of many of his rural allies. Hill detected an uncommon disdain in Byrd's unwillingness even to talk with him about the unfolding situation in Virginia. In contrast, he noted, Representative Dawson, of Chicago, brokered backdoor meetings between Herman E. Talmadge, of Georgia, who served as governor and then senator during the era, and black leaders in his state. Despite Talmadge's reputation as an unrepentant segregationist, Dawson "got people in the line together with Talmadge, and they started working out things." When the congressman tried to do something similar with Byrd, however, the senator refused. "Dawson did all he could to try to get Byrd to agree to just meet with me, just the two of us," recalled Hill. "He wouldn't even do that."[44]

Byrd's disdain for black aspirations surfaced several times in a warm correspondence with Sterling Hutcheson in the years after the judge's retirement. In one instance, the senator referred to the 1965 Voting Rights Act, introduced by President Lyndon Johnson in the wake of the Bloody Sunday march in Selma, Alabama, as "the worst bill that has been introduced in my thirty-two years in the Senate." The bill, which produced a revolution in black registration and voting, was viewed by many others as the supreme tool in granting full citizenship to blacks.[45]

As opposition to *Brown* hardened on one side of the divide, determination solidified on the other. On April 23, 1956, the NAACP lawyers filed yet another motion seeking desegregation in Prince Edward County schools. Three days later, they launched a court challenge in Newport News. And within weeks, similar lawsuits affecting Norfolk, Charlottesville, and Arlington schools were inserted into the judicial pipeline. "We feel we have been more than patient in giving time to comply with the Supreme Court decision. No one seems to want to do anything. We have no alternative but to resort to the courts," said Hill and Robinson in a joint statement announcing the litigation. "The new NAACP litigation brought tensions in Virginia to the exploding point," wrote the historian Brian Daugherity.[46]

A spark from an unexpected source lit the fuse. Federal Judge John Paul Jr., serving western Virginia, was no one's idea of a liberal. Educated as a civil engineer at the Virginia Military Institute, the bald, seventy-two-year-old jurist had been a federal prosecutor, an assistant US attorney general, and a Republican congressman before being nominated by Herbert Hoover for the judiciary. In a case handled by Martin in Roanoke a few years earlier Paul had seemed to agree with *Plessy v. Ferguson*, so NAACP expectations ran low when he was assigned the Charlottesville school case. They slipped further when the august former governor John Battle turned up as counsel for the city. The first inkling that the lawyers might have misjudged Paul came when Battle requested a three-week extension to file various papers. To Hill's surprise, Paul refused to play along. "I think we got ourselves a real judge," Hill told Robinson as they walked out of Paul's chambers.[47] The subsequent one-day trial on July 12 confirmed the suspicion. In court Battle and Almond tried a series of diversionary tactics. Paul sliced through the malarkey with a sharp-edged ruling. "I would close my eyes to the obvious facts if I didn't believe the state has been pursuing a deliberate, well-conceived plan of evasion," he said from the bench. The plaintiffs were entitled to the relief they sought, effective in the coming school term. Appeals could drag out the inevitable, but desegregation had become a matter of when, not if.[48]

Just days later, Judge Bryan wielded a similar blow. Ruling in the Arlington school case, he decreed that desegregation should begin the following January in county elementary schools and in September 1957 in junior and senior high schools. Again, appeals could extend the timetable, but not forever. Action still was pending in the Norfolk and Newport News challenges, but the segregationists had little cause for optimism from that quarter either. The previous summer, Judge Walter E. "Beef" Hoffman, assigned to hear those cases, had proved that he understood the Supreme Court's dim view of Jim Crow. When the state tried to skirt integration at the Seashore State Park in Virginia Beach by leasing the property to a private operator, Hoffman had issued a permanent injunction against such tactics. Robinson and attorney Ashe had defended Hoffman's order before the Fourth Circuit, which upheld the decision.[49]

Rather than retreat, Byrd and his allies dug deeper. In early July, Governor Stanley and key members of the Gray Commission traveled to Washington to confer with the senator and three Virginia congressmen. There, they committed to outright defiance even if it led to closing public schools. Acquiescing, Stanley announced a special session of the legislature to begin August 27, aimed at forging the legal tools needed for "unyielding

resistance" to school integration. On the eve of the assembly, addressing some two thousand constituents at an annual picnic in his apple orchard at Berryville, Byrd targeted his prime culprit. "It is no secret that
the NAACP intends to press first in Virginia" for integrated schools, he
said. "If Virginia surrenders, if Virginia's line is broken, the rest of the
South will go down too." He urged resisting "with every ounce of energy."[50] Two days later, states'-rights advocates waved Confederate flags
and packed the gallery of the House of Delegates for the start of the special session. Despite elevated passions, some lawmakers balked at outright
intransigence. On a key vote testing whether to allow localities to craft
their own integration policies, the shift of a mere two state senate votes
could have sent Virginia on a more moderate course. Nonetheless, support
for the Byrd-Stanley package held, and lawmakers adjourned with a firm
anti-integration, anti-NAACP program in place. Under the new laws, the
governor would close the public schools in any Virginia locality ordered by
the courts to integrate or voluntarily electing to do so. Public funds would
pay for private-school tuition grants for schoolchildren displaced by the
closures. A state Pupil Placement Board would assign pupils to particular
schools based on a variety of measures, but it was understood by all that
those assignments would not result in any racially mixed schools. In a
small nod to mollifying the courts, lawmakers approved a narrow loophole
under which a locality might integrate. That unlikely event would occur
without a penny of state funding.[51]

Lawmakers had one more task: to emasculate, if possible, the organization that had caused Virginia such turmoil. Fury at the NAACP spilled out
in rhetoric and in a package of seven bills aimed at crippling the association. "There is more affection and more desire to help the Negro in these
one hundred and forty members of the General Assembly than there is
in the entire NAACP," claimed Senator Albertis S. Harrison Jr., of Lawrenceville, a future governor, capturing the prevailing mood. In Orwellian
doublespeak, lawmakers proclaimed it the duty of government to promote
"interracial harmony and tranquility" and to protect its citizens from interracial tension and unrest. Toward that end, the Virginia General Assembly overwhelmingly approved bills demanding registration, including
disclosure of membership lists and financial data, by groups that advocated
on behalf of a particular race or engaged in activities that "cause or tend
to cause racial conflict or violence." The mandate might apply to several

groups, including the segregationist Defenders, but few doubted that the real target—and the group whose members and donors ran the greatest risk—was the NAACP. Lawmakers in Tennessee quickly copied Virginia's pioneering legislation almost verbatim, and politicians in Texas, Arkansas, and South Carolina soon adopted similar laws.[52]

Legislators also took direct aim at Hill, Robinson, and other NAACP attorneys by expanding the definitions of and setting criminal penalties for several practices in which lawmakers believed the black lawyers engaged: improperly soliciting business (known as "running and capping"); instigating lawsuits ("barratry"); and soliciting a lawsuit without having a direct interest in it ("maintenance"). The offenses essentially boiled down to drumming up and financing lawsuits for selfish purposes. Finally, modeling the House Un-American Activities Committee and the Senate subcommittee headed by Senator McCarthy, both of which had gained notoriety for their anti-Communist probes, lawmakers empowered two investigatory panels to turn a spotlight on NAACP practices. One of the few legislative critics of the commissions, Delegate John C. Webb, from northern Virginia, groused that the state did not need "a little Gestapo" to intimidate its citizens. His complaint drowned in a sea of support.[53]

Both Hill and Robinson had come to the *Brown* decision arguing that most Virginians would accept court-ordered integration—grudgingly no doubt, but ultimately with respect for the law. The 1956 special session of the Virginia legislature, coupled with a parallel hardening across the Deep South, proved them wrong. Initially, "we sensed that it was going to be some time" before full integration was achieved, but "I don't think the expectation at the beginning was that it was really going to be as slow as it was," Robinson recalled. As for Hill, he had trusted the voices of white acquaintances who claimed to endure segregation only because it was the law. But in the months and years after *Brown* II, he realized that "it was more than a law. . . . A lot of people just actually believed Negroes were inferior."[54] In the wake of *Brown* II, the South stood at the brink of unprecedented change. The forces of resistance were massing as never before. For Hill, Robinson, and their NAACP companions, there would be no retreat from what they believed millions of black Americans wanted, needed, and were entitled to receive.

FIFTEEN

A Fight to Survive

O. R. Phillips, of Columbia, South Carolina, spoke for countless fellow southerners in urging Governor Stanley to stand fast against the NAACP infidels. "The thing that should be done would be for every Southern State to outlaw the NAACP and not be allowed to operate in the South," he wrote in February 1957. "It is the most ungodly organization that ever drifted into the South and has brought more trouble than anything that ever happened in the South."[1] When it came to destroying the hated association, the overlords of Virginia and her kindred states tried their damnedest. In the ensuing years, they fought with equal ferocity to block school desegregation and to drive a stake into the heart of the "ungodly" organization championing that cause. In Virginia, for a time almost the entire weight of the political power structure bore down on the NAACP, targeting it for ruin, if possible, and crippling it, if not. Voices of moderation existed, but they were muted, eventually emerging from the shadows only because of the clarity of the federal judiciary, the tenacity of the black lawyers, and the dawning realization that Virginians could bow to the *Brown* edict or close public schools. The choice was as stark and simple as that.

For Robinson and Hill, men already challenged to meet vast community and professional commitments, the pressure and the stakes intensified. Even before the Virginia General Assembly convened on August 27, 1956, to adopt the underpinnings for Massive Resistance, the NAACP was priming for the fight. "Oliver is out of the city, but before leaving he asked that I write you as follows," Evalyn Shaed, Hill's sister-in-law and office administrator, advised Robert Carter six days before the session's start. Already some Virginia counties were pressuring NAACP chapters to disclose sensitive membership information, she reported. Hill and others were weighing a response. In the meantime, the national office should file paperwork with the State Corporation Commission identifying the NAACP Legal Defense and Educational Fund, Inc., as an out-of-state entity doing business in Virginia.[2] Previously, no one had questioned the organization's legal status; now they did.

The Virginians needed look no further than Louisiana and Alabama to glimpse what might be coming. In March, a Louisiana judge had dusted off a decades-old law to insist that the civil rights organization identify its members or close shop. Soon afterward, Alabama had accused the NAACP of violating state law by financing the then six-month-old Montgomery bus boycott and of paying Autherine Lucy Foster to sue the University of Alabama for admission. Roy Wilkins denied both claims, but a state judge ordered the NAACP to shut down anyway. He sealed the coffin with a contempt fine of one hundred thousand dollars for the group's refusal to turn over membership lists. In time, South Carolina would ban membership by public employees, including teachers, in the NAACP. Mississippi required teachers to file affidavits listing memberships in all organizations, including the NAACP. Texas accused the group in court of tax fraud and "engaging in illegal political activities." And Georgia jailed the president of the NAACP's Atlanta chapter and fined him twenty-five thousand dollars for refusing to turn over chapter records. "The war on the NAACP represented the gravest overt threat to basic civil liberties during the 1950's," concluded the historian Numan V. Bartley in his classic study of the era of Massive Resistance.[3]

The Virginia General Assembly's approval of the seven anti-NAACP bills during the 1956 special session validated Hill's worries. The delegate James M. Thomson, of Alexandria, had made the intent clear in the lead-up to their adoption: "With this set of bills . . . we can bust that organization . . . wide open." The legislative assault could not go unanswered. On November 29, after a flurry of conferences, the NAACP and the Legal Defense Fund filed companion lawsuits in federal court, seeking to block enforcement of the new laws. Carter and Hill represented the NAACP in *NAACP v. Almond,* which named the attorney general and several of the commonwealth's attorneys as defendants. Marshall and Robinson signed for the Legal Defense Fund. Only since the *Brown* decision, the groups noted, had state officials "concluded that the plaintiff's organization must be destroyed if segregation is to be preserved in this State."[4] The filings launched a six-year legal odyssey through state and federal courts.

The creation of the two investigatory panels particularly troubled the NAACP. The recent heavy-handed, inquisition-style congressional probes of Communist influence bred fear that similar tactics awaited witnesses called before the Virginia panels. The discovery over the next several months that the committees intended to hire former FBI agents and meet behind closed doors quickened dread. "It was a witch hunt," said Hill, describing the climate. He might have had even greater concern had he been privy to David Mays's diary entry on May 23, 1957, which read: "Two former FBI men—Simmons and Powell—played for us some samples of recordings of conversations with plaintiffs in the NAACP cases. These may prove very helpful in probable proceedings by the Bar Association against Oliver Hill and possibly others."[5] Clearly, the committees knew whom they were targeting. The Committee on Offenses Against the Administration of Justice, dubbed the Boatwright Committee, took its nickname from Chairman John B. Boatwright, a tobacco-chewing central Virginian whose district included the site of Robert E. Lee's surrender to Ulysses S. Grant in April 1865, ending the Civil War. Then seventy-four, the wily segregationist and powerful chairman of the House Committee on General Laws was not one to show restraint on bedrock principles, including social separation of the races.[6] Thomson, Boatwright's counterpart on the Committee on Law Reform and Racial Activities, was more than four decades his junior. Just thirty-two and with less than a year under his legislative belt, the younger lawmaker was every bit Boatwright's equal in intellect and cunning. He shared also an inflexible belief in the sovereign right of states to set their own course in matters of education and race. An outsized pugnacity, plus a political pedigree as the brother-in-law of Harry F. Byrd Jr., the senator's son, made Thomson a natural fit for the job. "Jim has a Spartan mentality," an acquaintance once said. "He either wants to come home with his shield or on top of it."[7] Despite slightly different missions and powers, the two committees had essentially one purpose: to collect information about the inner workings of the NAACP, thereby undermining an organization seen by most, and probably all, committee members as nefarious and up to no good.

The opening salvo from the Boatwright Committee arrived in the form of letters to the national and state offices of the NAACP dated January 14, 1957. The lawmakers requested a battery of information: names and addresses of all officers, employees, volunteers, donors, and service providers, plus certified statements listing all contributions and expenditures for 1956.[8] The letters launched a month-long game of cat and mouse. Hill politely requested a deadline extension until after the NAACP national board met on February 11. Meanwhile, behind the scenes a rash of meetings engaged the state and national legal staffs as they weighed a response to that request and to an even larger demand from the Thomson group, mailed January 30. The second appeal included an astonishing request for copies of all 1956 correspondence between the state conference and every Virginian to whom it had supplied legal aid "directly or indirectly," including litigants or prospective litigants in all school cases.[9]

News of the legislative assault stirred consternation. "Please inform me immediately of the legal status of the NAACP in the state of Virginia. . . . If we are to be confronted with imminent criminal action by the state, I should like to have the benefit of your opinion," urged Gregory Swanson, who had integrated the University of Virginia School of Law and now headed the Martinsville NAACP branch. "The NAACP is still a legally functioning organization in Virginia," replied Hill. However, because of recent Assembly action, the legal staff recommended limiting branch activities to fundraising and voter activity. Lawyers had requested a federal injunction halting enforcement of the new laws, he added. "We do not believe anyone is going to be prosecuted under these laws while this case is pending."[10] Still, caution was advised. Answering the Boatwright Committee, Wilkins offered to provide aggregate data on gifts and spending. He drew the line at naming members and donors as "an unwarranted invasion of our freedoms." Hill answered the Thomson Committee even more pointedly. The state conference had "nothing to hide," but it would not name names. "We know from previous experience that individuals in Virginia have been subjected to intimidation, harassment and economic reprisals for belonging to, or participating in activities sponsored by, this organization," he wrote.[11]

A swift rebuke arrived the next day in the form of subpoenas from the clerk of the Richmond Hustings Court. The court ordered Banks, among others, to appear before the Boatwright Committee prepared to hand over names and addresses. Alarmed, the NAACP lawyers scheduled a weekend conference in Washington; Robinson traveled north. There, the assembled group decided to show good faith by answering most of the committee's questions, while simultaneously pressing for an injunction blocking membership disclosure. With the injunction request pending before Judge Hutcheson, a phalanx of NAACP lawyers and officials, including Hill, Robinson, Marshall, and Banks, strode into the capitol for the February 20 hearing. In an environment where the only other black face was likely to belong to a janitor, the NAACP contingent typically traveled in pairs or groups, creating a bulwark of support in hostile terrain. Boatwright dismissed the crowd after ten minutes, allowing only cursory remarks from Marshall.[12] Temporarily, the court ploy had stayed the committee's hand. Behind the scenes, a shaken NAACP responded to fear of legislative overreach by transferring the assets of the Virginia conference—fourteen thousand dollars—to a New York bank and directing local branches to send their membership records for protection to Banks or Hill in Richmond.[13] An editorial in the *Richmond Afro-American* saw the proceedings for what they were: harassment of the NAACP. "It may be, that by sapping the organization's time and energies in meeting the demands of various legislative committees, its effectiveness will be minimized," the editorialist wrote. From a segregationist viewpoint, such a result probably was purpose enough.[14]

Even as Robinson, Hill, and their colleagues shouldered grueling school-desegregation caseloads during 1957 and 1958, they juggled an astonishing number of legal challenges involving the anti-NAACP laws. In late 1957 a Boatwright Committee lawyer complained that the group had had to go to court fourteen times in its first ten months to compel NAACP cooperation. If the committee was in court that many times, the NAACP presumably was as well. Moreover, the Boatwright interactions constituted but a single piece of the legal campaign to protect NAACP members against intimidation and its lawyers against claims of unethical behavior. Some three years after the initial meeting of the Boatwright group, Hill observed that the right of the NAACP to protect its membership lists remained "a matter of grave concern" and a principal issue in no fewer than six legal cases pending in varying postures before federal and state courts.[15] No wonder that, as David Mays reported with satisfaction, "the Negro lawyers seem to be physically exhausted."

With the tussle over membership lists stalled in court, the Boatwright and Thomson committees turned to another priority: discrediting the

NAACP lawyers. The legislative panels needed membership lists, they argued, to determine whether the NAACP had pressured or paid individuals to bring lawsuits. In mid-May, Robinson and Hill joined Carter and other worried observers in Washington for a full-fledged strategy huddle on the Virginia situation.[16] Meanwhile, over the next several months the legislative committees launched a series of closed-door hearings in Richmond, Charlottesville, Farmville, Arlington, and Norfolk, sites that formed ground zero for the school desegregation effort. Either Robinson or Hill, or both, attended most of the sessions. At times, the attorneys themselves spent hours in the witness box, explaining how they had initiated and funded lawsuits; at other times, they stood by, ready to offer legal assistance or perspective. Sometimes, Tucker, Ealey, and other members of the NAACP state legal committee helped monitor the hearings. The lawyers did not want any black citizen to face hostile legislators unattended.

The deliberations highlighted the 180-degree gap between what white lawmakers and the NAACP attorneys perceived to be principled behavior. To the astonishment of the private lawyers hired to staff the Boatwright Committee, Hill at one such session cheerfully and unapologetically acknowledged encouraging NAACP litigation. He saw such activity as defending constitutional rights; the probers saw it as unethical and illegal. Later, the Boatwright Committee released a partial transcript in an attempt to establish what they viewed as Hill's brazen wrongdoing.

Q: I am merely inquiring in what instance, as best you can now recall, has either the NAACP State Conference or any of its branches or its officers, acting in the capacity of officers, undertaken to either encourage such litigation or to persuade the commencement of such litigation?

HILL: It would be kind of hard to single out a single instance. I say that has happened on numerous occasions.

And later,

Q: Have you as an individual ever so addressed any gathering or any other person or group?

HILL: Oh, yes.

Q: Can you tell us when that occurred?

HILL: That would be most any time I have made a public speech, and they have been numerous.[17]

If urging citizens to insist that the government live up to the promise of the Constitution was a crime, then Hill pleaded guilty. While the NAACP lawyers answered confidently, some plaintiffs in the school-desegregation lawsuits did not. During a Charlottesville hearing in May, several witnesses confirmed Boatwright Committee suspicions by claiming not to have understood that signing NAACP petitions would make them parties to a desegregation lawsuit. One such witness, Reginald R. Moss, an employee of a local manufacturer, appeared "visibly shaken" after an hour with the committee, according to a news account. His discomfort stemmed in part from unexpectedly hearing his tape-recorded words from a prior interview with investigators played back to him. The committee unapologetically defended the secret tapings as necessary to ferret out lies.[18]

Whether backtracking by Moss and others reflected fear of economic reprisal from the white community, failure by the NAACP to properly explain its plans, or simple confusion remained an open question. The answer likely varied with the individual. To Hill's mind, however, there was little doubt that the legislative hearings had been rigged to put the NAACP in the worst possible light. "They get people with no experience in this kind of thing and ask leading questions," he said. "Nobody has an opportunity to examine witnesses to see if they understand the purport of what they're saying." Support for his claim lay in the selective, hand-picked nature of the Charlottesville witness list. Almost a dozen other plaintiffs, including a black doctor and the publisher of a small black weekly, men unlikely to be intimidated, were subpoenaed but not called to testify.[19] Why not? The explanation of Senator Earl Fitzpatrick, of Roanoke, a member of the committee, confirmed Hill's suspicion. "The committee knows what it is trying to develop. When it obtained information along the lines it wanted to develop, it didn't see any necessity to go any further," Fitzpatrick said.[20] As long as some plaintiffs were confused or misinformed, it did not matter whether others—or even most—understood their actions.

For months on end, scarcely a day passed without some new pleading or initiative to move school desegregation forward or block retaliatory action. Hill, as the head of the NAACP's state legal committee, and Robinson, as the Legal Defense Fund's regional representative, were at the center of it all. If a single week could showcase the three-ring circus that constituted their lives and those of their fellow NAACP attorneys during the period of Massive Resistance, it might be September 15–21, 1957. On the morning of Monday, September 16, the long-awaited trial in *NAACP v. Almond* and its companion LDF challenge to the constitutionality of the anti-NAACP laws opened in a federal courtroom in Richmond. For four days, Marshall, Carter, Robinson, and Hill squared off against the state's representatives, Mays and Henry Wickham. Meanwhile, in Arlington the Thomson Committee wrapped up two days of ill-tempered hearings with its chairman insisting that evidence sufficed to "bar the NAACP from the unauthorized practice of law." That same week, Judge Hutcheson granted Hill's request for an injunction protecting parents in Charlottesville and Richmond from overreach by new massive-resistance laws. Separately, Robinson and Hill filed an important brief challenging Hutcheson's latest ruling giving Prince Edward County virtually limitless time to begin desegregating its schools. And if all that was not enough, in northern Virginia Judge Bryan stayed his own recent order that Arlington must begin school desegregation the next week. Hill had argued against the stay a few days earlier, vowing in exasperation that if schools had to close to "bring Virginia to its senses, then the sooner we reach that crisis the better."[21] The avalanche of activity occurred alongside the routine demands of private law offices in which Robinson now shepherded the legal affairs of black financial institutions and Hill embraced a full-service civil and criminal practice. Unlike the lawyers at the NAACP and LDF headquarters in New York, the local attorneys did not have the luxury of focusing only on civil rights.

The trial testing Virginia's anti-NAACP bills proved to be a marquee event, crowding the federal courthouse in downtown Richmond and drawing wide media attention. The legal and political communities understood that the organization's survival in Virginia—and perhaps elsewhere—rested on the outcome. At issue were five bills, two requiring the forced disclosure of the names of members and donors and three targeting the ethics of the NAACP attorneys. Opening the NAACP testimony, Banks and Wilkins described the damage being done by the new laws. The Virginia conference had experienced a 30 percent drop in membership. Contributions also had slowed. "They have a fear of economic reprisals directed toward them," said Wilkins, attributing the decline in support to intimidation.[22] As for ethics, Marshall, Robinson, and Hill all denied that the NAACP lawyers had gone fishing for plaintiffs. "We have never gone out and solicited business in Virginia. We have never done any ambulance chasing," Hill insisted. Countering that point, Mays and Wickham introduced five *Davis* plaintiffs to testify that they had been made parties to the Prince Edward school case without their knowledge. Leonard Bland, a retired railroad worker, said he had learned his name was attached to the lawsuit six years after the fact, when "some men from the Boatwright Commission told me." Had he not attended a meeting at the Moton School after the strike? asked an incredulous Spot Robinson on cross-examination. "Yes," Bland replied. "Wasn't it discussed that you seek a lawsuit against segregation at that very meeting?" "I don't remember." The NAACP answered with four white witnesses from Arlington and Charlottesville who testified that they had endured threats, anonymous phone calls, and obscene remarks after becoming publicly identified with the school-desegregation movement.

Robinson's showcase moment came in debriefing Alabama's attorney general, John M. Patterson, an avowed segregationist who had played a key role in shutting down NAACP operations in his state. Mays had intended for his star witness to argue that registration laws such as Virginia's would help law enforcement keep track of dangerous white-supremacist groups, suggesting a more high-minded purpose to the new laws than discrediting a civil rights group. But the plan backfired when Robinson produced a newspaper clipping quoting Patterson as he headed for the Old Dominion. He was happy, Patterson had said, to help his friends in Virginia clip the wings of the NAACP. "He might as well have remained in Alabama," groused Mays in his diary.[23]

With the fate of the five bills resting in the judiciary, the Boatwright and Thomson committees began winding up their investigations. By mid-November their reports were ready for release. Thomson went first. Not surprisingly, the verdict damned the organizations behind the school-desegregation cases. The manner in which the NAACP, the Legal Defense Fund, and the state conference had acquired plaintiffs for their lawsuits was "in most cases, reprehensible," the report charged. The three groups "are now and have been engaged in the unauthorized practice of the law" with "enormous sums of money" spent to promote racial litigation. As if unearthing a scandal, the Thomson Committee reported that each of the desegregation lawsuits in Virginia "has been financed by these interlocking organizations." In no instance, it added ominously, had an individual plaintiff directly paid any part of the cost of litigation. The report did not mention that the NAACP had never contested the point or that in its view its actions had merely enabled the fulfillment of long-denied constitutional rights.[24]

The Boatwright Committee report, issued soon afterward, heaped fuel on the fire. It took direct aim at the practices undergirding the legal assault on Jim Crow and at specific lawyers, including Hill and Robinson. Members observed that various white segregationist groups had cooperated with the committee. In contrast, it claimed, the NAACP and its affiliates had operated egregiously at almost every turn. According to the report, the black lawyers had routinely solicited legal business, obtained plaintiffs by false pretenses, kept legal control of cases that should have been under the direction of their clients, and financed litigation at no cost to the plaintiffs.[25] The committee named its alleged culprits. Hill, Robinson, Banks, the NAACP, and its Virginia conference, among others, had committed barratry, punishable by fines and up to a year in jail. Hill, Robinson, Martin, and Tucker were guilty of "unprofessional conduct," punishable by the stripping of one's law license. Each of the other principal attorneys in the school-desegregation cases joined them in that offense. The report evaluated four additional crimes, all involving improperly promoting or directing litigation, and named more than a dozen alleged culprits, most of them local-branch activists. The NAACP and its offshoots were broadly culpable, the report said.[26]

Suddenly the campaign against the NAACP had entered new and hazardous terrain. Formally challenging professional ethics and alleging criminal activity propelled name-calling into a darker realm. The report not only chronicled complaints but also urged commonwealth attorneys in various localities to bring charges against the troublemakers and advised the Virginia State Bar to discipline those who had violated its code of ethics. Robinson, Hill, and their colleagues might hope that sounder judgment would prevail or that the federal courts would protect them from overreach. They might take comfort in community accolades such as Hill's selection as Omega Psi Phi's "Man of the Year" for 1957 or gain strength from moral certitude. They were, after all, pursuing a chosen aim and a noble purpose. Still, they were living in ugly times. No one could say how long it might take for justice to prevail or how much damage might be done to careers and fortunes before it did. A relentless bombardment of hate speech surrounded them. Campaigning for the governorship that fall, Lindsay Almond had asserted that the Republican Party and the NAACP had "cut the very heart out of Dixie." The scalpel rested in "the deft and ruthless fingers of the NAACP." Senator A. Willis Robertson, Byrd's Virginia colleague, trumpeted similar vitriol in a November address to the Richmond Bar Association, charging that the Communist Party was "trying to use the NAACP to destroy the nation's government by first destroying states' rights." Such diatribes in Virginia and elsewhere contributed to a sharp decline in open support for the group. By 1958 the organization had lost 246 branches in the South, and the proportion of NAACP members living in the region had declined from 50 percent to about 25 percent.[27]

And what of the lawyers caught in the crosshairs? What impact did such vitriol have on them? Assessing the damage, the historian Numan Bartley blamed the anti-NAACP campaign for hardening white southern sentiment against blacks and undermining valid dissent by linking human rights to Communist doctrine. But perhaps its most costly effect, he said, was that "it undermined Negro confidence in the basic commitment to justice by white men."[28] Dr. Ferguson Reid, Robinson's longtime friend, experienced such sentiment. Reid had returned to Richmond from military service in Korea in 1955, just in time for the devastating advent of Massive Resistance. "You play by the rules. You win, and then they come up with some other way to counteract it. It's something you never forget," said Reid, who believed Robinson and Hill shared his disillusionment, at least for a while.[29]

Former Virginia governor Wilder, who watched and learned from the older men, thought otherwise. He saw in Hill and Robinson a spark of belief in the ultimate promise of the Constitution that never wavered, he said. In his view, theirs was a vision shaped by Mordecai Johnson and "drilled into the minds of the civil rights' lawyers by Charles Houston that 'this is a fight to the end—an inevitable, endurable, everlasting engagement.'" The entire premise of a Howard Law education in the 1930s was that win or lose in the moment, if the Constitution meant what it said, fairminded men eventually would have no choice but to afford black people the same privileges as white. "I never felt they lost any sense of that," Wilder said. Hill and Robinson surely experienced times of exhaustion and acute disappointment. Consistent with Wilder's assessment, however, they showed no hint of giving up on the battle. "My father's main response to such nastiness was to fight," said Oliver Hill Jr. "He was always confident that through the law, all such efforts could be overcome." The surprise and regret the pair expressed in later years had to do with the extent to which racism blinded so many white southerners to the benefits of racial progress. Even then, they gave no public sign of losing faith in the power of the law itself to eventually overcome.[30]

As 1958 began, the law spoke with a forked tongue. On January 20 the Virginia Supreme Court of Appeals upheld the Boatwright Committee's demand for access to the NAACP membership rolls. The segregationists' celebration lasted just twenty-four hours. The next day, in a 2-1 decision, the three-judge federal panel weighing *NAACP v. Almond* ruled unconstitutional three of Virginia's anti-NAACP laws, including the two requiring membership disclosure. The majority also deemed the statute punishing barratry to be out of bounds. The remaining two laws were so vague as to need interpreting in state courts, they said. Dissenting, Hutcheson argued that all five should have been evaluated first by state judges.[31] Now, temporarily, it was the NAACP's turn to celebrate. The latest decision also would prove fickle. A final answer would come only after a long, circuitous wind through federal and state courts.

The NAACP attorneys had no time to dwell on personal woes. Since Judge Paul's ruling in Charlottesville and Judge Bryan's in Arlington in the summer of 1956, the school-desegregation cases had not languished. Even as lawmakers had worked overtime to create misery, the black lawyers had been steadily refuting motions, filing briefs, and arguing school cases. In March 1957 the Supreme Court upheld the desegregation rulings in Charlottesville and Arlington, sending the cases back to the lower courts for action. Meanwhile, Norfolk and Newport News joined the list of cities under a court order to desegregate. As predicted, Judge Hoffman had shown no patience with the pupil-placement scheme devised by the state. He recognized the law for what it was—a ruse to maintain segregation—and ruled accordingly. The Fourth Circuit validated his opinion in the summer of 1957. That fall the Supreme Court declined to review the decision. Through one gambit or another, the state managed to forestall school desegregation during the fall of 1957, but by early 1958 any realist could see that the days of delay were numbered.

Virginia's newly elected governor, Lindsay Almond, and the General Assembly reacted by hunkering down against the perceived forces of evil. Standing bare headed among a sea of top hats as he took the oath of office, Almond embraced the topic. There could be no compromise on integration, he said. "I cannot conceive such a thing as a 'little integration' any more than I can conceive a small avalanche or a modest holocaust." One breach and the floodgates would open. Lawmakers apparently concurred. In the legislative session that followed, they tightened their grip. Lamenting the chaos that had plagued Little Rock the previous fall when President Eisenhower reluctantly ordered the Army's 101st Airborne Division to usher nine black students into Central High School, the Virginians took aim against similar federal interference. With only four dissenting votes, they approved a so-called Little Rock Bill, shutting down any public school policed by military forces. Legislators also directed the Virginia State Bar to take all actions necessary to punish anyone guilty of the unethical and unauthorized practice of law. Conveniently, the Boatwright group had already spelled out who those individuals were.[32]

What the segregationists could not control, despite their best efforts, were the federal judiciary and the will of the NAACP and its allies. Two years of Massive Resistance had not subdued black leaders. Rather, it had made them only "more militant and determined in their demand for black civil rights," wrote the historian James Hershman. Meanwhile, the courts were methodically removing obstacle after obstacle to a showdown. By the summer of 1958 desegregation cases were moving forward in five principal localities: Arlington, Charlottesville, Norfolk, Newport News, and Prince Edward. Virginia's first school-desegregation case was proving stubbornly resistant to resolution. In January 1957, Judge Hutcheson had rejected the NAACP's appeal for a firm desegregation deadline in Prince Edward County. The following November, the Fourth Circuit had reversed that ruling, ordering Hutcheson to require a "prompt and reasonable start" on admitting black children to white schools. The Supreme Court had declined to intervene. In August 1958, with a new school year looming, Hutcheson complied with the appellate-court demand, but not in a way anyone had expected. Observing that the Athenian statesman Solon had traveled for a decade after introducing legal reforms in order to give citizens time to absorb the changes, Hutcheson insisted that Prince Edward needed a similar period for adjustment. "The hearts and minds of men cannot be controlled by legislation nor by force," he decreed, setting the desegregation launch for 1965.[33] So lax a timetable might never pass constitutional muster, but Hutcheson's opinion resolved one uncertainty. Four years after the *Brown* decision, another fall school opening was going to come and go without a single black child entering a white school in Prince Edward County. Once again, concern over the social upheaval of whites trumped respect for the fundamental rights of blacks.

In the NAACP's division of labor, Hill and Robinson served as primary counsel in the Prince Edward and Charlottesville cases. Victor Ashe and J. Hugo Madison took the lead on the Norfolk case, and Edwin Brown was the NAACP's principal attorney on the scene in Arlington. Hale Thompson and Phillip S. Walker primarily oversaw work in Newport News. Martin, Ealey, and, increasingly, Tucker played auxiliary roles in the central Virginia cases. However, as appeals moved forward, lines of distinction blurred. For example, Robinson, who excelled at appellate work, argued before the Fourth Circuit on the Norfolk case in April 1960, with Ashe, Madison, Hill, Marshall, and the local attorney Joseph A. Jordan assisting on the brief. In the Arlington case, Brown, Robinson, and Hill were listed as principal attorneys in 1956 and 1957, but in a critical 1958 hearing, Hill, Robinson, Reeves of the NAACP's national staff, and Otto Tucker of Alexandria handled the work. Assigning credit for specific victories in such fluid conditions proves problematic. In the largest sense, prosecuting the Virginia desegregation cases of the late 1950s was a collaborative effort, staffed by a team of attorneys in which Hill and Robinson, in conjunction with the NAACP national staff, played the lead roles.[34]

Surprisingly, the first Virginia school ordered to lock its doors proved to be none of the likely suspects. The dubious distinction went to Warren County High School in Front Royal, a scenic, mountain-encased community near the state's northwest corner. The county was among seventeen statewide with no black high school. A new facility was on the drawing board, but a group of parents inspired by the *Brown* decision saw no reason to wait. In mid-July 1958, without any preliminary drama, twenty-nine black children represented by Hill requested transfer into the county's white schools. The process moved forward with remarkable speed. When the school board refused the applications, Hill filed suit with thirteen-year-old Betty Kilby and her older brothers, James and John, as the first-named plaintiffs. In early September, Judge Paul barred the school board from denying admission; quickly, the Fourth Circuit jurist Simon E. Soboloff approved. The moment of truth had arrived. Either Governor Almond closed the high school or a group of black students would enroll.[35]

In July, Almond had affirmed that segregation superseded public schools in his mind. "We are not going to have government by the NAACP if I can prevent it," he pledged. Senator Byrd had stoked the resistance further at his annual picnic in Berryville at the end of August. The dread NAACP intended to first "bring Virginia to its knees" and then "march through the South singing 'hallelujah,'" he lamented. Byrd pledged to stand "firmly and four-square" with Almond to resist the onslaught.[36] On Friday, September 12, Almond made good on his promise. Neither black nor white students would attend public high school in Front Royal that fall, he decreed in a statement handed to the press at half past eight in the evening. The school was closed. Virginia had served notice: it remained the stalwart leader of the band of seven former Confederate states—along with Alabama, Florida, Georgia, Louisiana, Mississippi, and South Carolina—refusing to give an inch on school integration. Neighboring North Carolina, Maryland, West Virginia, Kentucky, and Tennessee might bow in token fashion to the courts, but Virginia intended to resist. Cigar and fedora in hand, Hill arrived at the Warren County courthouse the next day with seventeen black students in tow. While the young people waited outside, he went behind closed doors with Warren County school superintendent Q. D. Gasque and the county attorney to urge reconsideration. The rejection took five minutes. Leaving, Hill branded the school closing "unconstitutional" and pledged that the NAACP would use "every legal means" to fight it. Hill was more than ready to take the conflict to the next level.[37]

Dramatic as the Virginia events were, a similar scenario unfolding a thousand miles away in Little Rock overshadowed them. After a rare special session, the Supreme Court on September 12 ordered that city to abide by its desegregation plan, including the immediate integration of Little Rock's Central High School. The threat of white violence, the court said, did not justify depriving black children of their constitutional rights. The unanimous and unequivocal ruling sounded the death knell of Massive Resistance, but leading segregationists refused to hear. Arkansas governor Orville Faubus closed the city's four high schools effective Monday, September 15, rather than comply.[38] Almost simultaneously, two states and two governors had played the South's long-threatened trump card. The federal judiciary could order public schools to desegregate, but the decision on whether to fund public schools belonged to the states. Now the state and the nation would see how many Virginians favored segregation at any cost and how many had been sidestepping an aggravating problem, hoping that it would go away.

Emboldened by Faubus's example, Almond barreled forward. A week later, the governor shuttered Lane High School and Venable Elementary School in Charlottesville, displacing about seventeen hundred students. Eight days after that, on September 27, he took the boldest step of all, turning out the lights in six white junior and senior high schools in Norfolk and ordering some ten thousand students to stay home. By the end of September, thirteen public schools—nine in Virginia, serving about 12,700 students in three localities, and four in Little Rock—had ceased operating. No one knew how much further the mutiny would go. The anticipated crisis in Arlington had abated temporarily with Judge Bryan's decision to delay the desegregation of Stratford Junior High until the winter term. Winter was fast approaching, however. Meanwhile, desegregation cases in Richmond and Alexandria were moving forward rapidly under NAACP auspices.[39] Among whites, the calamity inspired both mean-spiritedness and soul-searching. "Why don't you go on over to Russia where you belong?" one Richmond resident inquired of Hill in a letter. "You should be shot as a traitor, as proven by you taking all those young Negroes to Warren County Courts and teaching them hate. . . . You are despised and held in contempt." But letters of another sort also were filtering into the dialogue. For several years, school-related constituent mail to Governors Stanley and Almond largely urged holding fast against desegregation. Now other voices emerged. J. E. Fitzgerald, the plastics-division manager of the Brunswick Balke Collender Company in Marion, wrote to Governor Almond as a business manager and a father. His company employed a large number of engineers and skilled technicians. Such professionals "I, am sure, will probably leave this area at once, if the public schools were closed or noticeably deteriorated," he said. Fitzgerald warned of a "disastrous effect" on a company employing twelve hundred people.[40]

In affected communities, parents scrambled to create alternate classrooms in church basements, neighborhood recreation centers, and private homes. While a hodgepodge of remedies provided schooling for most displaced children in Charlottesville and Warren County, approximately twenty-seven hundred Norfolk students went without formal education during the fall. The void prodded many white citizens and community leaders long tepid on the racial turmoil to find a voice. Suddenly their principal problem had less to do with race than with education. For many, sending their children to school with a few black students was a lesser evil than having no school to which to send them. Committees favoring public-school preservation cropped up across the state. In November, more than two dozen whites met in Richmond to form a statewide organization. Countergroups such as the Defenders of State Sovereignty and Individual Liberties also rallied. Meanwhile, newspaper editorial pages reflected the shifting sentiment. The *Virginian-Pilot* in Norfolk had long counseled moderation and reason. "The self-defeating nature of the massive resistance laws is too evident now to be concealed under any pretense," editor Lenoir Chambers advised in November. More defiant organs were starting to agree. State political leaders "know that they are licked," lamented the *Lynchburg News.* Even James Kilpatrick recognized the imperative to shift direction. "I believe the time has come for new weapons and new tactics," he counseled the Richmond Rotary Club on November 11.[41]

As the fall wore on, for the first time two non-NAACP lawsuits brought by white plaintiffs centered attention. In *Harrison v. Day*, Governor Almond and Attorney General Albertis Harrison asked Virginia's highest court to rule on whether the laws that had closed schools and transferred savings into private-school tuition grants passed muster under the state constitution. Meanwhile, in *James v. Almond*, a group of white parents aligned through the Norfolk Committee for Public Schools asked the federal courts to determine whether the state's school-closing law violated the Fourteenth Amendment. Some Norfolk public-school children were shut out of an education; for others, schools remained open. How, they asked, could that be justified under the Constitution?[42] While Virginia awaited resolution, fresh forces were moving in both the white and black communities. In late October, Frank Batten, the young publisher of the *Virginian-Pilot*, quietly began organizing the local business community to oppose the school closings. Meanwhile, Stuart T. Saunders, president of the Norfolk & Western Railway, convened a group of twenty-nine industrialists and businessmen concerned about the economic impact of the crisis. Meeting secretly with Virginia's three statewide-elected officials at Richmond's Rotunda Club in late December, the group initially felt rebuffed by Almond's response. Later, however, the governor acknowledged that the entreaty had profoundly influenced him.[43] Finally, more pragmatic, centrist views were gaining a toehold in white circles.

Among blacks, the concept of nonviolent protest, which had gained currency during the Montgomery bus boycott, made its way to Virginia. The Congress of Racial Equality (CORE) joined with the church coordinating committee of the NAACP to sponsor a New Year's Day march from Richmond's Mosque to the capitol. More than one thousand mostly black citizens walked five abreast under umbrellas during a cold, soaking rain to embrace racial reconciliation. Reaching the south portico, they sang "The Battle Hymn of the Republic" and urged Almond, who had declined to meet with them, to appoint a biracial committee to address school issues. Earlier in the day, the thirty-year-old minister who had gained national renown in Montgomery, Martin Luther King Jr., had praised the effort in a six-minute, recorded message. "What you are doing in Virginia is of utmost significance," he had encouraged the crowd. "You are making history."[44] The event, while under joint sponsorship of the NAACP, was an early sign in Virginia that the movement for civil rights already was broadening beyond legal challenges. As the 1960s arrived, direct action would accelerate with warp speed in many areas of the South, although not with equal force in Virginia. Astounding as it might have been to legions of white Virginians who detested the NAACP, the organization had long been a voice of moderation on the spectrum of black activism— "a moderate, elitist organization," in the words of the constitutional scholar Walter F. Murphy. As early as the late 1940s, youthful CORE workers had chaffed at Marshall's caution as they planned to travel south in the wake of the Irene Morgan decision, testing Jim Crow transportation laws. Tensions among various civil rights groups would intensify in the 1960s, but the Virginia State Conference of Branches remained the dominant black political force within the state. That clout was grounded in large measure in the successes of Hill, Robinson, and other NAACP attorneys, who by the 1960s had embraced direct action, as well as in the tireless efforts of leaders such as Banks, Tinsley, and Francis Griffin.[45]

In Virginia, the turning point in the fight against Massive Resistance arrived on January 19, 1959. Ironically, state and federal courts chose a state holiday honoring the birth of the Confederate hero Robert E. Lee to deliver back-to-back rulings affirming the futility of the school closings. By design, the Virginia Supreme Court of Appeals spoke first. The court responded to *Harrison v. Day* with a 5-2 ruling announced in midmorning. "However unfortunate the situation may be," state laws closing schools to avoid integration and then transferring public funds to private-school tuition grants did not pass muster under the Virginia constitution, the judges decreed. Later that day, a three-judge panel answered for the federal courts in *James v. Almond*. The Fourteenth Amendment did not permit communities to school some children while denying an education to others, the trio said. Astute observers had forecast the outcome for months. Still, the reality of defeat prompted a furious howl from the Executive Mansion, one described by Hershman as "probably the most overtly racist public remarks by a Virginia governor in over forty years." Speaking by a statewide television and radio hookup, Almond shocked many listeners by promising to openly defy the courts. He denounced those who "close their eyes to the livid stench of sadism, sex immorality, and juvenile pregnancy infesting the mixed schools of the District of Columbia and elsewhere." He accused integrationists of willingly substituting "strife, bitterness, turmoil, and chaos for the tranquility and happiness of an orderly society." And he pledged not to yield "to that which I know to be wrong and will destroy every semblance of education for thousands of the children of Virginia."[46]

The NAACP and its allies could not let the blast go unanswered. Five days later, Hill helped deliver a response in a fifteen-minute Sunday-evening speech televised by the National Broadcasting Company affiliate in central Virginia. For Hill, speaking as the NAACP's chief voice in Virginia, the telecast provided a moment of unprecedented media exposure. He began with a lesson in constitutional law and the primacy of individual rights over states' rights. Then he insisted that nothing worth preserving in southern tradition would be altered by desegregation. "All essential qualities based upon honesty, integrity, and the Christian ethics will not only be preserved, but strengthened," he argued. What, he asked, was so noble about "denying a patient treatment at a hospital, a traveler food and lodging, a spectator the right to sit in accordance with his individual preferences at places of public amusement and entertainment, the right of a man to secure employment?" Prudence trumped pique as Hill decided not to highlight the hypocrisy in Almond's critique of sexual mores in Washington, DC. According to a crossed-out section of a draft, he had considered saying: "When you are going to equate sexual morality, you not only have to consider illegitimacy statistics, but, I submit, you have to consider the million dollar abortion rings; the large amount of money spent on prophylactics and contraceptives used for illicit sexual relations; the number of sophisticates who enter hospitals under fictitious names and give birth to their children as married women."[47] The fighter in Hill recognized that white women also violated the strictures of sexual propriety in 1950s America; they simply had more resources for hiding it.

As for Almond, he appeared to find catharsis in his paroxysm of rage. When the General Assembly convened in special session a few days later, his anger seemed spent. Astonishing his audience once more, he counseled moving on. In what Muse called Almond's "finest hour," he reviewed the state's exhaustive efforts to block desegregation and insisted that no fair-minded person could fault him for failing to exercise powers he did not have. "I know of nothing more futile than a penal sentence that contributes to nothing but the ridiculous," he said, refuting those who urged his going to jail in protest. Almond's change of heart was heavily influenced by an eleventh-hour meeting with prominent businessmen who warned of economic repercussions if the resistance continued. But Hill believed that his speech also "helped to move the process along in a positive direction." In later years, Almond called his January 20 speech a mistake, a mishandling of his intention to help ease for segregationists the retreat from Massive Resistance. Senator Byrd never fully forgave the governor for his betrayal.[48]

In almost anticlimactic fashion, seventeen black students in Norfolk and four in Arlington entered previously white schools on the morning of February 2. "No crowds assembled, no violence broke out, no rowdy behavior marked the transition from the old to the new," reported the *Richmond News Leader*. Over the next weeks and months, the number of black students attending formerly white schools grew. Three schools in Alexandria desegregated on February 10. Warren County High School officially reopened on an integrated basis, although no white students attended until the following autumn. By fall, Charlottesville also had joined the list of schools with token integration. Still, only a few dozen of the more than two hundred thousand black children enrolled in Virginia's public schools attended integrated classrooms in the 1959–60 school term. Efforts to keep that number tamped down continued with all the gusto that previously had been devoted to keeping blacks out altogether. The legislative push to seize the NAACP's membership rolls and discredit its lawyers persisted. And black attorneys who once had fantasized that southern whites might accept court-ordered integration with a degree of magnanimity shed any remaining illusion that the racial caste system would go quietly.[49] Robinson, Hill, and their colleagues had won the war, but the opposing army acted as if it had not yet received news of its defeat. Many of the battles went on as ferociously as ever.

Nowhere was the disconnect between the Supreme Court's intentions and those of the local citizenry more evident than in Prince Edward County. The January 1959 court decisions ended overt defiance by the Virginia state government but did not silence local rebellion. By the spring of 1959, eight years had passed since Barbara Johns and her friends walked out of Moton High in protest of overcrowded, substandard conditions. A spanking new high school for blacks had opened in 1953, but most black elementary schools remained in disreputable condition. Leading whites acted as if there were no more to be done. For all the respect afforded him on both sides of the racial divide, Judge Hutcheson appeared to be enabling the foot-dragging. In 1948 Hutcheson had shown more resolve and foresight than any of his peers. He had recognized that *Plessy*'s separate-but-equal dictate was a two-sided equation. But now the Court of Appeals for the Fourth Circuit had twice directed the judge to kick-start progress in Prince Edward County. Instead, he had set an almost laughable desegregation deadline of 1965.

On May 5 the Fourth Circuit decreed that enough was enough. It rejected Hutcheson's latest order and instructed him to usher qualified black children into the white high school by the following fall. The appeals court would not be blackmailed by threats that the county was poised to shutter public schools. Once again, days passed without response from Hutcheson. Finally, Hill elected to act.[50] Driving two hours south from Richmond toward the North Carolina border, past verdant tobacco fields and along languid back roads, Hill arrived at the judge's hometown, Boydton. With only five hundred residents, the government seat of Mecklenberg County provided a quiet oasis from the frenzied pressures of courtroom life. Hutcheson retreated here whenever his schedule allowed. Pulling to a stop in front of the unpretentious white-frame cottage shared by Hutcheson and his wife, Betsy, Hill strode up the brick walk to a small side porch where the judge happened to be sitting. "Hey, Oliver," Hill later recalled their exchange, "what are you doing down here?" "Came down to see you, judge," he replied. Small talk followed, until Hutcheson finally asked, "What do you want?" Hill handed him the draft of an order directing county school officials to begin the desegregation process by fall. Hutcheson took in the document, shook his head, and handed it back. "You know I'm not going to sign this thing. You know I'm not going to sign it."[51]

Eleven years had passed since the Gloucester, Surry, and King George court cases, and Hutcheson was weary of it all. He was not Judge Bryan in Arlington or Judge Hoffman in Norfolk or even Judge Paul in western Virginia, where geography and density might insulate a jurist from the wrath of his peers. Most certainly, he was not Judge Waties Waring in South Carolina, who had shaken the state's social order and then moved north to New York City. Virginia's Southside was where Judge Hutcheson belonged and where he intended to stay. His roots were planted deep in county soil. These were his people and his culture. Oliver Hill, for his part, had spent years boldly ignoring color lines and societal taboos. Now here he was, sitting on the judge's side porch and challenging him, man to man, to set aside a lifetime of teaching and practice and, yes, prejudice. It was too much, and it was not going to happen. In July, just a step ahead of the inevitable showdown over Prince Edward County schools, Judge Hutcheson retired from full-time service on the federal bench. Anticipating such action months earlier, Senator Byrd had called himself "terribly distressed" at thoughts of Hutcheson's departure. "My admiration for you is unbounded, and you have done much to preserve what little we can from the aggressions of the powerful influences against us," Byrd had written.[52] The forces of progress and tradition were set on a collision course in Prince Edward County. Over the next several years, the conflict there would take its darkest turn yet. Hands other than Hill's and Robinson's would shepherd the case to its conclusion.

SIXTEEN

New Directions

As the 1950s ended, Hill and Robinson—like Virginia and America—stood poised for change. Two decades had passed since Hill arrived in Richmond as an eager, ambitious thirty-two-year-old determined to see whether the principles preached at Howard Law could crack the hidebound ways of the Old South. Four years later, as Hill marched off to war, Robinson had come forward to fill the older man's shoes. Between them, over the years, the pair had plucked a battalion of grassroots heroes from Virginia soil to advance the cause of equality. Irene Morgan, Barbara Rose Johns, Mahatma Corbin, and scores of others had given a human face to obscure legal claims. With the help of Martin Martin and others, they had tackled Jim Crow segregation in housing and transportation. In 1948 Hill had punctured a glass ceiling in electoral politics only to reveal two years later the severity of the restraints that remained. Together, through the school-equalization campaign, they had demonstrated to a national audience that efforts to make black and white education equal within a segregated system did not work. In *Brown v. Board of Education* they had joined Marshall, Carter, and others to wage the ultimate legal assault on segregated education in America. And in the five years since the court's 1954 decision, they had fought as never before to escape the crush of resistance.

Nationally, a new era of protest and confrontation loomed, although the dimensions of the direct-action movement had yet to take shape. The darker impulses of segregationists soon would collide with a hardened resistance, one swelling beyond the boundaries of courtroom civility. Unbeknownst to Robinson and Hill, a period of change awaited them as well. By mid-1961 each would be engaged in pursuits far from courtrooms and the malice of die-hard segregationists. Already, as a new school year opened in September 1959, Robinson appeared to be stepping back. He continued to play a vital part in several desegregation court cases, but as he built a law practice increasingly focused on black financial institutions and business clients, his day-to-day role in new civil rights matters lessened. Meanwhile, Hill, as the most visible champion of racial equality in Virginia, added new challenges to the obligations cramming his calendar.

Token school integration in Arlington, Norfolk, Alexandria, Warren County, and Charlottesville had pierced the myth that southern white children could not abide a single black classmate. The new legislative strategy aimed at holding such interactions to a minimum. A commission appointed by Almond in the wake of his capitulation on Massive Resistance crafted the plan. Dramatically, it passed the state senate by a single vote when a supporter recovering from abdominal surgery made a surprise appearance in the chamber. The plan gave parents and localities as much leeway as possible to avoid integration. It repealed the compulsory-school-attendance law, provided state-funded tuition grants for private schooling, and allowed school districts to defer to parental wishes in making school assignments. In effect, those so-called freedom-of-choice plans kept most children in segregated classrooms. A few black children gained admittance to white schools, but virtually no white parents elected to send their children to black schools. Hill had warned against such shenanigans during the commission's single public hearing, but he and other blacks acknowledged that the plan probably was the best the political climate would allow.[1]

Resistance to integration was far from dead. Prince Edward County confirmed that truth. On the heels of the federal appeals court's demand in May for "immediate steps" toward desegregation, county officials and the Prince Edward County School Foundation had swung into action. Carrying out a strategy arrived at four years earlier, the board of supervisors stripped the county budget of all funding for public schools. Meanwhile, the foundation activated plans to set up private, segregated classes for about fifteen hundred white children. The experiment launched on September 10, financed solely through donations for the first year. Classes would occur mostly in churches. Formal facilities would be added later. Roy R. Pearson, the foundation's full-time administrator, hailed area citizens as pathfinders shouldering the hopes of untold thousands. By sticking to their values, the segregationists were showing "the same courage as did our forefathers," he said.[2]

That perceived valor included no plans whatsoever for the education of seventeen hundred black children. At a press conference in early September, J. Barrye Wall, editor of the *Farmville Herald* and a driving force behind the public-school shutdown, asserted that whites were "as concerned about what the Negroes are going to do as anybody." Blanton Hanbury, president of the Prince Edward County foundation, urged blacks to "do exactly what we're doing: use their churches and civic halls." Left unsaid was the reality that African Americans had nowhere near the financial and institutional resources available to whites. Nor had they spent years creating a private-school infrastructure, in part because they did not want to acquiesce to such an arrangement. In Richmond, Hill predicted that the NAACP would go to court to force a reopening. But Prince Edward County itself provided the best possible evidence of how protracted any such court fight might be. Meanwhile, hundreds of black children faced immediate consequences. Every week or month of missed school represented dwindling opportunity.[3] Robert L. Hamlin, one of several dozen rising black seniors, recalled the autumn of 1959 as a time of uncertainty and fear. "It was really scary. I was concerned I wouldn't be able to graduate," Hamlin said more than a half century later. After staying home for several weeks, he learned that some classmates had enrolled at Kittrell College, a small, two-year institution some ninety miles away, near Henderson, North Carolina. Hamlin and his parents had never heard of the school, run by the AME Church, but the next weekend, they were in a loaded car heading south. Thus, Hamlin joined hundreds of children in a forced exodus from Prince Edward County, one that split families and altered life trajectories. "I had never been any place to be separated both from mom and dad at the same time," Hamlin recounted. "It was the loneliest feeling."[4]

Over the next several years, hundreds of black children duplicated Hamlin's experience. Some went to live out of state with relatives, some with Quaker families and other progressives dismayed at seeing children robbed of an education. Some found ways to enroll in nearby school districts, often by claiming the address of a relative. Yet, hundreds made do with makeshift study groups or simply gave up on formal education. Reverend Griffin, Hill, and other NAACP leaders argued that the dislocation would prove temporary. Even as children dispersed to Chicago, Philadelphia,

Boston, and elsewhere, those black leaders held out hope that the experiment with private education soon would collapse. When whites embarrassed by the controversy began urging creation of a parallel private school for blacks, Hill and other black elders, fearing the impact on their legal challenge, counseled parents to resist. As one thousand of Prince Edward County's black children gathered for an elaborate Christmas party in the first year of the closing, Hill led the chorus urging the community to stand firm. "All you will lose will be one or two years of Jim Crow education," he admonished. "In your leisure, you can gather more in basic education than you would get in five years of Jim Crow schools."[5] That claim would prove wildly optimistic. Had his father, Hill, and others in the NAACP hierarchy known the full scope of the sad and lengthy saga that awaited Prince Edward's children, Skip Griffin has observed, "my guess is they might have thought twice about it." Once again, the heaviest burden of the push for equality fell not on the NAACP lawyers but on ordinary people living out their lives in anonymity beyond the protections of a relatively privileged fraternity.[6]

Even if the human costs of the desegregation battles weighed most on ordinary citizens, the lawyers did not escape personal travails. Back in Richmond, pressure on the NAACP from the legislature and other arms of Virginia government continued unabated. There was no letup in the effort to dislodge NAACP membership records through the courts. Then, on September 23, 1959, threats of intimidation took the most serious turn yet. A district committee of the Virginia State Bar filed a formal complaint against Sam Tucker, accusing him of unprofessional conduct. The long arm of the oversight group had reached back to the early 1950s to find examples of clients who had not personally employed Tucker and who had not footed their own legal bills. Curiously, similar charges could have been brought against any member of the NAACP legal staff, including Robinson and Hill, yet only Tucker stood blamed. In dozens of cases over the decade, the civil rights organization had assigned lawyers and paid them for representing clients whose constitutional rights were in peril. Legal eagles at the state bar condemned such conduct as self-serving and unprofessional. In contrast, the NAACP viewed providing pro bono legal services as an essential tool in protecting disadvantaged populations against racial injustice. In attacking Tucker, the state bar was targeting a single, pivotal member of the state legal team. Why him and not the two leading members of that group? Emporia, where Tucker practiced, may have been considered more fertile territory for an assault than a larger city such as Richmond. Tucker was not identified with the inner circle of the national organization as directly as Robinson and Hill. He was not quite so polished a speaker or dresser. Even his darker skin, leading David Mays to derisively label him "Blue-Gum Tucker," may have contributed subtly to the bar's viewing him as an easier and more vulnerable target. If so, the organization did not reckon with Tucker's grit or the solidarity of the NAACP brotherhood.[7]

In early October, Hill advised the national staff that he had agreed to represent Tucker at an upcoming hearing before the bar's Fourth District Committee. "We have engaged our own court reporter and are preparing for a real battle," he said. At the conclusion of that hearing, the district committee drew up a formal complaint based on three cases. All dealt with criminal matters, not education. "I think this is deliberate," Robert Carter advised Roy Wilkins in a memo. He suspected that the bar preferred not to be seen as waging a vendetta over the *Brown* decision. In the first case, Tucker had represented a black sharecropper accused of slaying his white landlord. In the second, he had assisted in the prosecution of a white man accused of raping a sixteen-year-old black girl. And in the third, he had defended a black man involved in a fight with a white man. Given the state of 1950s justice, it is easy to imagine that none of those clients would have received adequate representation in court without Tucker. In each instance, his alleged offense had nothing to do with the quality of the legal representation. Rather, the concern centered on his having been retained and paid by the NAACP, not the client.[8] In January 1960, as disbarment proceedings approached, the NAACP national board of directors affirmed its belief in Tucker's "personal and professional integrity." The group pledged its full resources to his defense and warned that the situation posed "an ultimate test" of the state's power to crush lawyers trying to secure citizenship rights.[9]

On February 12, in a show of force, an estimated two hundred blacks crammed a Greensville County courtroom designed for an audience half that size to witness the high-profile prosecution. Tucker's four-man defense team was made up of Bob Ming of Chicago, Hill, Carter, and Herbert O. Reid of Washington. Ming, the lead attorney, was a skilled trial lawyer who had been the first black man to serve as a full-time faculty member at the University of Chicago Law School. A few months after the Tucker hearing, Ming would help win an acquittal from an all-white jury for Martin Luther King Jr. on perjury charges related to alleged tax evasion in Alabama. Ming focused on the vagueness of the allegations against Tucker. Nothing in the bill of particulars suggested that he had failed to properly represent his clients, the lawyer said. To the contrary, Tucker's defense had enabled individuals to exercise their constitutional rights. Apparently recognizing a problem, the judges ordered the commonwealth's attorney to draft amended charges, including a better explanation of what in Tucker's actions constituted improper conduct. It would be almost two years before the cast reassembled in a courtroom—a twenty-four-month period during which Tucker operated under a shadow of suspicion and intimidation.[10]

Coincidentally, as the Emporia lawyer faced attack, the technique he had pioneered in an Alexandria library two decades earlier was emerging at the fore of the national civil rights movement. On February 1, four students from the North Carolina Agricultural and Technical College unleashed a revolution as they sat down at a Woolworth's lunch counter in Greensboro, North Carolina, and refused to get up until the store closed for the night. The next day, their numbers had multiplied eightfold, and from there the student insurgency spread like sizzling oil across southern and border states. A little over a year later, the number of sit-in participants had swelled to more than seventy thousand, both black and white. "It was a watershed," wrote the civil rights scholar Harvard Sitkoff. "Race relations in the United States would never be the same."[11] The tsunami reached Richmond on February 20, eight days after the Tucker hearing. Early that Saturday morning an estimated two hundred students left the Virginia Union campus and walked downtown to the heart of the city's Broad Street business district. Thirty-four of them took seats reserved for whites at the Woolworth's lunch counter. Shortly thereafter, another seventy-four sat down in space designated for whites at the nearby G. C. Murphy store. As the sit-ins continued, some store managers shut down eating places; others closed their stores altogether. The largest of the businesses, the thriving Thalhimers Department Store, shuttered all four of its eating areas.[12] Two days later the students returned, their numbers more than doubled. This time store managers and the police were ready. After a series of lunch-counter closings throughout the downtown, the focus shifted to Thalhimers. Denied service at a fourth-floor tearoom and a first-floor lunch counter, a group of students—some of them carrying

small American flags—refused to budge. Police arrested thirty-four demonstrators, then booked and released them on a bond of fifty dollars each,
pending trial. Arrests, including that of Mrs. J. M. Tinsley, the elderly wife
of the former president of the state NAACP, continued the next day. "All of
us are shocked and outraged by this incredible demonstration of injustice,"
the NAACP lobbyist Clarence M. Mitchell Jr. telegraphed Tinsley.[13]

The following evening, February 24, an estimated three thousand angry
citizens overflowed the Fifth Street Baptist Church as organizers sought
to harness and focus the outrage. Outside, police monitored the throng
in response to a bomb threat. Loudspeakers transported the messages
of a dozen speakers into the street. Top billing went to Hill in the next
day's newspapers. For almost four years, he and his colleagues had endured a relentless assault by Virginia's political elite. They had weathered
countless legislative hearings and court appearances aimed at exposing
membership lists. The state bar had humiliated and endangered Tucker, a
principled NAACP attorney. As Hill began to speak, his frustration boiled
over. "What we ought to do tomorrow is get a picket line against one of
the most undemocratic institutions in Virginia, the General Assembly,"
he thundered.[14] As if envisioning the clashes that would sweep the region
over the next several years, he paid tribute to the student demonstrators
and cautioned against cowardice by their elders. "We've got to think in
terms of sacrifice—when these children went to jail, they made a sacrifice," he said. "I think the time has come when we should put this land of
the free and home of the brave on the spot—if we've got to go to jail, then
let's start thinking in terms of sacrifice and go to jail." A few days later, in
a rally at Cedar Street Memorial Baptist Church, Hill notched his rhetoric higher. The time had come, he said, to "let the world know Virginia is
not the birthplace of democracy, but the burying ground of democracy."
Neither Robinson nor Hill would ever be jailed in the cause of civil rights,
and there were limits to how far either man would go in accepting rad-
icalism. "Standing on a corner whooping and hollering never impressed
me," Hill said years afterward. However, his speech in the wake of the
Thalhimers student arrests signaled a growing acceptance of the limits of
court action as a means of forcing change. "The two things complemented
each other," Robinson said later, reflecting on the relationship between
court challenges and street protests. "You had to have a good, solid legal
foundation on a constitutional basis" before sit-ins and other forms of civil

disobedience worked.[15] Men who had spent more than two decades building the legal underpinnings for the end of Jim Crow segregation seemed to
recognize that a new form of action would impel the final push.

Personal passions steered Hill and Robinson down differing paths in the
months that followed. In midsummer, Howard University tapped the law-
school dean, James Nabrit, to assume the school presidency, creating a vacancy in the iconic academic post. For a replacement, trustees turned to the
forty-four-year-old Richmonder reputed to be one of the sharpest minds in
the battery of NAACP lawyers. More than a decade had passed since Robinson had left the law-school faculty to lead Marshall's school-equalization
campaign. Now the idea of guiding an institution that had given him such
focus and inspiration as a young man and that continued to play a critical
role in the pursuit of black aspirations offered appeal. In September the
university executive committee appointed him dean of the law school and
professor of law. With their children grown, the Robinsons divided their
time between residences in Washington and Richmond.[16]

Hill's horizons were expanding as well. His love of politics and his belief
in the ballot as an instrument of social change reasserted themselves as the
1960 presidential election approached. The National Bar Association had
named Hill its 1959 "Man of the Year," enhancing his national stature and
likely contributing to his appointment to the Democratic Party's biracial
Committee on Civil Rights. Spiteful Richmond Democrats voted to cen-
sure the national party chairman for the selection. Chaired by former First
Lady Eleanor Roosevelt, the Democratic panel drafted a far-reaching civil
rights plank for the upcoming party nominating convention in Los Angeles. Hill was not a convention delegate, but his growing prominence in
black political circles led him to plan an extensive family vacation in conjunction with the gathering. Bernie, Oliver Jr., and a young friend traveled
first to Saint Paul, Minnesota, for the national NAACP annual convention
and then wound their way to California. Hill's first choice for a presidential nominee had been the Minnesota senator Hubert H. Humphrey. As
was typical, Hill favored proven leadership over glamour or charisma. He
was not disappointed, however, when the Massachusetts senator John F.
Kennedy emerged with the nomination. The pair had met in Washington
prior to the convention, and Hill had been favorably impressed.[17] Driving
home through Arizona, the Hills experienced firsthand the kind of insult

that too often accompanied travel in the era for black citizens, no matter their stature. Entering a restaurant in Yuma, they waited—and waited—for service. Finally, a waitress informed them: "The manager says we don't serve Negroes." Agitated, Hill challenged the situation, to no avail. The travelers had no choice but to leave. Later, they listened over the car radio to a speech in which Arizona Senator Barry M. Goldwater denied the need in his state for various civil rights laws. "I think if I could have gotten my hands on him at that particular moment, I might have done him some physical damage," a still steaming Hill later wrote.[18]

Back in Richmond, Hill learned that Congressman William Dawson wanted to enlist him for an active role in the Kennedy effort. Relishing the opportunity to witness the inner workings of a national political campaign, he accepted a three-month assignment. Operating out of campaign headquarters at Fifteenth and K Streets in Washington, a team headed by Kennedy's brother-in-law R. Sargent Shriver assigned Hill to monitor campaigns for the black vote in Alabama, Florida, Georgia, Louisiana, North Carolina, Oklahoma, South Carolina, Tennessee, Texas, and Virginia. For a salary of $250 a week, he traveled the region, helping set up local organizations, trouble-shooting, and speaking on Kennedy's behalf when asked.[19] With the election won and a Democrat headed to the White House, Hill fielded queries about joining the new administration. Initially, he declined, deterred in part by a belief that Senator Byrd would block him in confirmation hearings. A few months later, a Shriver aide called offering a slot in the Federal Housing Administration. The commissioner needed an assistant for intergroup relations. The job primarily entailed working with minority and ethnic groups on housing issues. Fortunately, the post did not require Senate confirmation. Hill accepted.[20]

Not until a crowd had already assembled in Washington for his induction in May 1961 did Hill realize that he would have to resign from the Richmond law firm. He had expected to maintain a scaled-back legal practice, while spending most of his time in the capital. Immediately, he bargained for a six-month transition in which to close out affairs in Richmond while starting the new job.[21] Already, the law firm was in flux. For undisclosed reasons, Hill, Martin, and Olphin had disbanded their association in late 1960. For several months, Hill had operated solo at a new address in Jackson Ward. Then, he had cemented the partnership with Sam Tucker that had been percolating since the early 1940s. Hill had also invited young Henry Marsh, a recent Howard Law graduate, to join them. Marsh was the former Virginia Union student-body president who had so admired Hill's remarks to the legislature in late 1955. With Hill in Washington, the law firm would go forward with Tucker and Marsh at the helm. An August 20, 1961, letter typed by Evalyn Shaed confirmed the new arrangement. "I just said, 'If I close my eyes, I couldn't possibly know that Oliver wasn't still here,'" she quipped. "My new bosses have the same habit of getting their greatest inspiration and feeling the most industrious just before time to close the office!"[22]

Hill also stepped down from two decades at the helm of the legal committee of the Virginia State Conference of Branches of the NAACP. The leadership role passed to Tucker. In the same week that Hill arrived in Washington, youthful Freedom Riders met with violence outside Anniston, Alabama, providing a reminder of the ongoing stakes in the long battle for civil rights. An angry mob of whites waylaid a Greyhound bus on which several black and white Freedom Riders rode together, testing Supreme Court actions eliminating segregated interstate travel. The crowd set fire to the bus, burning it to the ground in broad daylight. Over the next days, beatings and arrests followed. Among the rulings being tested was the December 1960 Supreme Court decision in the Richmond case *Boynton v. Virginia*. The ruling had affirmed the right of blacks to dine in a bus-station restaurant designated for whites. Marshall had argued the case before the high court, but it was Martin of the Hill law firm who had shepherded it into the appellate courts.[23] Hill and Robinson might be gone, but the legacy of the law firm they founded lived on.

Almost simultaneously, Spot Robinson embarked on a new endeavor. In mid-April, President Kennedy nominated him to fill a vacancy on the US Commission on Civil Rights. Just four years old, the prestigious bipartisan commission had begun aggressively to dissect claims of discrimination based on race, color, religion, or national origin. Not surprisingly, it also had made enemies among southern congressmen, several of whom opposed elevating a known civil rights activist to the group. During floor debate, Senator Sam J. Ervin, of North Carolina, joined a half dozen southern senators protesting Robinson's nomination. Calling the selection "wholly inappropriate," Ervin complained that elevating Robinson would be "exactly on a par" with naming a member of a White Citizens' Council to the commission. Senator Talmadge of Georgia agreed. The nomination was "roughly equivalent to that of a litigant permitted to sit as judge in his own case," he said. For most, however, Robinson's mild and serious manner dispelled fear. Curiously, his supporters noted, the southern critics had raised no such alarms when former Virginia governor Battle, who represented Charlottesville in opposing desegregation in the mid-1950s, was named earlier to the same commission. The Senate confirmed Robinson by a 73-17 vote. Both Virginia senators, Harry Byrd and A. Willis Robertson, voted no.[24]

Both Hill's and Robinson's new appointments required background checks by the FBI. Those documents undermine southern segregationists' loud claims of links between the Virginia civil rights lawyers and the Communist Party. The Hill file dated from 1958, when the bureau secretly investigated him as part of a search labeled "Communist Infiltration of the National Association for the Advancement of Colored People." Neither that probe nor the 1961 update uncovered anything incriminatory. Sources advised the FBI that Hill had refused Communist support, other than from individuals, in his political campaigns and that he had "never [been] a CP [member] or CP front member." As for Robinson, several Communist informants said they knew of no connection with the party. One placed Robinson on a 1946 membership list of the District of Columbia chapter of the National Lawyers' Guild, accused by some in the McCarthy era of being a Communist front. Many others, however, saw that group merely as a progressive alternative to the American Bar Association, which did not at the time admit blacks. Such findings are consistent with the memory of Nina Robinson Govan. Once, when she was invited to an event honoring James Jackson Jr., a former Richmond neighbor, civil rights activist, and avowed Communist, her father forbade her from going. "Dad said, 'You can't go because he's a Communist,'" she recalled.[25]

Just as Hill's government job precluded outside legal work, so Robinson's new task required laying down the civil right cases that had dominated his professional life. In a letter to Marshall, Robinson formally withdrew as NAACP counsel in the handful of Virginia cases in which he remained active.[26] For the first time in more than two decades, neither Hill nor Robinson was an active participant in a lawsuit involving state or federal civil rights. Marshall also withdrew from advocacy, accepting an appointment that autumn to the Court of Appeals for the Second Circuit. Three of the lions of the legal assault on Jim Crow segregation had moved on to new challenges. An era had ended.

Matters that had engaged Robinson's and Hill's attention were not so quickly dispatched. It would be several more years before remaining legal cases—the Sam Tucker disbarment proceedings, the Prince Edward school closings, and the various NAACP court battles with the Virginia power structure—were resolved. Hill and Robinson could offer advice from the sidelines, but others carried the load. After lengthy skirmishing, the principals in the Tucker case reassembled for trial in January 1962. Once again, the NAACP brain trust spun into action. Ming arrived from Chicago to head the legal team. Wilder recalled his awe, as a young attorney, in witnessing an intense strategy session preceding the trial. Marsh voiced similar admiration as he described a moment when some in the group, worried that Tucker would be railroaded by segregationist judges, favored making a prominent white attorney their front man in court. Tucker was adamant. He would rather lose, he insisted, than give credence to the notion that black men could not stand alone in a court of law.[27]

Marsh cited Ming's stirring defense of Tucker, delivered in a Sussex County courtroom packed with black supporters, as the "greatest speech I have ever heard in a courtroom." Tucker's only "crime" had been to defend the poor and the powerless, Ming argued. He had upheld the noblest aspirations of the legal profession. If anyone should be disbarred, it was the commonwealth's attorney, for perpetuating such a fraud on justice. The judges responded by dismissing all three NAACP-related claims against Tucker. They saved a bit of face for the commonwealth by chastising Tucker for a murky, late-arriving complaint involving an estate settlement for a client believed to have died without an heir. After an heir appeared, according to the complaint, Tucker had met with him and watched as the man signed a statement allowing Tucker to continue as administrator of the estate. According to the bar, the man's lawyer should have been present.[28] Stung, Tucker never forgot or forgave the assault on his integrity. Receiving an award a quarter century later, he first apologized for what he was about to say and then reminded the audience that he had once been prosecuted for the very actions now earning commendation. "A committee of this bar allowed itself to be used for such nefarious purposes," he lamented, warning against future shortsightedness.[29]

The school situation in Prince Edward County continued even longer than Tucker's trials, and with more dire consequences, given the hundreds of children affected. Astonishingly, the public schools did not reopen until the fall of 1964, five years after their closing. In May 1961, just after resigning as counsel in the case, Hill delivered a fiery speech in Farmville observing the seventh anniversary of the *Brown* decision. He offered no apology for the NAACP's urging black families to resist the lure of separate schools for their children. And he equated the willingness of officials and "the so-called 'good people' of this county" to sacrifice the educations of hundreds of black children with the outrages of Nazi Germany. His language reflected personal fury as well as the volatile tenor of the times. "In my opinion, they are guilty of 'a crime against humanity' no different than the crimes perpetrated by Eichmann and his Nazi cohorts, except in the matter of the degree of the offense," he charged. The Prince Edwardians had not taken anyone's life, but they had robbed many of their futures. Heated rhetoric aside, Hill had not lost his penchant for prudence. He urged looking at the matter "from the point of view of ordinary common sense." In a world broadly populated by peoples of color, a segregated America strengthened the propaganda of totalitarian enemies. "The faster we break down notions of racial segregation, the more rapidly we build bulwarks to strengthen democracy," he said.[30] The Prince Edward speech reflected, once again, the poles of Hill's personality—a passion, even rage, in the face of injustice tempered by an ability to calm provocation, think logically, and extend sympathy to adversaries stunted by misunderstanding.

Finally, in mid-1963, the embarrassment of an American community in which black children had gone unschooled for four years proved too mortifying to ignore. The transition came as a mood of profound unease gripped the nation. In May, images of the Birmingham commissioner of public safety, T. Eugene "Bull" Connor, unleashing police dogs and fire hoses on black demonstrators, including children, had shocked many Americans. The June murder of the Mississippi NAACP field secretary, Medgar Evers, elevated tensions. Police violence and mass arrests greeted major demonstrations in Danville, Virginia, that summer. And in Farmville, anger swelled as a series of street demonstrations in late July and early August climaxed with almost four dozen arrests over several days. After months of planning, spearheaded by the US Department of Justice and local black leaders, including Reverend Griffin, Governor Albertis Harrison on August 14 announced the formation of the Prince Edward Free Schools Association. Funded by private donations and open to all children, both black and white, the schools would return universal education to Prince Edward for the first time since the spring of 1959. Classes opened on September 16, one day after four black girls met their deaths in a Sunday morning bombing at the Sixteenth Street Baptist Church in Birmingham. Before the school year ended, more than fifteen hundred students, just eight of them white, would take advantage of the opportunity. Many of the students arrived with skills far below what should have been expected for children of their age; some never recovered.[31]

Nine months later, on May 25, 1964, the Supreme Court ordered Prince Edward County to reopen its schools. Carter had argued the case, with Tucker and Reeves assisting on the brief. Closing the public schools while at the same time giving tuition grants to white children attending segregated private schools denied black children the equal protection of the law guaranteed by the Fourteenth Amendment, the court said. A county could not close its schools to "avoid the law of the land" while the state kept other schools open at taxpayers' expense.[32] Almost thirteen years to the day after Robinson filed the challenge prompted by Barbara Johns and her classmates at the federal courthouse in Richmond, their efforts gained redemption. Still, the victory was far from complete. At the end of 1964 approximately 2 percent of the black children in the public schools of the eleven former Confederate states were attending school with white children. In Virginia in 1965, only about 5 percent of almost a quarter million black students attended desegregated schools. As far as the South had come, it had much further to go.[33]

The NAACP legal battles with the Virginia power structure also proved prolonged. The most consequential of the cases had begun in 1956 as companion lawsuits, *NAACP v. Almond* and *NAACP Legal Defense & Education Fund, Inc., v. Almond*, shepherded respectively by Carter and Hill and by Marshall and Robinson. The cases ended in the Supreme Court four attorneys general later as *NAACP v. Button*. The odyssey of more than six years wound through federal courts up to the Supreme Court, back down to a variety of state courts, and finally up to the nation's highest court again. The journey occurred against a backdrop of tension between Marshall, who headed the Legal Defense Fund, and Carter, serving as general counsel for the parent NAACP. Federal tax policy dictated the need for separation between the two groups, but the split went further. "The Legal Defense Fund was getting most of the money, so the NAACP people were a little disgusted about it," Hill recalled. "There came a little rift between Thurgood and Bob, and all through the years, when I'd go to New

York, I used to stay with Bob. And when Thurgood came down, he would stay with Spot." For Hill's part, that division reflected the work they were doing, not any personal conflict. "There was no way a rift [could come] between me and Thurgood," he said. The division had one consequence relative to the *Button* case. In the end, it was the lawsuit brought by Carter and Hill for the NAACP, rather than the Robinson-Marshall case for the Legal Defense Fund, that the Supreme Court decided. Late in the proceedings, the groups had split over whether to take a Virginia court ruling directly to the Supreme Court or let the matter work its way through lower federal courts. Ever the legal purist, Robinson saw the longer route as the safer course. So when the Supreme Court handed down its long-awaited ruling on January 14, 1963, it was the NAACP lawsuit that prevailed.[34]

By that point, all of the legislature's anti-NAACP bills had been dispatched except the barratry statute. As in the Tucker trial, the issue was whether an advocacy organization such as the NAACP could constitutionally encourage and finance lawsuits. Or as the state framed it, did such action constitute "drumming up business" in violation of legal ethics? Also, did state legislatures and lawyers have the right to determine their own ethical standards in such matters? By a 6-3 count, the justices answered no to both questions. The Virginia statute entailed "the gravest danger" of smothering the rights of blacks, the opinion said. "A state may not," under the "guise" of regulating professional conduct, "ignore constitutional rights," the court held.[35] Triumphant, the NAACP hailed the ruling as a death blow to a host of similar statutes approved in the mid-1950s by southern legislatures. Two months later, the Supreme Court handed segregationists another defeat. The court overturned the conviction of a Florida NAACP official who had refused to divulge membership lists to a legislative commission. Mark Tushnet described the combined victories in *Button* and *Gibson v. Florida Legislative Investigative Committee* as "the last chapter" in the NAACP's triumph over southern lawmakers. Still, the exhaustive court battles had taken a toll. As the Virginia experience had shown, "the years consumed in responding to the attack, and in attempting to implement *Brown,* were years in which Marshall and his staff could do little else," Tushnet wrote.[36]

Once again, the Virginia power elite did not know when to admit defeat. Responding to the prodding of the Boatwright Committee, the Virginia State Bar had challenged the NAACP legal practices in state court.

To handle the matter, the oversight agency had employed the prominent Richmond attorney Aubrey R. Bowles Jr., described by the executive secretary of the Virginia Supreme Court of Appeals as "one of the fathers of the movement to improve the administration of justice in Virginia." Despite Bowles's clout, the matter dragged on. Minutes of the bar's executive committee from October 1961 reflect that the lawsuit was pending in chancery court. By July 1962, Bowles was hoping to get the litigation "wound up or at least well underway this fall." Half a year later, when the *Button* decision came down, matters remained on hold. Undaunted, Bowles pressed forward. Ten months later, with the case still stalled, the bar secretary recorded Bowles's by then almost amusing exasperation: "Every time it seemed that we were almost ready to get the cases set for hearings, one of the NAACP lawyers would be promoted to a judgeship or a deanship or some high ranking government job, and the new counsel, of course would plead his unfamiliarity with the litigation."[37]

Not until April 16, 1964, did the bar finally approve a face-saving motion authorizing Bowles "to enter into the best possible agreement and have the suits dismissed." The legislative assaults also faded away over time. The Committee on Offenses Against the Administration of Justice issued its last significant report on November 1, 1963. Unrepentant, the group complained that much of its time had been wasted in litigation owing to "contemptuous refusals of witnesses to answer pertinent and proper questions."[38] The committee had burdened the NAACP with endless rounds of litigation, but the civil rights group's stalling tactics ultimately prevailed. Its membership lists were not violated. Finally, in 1973, lawmakers erased the nefarious and defunct committee from the state code.

In the years that followed, Robinson and Hill continued their quest to improve the racial landscape of America, each in his own way. Less than two months before his assassination, President Kennedy nominated Robinson to a seat on the US District Court for the District of Columbia. The chairman of the Senate Judiciary Committee, James O. Eastland of Mississippi, true to his segregationist core, refused to take up Robinson's nomination and that of his fellow African American civil rights activist A. Leon Higginbotham Jr. to a similar post. As a harbinger of the push for racial equality that would animate Lyndon B. Johnson's presidency, the new chief executive responded with recess appointments of the two in January 1964. The action came less than an hour before the Senate was scheduled to convene for the second session of the Eighty-Eighth Congress. Standing by in Richmond, Judge John D. Butzner Jr., of the federal district court, swore in Robinson before a noon deadline, making him the first black jurist on the District of Columbia court and one of only a handful in the entire federal judiciary.[39] Six months later, the Senate quietly affirmed Robinson's formal nomination to the post. Two years after that, the body approved Johnson's recommended elevation of Robinson to the US Court of Appeals for the District of Columbia Circuit, a panel considered by many to be second only to the Supreme Court in importance. The thin-faced, balding jurist who peered out soberly through black-rimmed glasses came "highly recommended" by an assortment of peers, an FBI background report concluded. Summary memos described him as "exceptionally brilliant" and "honest, able, serious, discreet, industrious and morally upright."[40]

Robinson would serve capably on federal courts for more than a quarter century. In his outsized work ethic and almost monastic retreat from the public arena, he epitomized his own prescription for judicial excellence. Those called to the judiciary "may no longer participate in the daily intercourse of life as freely as do others," Robinson wrote. "They have a duty to the judicial system in which they have accepted membership fastidiously to safeguard their integrity." The years of advocacy had ended; Robinson would serve his race with professionalism and a code of ethics so strict that he disapproved when a clerk dismissed a legal brief as boring and, by reputation, refused even to jaywalk. "That sense of ethics pervaded his whole self," said former clerk Stephen Carter. "It was not a view most people would follow, but it was in a certain way intrinsic to who he was." In 1981 Robinson began a five-year stint as chief judge of the circuit court. Again, he broke ground, becoming the first of his race to fill the lofty slot and only the second black man ever to become chief judge of one of the nation's eleven circuits. In September 1989, faced with Marian's mounting health problems, Robinson took senior status in order to better care for his ailing wife. Nine years later, on October 11, 1998, while at home in Richmond, he suffered a heart attack and died at age eighty-two. Marian, whose health had been considered to be at greater risk than her husband's, outlived him by several years. Both Robinson children survived their parents.[41]

Hill's stint in Washington lasted five years, a period he recalled with less satisfaction than the earlier decades practicing law. In his absence, Tucker and others carried on the work of the NAACP state legal committee, minus a key member. Unexpectedly, Martin died of a heart attack at his home in Richmond in April 1963, depriving the state of one of its most accomplished trial lawyers. His death cut short a career that complemented Hill's and Robinson's and that likely would have garnered additional acclaim had he lived beyond age fifty-two.[42] Returning to Richmond in 1966, Hill joined his friends to form the state's premier civil rights law firm, Hill, Tucker & Marsh. He engaged actively in Democratic politics, and—in keeping with the growing clout of black voters and his own stature—won appointment in 1968 to the commission assigned to author a revised state constitution. The coveted selection by Governor Mills Godwin, a leader in Massive Resistance, reflected changing times. Governor Holton in the early 1970s briefly considered naming Hill to a state judgeship before opting for a Republican loyalist. Hill himself seemed not to mind. His love of the political arena would have made his preferred achievement a seat in Congress had political realities allowed.[43]

Fittingly, the Hill law firm emerged in the forefront when the Supreme Court moved school desegregation into its next phase. In 1965 Tucker and Marsh filed *Green v. County School Board of New Kent County,* a challenge to continued racial isolation in the schools of a rural county east of Richmond. A decade after the Supreme Court ordered localities to move toward school desegregation with "all deliberate speed," New Kent had made no progress whatsoever. It maintained just two schools, one solidly black, one solidly white. Faculty, staff, transportation, and extracurricular activities remained similarly segregated. Armed with the landmark Civil Rights Act of 1964, which allowed federal officials to withhold funds from segregated school systems, Tucker and Marsh went to court. Later, Hill would join their effort. Confronting the federal threat, New Kent had adopted a "freedom of choice" plan in which parents could choose a preferred school. As late as the spring of 1968, when Tucker argued the case before the Supreme Court, not a single white child had chosen to attend New Kent's black school, and only about 15 percent of black children attended the white school. There could be no more delays, the court decreed. The time had come for New Kent—and by implication many similarly procrastinating school districts—to create a unitary system. School districts must take immediate steps to eliminate discrimination, "root and branch," the court said. The decision would prove to be the most momentous school ruling since the two *Brown* decisions. Districts could no longer hide behind the facade of choice.[44]

As the ruling took hold, the percentage of southern black students attending majority white schools jumped from less than 14 percent in 1967 to one-third in 1970. Soon, some jurists and local officials turned to cross-town and interdistrict busing as tools to further speed school integration. By leaping district boundaries, they sought to overcome the effects of entrenched housing segregation, consequences that had become even more distinct as whites evacuated core cities for suburban enclaves in the 1950s and 1960s. As Hill had foreseen two decades earlier, without adjustment, segregated neighborhoods could not produce integrated schools. The strategies ignited a furious backlash. Unrepentant segregationists joined forces with white suburban parents concerned about subjecting their children to long bus rides and inferior schools. Ruling against cross-district busing in a 1974 Detroit decision, *Milliken v. Bradley,* the Supreme Court brought to a halt the most aggressive of those efforts. Over the next decade and a half, the nascent forces of school integration stalled. Battered by extensive white flight to suburban counties and a Supreme Court hostile to cross-jurisdictional desegregation orders, progress on school integration began to reverse course.[45]

As he evolved from front-line activist to elder statesman, Hill reaped the rewards of his earlier work. A host of organizations lavished him with praise. A man who had spent the first two-thirds of his life fighting Jim Crow segregation spent his final years collecting accolades from many of the groups he had once challenged. Observing that transformation, Governor Timothy M. Kaine took the rare step of arranging for Hill to lie in state at the Governor's Mansion in the wake of his death at home over breakfast with his son, Oliver Jr., and daughter-in-law, Renee, on August 5, 2007. Bernie had predeceased her husband by more than a decade. A centenarian at his death, Hill had collected the highest honors bestowed by the American Bar Association and the NAACP. He had seen a juvenile courts building and a historic Capitol Square building named in his honor. And he had received a Presidential Medal of Freedom from William J. "Bill" Clinton, who applauded him as one who "stood up for everything that is necessary to make America truly one, indivisible, and equal."[46]

Robinson's later years and his passing also brought tributes, although his name and face remained far less familiar than Hill's to the public at large. Adhering to his judicial code, he refused all but the rare interview in the last three decades of his life. The relative silence contributed to his achievements' often being conflated with those of Hill into a single narrative. Yet he rightly remained a revered presence among the architects of the legal assault on Jim Crow and a valued colleague among federal jurists. Along the way, he earned honorary degrees from Howard, Georgetown University, and the New York Law School. A new federal courthouse for the US District Court for the Eastern District of Virginia dedicated in 2008 in downtown Richmond bears his name, along with that of the federal district judge Robert R. Merhige Jr., who in 1972 ordered cross-district busing in Richmond and neighboring counties. The Court of Appeals for the Fourth Circuit later overturned the decision, and the Supreme Court affirmed the circuit-court ruling with a 4-4 tie, essentially cementing in place racial divisions among area school systems that remain.[47]

Hill and Robinson stand together, merging at the arm and shoulder in what may prove to be their most timeless tribute. Jointly, they gaze out over the grounds of the Virginia Capitol from a civil rights memorial dedicated in 2008 to the memory of the students who led the Prince Edward strike and the men who ushered that case into the annals of American history. In artist Stanley Bleifeld's rendering, Hill, the activist, stands slightly to the fore, a hint of a smile illuminating his face, a document—probably the *Brown* ruling—thrust high in his right hand. Beside him, Robinson, the intellectual, carries a weighty briefcase and stares impassively ahead. Neither man looks angry or alarmed. The message seems clear. They have no need to be. Their faith in the promise of the Constitution and the power of the law sustains them. The sculpture captures the essence of men who chaffed at hateful politicians and angry segregationists during their long careers but never succumbed to cynicism. Even in the wake of a series of Supreme Court setbacks to school integration, Robinson remained serene. "One remarkable thing about our country—if you're right, you stand a fairly good chance of changing minds," he said in 1989, just as he was moving into senior status on the appeals court. Given ample provocation to lose trust in democratic institutions, they did not. Late in life, Hill continued to rail against injustices, but both he and Robinson believed in rationality as a force stronger than temporary failure or fear. And when, at their deaths, the nation still seemed trapped in wells of inequality and separation, they appeared satisfied to have done their part in their time.[48]

Did they resolve racial inequities? No, they did not even come close. But those who from a twenty-first-century perspective dismiss the importance of eliminating de jure segregation while de facto segregation remains did not experience the humiliation, fear, and repression in the earlier era. In every phase of the NAACP assault on legalized segregated life in America—from education to housing to transportation to voting—Robinson and Hill contributed in important ways. And when with their help *Brown v. Board of Education* cemented the seismic shift away from enforced segregation into a period of desegregation, they held fast against the furious aftershocks created within a reeling white southern culture. When desegregation did not lead quickly to full integration, as it has not even yet, they cautioned against despair. "It's unrealistic to think in any evolutionary fashion that there would be any substantial change in control in such a short period of time. The only way for that to happen is violent revolution," Hill said three decades after the *Brown* verdict. It was enough that he and Robinson and scores of associates, high and low, had advanced the cause of freedom and justice. "We are now in a period of desegregation, and must remember that integration is a social process that is quite different, and which will come slowly with the passage of time," Hill told an assembly of black college students in Bluefield, West Virginia, in May 1959. Perhaps the strongest mark of the lawyers' resolve was their expectation that future generations would keep the torch aflame.[49]

The liner on Hill's casket bore a simple inscription consistent with the philosophy of two men who elevated ideas and principles above monetary gain or personal comfort. Tributes and acclaim, it seemed to say, matter little in the long arc of history. What counts are the acts themselves, the accumulation of day-to-day, year-to-year decisions and deeds that, with time, reveal a life. "Let the Work I've Done Speak for Me," read Hill's chosen epitaph. The work did—and does. Over decades, in countless courtrooms and with a power born of right conviction, it announced Oliver Hill and Spottswood Robinson to be among the best of their generation. Or any other.

EPILOGUE

2016

On a warm spring day in 2016 the nation's newly installed secretary of education crossed downtown Washington to address a packed gathering of teachers, school administrators, academics, and policy strategists about one of the nation's most pressing and persistent problems. More than sixty years after the Supreme Court decision in *Brown v. Board of Education* held out the promise of an educational system with equal opportunity for all, in many settings the vision and the reality diverged as sharply as ever. After a surge of progress on both school integration and minority-student achievement in the 1970s and 1980s, momentum had stalled. Too often, gains appeared to be dialing backward. Widespread school integration still seemed an impossible dream. Disillusioned by years of disappointment, large numbers of blacks, as well as whites, did not even consider it to be a desirable goal. John B. King Jr. was not among them. Years earlier, the deaths of both his parents before he turned twelve had placed a man destined to become a New York state education commissioner and then cabinet secretary at risk of disappearing into a big-city swirl of dysfunction. He credited his deliverance to public schools, and he wanted a quality education to be a life preserver available to every child. "If not for those teachers at P.S. 276, I wouldn't be alive today," King said. And so the secretary had become an apostle of the newest version of an old idea: the belief that socioeconomic and racial diversity in schools could herald a better society for all. After years of sojourning in the backwater of education-policy research, with King's help, integration was poised for resurgence as a national strategy in the final year of Barack Obama's presidency. "The evidence is clear," King told the assembled group. School integration "is a policy direction that stands to benefit all our students. We have to seize this moment."[1]

Much had changed in the days since Spottswood Robinson and Oliver Hill advanced the cause of integration by dismantling the legal barriers to desegregation. Beginning in the early 1970s, the courts on which the pair and their contemporaries depended had halted the most aggressive forms of enforced racial integration in schools, particularly interdistrict, urban-suburban busing. In 2007, in a disappointing 5-4 ruling involving Seattle and Louisville, the Supreme Court had restricted even voluntary school-integration efforts designed around race. Adapting to the changed reality, the new integration advocates largely stressed socioeconomic diversity, although many still saw merit in a racial and ethnic mix. Moreover, the modernists operated within a milieu that hardly would have been recognizable in Hill and Robinson's heyday. Large numbers of Latinos and Asians had brought a rainbow hue to school populations once shaded mostly in black and white. In 2016, at the sixty-second anniversary of *Brown*, the Civil Rights Project at the University of California, Los Angeles, reported a revolution in the racial makeup of the nation's classrooms between 1970 and 2013. Whites made up just 50 percent of the school population in 2013, down from 79 percent four decades earlier. The black population remained relatively stable at about 15 percent, while the Latino population had exploded from 5 percent to 25 percent and the Asian population had increased from less than 1 percent to 5 percent.[2]

The jettisoning of legal segregation several generations earlier had produced a degree of progress. Substantial numbers of black children enjoyed access to the opportunities of which Hill and Robinson had dreamed. That very real accomplishment remained. But segregated housing patterns and troubled inner-city economics shackled many others to inferior schools and a dim future as surely as law and custom had constrained earlier generations. Worryingly, the percentage of "intensely segregated nonwhite schools"—defined as those in which 10 percent of students or fewer were white—had more than tripled, from less than 6 percent in 1988 to almost 19 percent of all public schools in 2013. Despite exceptions, too many schools were diverging into African American and Latino bastions of poverty and Caucasian and Asian citadels of means. Forty-eight percent of Hispanic students and 30 percent of black students attended high-poverty schools in the 2013–14 school year, compared with just 15 percent of whites and 4 percent of Asian students, according to federal data.[3]

What would Hill and Robinson make of that altered landscape? History suggests that they would decry the increasing intersection of socioeconomic and racial isolation and call, as they did many years ago, for integrated classrooms and neighborhoods. Their basic premises still hold. In 1950 Robinson repudiated the idea that separate schools for black and white children ever could be made truly equal across a broad plain. The levers of power were simply too imbalanced to think that resources and outcomes could be equalized within an apartheid system, his experiences had taught. Simultaneously, Hill argued that all children, but particularly those whose life experiences deprived them of mainstream opportunities, benefited from diversity. "I never had a class with white folks, and I never believed Negro children had to go to school with white children in order to learn," he said. "But I fought for school integration because I believed that for the Negro to enjoy the full advantages of our culture, he needed to be associated with people who run that culture."[4]

Hill and Robinson spoke primarily from the perspective of race, while most of the newer integration disciples emphasize socioeconomic class. Still, the generational divide does not preclude shared understandings. Like Hill, the new advocates recognize that myriad benefits, tangible and intangible, flow from access to the dominant culture and that the rewards run in two directions. Advantaged children—and civic society as a whole—benefit when education reflects a range of real-world experiences and perspectives. Meanwhile, just as Robinson might have predicted, separate but equal has performed no better in the modern day than in his. Since the Nixon administration in the 1970s, the nation's unwritten pact has been to invest cash, sometimes massive amounts, in poorer, urban schools in return for dropping any threat of merger with middle-class, suburban schools. Yet performance within many of those islands of disadvantage has, if anything, worsened. "The basic truth is that we have tried for more than three decades to make schools of concentrated poverty work, and we have largely failed," observed James E. Ryan, dean of the Harvard Graduate School of Education.[5]

A wealth of social-science research dating from the 1960s buttresses the claim. For those looking for a path out of failure, the preponderance of evidence points to a simple truth: poor children do better academically in a middle-class school than in a predominantly poor school. Meanwhile, the more advantaged children are not harmed so long as the middle-class presence remains strong. That was the finding of the education sociologist

James S. Coleman in his landmark 1966 study of educational opportunity in America. Even as some of Coleman's methodologies have come under fire, numerous other research studies strengthen the case. When Geoffrey Borman and Maritza Dowling, of the University of Wisconsin at Madison, applied updated statistical techniques to Coleman's data in 2010, for example, they found that the socioeconomic status of a school has even more of an effect on student achievement than Coleman suggested. And an unusual zoning program in wealthy Montgomery County, Maryland, allowed the Rand Corporation researcher Heather Schwartz to observe that poor children randomly assigned to high-advantage schools in 2001–7 "far outperformed" poor children assigned to low-advantage schools even when the higher-poverty schools had the benefit of substantially higher per-pupil funding.[6]

Such findings might prompt skepticism among middle- and upper-class parents whose children profit from current educational structures. They might anger minority parents and activists who dispute the notion that a segregated education disadvantages minority youth. But the results, observed Ryan, are the results. "Education scholars and commentators of every political stripe acknowledge the robustness and consistency of these findings," he wrote.[7] Richard Kahlenberg concurs. A senior fellow at the Century Foundation, the progressive think tank that sponsored the education symposium attended by King, Kahlenberg describes a "tragic paradox" surrounding school integration in the early twenty-first century: social scientists largely agree that socioeconomic and racial mixing benefits children and, by extension, democratic society. Yet an equally durable consensus dismisses school integration as a political nonstarter.[8] A growing number of education analysts and practitioners have begun to reject the second part of that dichotomy. Just as Robinson and Hill persisted against daunting odds because they believed desegregation served the commonweal, so groups including the Century Foundation and the National Coalition on School Diversity—uniting more than two dozen national civil rights organizations, university-based research centers, and state and local coalitions—refuse to succumb to modern-day naysayers on integration. The evidence in its favor is too strong, they say. Socioeconomic and, to the extent legally possible, racial integration serve the national interest, both by exposing poor children to advantages middle-class youth assume and by creating classrooms that mirror the complex world through which democracy weaves.[9]

The 2016 national elections wielded a blow to such ideas. Representative Bobby Scott of Virginia, the ranking Democratic member in 2016 of the House Committee on Education and the Workforce, was among those who had hoped that a realigned Supreme Court might revisit the narrow 2007 decision in *Parents Involved in Community Schools v. Seattle School District No. 1*, which limited consideration of race in even voluntary school-assignment plans. Presumably, under the administration of President Donald J. Trump, that was not to be. "A meaningful change in direction is unlikely politically," Scott lamented in the election's aftermath. Still, Kahlenberg saw slivers of hope, both in the potential for ongoing progress at the state and local, if not federal, levels and in postelection laments over evidence of a deeply fractured nation. "Ironically, Trump's election could spur more efforts at school integration, not because of federal support, but because people see a strong need to find ways to bring the county together," he said. "Even some conservatives may see value in school integration by choice as a way of promoting social cohesion."[10] Any such effort by necessity would be designed around socioeconomics, not race. How might Hill and Robinson regard such a shift? While their writings do not say, nothing suggests that they would reject solutions predicated on economic disparity. While the pair were passionately committed to the advancement and equal treatment of black children and adults, they were not driven by race alone. "We are battling the segregationists, not the white race," Hill said repeatedly during the years of Massive Resistance. Similarly, said Ferguson Reid, Robinson was "militant against the system, not the people perpetrating the system." Moreover, the men were pragmatic, strategic thinkers, not ideologues. The societal revolution they spawned occurred within established institutions. Racial integration would no doubt remain a priority for them if they were alive today. But Robinson and Hill were practical enough to recognize the empirical benefits of middle-class schools to poor children of any race, as well as the advantages of voluntary racial mixing. Race and poverty are "so overlapping that if you do one, you do the other," acknowledged Scott.[11]

Drawing on extensive research, Kahlenberg identified three reasons why middle-class schools benefit children: motivated peers, involved parents, and high-quality teachers. All three "correlate much more with socioeconomics than with race," he said. In more prosperous settings, peers are less likely to engage in disruptive behaviors and more apt to value learning. Parents are more likely to have time to volunteer in classrooms and to know how to pull the levers of power when problems arise. And stable, high-quality teachers are more likely to make up the faculty, because satisfaction increases when discipline and learning issues decline. All those qualities are invaluable to learning, and none can be easily or consistently duplicated in high-poverty schools, Kahlenberg said.[12] Lack of racial diversity in education also handicaps children coming of age in a complex, global world. "My daughter is going to grow up in a society with no racial majority. She has to know how to get along with and work with other people," said Genevieve Siegel-Hawley, a Virginia Commonwealth University education scholar who has written extensively about the imperative of diverse schools. With nine of ten American youth attending public schools, there is no better laboratory for building understanding, she said.[13]

Even as the testing-and-accountability movement dominated educational policy in the early twenty-first century, school-integration plans focused on socioeconomics have quietly taken hold in settings as diverse as Louisville; Hartford, Connecticut; and Berkeley, California. The number is growing. When the Century Foundation began seeking out such integration programs in 1996, it could find only two districts consciously pursuing that aim. By 2007 the number had grown to about forty. And a 2016 update identified ninety-one such plans in thirty-two states. More than 4 million students, roughly 8 percent of the nation's school population, attended school districts or charter schools using socioeconomic status as a factor in school assignments.[14]

The diversity programs fit into five basic categories.[15] The most common strategy involves redrawing school-attendance zones to promote socioeconomic variety. Many school-zone boundaries were set, consciously or unconsciously, to protect racially segregated housing. Adjusting them often can create more diverse schools. Districtwide choice policies designed to foster diversity are a second alternative. Cambridge, Massachusetts, pioneered the concept to aid racial integration in the 1980s. Under a typical choice plan, officials establish a series of magnet schools, each promoting a certain learning track or theme. Districts make student assignments based on both family wishes and an algorithm that strives to spread socioeconomic diversity. In the most adventurous such programs, jurisdictions partner voluntarily with a neighboring locality to create a greater socioeconomic range. City schools in Louisville, Kentucky, and suburban schools in surrounding Jefferson County, for instance, operate as a single school system for that purpose. "There are no struggling inner-city schools here," reported a 2015 *Atlantic* magazine article describing the Louisville–Jefferson County program. Rather, many attribute the city's vibrancy in part to its racial and economic mix in schools.[16]

The third and fourth categories include school systems that make socioeconomic diversity part of the criteria for attending a specific magnet or charter school. Two of the boldest such plans exist in Connecticut, where the Hartford and New Haven school systems operate cross-district magnet schools that draw students from both the inner city and the suburbs. A final category of diversity plans gives preference to school-transfer requests that increase socioeconomic balance. Fraught as the focus on school integration might be, school districts willing to promote diversity embrace a reality ignored at the nation's peril. Education remains the great equalizer in American society, the force that allows children to rise above accidents of birth, creating vibrancy through economic and class mobility. Yet tragically, in far too many settings the fortunes of poor children increasingly are calcified in no-exit communities and schools. "Segregation in public K-12 schools isn't getting better, it's getting worse, and getting worse quickly," warned Scott.[17]

No education strategy offers a panacea, and extensive socioeconomic integration may prove impossible in many settings. The nexus of segregated housing and limited transportation with segregated schools creates formidable challenges. Yet, the experiences of dozens of school districts nationwide show that creative, voluntary steps in the direction of school integration can be taken in almost any community willing to try. The changing demographics of America and the demands of an increasingly global society point to an inescapable truth: it is past time for far more communities to make the commitment. Creating economically and, where legally possible, racially diverse schools should become the twenty-first-century extension of the school-equality movement shouldered by Hill, Robinson, and their fellow civil rights attorneys.

Hill recognized the imperative. In the last third of his life, he often mused about the need to see past artificial constructs of difference, including nationality, race, and class. As early as the late 1970s, in a speech at Saint Paul's College, a small, impoverished black school in southern Virginia, he proposed creating a "Universal Society for the Advancement of Human

Earthlings." Around 1990 he incorporated an entity named Evolutionary Change, Inc., and dedicated it to educating those so-called earthlings about "the inevitability of change and the importance of peaceful solutions to problems." His focus on the concept quickened as he aged. "We've got to stop thinking in terms of ourselves as blacks and whites and Americans and Jews and Chinese and Russians, and think of ourselves in terms of being human beings," he urged. "I don't care what you're doing or what you think. It's going to change. So, then, how can we keep the change moving in a way that's beneficial to humanity, rather than just try to hold on to what we have and enjoy that at the expense of everybody else?"[18]

By helping to sound the death knell of Jim Crow segregation, Oliver Hill and Spottswood Robinson answered that question for their time. Time and circumstance are never static, however. The challenge they pose for this and future generations is to do the same, with equal fearlessness, in ours.

NOTES

JW	Juan Williams
LB	Lester Banks
LR	Leon "Andy" Ransom
MM	Martin Martin
OH	Oliver Hill
RC	Robert Carter
RP	Rupert Picott
RW	Roy Wilkins
SR	Spottswood Robinson III
ST	Sam Tucker
TM	Thurgood Marshall
WH	William Hastie
WW	Walter White

NEWSPAPERS AND JOURNALS

GJ	*Gloucester Gazette–Matthews Journal*
HSWVJ	*Historical Society of Western Virginia Journal*
JG	*Journal and Guide*
NYT	*New York Times*
RAA	*Richmond Afro-American*
RNL	*Richmond News Leader*
RTD	*Richmond Times-Dispatch*
RT	*Roanoke Times*
SSN	*Southern School News*
VMHB	*Virginia Magazine of History and Biography*
VP	*Virginian-Pilot*
VTB	*Virginia Teachers Bulletin*
WAA	*Afro-American (Washington ed.)*
WP	*Washington Post*

Introduction

1. Charles Scarborough, "Botetourt Principal Says Classes Full," *RNL*, Sept. 9, 1948, 2; "Schools of Virginia Continue Discrimination in County" and "Civic Leaders' Tour Reveals Conditions Little Changed," both in *RAA*, Sept. 18, 1948, sec. 2, p. 4; "Attorneys Find No Substantial Changes in Negro Schools," *GJ*, Sept. 16, 1948, 1; *Ashley v. Sch. Bd. of Gloucester County*, 82 F. Supp. 167 (E.D. Va. 1948).

2. "Court Orders Surry Schools Be Equalized," *RTD*, Mar. 31, 1948, 1; "Court Rules Discrimination in 3 Counties," *RNL*, Apr. 8, 1948, 1; "Mixed School Classes Held Possible in Gloucester, King George," *RNL*, July 30, 1948, 1. In the first of the rulings, on March 30, 1948, Hutcheson ordered the Surry school board to make immediate plans to equalize facilities and opportunities for black children. Equal-

ization rulings directed toward Gloucester, King George, and Chesterfield Counties followed.

3. While various acquaintances spelled the nickname "Spott" or "Spotts," Robinson signed his letters "Spot."

4. See series of photographs in *RAA*, Sept. 18, 1948, 1, and sec. 2, 1.

5. Richard Kluger, *Simple Justice* (New York: Vintage Books, 1975), 472; Carl Rowan, *Dream Makers, Dream Breakers* (Boston: Little, Brown, 1993), 6; Mark Tushnet, *The NAACP's Legal Strategy against Segregated Education, 1925–1950* (Chapel Hill: University of North Carolina Press, 1987), 110.

6. George Booth, telephone interview by author, Nov. 26, 2012, Brooklyn, NY.

7. Scarborough, "Botetourt Principal Says Classes Full," 2; "Negroes Ask Admission to Schools for Whites," *RTD*, Sept. 10, 1948, 1.

8. "Tuck Urges Calm, Tolerant Handling of School Problem," *RTD*, Sept. 10, 1948, 1.

9. Mark Tushnet, *Making Civil Rights Law: Thurgood Marshall and the Supreme Court, 1936–1961* (New York: Oxford University Press, 1994), 13, 116; Larissa Smith, "A Civil Rights Vanguard: Black Attorneys and the NAACP in Virginia," in *From the Grassroots to the Supreme Court: Brown v. Board of Education and American Democracy*, ed. Peter Lau (Durham, NC: Duke University Press, 2004), 131, 144. Houston insisted on the title "vice-dean" rather than "dean" (see ch. 2, n. 12).

10. OH, interview by Kendall Thomas, Feb. 2, 2004, Columbia Law School, OHC. The author was the first researcher to review the Hill papers at VSU; they were unprocessed at the time.

11. In *Sweatt v. Painter*, 339 U.S. 629 (1950), the court ruled that a separate law school established by Texas for black students did not offer substantially equal education. In *McLaurin v. Oklahoma State Regents*, 339 U.S. 637 (1950), the court rejected a scheme by which a black student seeking a doctorate in education at the University of Oklahoma was forced to endure segregated seating.

12. RC, telephone interview by author, Apr. 1994, New York; Patricia Sullivan, *Lift Every Voice: The NAACP and the Making of the Civil Rights Movement* (New York: New Press, 2009), 341.

13. Rick Sauder, "Oliver Hill: A Journey Down the Civil Rights Road," *RNL*, Jan. 15, 1992, 1; Michael Williams, "Hill To Get Medal of Freedom," *RTD*, Aug. 6, 1999, B4; Kluger, *Simple Justice*, 471, 473; Benjamin Muse, "Negro Crusaders Should Relax Awhile," *WP*, June 6, 1954, B2.

14. Sullivan, *Lift Every Voice*, 419; Kluger, *Simple Justice*, 553, 645 (quotation).

15. *NAACP v. Button*, 371 U.S. 415 (1963), began in 1956 as companion suits by the NAACP and its Legal Defense and Educational Fund.

16. Jack Greenberg, telephone interview by author, May 5, 2011, New York.

17. Any complete list of pivotal, southern civil rights lawyers includes Fred D. Gray of Montgomery, Alabama, who first gained renown during the 1955 Montgomery bus boycott. Only twenty-four at the time, Gray was not part of the older

group named here, which formed a network of support for the NAACP beginning in the 1930s and 1940s. Gray tells his story in *Bus Ride to Justice* (1995; reprint with a new foreword, Montgomery, AL: NewSouth Books, 2013).

18. "Time for Tolerance and Calm Thinking," *GJ*, Sept. 16, 1948, 2.

19. Frederick Carter, "A Gift of God," unpublished manuscript made available to author by Carter.

20. "Coming Events," "Trial Justice," and "Among the Colored," *GJ*, Sept. 16, 1948, 1, 1, 8.

21. "Contempt Proceedings Set for Va. School Officials," *RAA*, Oct. 2, 1948, 1; "Hear School Case Friday in Richmond," *GJ*, Oct. 21, 1948, 1.

22. "Gov. Tuck Joins Dixiecrats in Defiant Tirade," *RAA*, Oct. 23, 1948, 1.

23. Herbert Hutcheson Jr. to Sterling Hutcheson, July 31, 1954, CSH, Accession No. 32432, Box 3A.

24. "Gloucester School Case Continued Until November," *GJ*, Oct. 28, 1948, 1; "Contempt Ruling Against Virginia School Officials Delayed," *RAA*, Oct. 30, 1948, 12; Bill Foster, "Gloucester Contempt Is Denied," *RNL*, Dec. 14, 1948, 1.

25. "Gloucester County School Contempt Case Continued," *RAA*, Dec. 18, 1948, 5; Foster, "Gloucester Contempt Is Denied," 1.

26. *Ashley v. Sch. Bd. of Gloucester County,* 82 F. Supp. 167 (E.D. Va. 1948), order Jan. 13, 1949.

27. "White Lawyer Who Lost School Case Hurls Taunt," *RAA*, Jan. 22, 1949, 6; "Editorial Response to Contempt Order," *GJ*, Jan. 20, 1949, 2.

28. "School Officials Are Left in Embarrassing Position," *GJ*, Apr. 7, 1949, 1; William Foster, "Way Cleared for Additional School Suits," *RNL*, May 5, 1949, 1.

29. "One For, One Against," *RAA*, May 14, 1949, 4.

30. "White Lawyer Who Lost School Case Hurls Taunt," 6.

31. Foster, "Way Cleared for Additional Law Suits," 1; John Popham, "Negro, White Schools in the South Held $545,000,000 Apart in Value," *NYT*, Jan. 26, 1949, 10; "$545 Million Due Schools," *RAA*, Jan. 29, 1949, 1.

1. A World Split by Law and Custom

1. "Undaunted by Downpours of Rain, Visiting Thousands Enjoy Reunion Day," *RTD*, June 1, 1907, 1; "Thousands Greet General Lee on His Arrival Here," *RTD*, May 29, 1907, 1. Dozens of related articles filled the *Richmond Times-Dispatch* and the *Richmond News Leader* during the reunion.

2. "Reunion Ends with Grand Parade and Unveiling of Davis Monument," *RTD*, June 4, 1907, 1; "Confederate Army Gathers at Statue of Gallant Stuart," *RTD*, May 31, 1907, 1; "Monument is Unveiled Amid Roar of Cannon," *RNL*, June 3, 1907, 1.

3. Change-of-name order, Charles B. White, Oct. 1, 1942, Richmond Hustings Court, General Index to Deeds, Reel 434D, 129.

4. Michael Chesson, *Richmond After the War, 1865–1890* (Richmond: Vir-

ginia State Library, 1981), xv; Virginius Dabney, *Richmond* (Garden City, NY: Doubleday, 1976), 254, 272; *Encyclopedia Virginia*, s.v. "Anti-Lynching Law of 1928," by Douglas Smith, accessed Mar. 19, 2017, www.encyclopediavirginia.org /Antilynching_Law_of_1928.

5. Charles Dew, *The Making of a Racist: A Southerner Reflects on Family, History, and the Slave Trade* (Charlottesville: University of Virginia Press, 2016), 140–45; Chesson, *Richmond After the War*, 7–10; Ben Campbell, *Richmond's Unhealed History* (Richmond: Brandywine, 2012), 109, 137; Peter Wallenstein, *Cradle of America: Four Centuries of Virginia History* (Lawrence: University of Kansas Press, 2007), 253. For additional discussion of the 1902 constitution, which disenfranchised not only blacks but also poor whites, see J. Douglas Smith, *Managing White Supremacy: Race, Politics, and Citizenship in Jim Crow Virginia* (Chapel Hill: University of North Carolina Press, 2002), 24–26.

6. Ronald Heinemann, John Kolp, Anthony Parent Jr., and William Shade, *Old Dominion, New Commonwealth: A History of Virginia, 1607–2007* (Charlottesville: University of Virginia Press, 2007), 301.

7. Marie Tyler-McGraw, *At the Falls: Richmond, Virginia, and Its People* (Chapel Hill: University of North Carolina Press, 1994), 213–15, 227, 229–30; Chesson, *Richmond After the War*, 101–2; Dabney, *Richmond*, 271; Oliver Hill, "Rights Movement Started in Virginia," *RTD*, Mar. 17, 2002, E1; Wallenstein, *Cradle of America*, 286–87; Ann Alexander, *Race Man: The Rise and Fall of the "Fighting Editor," John Mitchell Jr.* (Charlottesville: University of Virginia Press, 2002), 131–41, 174.

8. J. Douglas Smith, *Managing White Supremacy*, 87–100, 107–29; Wallenstein, *Cradle of America*, 298–99.

9. Alexander, *Race Man*, 186; Virginius Dabney, *Virginia: The New Dominion* (Garden City, NY: Doubleday, 1971), 474; *Bliley v. West*, 42 F.2d 101 (1930); J. Douglas Smith, *Managing White Supremacy*, 140–41.

10. Thelma Fant, interview by author, May 29, 2013, Richmond.

11. Chris Silver and John Moeser, *The Separate City: Black Communities in the Urban South, 1940–1968* (Lexington: University Press of Kentucky, 1995), 30, 147.

12. OH, interview by Carolyn Oliver, June 9, 1999, VPF, recording made available to author by Carolyn Oliver; Oliver Hill, *The Big Bang: Brown v. Board of Education and Beyond* (Winter Park, FL: Four-G, 2000), 2, 1–12.

13. History of Mount Carmel Baptist Church, accessed May 16, 2013, http:// www.themountcarmel.org/church_history; Fant, interview by author, May 29, 2013.

14. Virginia Bureau of Vital Statistics, Marriage Index—Husbands, 1900–1911, Reel 5, LVA; Oliver Hill Jr., interview by author, July 28, 2011, Ettrick, VA.

15. Hill, *Big Bang*, 4–5. In some interviews, Hill said he moved to Roanoke at age five.

16. Rand Dotson, *Roanoke, Virginia, 1882–1912: Magic City of the New South*

(Knoxville: University of Tennessee Press, 2007), 6–10; John Kern, "Oliver White Hill, Civil Rights Attorney in Roanoke and Throughout Virginia," *HSWVJ* 19 (2010): 1.

17. Dotson, *Roanoke, Virginia, 1882–1912*, 132–52.

18. OH, handwritten notes for 1993 acceptance speech, OHC.

19. Hill, *Big Bang*, 36.

20. OH, interview by Oliver, June 9, 1999.

21. Lelia Pentecost to OH, June 21, 1939, OHC; Mike Hudson, "Civil rights veteran: Today's battles 'more complicated,'" *Roanoke Times & World-News*, Jan. 31, 1993, 1; Hill, *Big Bang*, 16.

22. Hill, *Big Bang*, 33–35.

23. Ibid., 9.

24. OH, interview by Oliver, June 9, 1999.

25. Hill, *Big Bang*, 20–32; OH, interview by Leon Higginbotham, May 25, 1985, CRLP, Accession No. 12801-a, Box w/8606-h, 404–6.

26. Hill, *Big Bang*, 36–72; OH, "List of employers, 1918–1935" (handwritten), and Howard student records, spring quarter 1927, both in OHC; OH, interview by Higginbotham, May 25, 1985, 406.

27. Hill, *Big Bang*, 69.

28. Daniel Lissner, "The American Way: Oliver Hill and the Desegregation of Public Schools in Prince Edward County, Virginia," May 1, 1997, unpublished paper, OHC.

29. Kenneth Mack, "Rethinking Civil Rights Lawyering and Politics in the Era Before *Brown*," *Yale Law Journal* 115 (Nov. 2005): 264–69. Mack argues that the scholarly view of black lawyering in the early twentieth century as a court-based, rights-centered exercise aimed at the elimination of de jure segregation took root popularly only after the *Brown* decision. Even though "no one would deny" that Hill, Marshall, and their colleagues entered the legal profession hoping to improve African American lives, injecting the Fourteenth Amendment into the narrative in the mid- to late 1920s may be premature.

30. Robinson family tree maintained by Nina Govan; "The Frightful Calamity at Richmond, Va.," *Frank Leslie's Illustrated Newspaper*, May 14, 1870, 134.

31. Nina Govan, telephone interview by author, Oct. 2008, and interview by author, Apr. 20, 2011, Washington, DC.

32. Spottswood W. Robinson III, "Spottswood William Robinson, Jr.," in *Legal Education in Virginia, 1779–1979*, by William Bryson (Charlottesville: University Press of Virginia, 1982), 553–56.

33. Ibid., 555.

34. Nina Govan and Oswald Govan, interviews by author, Apr. 20, 2011, Washington, DC; copy of FBI background check on SR, conducted in 1963 and obtained by author under Freedom of Information and Privacy Acts.

35. "Mrs. Inez C. Robinson succumbs at 100," *Richmond Free Press*, Feb. 17, 1994.

36. Cameron McWhirter, *Red Summer: The Summer of 1919 and the Awakening of Black America* (New York: Henry Holt, 2011), 20, 127–48; Scott Ellsworth, "Tulsa Race Riot," in *Encyclopedia of Oklahoma History and Culture,* accessed Mar. 19, 2017, www.okhistory.org/publications/enc/entry.php?entry=TU013; Alexander, *Race Man,* 181.

37. For images of Jackson Ward, see Elvatrice Belsches, *Richmond, Virginia* (Charleston: Arcadia, 2002); and Seldon Richardson, *Built by Blacks: African American Architecture and Neighborhoods in Richmond* (Charleston: History Press, 2008).

38. "14th Census of the United States, 1920," National Archives and Records Administration, Microfilm Publication T625.

39. Ferguson Reid, interview by author, Jan. 18, 2013, Richmond.

40. Ibid.

41. Richardson, *Built by Blacks,* 99–103.

42. Ruth Jenkins, "Nobody Raises Eyebrows When U.S. Judge Calls His Secretary 'Honey,'" *RAA,* Oct. 26, 1963; Nina Govan, interview by author, Apr. 20, 2011; Reid, interview by author, Jan. 18, 2013.

43. Armstrong High School ledger in possession of Thelma Fant, accessed June 1, 2013, Richmond.

44. SR, interview by JW, n.d., JWC. Williams conducted three taped interviews with Robinson while researching a book on Thurgood Marshall. Two dated interviews were conducted in 1989 and 1993. The third interview, undated, appears from the text to have been conducted between the other two.

45. Catalog of Virginia Union University, 1932–33, VUUA.

46. Ray McAllister, "A Life on the Law's Cutting Edge," *RTD,* July 26, 1986, F1; SR, interview by JW, n.d.

2. A First-Class Law School

1. Elizabeth Abbott, *A History of Celibacy* (Cambridge, MA: Da Capo, 2001), 158. Hill spoke of eating with Marshall at Father Divine's in many interviews, as well as in *Big Bang,* 79.

2. Juan Williams, *Thurgood Marshall: American Revolutionary* (New York: Times Books, 1998), 53; Larry Gibson, *Young Thurgood: The Making of a Supreme Court Justice* (Amherst, MA: Prometheus Books, 2012), 107, 117; OH, interview by Ronald Carrington, Nov. 13, 2002, VFDC, dig.library.vcu.edu/cdm/ref/collection/voices/id/5.

3. Gibson, *Young Thurgood,* 113; Hill, *Big Bang,* 80–81.

4. OH, interview by Richard Kluger, Richmond, Apr. 4, 1971, BBEC, MS 759.

5. Sauder, "Oliver Hill," 1; Hill, *Big Bang,* 62; "Howard Law Class Split in Factions," *WAA,* Oct. 17, 1931.

6. Hill, *Big Bang,* 74.

7. OH, interview by Higginbotham, May 25, 1985, 407; OH, interview by Car-

rington, Nov. 13, 2002; Genna Rae McNeil, *Groundwork: Charles Hamilton Houston and the Struggle for Civil Rights* (Philadelphia: University of Pennsylvania Press, 1983), 64; Gibson, *Young Thurgood,* 107.

8. Rayford Logan, *Howard University: The First Hundred Years, 1867–1967* (New York: New York University Press, 1969), 249; "Howard University Law School announces Legal Survey," press release, 1927, CHHC, Box 163–6; J. Clay Smith Jr., *Emancipation: The Making of the Black Lawyer, 1844–1944* (Philadelphia: University of Pennsylvania Press, 1993), 9; Gibson, *Young Thurgood,* 355–56.

9. Gibson, *Young Thurgood,* 108.

10. Robert Carter, "In Tribute: Charles Hamilton Houston," *Harvard Law Review* 3 (June 8, 1998): 2150–51.

11. Charles Houston, "The Need for Negro Lawyers," *Journal of Negro Education* 4 (Jan. 1935): 49, 51.

12. Some researchers say Houston insisted on the title "vice-dean" because he was dissatisfied with his compensation; others say he was protesting inadequate faculty pay. Since money was not a primary motivator for Houston, the latter seems more likely. McNeil, *Groundwork,* 79, embraces that view.

13. Rowan, *Dream Makers, Dream Breakers,* 67; Williams, *Thurgood Marshall,* 54; Charles Houston, "Faculty Bulletin," Oct. 9, 1931, CHHC, Box 163–6.

14. Circular of information, May 1930, CHHC, Box 163–6.

15. McNeil, *Groundwork,* 82; OH, interview by Oliver, June 9, 1999; Logan, *Howard University,* 267–68.

16. Kenneth Mack, *Representing the Race: The Creation of the Civil Rights Lawyer* (Cambridge, MA: Harvard University Press, 2012), 68; Gibson, *Young Thurgood,* 108; McNeil, *Groundwork,* 84–85; Sullivan, *Lift Every Voice,* 161.

17. Sullivan, *Lift Every Voice,* 161; list of Howard Law faculty, 1931, CHHC, Box 163–6.

18. Gibson, *Young Thurgood,* 110; Williams, *Thurgood Marshall,* 57; OH, interview by Thomas, Feb. 2, 2004.

19. OH, interview, Nov. 5, 2008, Omega Psi Phi Fraternity, http://thedefender online.org/2008/11/05/oliver-hill-documentary (the author retains a transcript of the interview, which has since been removed from the website); Gibson, *Young Thurgood,* 110; McNeil, *Groundwork,* 82.

20. Gilbert Ware, *William Hastie: Grace Under Pressure* (New York: Oxford University Press, 1984), 154.

21. Hill, *Big Bang,* 77–78.

22. Marybeth Gassman and Roger Geiger, eds., *Higher Education for African Americans Before the Civil Rights Era, 1800–1964* (New Brunswick, NJ: Transaction, 2012), 21–25.

23. "Samuel Peyton Brown Family Tree," OHC.

24. Ibid.; Hill, *Big Bang,* 280; OH, interview by JW, Dec. 17, 1992, JWC.

25. OH, interview by Thomas, Feb. 2, 2004.

26. OH, interview by Kluger, Apr. 4, 1971; OH, interview by Carrington, Nov. 13, 2002; Conrad Pearson, interview by Walter Weave, Apr. 18, 1979, Southern Oral

History Program, Interview H-0218, University of North Carolina at Chapel Hill, http://docsouth.unc.edu/sohp/H-0218/menu.html. A major roadblock was the refusal of the black president of the North Carolina College for Negroes to turn over Hocutt's transcript.

27. List of Howard Law School graduates, prepared by archivist Seth Kronemer, in author's possession; "Sun Broils 2,000 at H. U. Commencement," *WAA*, June 17, 1933, 1; OH, interview by JW, Dec. 17, 1992.

28. Williams, *Thurgood Marshall*, 59; "Sun Broils 2,000 at H. U. Commencement," 1.

29. J. Douglas Smith, *Managing White Supremacy*, 259–70; ST, interview by William Elwood, Feb. 18, 1985, CRLP, Accession No. 12801-a, Box w/8606-h, 852, 856.

30. J. Douglas Smith, *Managing White Supremacy*, 260–61; ST, interview by Elwood, Feb. 18, 1985, 859–60.

31. Hill, *Big Bang*, 85–86; OH, interview by Carrington, Nov. 13, 2002.

32. OH, interview by Elwood, Oct. 1987, CRLP, Accession No. 12801-a, Box w/8606-h, 909–11; Hill, *Big Bang*, 86–88.

33. Hill, *Big Bang*, 88–89; OH, interview by Elwood, Oct. 1987, 911.

34. Hill, *Big Bang*, 85; Gibson, *Young Thurgood*, 264–66.

35. Hill, *Big Bang*, 283; marriage license no. 179826, issued Sept. 4, 1934, Vital Records, Washington, DC, Superior Court.

3. A Gamble on Roanoke

1. BH to OH, n.d., OHC. The letter is among more than two hundred written by the couple between September 1934 and July 1936 and contained in the collection. The Louis-Baer match occurred in September 1935.

2. University of Virginia, Geospatial and Statistical Data Center, "Historical Census Browser," accessed July 24, 2012, http://mapserver.lib.virginian.edu/collections; Houston, "Need for Negro Lawyers," 49. In *Big Bang*, 99, Hill states that in the 1930s there were five black lawyers in Roanoke and about forty statewide.

3. Clarence Dunnaville Jr., "Gainsboro and its Outstanding Black Citizens," *HSWVJ* 16 (2004): 38; Raymond Barnes, *A History of the City of Roanoke* (Radford, VA: Commonwealth, 1968), 744–49.

4. Hill, *Big Bang*, 90–91. For discussion of life in the Gainsboro neighborhood, see Erin Baratta, "Gainsboro Neighborhood, 1890–1940," *HSWVJ* 14 (1999): 40–50; Alice Roberts and Margaret Roberts, "Gilmer Avenue, Northwest," ibid., 51–52; and Dunnaville, "Gainsboro," 36–41. Hill's letterhead stationery and the return addresses on various letters identify his office address as 40 High Street; however, *Hill's Roanoke City Directory 1935* (Richmond, 1935) identifies Hill's business address as 40 Center Avenue NW. According to Baratta, "Gainsboro Neighborhood," 49, two sections of Center Avenue "were together previously High Street."

5. Hill, *Big Bang*, 90–91.

6. OH to BH, Oct. 3 and 8, 1934, and BH to OH, Oct. 10, 1934, all in OHC.

7. J. A. Reynolds to WW, Feb. 28, 1934; unsigned letter to Reynolds, Mar. 5, 1934; and Reynolds to WW, May 9, 1934, all in NAACP Papers, Group I, Box G-212.

8. In a letter to the national office dated June 25, 1934, Reynolds observed that "most people [would] be surprised to know how many of our educated people are fighting against the N.A.A.C.P." Ibid.; OH to BH, Dec. 14, 1934, and BH to OH, Dec. 16, 1934, both in OHC.

9. Roanoke branch report to national NAACP, Feb. 27, 1935, NAACP Papers, Group I, Box G-212.

10. Larissa Smith, "Civil Rights Vanguard," 130–32; Tushnet, *Making Civil Rights Law*, 12–13.

11. Tushnet, *Making Civil Rights Law*, 12–13. See also McNeil, *Groundwork*, 114–17; and Sullivan, *Lift Every Voice*, 156–57.

12. Larissa Smith, "Civil Rights Vanguard," 133.

13. BH to OH, Sept. 28, 1934, OHC.

14. OH to BH, Oct. 3, Nov. 14, Dec. 16, Nov. 11, 1934, OHC.

15. OH to BH, Nov. 16, 1934, and BH to OH, May 7, 1935, OHC.

16. OH to BH, Oct. 22, 1934, Jan. 13, 1935, OHC.

17. OH to BH, n.d., probably late 1934 or early 1935; OH to BH, n.d.; and BH to OH, n.d., probably Jan. 1935, OHC.

18. OH to BH, Nov. 11, 1934; Reginald Shareef, *Roanoke Valley's African-American Heritage* (Virginia Beach, VA: Donning, 1996), 75.

19. OH to BH, Jan. 13, Oct. 20, Nov. 11, 1935, all in OHC.

20. OH to BH, Feb. 24, 1935, OHC. The back-and-forth letters continued over the next week, concluding on the following Sunday, March 3.

21. OH to BH, May 5, 1935, OHC.

22. BH to OH, June 17, 1935, OHC.

23. "Negro is Given Death Sentence," *RT*, Sept. 24, 1935, 4.

24. OH to BH, Sept. 24, 1935, OHC.

25. Frank Clarke to Charles Houston, Sept. 17, 1935, NAACP Papers, Group I, Box G-212, brackets and parentheses in the original.

26. Alexander Leidholdt, "'Never Thot This Could Happen in the South!': The Anti-Lynching Advocacy of Appalachian Newspaper Editor Bruce Crawford," *Appalachian Journal* 38 (Winter/Spring 2011): 206–7.

27. Correspondence regarding Little case, Sept. 20 to Oct. 1, 1935, NAACP Papers, Group I, Box G-212.

28. OH to BH, Oct. 19, 1935, OHC.

29. OH, interview, Nov. 5, 2008, Omega Psi Phi.

30. This account is found in "A Summary of the Evidence Introduced by Commonwealth in Case of Commonwealth v Harrison Little," Secretary of the Commonwealth Executive Papers, Dec. 23, 1936, Accession No. 24938, Box 1028, LVA. For an additional account, see "Two Shoot It Out in Darkened Room," *RT*, Sept. 17, 1935, 3.

31. "Application for Pardon or Parole," Secretary of the Commonwealth Executive Papers, Dec. 23, 1936, LVA; J. A. Anderson to OH, Oct. 30, 1935, OHC.

32. C. J. Williams to Gov. George Peery, and Horace Sutherland to Peery, both in Secretary of the Commonwealth Executive Papers, Dec. 23, 1936, LVA.

33. List of Pardons, Commutations, and Reprieves, H. D. Doc. 12 (1938), 51.

34. Hill, *Big Bang*, 97.

35. OH to BH, Nov. 15, 1935, OHC; Houston to OH, Nov. 20, 1935, AFPS Papers, Group I, Box C-203.

36. OH to BH, Oct. 20 and Nov. 25, 1935, OHC.

37. "Colored Teachers End Meeting Today," *RT*, Nov. 29, 1935, 4. The *Roanoke Times* was not alone in ignoring the NAACP gathering. The *Journal and Guide*, then the state's premier black newspaper, did so also, suggesting a deliberate decision not to alert outsiders to NAACP strategy.

38. Luther P. Jackson, *A History of the Virginia State Teachers Association* (Norfolk, VA: Guide Publishing, 1937), 108; Sullivan, *Lift Every Voice*, 212–13. See also "Virginia Teachers Take Important Step at Convo," *JG*, Dec. 7, 1935, 1.

39. "Virginia Teachers Take Important Step at Convo," 1.

40. Sullivan, *Lift Every Voice*, 208–10; *Murray v. Pearson*, 169 Md. 478 (1936).

41. Williams, *Thurgood Marshall*, 62; Gibson, *Young Thurgood*, 246.

42. For a full account of the Jackson application, see J. Douglas Smith, *Managing White Supremacy*, 244–48; and Fred Scott to Alice Jackson, Oct. 5, 1935, AFPS Papers, Group I, Box C-203.

43. Houston to Professor C. H. Hamlin, Dec. 9, 1935, AFPS Papers, Group I, Box C-203.

44. BH to OH, Jan. 21, 1936, OHC. The selection of Hill is surprising since the Richmond attorney Byron Hopkins corresponded with Houston throughout the fall of 1935 regarding efforts to integrate Virginia colleges. That correspondence can be found in AFPS Papers, Group I, Box C-203.

45. "30 Negroes Get Educational Aid Under New Law," *RTD*, July 30, 1936, 12.

46. BH to OH, Jan. 17 and Feb. 9, 1936, and OH to BH, Feb. 13, 1936, all in OHC.

47. OH to BH, May 1936, and BH to OH, May 14, 1936, OHC.

48. OH to BH, Apr. 20, 1936, OHC.

49. BH to OH, Apr. 21, 1936, OHC.

50. BH to OH, June 28 and June 1, 1936, OHC.

51. OH to BH, July 21, 1936, OHC.

52. Clifton Woodrum to James Farley, July 23, 1936, OHC.

4. "The Best Student I Ever Taught"

1. Olivia Hill to OH, Apr. 21, 1936, OHC.

2. SR, interview by JW, n.d.

3. Ibid.; catalogs of Virginia Union University, 1932–33, 1933–34, 1934–35, and 1935–36, VUUA.

4. SR, interview by JW, n.d.; J. Clay Smith Jr., *Emancipation*, 52.

5. Marriage license no. 190808, May 5, 1936, Vital Records, Washington, DC, Superior Court. Curiously, the license reads, "Spottswood Wm. Robinson, 3rd, and Bernice Marian Lott," which is not Marian's correct surname. Jenkins, "Nobody Raises Eyebrows When U.S. Judge Calls His Secretary 'Honey'"; SR, interview by JW, Aug. 22, 1989, JWC; Oswald Govan, interview by author, Apr. 20, 2011.

6. SR, interview by JW, n.d.

7. Logan, *Howard University*, 377; J. Clay Smith Jr., *Emancipation*, 50.

8. "Law Alumni at H.U. Criticize Dr. Flexner," *WAA*, June 17, 1933, 9.

9. Laura Kiernan, "The Fire Still Burns," *WP*, May 27, 1981, 1.

10. SR, interview by JW, n.d.

11. Ibid.

12. "Presentation of Portrait, Hon. Spottswood W. Robinson III," June 9, 1989, US Courthouse, Washington, DC, document in author's possession, courtesy of Nina Govan.

13. Ibid.

14. Description of Nabrit's course, CHHC, Box 163–6; Tushnet, *Making Civil Rights Law*, 87; SR, interview by JW, Aug. 22, 1989; Kluger, *Simple Justice*, 472.

15. SR, interview by JW, Aug. 22, 1989.

16. *Missouri ex rel. Gaines v. Canada*, 305 U.S. 337 (1938).

17. Ibid.; Sullivan, *Lift Every Voice*, 233. The quotation is attributed to Pauli Murray. See also McNeil, *Groundwork*, 149–50.

18. SR, interview by JW, n.d.; Carter, "In Tribute: Charles Hamilton Houston," 2153.

19. Carter, "In Tribute: Charles Hamilton Houston," 2153.

20. OH, interview by Higginbotham, May 25, 1985, 410; OH, "List of employers, 1918–1935."

21. OH to Lelia Pentecost, May 23, 1938, OHC.

22. Williams, *Thurgood Marshall*, 83–85.

23. OH, interview by JW, Dec. 17, 1992, JWC.

24. Williams, *Thurgood Marshall*, 79–80; J. Byron Hopkins to OH, Aug. 12, 1938, OHC.

25. OH's handwritten minutes of the Waiter's, Cook's and Bellman's Club, May 16, 1938, OHC.

26. OH, interview by Oliver, June 9, 1999; OH, interview by Higginbotham, May 25, 1985, 410–11; Hill, *Big Bang*, 99–100.

27. Hill, *Big Bang*, 100–101; Larissa Smith, "Civil Rights Vanguard," 138.

28. For a full account, see Raymond Arsenault, *The Sound of Freedom: Marian Anderson, the Lincoln Memorial, and the Concert that Awakened America* (New York: Bloomsbury, 2009).

29. "237 Grads Given Howard Degrees," *WAA*, June 17, 1939, 15. The Howard Law archivist Seth Kronemer could not verify the distinction of "highest grade point average in law school history," in part because of evolving grading standards

between the school's founding in 1869 and Robinson's graduation in 1939. However, the statement was so widely repeated at the time and later that it seems safe to assume that Robinson held the record at least for the period from the time an accredited, full-time day program began, in the early 1930s, and probably longer. In 2010, Ritu Narula surpassed Robinson by graduating summa cum laude.

30. J. Clay Smith Jr., *Emancipation*, 52; Ware, *William Hastie*, 188; SR, interview by JW, n.d.

31. BH to OH, Sept. 29, 1939, OHC.

32. SR, interview by JW, n.d.

33. SR, interview by JW, Aug. 22, 1989.

34. Ibid.

35. Ibid.

5. Breakthrough in Norfolk

1. Front-page stories in *RTD*, May 1, 1939, included "Hitler Seen Demanding 15-Mile-Wide Roadway Across Polish Border" and "Roosevelt Rededicates United States to Peace"; "Still for 'Carry Me Back,'" an editorial, appeared on p. 10. See also, "Ku Klux Parade 'Inspires' Negroes in Miami to Vote," *RTD*, May 3, 1939, 1.

2. OH to BH, May 8, 1939, OHC; Hill, *Big Bang*, 101–2.

3. Hill, *Big Bang*, 101–2; BH to OH, July 28, 1939, OHC.

4. Hill, *Big Bang*, 101; BH to OH, June 3, 1939, OHC.

5. BH to OH, June 3 and July 15, 1939, OHC.

6. L. F. Palmer, "Negro Education in 1939," *VTB*, Jan. 1940, 2.

7. "*Afro*'s 1939 Richmond Honor Role," Feb. 3, 1940, *RAA*, 11; "Petition in Behalf of Brother J. M. Tinsley," OHC; Larissa Smith, "Civil Rights Vanguard," 141; TM to RW, Feb. 14, 1940, NAACP Papers, Group II, Box C-210; "State NAACP Called Model," *RAA*, Nov. 30, 1940, 14.

8. J. Douglas Smith, *Managing White Supremacy*, 258–59; "First Lady Gives Medal to Contralto," *RTD*, July 3, 1939, 1; "5,000 See Mrs. Roosevelt Present NAACP Medal to Marian Anderson," *RAA*, July 8, 1939, 1.

9. Earl Lewis, *In Their Own Interests: Race, Class, and Power in Twentieth-Century Norfolk, Virginia* (Berkeley: University of California Press, 1991), 157.

10. Rupert Picott, *History of the Virginia Teachers Association* (Washington, DC: National Education Association, 1975), 108. For discussion of the Maryland cases, see Gilbert Ware, "Equal Pay for Black Teachers," *Crisis*, Mar. 1984, 40–41; and Gibson, *Young Thurgood*, 309–23.

11. TM, memo to WW, Nov. 29, 1937, NAACP Papers, Group I, Box D-91; Picott, *History of the Virginia Teachers Association*, 108; Lewis, *In Their Own Interests*, 155–57.

12. Lewis, *In Their Own Interests*, 158; Peter Wallenstein, *Blue Laws and Black Codes: Conflict, Courts and Change in Twentieth-Century Virginia* (Charlottes-

ville: University of Virginia Press, 2004), 90; Kluger, *Simple Justice*, 215; Tushnet, *NAACP's Legal Strategy against Segregated Education*, 78.

13. Judge James Benton, ret., interview by author, Jan. 22, 2013, Richmond.

14. "Extended School Equality Fight" and "Surry, Pulaski, Middlesex and Alleghany Begin Action," *RAA*, Feb. 11, 1939, 13; "Covington Citizens Deplore Public School Discriminations," *JG*, Mar. 25, 1939, 1; "Virginia Principals Ponder Unequal School Cases," *RAA*, Feb. 25, 1939, 13; "Cumberland County is Robbing Right and Left," *RAA*, May 13, 1939, 17; Nat Turner, "Minority Robs the Majority in Essex," *RAA*, May 27, 1939, 13.

15. "Court Denies Salary Claim of Teacher," *VP*, June 1, 1939, 18.

16. BH to OH, June 3, 1939, OHC.

17. "Miss Black is Dropped" and "NAACP Statement from New York," *RAA*, June 24, 1939, 1.

18. Jeffrey Littlejohn and Charles Ford, *Elusive Equality: Desegregation and Resegregation in Norfolk's Public Schools* (Charlottesville: University of Virginia Press, 2012), 8–9; "School Board Condemned by Negroes," *VP*, June 26, 1939, 12; "School Board is Urged to Reappoint Fired Teacher," *JG*, July 1, 1939, 1; "Let the School Board Reconsider," *VP*, June 27, 1939, 6.

19. "Salary Fight is Renewed as Three More Lose Jobs," *RAA*, June 24, 1939, 13.

20. Hill told versions of the story many times, including in his Nov. 13, 2002, interview by Carrington and in *Big Bang*, 215–17.

21. *Bliley v. West*, 42 F.2d 101 (1930); Wallenstein, *Blue Laws and Black Codes*, 173–77; Henry Suggs, "P. B. Young and the Norfolk Journal and Guide, 1910–1954" (PhD diss., University of Virginia, May 1976), 144.

22. Frank Green, "'It Wasn't a Good Time Back Then,'" *RTD*, Mar. 2, 2014, 1.

23. Lisa Lindquist Dorr, *White Women, Rape, and the Power of Race in Virginia, 1900–1960* (Chapel Hill: University of North Carolina Press, 2004), 30; J. Douglas Smith, *Managing White Supremacy*, 156; Sullivan, *Lift Every Voice*, 229; Michael Klarman, *From Jim Crow to Civil Rights: The Supreme Court and the Struggle for Racial Equality* (Oxford: Oxford University Press, 2004), 158.

24. OH, interview by Carrington, Nov. 13, 2002; Hill, *Big Bang*, 216–17; Wallenstein, *Blue Laws and Black Codes*, 87–88.

25. S. J. Ackerman, "The Trials of S. W. Tucker," *Washington Post Magazine*, June 11, 2000, W14ff.; J. Douglas Smith, *Managing White Supremacy*, 259–70; Wallenstein, *Blue Laws and Black Codes*, 88–89; *Out of Obscurity: The Story of the 1939 Alexandria Library Sit-in*, video by River Road Productions, 1999, viewed by author at Alexandria Black History Museum, formerly the Robert H. Robinson Library, summer 2013.

26. Littlejohn and Ford, *Elusive Equality*, 18–19; Lewis, *In Their Own Interests*, 161.

27. Minutes of the Joint Committee, Sept. 15, 1939, OHC.

28. Gibson, *Young Thurgood*, 322–26.

29. RW to Thomas Hewin and OH, Jan. 24, 1940, NAACP Papers, Group II, Box B-181; "Negro Seeks Injunction in Salary Fight," *VP*, Nov. 3, 1939, pt. 2, p. 12.

30. OH to TM, July 12, 1940; TM to OH, June 29, 1940; and OH to TM, July 1, 1940, all in NAACP Papers, Group II, Box B-181.

31. Alfred Anderson to TM, Jan. 13, 1940, ibid.

32. John Peters, *From Marshall to Moussaoui: Federal Justice in the Eastern District of Virginia* (Petersburg, VA: Dietz, 2013), 123.

33. Hill, *Big Bang*, 126; "Negroes Lose Suit for Equal Pay to Schoolteachers," *VP*, Feb. 13, 1940, 1; opinion, *Alston v. Sch. Bd. of Norfolk*, Feb. 12, 1940, NAACP Papers, Group II, Box B-182; TM to Carl Murphy, Feb. 13, 1940, and TM to Mark Ethridge, Feb. 15, 1940, both in ibid., Box B-181.

34. Hill, *Big Bang*, 126–27; *Chambers v. Florida*, 309 U.S. 227 (1940).

35. TM to WH and LR, Mar. 12, 1940, NAACP Papers, Group II, Box B-181.

36. OH to TM, Feb. 19, 1940, ibid.

37. TM to OH, Mar. 19, 1940, ibid.

38. TM to RW and TM to OH, both Mar. 25, 1940, ibid.

39. Alfred Anderson to OH, Mar. 20, 1940, ibid.

40. TM to OH, Mar. 25, 1940.

41. OH, interview by Carrington, Nov. 13, 2002; Hill, *Big Bang*, 127–28.

42. Suggs, "P. B. Young and the Norfolk Journal and Guide," 157.

43. Ibid.; OH, interview by Higginbotham, May 25, 1985, 415; Hill, *Big Bang*, 128–30.

44. OH to WH, LR, and TM, Apr. 12, 1940, and TM to OH, Apr. 13, 1940, both in NAACP Papers, Group II, Box B-181.

45. TM to members of the Joint Committee, Apr. 13, 1940; TM to RW, Apr. 24, 1940; and RW, memo, Apr. 26, 1940, ibid.

46. Melvin Alston to TM, Apr. 30, 1940; TM to OH, May 1, 1940; and OH to Alston, May 2, 1940, ibid.

47. TM to LR and WH, May 28, 1940, and TM to Mrs. L. B. Michael, June 10, 1940, ibid.

48. "School Wage Case Argued Before Court," *VP*, June 14, 1940, pt. 2, p. 1.

49. *Alston v. Sch. Bd. of Norfolk*, 112 F.2d 992 (1940); "School Teachers Pay Differential Unconstitutional," *VP*, June 19, 1940, 20; Lewis, *In Their Own Interests*, 163.

50. OH to TM, June 18, 1940, NAACP Papers, Group II, Box B-181.

51. TM to Norfolk Teachers Association, Sept. 24, 1940, ibid.

52. TM to L. F. Palmer, Oct. 5, 1940, and Palmer to TM, Oct. 12, 1940, both in NAACP Papers, Group II, Box B-182.

53. *Alston v. Sch. Bd. of Norfolk*, 311 U.S. 693 (1940); LR to OH, Oct. 28, 1940, NAACP Papers, Group II, Box B-182; L. F. Palmer, "Our Great Victory," *VTB*, Nov. 1940, 2.

54. *Mills v. Bd. of Ed. of Anne Arundel County*, 30 F. Supp. 245 (1939); Gibson,

Young Thurgood, 323–26. Following the *Mills* decision, the Maryland legislature equalized teacher salaries statewide in 1941.

55. Suggs, "P. B. Young and the Norfolk Journal and Guide," 1–3, 135, 173.

56. LR to TM, Nov. 1, 1940, and P. B. Young to TM, Nov. 26, 1940, both in NAACP Papers, Group II, Box B-182.

57. TM to WW and RW, Nov. 8, 1940, and TM, undated memo covering events of Oct. 18–Nov. 27, 1940, in Norfolk teachers' case, ibid.

58. TM, undated memo covering events of Oct. 18–Nov. 27, 1940, ibid.

59. TM to RW, Nov. 22, 1940; P. B. Young to TM, Nov. 16, 1940; and TM to P. B. Young, Nov. 18, 1940, NAACP Papers, Group II, Box B-182.

60. TM to WH, LR, and OH, Nov. 28, 1940; TM, undated memo covering events of Oct. 18–Nov. 27, 1940; and TM to Alston, Dec. 4, 1940, ibid.

61. Alfred Anderson to OH, Jan. 6, 1941, and OH to LR, Jan. 31, 1941, ibid.

62. Alston to TM, Feb. 3, 1941, ibid.

63. LR to RW, Feb. 6, 1941, ibid.; "Renewal of Court Fight Threatens Va. Teachers," *RAA*, Feb. 8, 1941, 13.

64. OH to LR and TM, Feb. 18, 1941, NAACP Papers, Group II, Box B-182; Sullivan, *Lift Every Voice*, 248.

65. Minutes of the Joint Committee, Nov. 10, 1940, OHC.

66. Hill, *Big Bang*, 132.

6. Storm Clouds Near and Far

1. Tushnet, *Making Civil Rights Law*, 72.

2. Ruth Bader Ginsburg, interview by author, Dec. 17, 2013, Washington, DC.

3. Judge Harry Edwards, comments, "Proceedings of the Memorial Ceremony Celebrating the Life and Work of the Honorable Spottswood W. Robinson III [May 12, 1999, Prettyman Courthouse, Washington, DC]," document in author's possession, courtesy of Nina Govan.

4. LaVerne Williams, interview by author, Jan. 7, 2014, Hyattsville, MD.

5. Stephen Carter, telephone interview by author, Feb. 20, 2014.

6. "Spottswood W. Robinson III, Personal Data Questionnaire," June 18, 1963, prepared in conjunction with his nomination to the federal judiciary, copy in author's possession, courtesy of Nina Govan; "Robinson, Spottswood W(illiam) 3D," in *Current Biography*, Mar. 1962, 33–34; Bobby Stafford, telephone interview by author, Sept. 2008.

7. 1940 US Census, accessed through ancestry.com, June 3, 1013; "Spottswood W. Robinson III, Personal Data Questionnaire," June 18, 1963; Nina Govan, interview by author, Apr. 20, 2011.

8. *Buchanan v. Warley*, 245 U.S. 60 (1917); *Corrigan v. Buckley*, 271 U.S. 323 (1926); Clement E. Vose, *Caucasians Only: The Supreme Court, the NAACP, and the Restrictive Covenant Cases* (Berkeley: University of California Press, 1967), 65–66; Leland Ware, "Invisible Walls: An Examination of the Legal Strategy of

the Restrictive Covenant Cases," *Washington University Law Review* 67 (1989): 739–41.

9. Ware, "Invisible Walls," 748.

10. McNeil, *Groundwork,* 177.

11. L. Douglas Wilder, interview by author, Apr. 13, 2011, Richmond.

12. Ware, *William Hastie,* 154.

13. SR, interview by JW, Aug. 22, 1989.

14. James Cephas to WW, Apr. 29, 1942; TM to Cephas, May 1, 1942; W. F. Turner to WW, May 5, 1942; SR to Turner, May 8, 1942; WW to Mary Gibson Hundley, Apr. 19, 1942; and Hundley to WW, Apr. 12, 1942, all in NAACP Papers, Group II, Box B-132.

15. *Hundley v. Gorewitz,* 132 F.2d 23 (D.C. Circuit, 1942).

16. OH, interview by Carrington, Nov. 13, 2002.

17. "U.S. Executions from 1608–2002," ProCon.org, accessed May 19, 2016, http://deathpenalty.procon.org/view.resource.php?resourceID=004087; "Salary Fight is Renewed as Three More Lose Jobs," 13; John Jordan, "School Board Fires 4," *JG,* June 21, 1941, 1; "Fredericksburg Fires Teachers in Pay Fight," *RAA,* May 2, 1942, 15; "Six Teachers Fired," *RAA,* May 22, 1943, 1.

18. Linwood Holton Jr., interview by author, May 28, 2014, Irvington, VA. Bilbo, who twice served as governor of Mississippi before election to the Senate, was an unapologetic white supremacist and race-baiter.

19. V. O. Key, *Southern Politics in State and Nation* (New York: Alfred Knopf, 1950), 19–20.

20. Andrew Buni, *The Negro in Virginia Politics, 1902–1965* (Charlottesville: University of Virginia Press, 1967), 124–25; Heinemann et al., *Old Dominion, New Commonwealth,* 298–310; Brent Tarter, *The Grandees of Government: The Origins and Persistence of Undemocratic Politics in Virginia* (Charlottesville: University of Virginia Press, 2013), 281–304.

21. Tarter, *Grandees of Government,* 283.

22. Luther Jackson, "The Voteless School Teachers of Virginia," *VTB,* Nov. 1941, 12. According to Campbell Gibson and Kay Jung, "Historical Census Statistics on Population Totals by Race, 1790 to 1990" (US Census Bureau Working Paper Series, 56, Sept. 2002), Virginia's black population fell from about 36 percent in 1900 to 27 percent in 1930, 25 percent in 1940, and 22 percent in 1950. It stabilized at about 19 percent in the late twentieth century.

23. Hill, *Big Bang,* 105–6; Emma Edmunds, field notes, May 22, 2004, contained in "Mapping Local Knowledge: Danville, Virginia, 1945–75," undated document created by the Carter G. Woodson Institute for African-American and African Studies, University of Virginia, in author's possession, courtesy of Edmunds.

24. Edwina Martin and Paula Martin Smith, telephone interviews by author, both Sept. 10, 2013; MM to Hill, Martin & Robinson law firm, n.d., OHC.

25. "Atty. Martin eulogized as an 'illustrious son,'" undated newspaper clipping, OHC; Larissa Smith, "Civil Rights Vanguard," 142; BH to OH, Oct. 2, 1939, OHC.

26. "Bradshaw Fight Seen Aiding Halifax County," *RAA*, Nov. 25, 1939, 15; OH to TM, Mar. 2, 1940, NAACP Papers, Group II, Box B-181; *Bradshaw v. Commonwealth*, 174 Va. 391 (1939).

27. Hill, *Big Bang*, 106; Branch News, *Crisis*, Nov. 1941, 359.

28. Richard Sherman, *The Case of Odell Waller and Virginia Justice, 1940–1942* (Knoxville: University of Tennessee Press, 1992), offers a full account of the Waller case; for Martin's role, see pp. 90–91.

29. "NAACP to Defend Youth, 15, on Rape Charges," *California Eagle*, Dec. 12, 1940, 1; "Youth, 15, to Die in Chair for Attack," *RAA*, Dec. 28, 1940, 1; Dorr, *White Women, Rape, and the Power of Race in Virginia*, 40; Hill, *Big Bang*, 122.

30. "Virginia Youth Doomed to Die Unless Mass Protests Halt His Legal Lynching, Feb. 21," *New York Age*, Feb. 1, 1941, 1; "Slated to Die, Boy, 15, Gets Writ of Error," *RAA*, Mar. 8, 1941, 1; "Commutation of Sentence of Joseph R. Mickens," Secretary of the Commonwealth Executive Papers, Dec. 29, 1941–Jan. 9, 1942, Accession No. 24938, Box 1189, LVA.

31. "Parole board pardon report" and "Grant of conditional pardon," both in Secretary of the Commonwealth Executive Papers, Dec. 20–29, 1961, Accession No. 26519, Box 1452, LVA.

32. "Mrs. Oliver W. Hill," *RAA*, Sept. 14, 1940, 3; "Omega Phi [*sic*] Phi Chapter Dance in Novelty Setting," *RAA*, May 24, 1941, 13.

33. BH to OH, Apr. 30 and July 12, 1939, OHC.

34. ST, interview by Elwood, Feb. 18, 1985, 857.

35. Ibid.

36. "Portsmouth Acts to Obtain Equal Teachers Pay," *RAA*, Dec. 14, 1940, 2; "Two More Groups Ask for Pay Parity," *RAA*, Dec. 21, 1940, 1; L. F. Palmer, "The Present Status of Salary Equalization," *VTB*, Jan. 1941, 3.

37. Holton, interview by author, May 28, 2014.

38. Douglas Summers Brown, Virginia Lee Baker, Eleanor Little Eanes, and L. Ralph Slagle, eds., *Sketches of Greensville County Virginia, 1650–1967* (Richmond: Whittet & Shepperson, 1968), 130–31.

39. "File Bus Suit in Greensville Co.," *JG*, Mar. 15, 1941, 2; "Father to Get Bus for School Child in the South," *Crisis*, Apr. 1941, 136; *Branch v. Sch. Bd. of Greensville County*, Mar. 11, 1941, Civil Action 139, records retrieved from PFRC; TM, memo to RW, Mar. 14, 1941, NAACP Papers, Group II, Box B-147.

40. OH to LR, WH, TM, and Bob Ming, Mar. 18, 1941, ibid.

41. Jordan, "School Board Fires 4," 1; John Jordan, "Norfolk County Faces Suit Over School Busses," *JG*, Nov. 22, 1941.

42. "Residents of County to Act Minus NAACP," *JG*, Jan. 10, 1942, 10; "County School Board Sued by Three Principals," *JG*, Jan. 17, 1942, 10; "Board Answers Complaint of Fired Teachers," *JG*, Feb. 28, 1942, 10; OH to TM and LR, Jan. 20, 1942, NAACP Papers, Group II, Box B-182; *Overton v. Sch. Bd. of Norfolk County*, order issued Oct. 9, 1943, Chancery Order Book No. 20, Norfolk County, June 6, 1941–Oct. 23, 1943, Chesapeake Circuit Court, Records Room, 585.

43. OH, interview by Carrington, Nov. 13, 2002; Oliver Hill, "A Symposium on Charles Hamilton Houston: Oral History," *New England Law Review* 27 (Spring 1993): 675–76. See also Gary M. Williams, *Sussex County, Virginia: A Heritage Recalled by the Land* (Petersburg, VA: Dietz, 2012), 231–33; Wallenstein, *Blue Laws and Black Codes,* 95–96; and "Pupils Sue for Admission to White Virginia County Schools," *RAA,* Sept. 19, 1942, 1.

44. *Speed v. Sch. Bd. of Sussex County,* Sept. 14, 1942, Civil Action 240, PFRC.

45. Ibid.

46. OH, interview by Carrington, Nov. 13, 2002; Gary M. Williams, *Sussex County, Virginia,* 232. In the November 13 interview, Hill recalled the judge as Garland Pollard, a former governor, but Robert Nelson Pollard served on a federal district court in Virginia from 1936 until 1954.

47. OH, interview by Carrington, Nov. 13, 2002

48. "Supplemental Answer filed by Defendants," *Speed v. Sch. Bd. of Sussex County,* Nov. 14, 1942, Civil Action 240, PFRC.

49. Kenneth Mack, "First 100 Years of the NAACP," Feb. 26, 2010, C-SPAN video library, http://www.c-span.org/video/?292293-1/first-100-years-naacp. Mack argues that courtrooms "remained open to a crossing of racial barriers in a way most public venues were not." The mechanics of courtroom procedure, if not verdicts, often were color neutral.

50. Frederic Carter to Justice Preston Campbell, Dec. 23, 1940, and "The Old Dominion Bar Association (The Early Years, 1940–1950)," both in OHC.

51. "Old Dominion Bar Association (The Early Years, 1940–1950)," OHC.

52. "Negro Teachers Seek Injunction," *RTD,* Feb. 19, 1942, 8; "Teacher Salaries To Be Equalized," *RTD,* Jan. 22, 1943, 9; OH, interview, Nov. 5, 2008, Omega Psi Phi; Along the N.A.A.C.P. Battlefront, *Crisis,* Mar. 1943; Peters, *From Marshall to Moussaoui,* 131.

53. J. Douglas Smith, *Managing White Supremacy,* 138–39; Adam Fairclough, *A Class of Their Own: Black Teachers in the Segregated South* (Cambridge, MA: Belknap Press of Harvard University Press, 2007), 345.

54. "Dr. L. F. Palmer Dies in Virginia," *RAA,* Nov. 25, 1950, 1; Picott, *History of the Virginia Teachers Association,* 117; "NN Schools Named for Activists," Newport News Public Schools press release, Feb. 28, 2011; J. Douglas Smith, *Managing White Supremacy,* 273.

55. "School Board Appointment Action Hit," *RTD,* May 18, 1943, 7; "Negro Leaders Protest Action in School Case," *RTD,* May 19, 1943, 6; Along the N.A.A.C.P. Battlefront, *Crisis,* June 1943, 180.

56. Dorothy Palmer Smith, *A Lonely Place in the Sky* (Chicago: Third World, 1989), p. II.

57. Wallenstein, *Blue Laws and Black Codes,* 92; L. F. Palmer, "Again, Victory in Newport News," *VTB,* Sept. 1945, 101; *Roles v. Sch. Bd. of Newport News,* 61 F. Supp. 395 (1945).

58. OH to LR and OH to Wendell Walker Jr., Nov. 13, 1945, OHC.

59. Hill, *Big Bang*, 190; OH, interview by Carrington, Nov. 13, 2002.

60. In a letter of May 28, 1942, to the local draft board, OHC, Hill said that he "will enlist in some branch of the service prior to Aug. 1, 1942." It is unclear how that timeline was extended to June 1943.

61. Hill, *Big Bang*, 191; OH, interview by Carrington, Nov. 13, 2002; Tushnet, *Making Civil Rights Law*, 72.

62. SR to OH, Oct. 9, 1942, OHC.

63. OH to JT, June 25, 1943, OHC.

64. Minutes of the Joint Committee, Apr. 18, 1943, OHC.

65. Photo of Martin Martin, *RAA*, June 12, 1943; "Suspect to Go Free After Year in Death Row," *RAA*, June 19, 1943, 3; "Doomed Virginia Man Freed," *RAA*, June 26, 1943, 9; Eric. W. Rise, *The Martinsville Seven: Race, Rape, and Capital Punishment* (Charlottesville: University Press of Virginia, 1995), 73.

66. "Detroit Race Riots 1943," *American Experience*, PBS, accessed Apr. 8, 2014, https://www.google.com/search?q=Detroit+riots+%2B+1943+&ie=utf-8&oe=utf-8&aq=t&rls=org.mozilla:en-US:official&client=firefox-a&channel=sb.

67. OH to Pentecost, Apr. 9, 1943, OHC.

68. [Dorothy Scott], unsigned letter to BH, July 2, 1943, OHC.

7. Robinson at the Helm

1. TM to SR, May 2, 1944, NAACP Papers, Group II, Box B-135.

2. SR to TM, May 19, 1944, ibid.

3. "Howard Walker Dies in Chair," *RAA*, June 3, 1944, 10; "What Was It Like?," Shenandoah University exhibit resulting from student-faculty investigation headed by Dr. Warren Hofstra, Nov. 2013.

4. "NAACP Promises to Test Democratic Party Action," *RAA*, July 15, 1944, 1; "Ousted Va. School Group to Appeal," *RAA*, Apr. 22, 1944, 9; "NAACP May Aid in Jim Crow Case," *RAA*, Aug. 5, 1944, 8.

5. Tushnet, *Making Civil Rights Law*, 72. Catherine Barnes, in *Journey from Jim Crow: The Desegregation of Southern Transit* (New York: Columbia University Press, 1983), 41, says that the NAACP considered challenging Jim Crow laws on the basis of the Commerce Clause "at least as early as 1919." She credits a memorandum prepared by attorney Milton Konvitz in 1943 for "a stepped-up NAACP attack on the problem."

6. *Hall v. DeCuir*, 95 U.S. 485 (1877).

7. *Mitchell v. United States*, 313 U.S. 80 (1941); Catherine Barnes, *Journey from Jim Crow*, 1–2, 6, 32.

8. R. H. Cooley Jr. to Houston, Mar. 24, 1940; Cooley to TM, Apr. 3, 1940; TM to Cooley, Apr. 5, 1940; secretary to Thurgood Marshall to OH, Apr. 6, 1940; TM, memo to OH, Apr. 22, 1940; and "Summary of Facts Leading Up to Arrest of Pauli Murray and Adelene McBean," Mar. 24, 1940, all in NAACP Papers ,Group II, Box B-190.

9. Ware, *William Hastie*, 186.

10. RW to TM, May 17, 1944, NAACP Papers, Group II, Box B-99.

11. Seaboard Railway timetable, 1939, NAACP Papers, Group II, Box B-186; Catherine Barnes, *Journey from Jim Crow*, 15–16.

12. Lawrence Jackson, *The Indignant Generation: A Narrative History of African American Writers and Critics, 1934–1960* (Princeton, NJ: Princeton University Press, 2011), 150–51; "Ga. Educator Thrown off Train, Beaten," *RAA*, Sept. 5, 1942, 1; Prentice Thomas to Professor Hugh Gloster, Sept. 11, 1942, NAACP Papers, Group II, Box B-184.

13. "Solons Asked to Abolish Jim-Crow Law," *RAA*, Feb. 5, 1944, 1; "Virginians Speak on J. C.," *Crisis*, Feb. 1944, 47ff.; J. Douglas Smith, *Managing White Supremacy*, 280–82.

14. "Protest Against Jim Crow Brings 90-Day Jail Term," *RAA*, Mar. 11, 1944, 1.

15. Hill, *Big Bang*, 138.

16. OH, interview by Elwood, Oct. 1987, 893–94.

17. Ibid., 897–98.

18. Gunnar Myrdal, *An American Dilemma: The Negro Problem and Modern Democracy* (1944; reprint, New York: Harper & Row, 1962), 635.

19. Petition for writ of error, *Morgan v. Commonwealth*, 184 Va. 24, 34 S.E.2d 491 (1945); Patrick Lackey, "Woman's Influence Surpasses Fame," *VP*, Mar. 8, 1992, 1; Cleo Gregory Warren, interview by author, Feb. 26, 2013, Gloucester County, VA. For accounts of Irene Morgan's case, see Connie Coling, *Irene Morgan's Bus Ride* (Gloucester, VA: Gloucester County Friends of the Museum, 2012); Ware, *William Hastie*, 185–90; and Catherine Barnes, *Journey from Jim Crow*, 45–48.

20. J. Douglas Smith, *Managing White Supremacy*, 69; 1930 Virginia Acts of Assembly, ch. 128, secs. 4097z–4097dd.

21. *Plessy v. Ferguson*, 163 U.S. 537 (1896); J. Douglas Smith, *Managing White Supremacy*, 28.

22. Warren, interview by author, Feb. 26, 2013.

23. Petition for writ of error, *Morgan v. Commonwealth*, 184 Va. 24, 34 S.E.2d 491 (1945).

24. Larry Chowning, *Signatures in Time: A Living History of Middlesex County, Virginia* (Saluda, VA: Middlesex County Board of Supervisors, 2012), 322.

25. Lackey, "Woman's Influence Surpasses Fame," 1.

26. *Morgan v. Commonwealth*, Common Law Order Book No. 7, Cases 330 and 331, Middlesex County Circuit Court, Saluda, VA; Clerk C. W. Eastman to Hon. Douglas Mitchell, Oct. 19, 1944, Middlesex Circuit Court Records, "Law & Com" Box, File 40, Docket 330 (1944).

27. SR to TM, Jan. 11, 1945, and TM to SR, Jan. 15, 1945, NAACP Papers, Group II, Box B-190.

28. SR to TM, Apr. 26, 1945, ibid.; opinion, *Morgan v. Commonwealth*, 184 Va. 24, 34 S.E.2d 491 (1945).

29. TM to Richard Westbrooks, June 20, 1945, NAACP Papers, Group II, Box B-190.

30. MM to OH, July 26, 1945, OHC.

31. Dorothy Scott to OH, July 23, 1945, OHC.

32. SR to TM, and "Memorandum to Mr. Wilkins from Thurgood Marshall," both Nov. 28, 1945, both in NAACP Papers, Group II, Box B-190.

33. TM to SR, May 2, 1944; SR to TM, May 19, 1944.

34. TM to SR, Dec. 16, 1944, NAACP, Group II, Box B-135.

35. "Court Upholds Death Penalty," *RAA*, Oct. 14, 1944, 1; "Pardon Board Hears Plea in Rogers Case," *RTD*, Sept. 18, 1945, 5.

36. "Court Upholds Death Penalty," 1.

37. Dorothy Scott to OH, Sept. 13, 1944, OHC.

38. Marian [Robinson] to OH, Jan. 7, 1945, and BH to OH, Aug. 5, 1945, both OHC.

39. "Induction Record of Oliver White Hill," OHC; Hill, *Big Bang*, 197–205.

40. Hill, *Big Bang*, 205–10.

41. Ibid., 200–201.

42. OH, interview by William Elwood, Oct. 1987, CRLP, 895; "Black Soldiers Battled Fascism and Racism," *WP*, May 26, 2004, B1; *The Perilous Fight: America's World War II in Color*, accessed May 5, 2014, http://www.pbs.org/perilousfight/social/african_americans/.

43. OH, interview by JW, Dec. 17, 1992.

44. Jeffrey Gonda, *Unjust Deeds: The Restrictive Covenant Cases and the Making of the Civil Rights Movement* (Chapel Hill: University of North Carolina Press, 2015), 21.

45. Vose, *Caucasians Only*, 57; Gonda, *Unjust Deeds*, 41; *Mays v. Burgess*, 147 F.2d 869 (1945).

46. Dissenting opinion, J. Edgerton, Jan. 29, 1945, *Mays v. Burgess*, 147 F.2d 869 (1945).

47. Vose, *Caucasians Only*, 55–56; *Hansberry v. Lee*, 311 U.S. 32 (1940).

48. Ware, *William Hastie*, 168–70; minutes of Chicago restrictive-covenant conference, July 9, 1945, NAACP Papers, Group II, Box B-132; TM to Henry Landry, Apr. 2, 1945, ibid., Box B-135.

49. H. B. Willey to TM, May 28, 1945, NAACP Papers, Group II, Box B-135; minutes of Chicago restrictive-covenant conference, July 9, 1945.

50. Notes on Loren Miller presentation to Chicago restrictive-covenant conference, July 9, 1945, NAACP Papers, Group II, Box B-132. For full treatment of Miller's career, see Amina Hassan, *Loren Miller: Civil Rights Attorney and Journalist* (Duncan, OK: McCasland Foundation, 2015).

51. "Memorandum to the National Legal Committee," June 13, 1945, NAACP Papers, Group II, Box B-132; Gonda, *Unjust Deeds*, 104.

52. SR to TM, June 28 and July 24, 1945, both in NAACP Papers, Group II, Box B-132; "Carrier Planes Swoop on Tokyo Area; B-29s Also Score; Truman at Sea on Way to Big Three Parley," *NYT*, July 10, 1945, 1.

53. Notes on presentation by Spottswood Robinson to Chicago restrictive-covenant conference, July 9, 1945, NAACP Papers, Group II, Box B-132.

54. Notes on Charles Houston's presentation to Chicago restrictive-covenant conference, July 9, 1945, ibid.

55. "Pardon Board Gets Dramatic Plea for Rogers," *RNL*, Sept. 17, 1945, 3; "Pardon Board Hears Plea in Rogers Case"; "Silas Rogers Parole Plea Stumps Va. Pardon Board," *RAA*, Sept. 22, 1945, 1.

56. "Rogers Death Sentence Cut to Life Term," *RNL*, Oct. 13, 1945, 2; "Pardon Board Commutes Death Penalty," *RTD*, Oct. 14, 1945, sec. 2, 1. In 1953, after a two-year campaign headed by James J. Kilpatrick, editorial-page editor of the *Richmond News Leader*, Rogers was set free. Several years later, he was convicted of raping a woman in New Jersey and sent back to prison.

57. TM to Louis Wirth, Apr. 23, 1947, NAACP Papers, Group II, Box B-132. See also Edward Dudley to Margaret Cressaty, Aug. 17, 1945, ibid., Box B-135; TM to Rev. F. D. Gholston, Sept. 26, 1945, ibid., Box B-132; Marian W. Perry to Alexander Allen, June 1, 1946, ibid. Sullivan, *Lift Every Voice*, 300, suggests that the study was completed in the fall of 1945; however, NAACP files on restrictive covenants contain no evidence of its completion.

8. Rising Expectations

1. OH to BH and OH to Hill, Martin & Robinson, both Oct. 25, 1945, OHC; Hill, *Big Bang*, 212–13.

2. BH to OH, July 28, 1945, OHC.

3. OH to Albert Miller, Dec. 4, 1945, OHC.

4. Marvin Caplan, *Farther Along: A Civil Rights Memoir* (Baton Rouge: Louisiana State University Press, 1999), 23–24.

5. Ibid., 25–26.

6. Ibid., 33–34.

7. Ibid., 63.

8. OH, interview by Higginbotham, May 25, 1985, 421.

9. Gilbert King, *Devil in the Grove: Thurgood Marshall, the Groveland Boys, and the Dawn of a New America* (New York: HarperCollins, 2012), 120–22; Catherine Barnes, *Journey from Jim Crow*, 62.

10. Ware, *William Hastie*, 188; Tushnet, *Making Civil Rights Law*, 73; NAACP Press Service, "Virginia 'Jim-Crow' Law Argued before Supreme Court," Mar. 28, 1946, NAACP Papers, Group II, Box B-190.

11. Ware, *William Hastie*, 189.

12. TM to WH and Gloria Samuels to SR, both Apr. 23, 1946, NAACP Papers, Group II, Box B-190.

13. *Morgan v. Virginia*, 328 U.S. 373 (1946). For analysis of behind-the-scenes pressures on the court in the *Morgan* decision, see Tushnet, *Making Civil Rights Law*, 73–74; Catherine Barnes, *Journey from Jim Crow*, 46–48; and Klarman, *From Jim Crow to Civil Rights*, 221–22. Despite a growing interest in safeguarding mi-

nority rights, the Court was not yet ready to overturn separate but equal, historians broadly agree.

14. "JC Bus Travel Outlawed," "Jurists Rule State Laws Place Undue Burden on Interstate Travel," and "Attorneys Hail Morgan Decision," all in *RAA*, June 8, 1946, 1; Western Union mailing list, n.d., NAACP Papers, Group II, Box B-190.

15. 1946 Virginia Acts of Assembly, 494. For discussion of Cooke's adaptation to changing Virginia politics as House of Delegates Speaker from 1968 to 1980, see Tarter, *Grandees of Government*, 358.

16. "Memorandum to Mr. White from Robert L. Carter," Sept. 20, 1946, NAACP Papers, Group II, Box B-99.

17. "Memorandum to the Board of Directors from Mr. White," Sept. 9, 1946, ibid.

18. "Memorandum to Mr. White from Robert L. Carter," Sept. 20, 1946.

19. Ralph Matthews, "23 Suits Aimed at Bias Ask $250,000 in Damages," *RAA*, Aug. 23, 1947, 1. Matthews reported that eighteen of twenty-three recent lawsuits attacking Jim Crow transportation statewide had been filed by Hill, Martin & Robinson. See also Catherine Barnes, *Journey from Jim Crow*, 63, 197.

20. Benjamin E. Mays, *A Long Journey: Dr. Benjamin E. Mays Speaks on the Struggle for Social Justice in America*, ed. Freddie Colston ([Bloomington, IN]: Xlibris, 2011), 29–34; Perry to Cyrus Johnson, May 23, 1947, NAACP Papers, Group II, Box B-186; "Report of the Legal Department," May 1946, ibid., Box B-97.

21. OH, interview by Higginbotham, May 25, 1985, 419; Wallenstein, *Blue Laws and Black Codes*, 97–98; "Hustings Court Reverses Case of Negro Convicted for Disturbance on Bus," *RTD*, Jan. 22, 1947, 2.

22. *Taylor v. Commonwealth*, 187 Va. 214, 46 S.E.2d 384 (1948); "Appellant Wins Jim Crow Bus Verdict," *RTD*, Mar. 2, 1948, 1; Lester Banks, "This Is Your NAACP," *RAA*, Apr. 14, 1951, 6.

23. *New v. Atlantic Greyhound Corp.*, 187 Va. 726, 43 S.E.2d 872 (1947); "Virginia Supreme Court Reverses Murder Conviction found in Rockingham County," *RTD*, Sept. 4, 1947, 2.

24. *Day v. Atlantic Greyhound Corp.*, 171 F.2d 59 (1948); Banks, "This Is Your NAACP," 6.

25. *Chance v. Lambeth*, 186 F.2d 879 (4th Cir. 1951); *Atlantic Coast Line Railroad v. Chance*, 341 U.S. 941 (1951); Catherine Barnes, *Journey from Jim Crow*, 81.

26. *Browder v. Gayle*, 352 U.S. 903 (1956).

27. George Houser and Bayard Rustin, "Journey of Reconciliation: A Report," n.d., NAACP Papers, Group II, Box B-190; Bayard Rustin, "I Spent 22 Days on a Chain Gang," *RAA*, Aug. 20, 1949, 1; *Boynton v. Virginia*, 364 U.S. 454 (1960); Catherine Barnes, *Journey from Jim Crow*, 144–51.

28. Tom Chillemi, "Breakthrough in civil rights for blacks," *Southside Sentinel*, Jan. 16, 1992, 1; Lackey, "Woman's Influence Surpasses Fame," 1; Warren, interview by author, Feb. 26, 2013.

29. "AFRO Honor Roll," *RAA*, Feb. 22, 1947, 14.

30. Vera Dean to WW, Aug. 10, 1950, NAACP Papers, Group II, Box B-186.

31. An analysis by Doxey Wilkerson in the *Journal of Negro Education* 29 (Winter 1960): 19, put salaries for Virginia's black female teachers at 69 percent of those for white female teachers in 1940–41 and salaries for black male teachers at 57 percent of those for white male teachers. By 1945–46 the gap had lessened, with black female teachers receiving salaries equal to 95 percent of those for white female teachers and black male teachers receiving salaries equal to 98 percent of those for white male teachers, on average, according to the report. However, when Hill, Martin & Robinson embarked on a major school-equalization campaign in 1946 and 1947, black teachers were still paid considerably less than whites in multiple communities, casting doubt on Wilkerson's statistics.

32. TM to WW, Oct. 24, 1945, NAACP Papers, Group II, Box B-99.

33. RC to TM, Jan. 16, 1946, ibid., Box B-171.

34. LR to TM, Apr. 3, 1946; Samuels to LR, Apr. 5, 1946; and TM to officers of state conferences and branches, Apr. 1, 1946, all in ibid., Box B-137.

35. "Confidential Digest of Proceedings in Atlanta Conference," memo prepared by RC, ibid.

36. Ibid.

37. "Memorandum to Executive Staff from Thurgood Marshall," Apr. 30, 1946, and "NAACP Lawyers Survey Jim Crow in Education," Apr. 27, 1946, ibid.

38. Sterling Hutcheson, "Supplemental Findings of Fact," July 29, 1948, *Freeman v. County Sch. Bd. of Chesterfield County,* 82 F. Supp. 167 (1948); Arthur M. Freeman to RP, Sept. 19, 1946, OHC.

39. RP to H. E. Fauntleroy, Sept. 21, 1946, OHC.

40. MM to RP, Sept. 26, 1946, OHC.

41. Complaint, *Smith v. Sch. Bd. of King George County,* Oct. 14, 1946, Civil Action 631, Box 66, PFRC.

42. Ibid.

43. Sullivan, *Lift Every Voice,* 319; "Looking Behind Tragedy at Moore's Ford Bridge," accessed Aug. 30, 2014, http://www.nbcnews.com/id/13905047/ns/us _news-life/t/looking-behind-tragedy-moores-ford-bridge/#.VAI34GPG_2Y.

44. "Branch Action Letter," Nov. 25, 1946, NAACP Papers, Group II, Box B-99; Williams, *Thurgood Marshall,* 131–32, 139–40; King, *Devil in the Grove,* 15–20; Sullivan, *Lift Every Voice,* 324–25.

45. Harry Truman, address to the NAACP, 1947, American Experience, accessed Aug. 31, 2014, http://www.pbs.org/wgbh/americanexperience/features/primary -resources/truman-naacp47/.

46. John Taylor, *Freedom to Serve: Truman, Civil Rights, and Executive Order 9981* (New York: Routledge, 2013), 82; Buni, *Negro in Virginia Politics,* 158–61; "Special Message to the Congress on Civil Rights," Feb. 2, 1948, http://www .presidency.ucsb.edu/ws/?pid=13006; "President Harry Truman Seeks Support for his Civil Rights Legislation," accessed Aug. 31, 2014, http://www.raabcollection .com/harry-truman-autograph/president-truman-seeks-support-civil-rights -legislation.

47. Tushnet, *NAACP's Legal Strategy against Segregated Education*, 120–23; Sullivan, *Lift Every Voice*, 337–38. For a full account, see Cheryl E. B. Wattley, *A Step toward* Brown v. Board of Education: *Ada Lois Sipuel Fisher and Her Fight to End Segregation* (Norman: University of Oklahoma Press, 2014).

48. Tushnet, *NAACP's Legal Strategy against Segregated Education*, 125–26; Sullivan, *Lift Every Voice*, 340–41. For a full account of the *Sweatt* case, see Gary Lavergne, *Before Brown: Heman Marion Sweatt, Thurgood Marshall, and the Long Road to Justice* (Austin: University of Texas Press, 2010).

49. Loren Miller, "Covenants for Exclusion," *Survey Graphic*, Oct. 1947, NAACP Papers, Group II, Box B-132.

50. Minutes on restrictive-covenant conference, Jan. 26, 1947; Loren Miller to TM, Feb. 3, 1947, NAACP Papers, Group II, Box B-132; Vose, *Caucasians Only*, 126.

51. Vose, *Caucasians Only*, 109–19.

52. Ibid., 157; Kluger, *Simple Justice*, 249.

53. Kluger, *Simple Justice*, 253.

54. SR to Perry, Sept. 11, 1947; Perry to SR, Sept. 29, 1947; and Perry to Houston, Sept. 29, 1947, all in NAACP Papers, Group II, Box B-132.

55. "Presentation of Portrait, Hon. Spottswood W. Robinson III."

56. Executive Committee minutes, LDF, June 9, 1947, NAACP Papers, Group II, Box B-99.

57. NAACP Press Office, "Special Release," Oct. 31, 1947, ibid., Box C-211. See also SR to TM, Sept. 11, 1947; TM to SR, Sept. 15, 1947; and SR to TM, Sept. 22, 1947, all in LDF Papers, Box 32.

9. "A Man among Men"

1. Edwin Slipek, "Race and Reservations," *Style Weekly*, July 25, 2012, 12ff.; Belsches, *Richmond, Virginia*, 121; Tyler-McGraw, *At the Falls*, 277.

2. Caplan, *Farther Along*, 52–53; "AVC Chairman to Speak Here," *RTD*, Nov. 27, 1946, 5.

3. Slipek, "Race and Reservations," 15.

4. Hill, *Big Bang*, 230.

5. Buni, *Negro in Virginia Politics*, 124; Larissa Smith, "Where the South Begins: Black Politics and Civil Rights Activism in Virginia, 1930–1951," abstract of doctoral dissertation submitted to Emory University Department of History, 2001, LVA.

6. J. Douglas Smith, *Managing White Supremacy*, 230–31; Branch News, *Crisis*, Sept. 1944, 258; Buni, *Negro in Virginia Politics*, 130.

7. *Smith v. Allwright*, 321 U.S. 649 (1944); Steven Lawson, *Black Ballots: Voting Rights in the South, 1944–1969* (New York: Columbia University Press, 1976), 41–46; "Texas Primary Decision," *Crisis*, June 1944, 186ff. For South Carolina's efforts to evade the ruling, see Lawson, *Black Ballots*, 48–52.

8. Buni, *Negro in Virginia Politics*, 146, 131, 128.

9. Ibid., 150–51.

10. Sullivan, *Lift Every Voice*, 317; Buni, *Negro in Virginia Politics*, 151–53.

11. Contract between Oliver and Beresenia Hill and R. V. Dorsey, Feb. 1, 1947, OHC.

12. Hill, *Big Bang*, 288.

13. Ibid., 286.

14. Ibid.; OH, interview by Elwood, Oct. 1987, 908.

15. Hill, *Big Bang*, 220; Buni, *Negro in Virginia Politics*, 154.

16. "Hill's Election Chances Boosted," *RAA*, June 21, 1947, 1; Buni, *Negro in Virginia Politics*, 153–54; "8000 Qualify to Vote in Primary," *RAA*, July 12, 1947, 1.

17. "Withdrawal is Denied by Huntley," *RNL*, Aug. 1, 1947, 15.

18. "Voting Slows Down After Brisk Start," *RNL*, Aug. 5, 1947, 1.

19. Jack Kilpatrick, "Negro Vote Proves Heavy in City Primary," *RNL*, Aug. 6, 1947, 1; "City Nominates Four Newcomers for Assembly," *RTD*, Aug. 6, 1947, 1; "Morning After: Hard Work Pays Off at the Polls," *RNL*, Aug. 6, 1947, 1. Newspaper accounts put Murray's margin over Hill variously at 193, 190, or 187 votes. The Richmond registrar and city clerk no longer retain 1947 election records.

20. Ralph Matthews, "Hill Nosed Out by 187 Votes," *RAA*, Aug. 9, 1947, 1.

21. Ibid.; Nat Turner, "Lawyer Misses Nomination by Hair," *RAA*, Sept. 6, 1947, 16.

22. "Oliver Hill Backs Charter, Urges Support for Murray," *RAA*, Nov. 1, 1947, 9.

23. "Richmond's Negro Vote and the Future," *RTD*, Aug. 7, 1947, 10.

24. "150 Present to Support Race Bills," *RNL*, Feb. 20, 1948, B1; "Repeal of Virginia's 'Jim Crow' Laws Urged by 8 Speakers at House Committee Hearing," *RTD*, Feb. 21, 1948, 3; "Not One Person Protests Bill," *RAA*, Feb. 28, 1948, 1.

25. "Hats Off to Va. Lawmakers," *RAA*, Feb. 28, 1948, 1.

26. "Clergy, Educators Ask Revision of Existing Segregation Laws," *RNL*, Feb. 26, 1948, 1; "Segregation End is Urged by Group Here," *RTD*, Feb. 27, 1948, 7; "Tuck Urges Truman, Wallace Elimination on Ballot," *RTD*, Feb. 27, 1948.

27. "Byrd Backs Tuck Proposal to Bar Truman, Wallace From Ballot," *RNL*, Feb. 26, 1948, 1; "House Committee Buries Bills to End Racial Segregation," *RTD*, Mar. 2, 1948, 4; "Murray Bills Die Despite Support," *RAA*, Mar. 6, 1948, 1; "House Adopts Boatwright's Bill on South," *RTD*, Mar. 6, 1948, 2.

28. Tyler-McGraw, *At the Falls*, 283; "Richmond Awaits First Non-Partisan Election," *RAA*, May 22, 1948, sec. 2, 1.

29. "Charter Wins Approval by Overwhelming Majority," *RTD*, Nov. 5, 1947, 1.

30. Tyler-McGraw, *At the Falls*, 283; Hill, *Big Bang*, 225.

31. "RCA Slate Disappoints Minorities," *RNL*, Mar. 25, 1948, 1.

32. Ibid.

33. Hill, *Big Bang*, 226; "Hill to Run for Post on City's New Council," *RTD*, Mar. 21, 1948, sec. 2, 1; "Hill Seeking Council Seat," *RAA*, Mar. 27, 1948, 1.

34. Hill, *Big Bang*, 226.

35. "10,000 Qualify to Vote in Richmond," *RAA*, Feb. 7, 1948, 1; Caplan, *Farther Along*, 82; "Whites to Help Elect Hill," *RAA*, June 5, 1948, 12.

36. Overton Jones, "Rash of Speeches to End Campaign for New Council," and Hill ad, *RTD*, June 6, 1948, sec. 2, 1 and 2.

37. "Candidates for Council Make Last-Minute Pleas on 13 Radio Programs," *RTD*, June 8, 1948, 1.

38. Ibid.; "Stadium Fete Will Feature Joan Brooks," *RTD*, June 6, 1948, sec. 2, 1.

39. "Richmond's Great Opportunity," *RTD*, June 6, 1948, sec. 4, 2; "Birth of New Council Given Gala Greeting at Stadium," *RTD*, June 9, 1948, 5; "Eight of Citizens Slate, Hill Elected to Council," *RTD*, June 9, 1948, 1.

40. "Hill Given Support by Wealthier Whites," *RAA*, June 19, 1948, 1.

41. Ibid.; "Election Results," *RTD*, June 9, 1948, 5; Buni, *Negro in Virginia Politics*, 157; "Richmond Elects Negro to Council," *NYT*, June 10, 1948, OHC. W. A. Lawrence was elected to the Nansemond County Board of Supervisors in 1947, a year ahead of Hill.

42. "Eight of Citizens Slate, Hill Elected to Council," 1.

43. Telegrams and newspaper clippings, OHC.

44. "Richmond Elects Negro to Council," undated newspaper clipping, OHC; Overton Jones, "Only Living Negro City Councilman Recalls Local Political Highlights of Bygone Days," *RTD*, June 9, 1948, 4; "Hill Given Support by Wealthier Whites," 1; "Oliver Hill Elected to Council by 9,097 Votes," *RAA*, June 12, 1948, 1; Buni, *Negro in Virginia Politics*, 157.

45. Hill, *Big Bang*, 231–32; DNC publicity division, "Statement by the Honorable Oliver W. Hill," Sept. 30, 1948, OHC.

46. "Hill Is Typical of the New Southern Negro," *Color* 4 (Jan. 1949), OHC.

47. *Rice v. Elmore*, 165 F.2d 387 (1947).

48. Gonda, *Unjust Deeds*, 182–89; *Shelley v. Kraemer*, 334 U.S. 1 (1948); *McGhee v. Sipes*, 334 U.S. 1 (1948); *Hurd v. Hodge*, 334 U.S. 24 (1948).

49. Vose, *Caucasians Only*, 212–14.

10. Farewell to Separate but Equal

1. NAACP Press Office, "Special Release," Oct. 31, 1947.

2. Kluger, *Simple Justice*, 472–73; "Miller Cites Gains by Negro Schools in Reply to Suits," *RTD*, Sept. 19, 1949, sec. 2, 1.

3. "Fairfax," *VTB*, Jan. 1946, 1–4.

4. Caplan, *Farther Along*, 55–56; Brian J. Daugherity, *Keep on Keeping On: The NAACP and the Implementation of* Brown v. Board of Education *in Virginia* (Charlottesville: University of Virginia Press, 2016), 11–12; *Encyclopedia Virginia*, s.v. "William Lester Banks," accessed Oct. 23, 2014, http://www.encyclopediavirginia.org/Banks_William_Lester_1911-1986.

5. Kluger, *Simple Justice*, 472–73; LB, interview by Richard Kluger, Apr. 4, 1971, BBEC, MS 759; Robert Pratt, "New Directions in Virginia's Civil Rights History," *VMHB* 104 (Winter 1996): 152; "Charges Dropped Against Lester Banks," *Crisis*, Dec. 1961, 630.

6. LB, interview by Kluger, Apr. 4, 1971.

7. Jack Gravely, interview by author, Feb. 4, 2013, Richmond; LaVerne Williams, interview by author, Jan. 7, 2014.

8. Reeda Butler, interview by author, Jan. 7, 2014, Hyattsville, MD.

9. Lucy Thornton Edwards, interview by author, Sept. 30, 2014, Richmond.

10. Larissa Smith, "Civil Rights Vanguard," 145. Gloster Current to TM, June 10, 1947; JT, OH, and LB to NAACP Board of Directors, Sept. 5, 1947; and JT and LB to Hon. T. Delany, May 3, 1948, all in NAACP Papers, Group II, Box C-211.

11. WW to Madison Jones, June 17, 1946, ibid., Box B-190.

12. W. E. B. Du Bois, "Does the Negro Need Separate Schools?," *Journal of Negro Education* 4 (July 1935): 328–35; Tushnet, *NAACP's Legal Strategy against Segregated Education,* 115–16.

13. Tushnet, *NAACP's Legal Strategy against Segregated Education,* 115–16.

14. "Preliminary Statement of Thurgood Marshall," meeting of Texas State Conference of Branches, Sept. 5, 1947, NAACP Papers, Group II, Box B-99.

15. "Statement of Policy Concerning the N.A.A.C.P. Education Cases," Sept. 1947, and "Board Statement on Education," June 7, 1948, both ibid.

16. "Court Orders Surry Schools Be Equalized," 1; "Equal Educational Facilities Are Ordered in Surry County," *RNL,* Mar. 31, 1948; complaint (July 17, 1947) and answer (Aug. 14, 1947), *Kelly v. Sch. Bd. of Surry County,* Civil Action 730, PFRC.

17. Final judgment, *Kelly v. Sch. Bd. of Surry County,* Mar. 30, 1948, PFRC.

18. *Arthur Freeman v. Sch. Bd. of Chesterfield County,* Civil Action 644; *Smith v. Sch. Bd. of King George County,* Civil Action 631; and *Ashley v. Sch. Bd. of Gloucester County,* Civil Action 175, all Apr. 7, 1948, PFRC.

19. Virginius Dabney, "The Court Calls for Better Negro Schools," *RTD,* Apr. 5, 1948, 10.

20. TM to JT, June 3, 1948, NAACP Papers, Group II, Box A-36.

21. Minutes of the Joint Committee, June 13, 1948, OHC.

22. Final judgments, *Smith v. Sch. Bd. of King George County* and *Ashley v. Sch. Bd. of Gloucester County,* both July 29, 1948, PFRC; "Great Dilemma in Virginia," *Virginia Education Bulletin,* Oct. 1948, 48; "Negroes Ask Admission to Schools for Whites," 1; Bill Foster, "Attorney's Request Held Unreasonable," *RNL,* Sept. 9, 1948, 1.

23. Transcript of testimony on rule to show cause, *Smith v. Sch. Bd. of King George County,* Oct. 22, 1948, PFRC.

24. Transcript of testimony and answer of the defendants, *Smith v. Sch. Bd. of King George County,* Nov. 20, 1946, PFRC.

25. Transcript of testimony, *Smith v. Sch. Bd. of King George County,* Oct. 22, 1948, PFRC. Note that the original *Q* and *A* have been replaced with *Martin* and *Picott,* and colons have been added for clarity.

26. Nat Turner, "King George Promises Equal Schools by Sept. 1949," *RAA,* Nov. 20, 1948, 8; "King George School Case Continued to Sept., 1949," *RAA,* Dec. 11, 1948, 9; order removing case from docket, *Smith v. Sch. Bd. of King George County,* Sept. 16, 1949, PFRC.

27. "Sterling Hutcheson Memorandum Order," *Ashley v. Sch. Bd. of Gloucester*

County, Jan. 13, 1949, PFRC; Foster, "Way Cleared for Additional School Suits," 1; "Equalization Efforts Cited by Gloucester," *RNL*, May 4, 1949, 1.

28. "Three U. of Va. Students Fined $650 Each," *RNL*, May 5, 1949, 2; "$50,000 More Okayed for Gloucester County Schools," *RAA*, May 28, 1949, sec. 2, 4; "Gloucester Co. Board Pays Fines of School Officials," *RAA*, June 11, 1949, 9.

29. SR to RC, June 18, 1949, and "Techniques in the Handling of School Facilities Cases," both in LDF Papers, Box 32.

30. Brief on behalf of the plaintiffs, *Corbin v. Sch. Bd. of Pulaski County*, Dec. 16, 1948, Civil Action 341, PFRC.

31. Beth Macy, "Dr. Corbin's Fight," *RT*, Feb. 15, 2004, Extra-1; *Encyclopedia Virginia*, s.v. "Percy Casino Corbin," accessed Nov. 5, 2014, http://www .encyclopediavirginia.org/Corbin_Percy_Casino_1888–1952; transcript of trial, *Corbin v. Sch. Bd. of Pulaski County*, Oct. 13, 1948, PFRC.

32. *Corbin v. Sch. Bd. of Pulaski County*, 84 F. Supp. 253 (1949). Biographical information about Barksdale can be found in introductions to his papers at the University of Virginia Law Library and Virginia Military Institute Library Archives: archives.law.virginia.edu/person/alfred-d-barksdale (accessed Mar. 19, 2017) and http://ead.lib.virginia.edu/vivaxtf/view?docId=uva-sc/viu00129.xml;query= (accessed Nov. 21, 2014).

33. Brief on behalf of the plaintiffs, *Corbin v. Sch. Bd. of Pulaski County*; opinion, *Corbin v. Sch. Bd. of Pulaski County*, 84 F. Supp. 253 (1949).

34. *Corbin v. Sch. Bd. of Pulaski County*, 177 F.2d 924 (1949).

35. "Stunning Decision in Pulaski," *RNL*, Nov. 23, 1949, 10.

36. "School Desegregation and Civil Rights Stories: Pulaski County, Virginia," Education Resources on School Desegregation, Box 33A, PFRC.

37. Transcript of trial, *Carter v. Sch. Bd. of Arlington County*, Sept. 6, 1949, Civil Action 331, PFRC; *Carter v. Sch. Bd. of Arlington County*, 182 F.2d 531 (1950).

38. *Carter v. Sch. Bd. of Arlington County*, 182 F.2d 531 (1950).

39. *Carter v. Sch. Bd. of Arlington County*, 87 F. Supp. 745 (1949).

40. *Carter v. Sch. Bd. of Arlington County*, 182 F.2d 531 (1950).

41. "Spectators Far and Near Vie for High Court Seats," *RAA*, Apr. 8, 1950, 13; "No Equality in Jim Crow," *RAA*, Apr. 8, 1950, 1; Sullivan, *Lift Every Voice*, 341, 380; Kluger, *Simple Justice*, 275–77.

42. "Spectators Far and Near Vie for High Court Seats," 13; SR to TM, Mar. 20, 1950, and TM to SR, Mar. 22, 1950, both in LDF Papers, Box 32.

43. "Heart Attack Fatal to Charles Houston," *Baltimore Afro-American*, Apr. 29, 1950, 1; Williams, *Thurgood Marshall*, 184; Sullivan, *Lift Every Voice*, 382–83; Peter Irons, *Jim Crow's Children: The Broken Promise of the Brown Decision* (London: Penguin Books, 2002), 102.

44. Arthur Krock, "An Historic Day in the Supreme Court," *NYT*, June 6, 1950, 28; *Sweatt v. Painter*, 339 U.S. 629 (1950).

45. *McLaurin v. Oklahoma State Regents*, 339 U.S. 637 (1950).

46. *Henderson v. United States*, 339 U.S. 816 (1950).

47. Tushnet, *NAACP's Legal Strategy against Segregated Education*, 135–37.

48. Kluger, *Simple Justice*, 290–91.

49. SR, interview by JW, Aug. 22, 1989; Larissa Smith, "Civil Rights Vanguard," 147. Smith's quotation from Robinson is taken from "Policy in the Program against Jim Crow Education," *Historical Souvenir Program*, 41, NAACP Papers, Group II, Box C-212. Also addressing Robinson's disaffection with the equalization campaign are Sullivan, *Lift Every Voice*, 379–80; and Tushnet, *NAACP's Legal Strategy against Segregated Education*, 110.

50. SR, interview by JW, Aug. 22, 1989.

51. Ibid. An account of this meeting also appears in Williams, *Thurgood Marshall*, 195–96. While I have found no other record of the incident, Robinson's general scrupulousness in describing his work supports its accuracy. Kluger, *Simple Justice*, 291–93, describes a large gathering of NAACP lawyers called by Marshall the week after the *Sweatt* and *McLaurin* decisions. Given the timing, this was likely the same event. In Kluger's telling, from the start the purpose of the gathering was to "ponder the best way 'to end segregation once and for all.'" Like Robinson, Kluger describes sentiment among the assembled group as "by no means unanimous." He credits Robinson with being one of those who, throughout the pivotal period, encouraged still-uncertain Marshall to launch a full-fledged assault on segregated schools.

52. OH, interview by Kluger, Apr. 4, 1971; OH, interview by JW, Dec. 17, 1992; OH, interview by Carrington, Nov. 13, 2002. In a tribute to Thurgood Marshall in *Harvard Law Review* 105 (Nov. 1991): 40, called to the author's attention by James Hershman Jr., Robert Carter asserted that Martin Martin and Oliver Hill had resigned from the LDF's National Legal Committee in protest of the decision to take no more school-equalization lawsuits. I could find no evidence to support the claim. Hill appears on lists of Legal Committee members in both 1950 and 1951; as Martin was not a member of the Legal Committee in 1950, he could not have resigned.

53. Sullivan, *Lift Every Voice*, 381–82; Kluger, *Simple Justice*, 293–94; Tushnet, *NAACP's Legal Strategy Against Segregated Education*, 136; Gloster Current, memo to RC outlining NAACP policy on segregation in education, Sept. 11, 1957, NAACP Papers, Group III, Box A-282.

54. "Keeping an Eye on What Politicians are Doing," *RAA*, June 3, 1950, 9; Hill, *Big Bang*, 232; Buni, *Negro in Virginia Politics*, 168–69.

55. Silver and Moeser, *Separate City*, 60; Harry Kollatz Jr., "The Curve Around the Station," Dec. 23, 2013, http://richmondmagazine.com/news/richmond-history/I-95-cross-into-Shockoe/; "Segoe Plan Foes to Meet at 8 Tonight," *RTD*, June 1, 1950, 4.

56. Hill, *Big Bang*, 232–36; "Oliver Hill, Expressway Beaten," *RAA*, June 17, 1950, 1; "Oliver W. Hill Bows Out of Richmond City Council," *RAA*, July 8, 1950, 12.

57. "Hill Lost; We Gained Ground," *RAA*, June 24, 1950, 3; "A Good Council—But Hill or Wilson Will be Missed," *RTD*, June 15, 1950, 12.

58. W. Stirling King to OH, June 14, 1950; T. Coleman Andrews to OH, June 23, 1950; and C. Merle Luck to OH, June 15, 1950, OHC. These are among many condolence letters in Hill's papers, OHC.

59. "Council Race is Lily-White," *RAA*, Mar. 17, 1951, 1; OH, interview by Elwood, Oct. 1987, 901; Buni, *Negro in Virginia Politics*, 179.

60. Hill, *Big Bang*, 288; Oliver Hill Jr., interview by author, July 28, 2011; LB, "Helping Ourselves by Helping Others," Oct. 17, 1949, NAACP Papers, Group II, Box C-211.

61. Hill, *Big Bang*, 288; Oliver Hill Jr., interview by author, July 28, 2011.

62. "Va. University Ignores Warning, Bars Lawyer," *RAA*, July 22, 1950, 3; "U. Va. Faces Suit for Rejection of Negro as Law School Student," *RTD*, July 26, 1950, 1; "U.S. Court Opens Va. U. Law School," *RAA*, Sept. 9, 1950, 1; "Martinsville Negro Lawyer is Admitted to University," *RTD*, Sept. 16, 1950, 4. For additional background, see SR, "Memo to Thurgood Marshall," Aug. 3, 1950, and SR to RC, Aug. 22, 1950, both in LDF Papers, Box 247.

63. "Gregory H. Swanson: First African American Admitted to U. Va. (1950)," accessed Nov. 18, 2914, http://www.virginia.edu/woodson/projects/kenan/swanson/swanson.html.

64. Klarman, *From Jim Crow to Civil Rights*, 279; Rise, *Martinsville Seven*, 2; "Five Doomed, 2 More Face Trial," *RAA*, May 7, 1949, sec. 2, 1.

65. Virginia State Conference of Branches, press release, May 13, 1949, NAACP Papers, Group II, Box C-211; Rise, *Martinsville Seven*, 64–66; "Lawyers Refuse to Stay in Va. Case with CRC," *RAA*, June 23, 1949, 3.

66. "Supreme Court to Review Cases of Martinsville Seven," *RAA*, Dec. 24, 1949, 14; "Martinsville Seven Case Argued," *RAA*, Jan. 14, 1950, 1; Rise, *Martinsville Seven*, 81–82, 99.

67. Rise, *Martinsville Seven*, 102, 118; Sullivan, *Lift Every Voice*, 398; "'Dual Justice' Basis of Martinsville Seven Plea," *RAA*, Aug. 5, 1950, 6; Klarman, *From Jim Crow to Civil Rights*, 279.

68. "Execution of Four Set Today," *RTD*, Feb. 2, 1951, 1; "Four of Seven Martinsville Men Executed," *RTD*, Feb. 3, 1951, 1; Rise, *Martinsville Seven*, 143–48.

69. Nina Govan, interview by author, Apr. 20, 2011.

11. Child Crusade in Prince Edward County

1. Robinson and Hill told slightly different stories about how they first made contact with the students. Robinson said that the Johns-Stokes letter provided the initial connection. Hill recalled receiving a telephone call from Barbara Johns on the day of the strike, seeking assistance. In the earliest and still most detailed account of the strike, Bob Smith's *They Closed Their Schools: Prince Edward County, Virginia, 1951–1964* (1965; reprint, Farmville, VA: Martha E. Forrester Council of Women, 1996), Johns said she did not telephone the attorneys that day. However, Smith confirmed through school records that a call was placed from Moton High to the Hill, Martin & Robinson law firm on April 23. At the trial growing out of

the student strike, Hill observed: "We knew nothing about this strike until we got a letter asking us to come up there because the children were out on strike." Several years later, during testimony in *NAACP v. Patty* and in many subsequent interviews, Hill described a telephone call. The text of the Johns-Stokes letter appeared in *RTD*, Apr. 2, 1967, B4.

2. Jill Titus, *Brown's Battleground: Students, Segregationists, and the Struggle for Justice in Prince Edward County, Virginia* (Chapel Hill: University of North Carolina Press, 2011), 3; Kluger, *Simple Justice*, 459–60; Edwilda Allen Issac [*sic*], interview by George Gilliam and Mason Mills, The Ground Beneath Our Feet Project, VCDH, 2000.

3. "Teachers Hit Segregation But Balk at Mixed Schools," *RAA*, Nov. 11, 1950, 1.

4. "Va. Advisory Forum Asks Mixed Schools," *RAA*, Jan. 27, 1951, 12.

5. "NAACP Geared for Public School Fight," *RAA*, Apr. 28, 1951, 12.

6. John Stokes, *Students on Strike: Jim Crow, Civil Rights, Brown, and Me* (Washington, DC: National Geographic, 2008), 61–62.

7. Taylor Branch, *Parting the Waters: America in the King Years, 1954–63* (New York: Simon & Schuster, 1988), 7–26; Kluger, *Simple Justice*, 454–55.

8. Kluger, *Simple Justice*, 460–62; Francis Mitchell, "L. Francis Griffin Maintains a Martyr's Date with Destiny," *Jet Magazine*, May 18, 1961, 20–25.

9. Mitchell, "L. Francis Griffin Maintains a Martyr's Date with Destiny"; Kluger, *Simple Justice*, 462–63; Christopher Bonastia, *Southern Stalemate: Five Years without Public Education in Prince Edward County, Virginia* (Chicago: University of Chicago Press, 2012), 29–30.

10. Leslie F. "Skip" Griffin Jr., interview by author, July 23, 2014, Cambridge, MA.

11. Bonastia, *Southern Stalemate*, 31; Haldore Hanson, "No Surrender in Farmville, Virginia," *New Republic*, Oct. 10, 1955, 13.

12. Joan Johns Cobbs, telephone interview by author, Jan. 13, 2015.

13. Bonastia, *Southern Stalemate*, 33; Tushnet, *Making Civil Rights Law*, 152; Kara Miles Turner, "'Liberating Lifescripts': Prince Edward County, Virginia, and the Roots of *Brown v. Board of Education*," in Lau, *From the Grassroots to the Supreme Court*, 96–97.

14. Numerous written accounts exist of the Moton student strike, including, Smith, *They Closed Their Schools*, 27–44; Kluger, *Simple Justice*, 468–71; Stokes, *Students on Strike*, 54–70; Kara Miles Turner, "Liberating Lifescripts," 88–100; Bonastia, *Southern Stalemate*, 33–35; and Irons, *Jim Crow's Children*, 80–87. Both Smith and Kluger conducted personal interviews with Barbara Johns, who died in 1991. Those accounts are augmented by student interviews and papers, including Edwilda Allen Issac [*sic*], interview by Gilliam and Mills; and John Watson Jr., "The Students' Role in the Prince Edward County Case," n.d., NAACP Papers, Group II, Box C-212.

15. Cobbs, telephone interview by author, Jan. 13, 2015.

16. Joy Cabarrus Speakes, interview by author, Jan. 9, 2015, Farmville, VA. See also above, n. 14.

17. "Enemy Opens Major Offensive in Korea," *RTD*, Apr. 23, 1951, 1; "Mac-

Arthur Gets Greatest U.S. Acclaim from 7,500,000 in New York Parade," *RTD*, Apr. 21, 1951, 1; "Guns Blaze on Carolina Strike Front," *RTD*, Apr. 28, 1951, 1.

18. "Negro Pupils at Farmville Go On Strike," *RTD*, Apr. 25, 1951, 7.

19. Once again, Robinson's and Hill's memories differ in detail. In *Big Bang*, 150, and elsewhere, Hill said he had agreed during Johns's telephone call to meet with the students while en route to Pulaski. However, in Robinson's August 22, 1989, interview by Juan Williams, JWC, the attorney said that after receiving the Johns-Stokes letter, the lawyers had contacted the students and arranged a meeting. By a third interpretation, that of John Stokes in *Students on Strike*, 79, the lawyers set up the meeting through Reverend Griffin.

20. SR, interview by JW, Aug. 22, 1989. Other descriptions of the visit include OH, interview by Higginbotham, May 25, 1985, 424; OH, interview by Gilliam and Mills, The Ground Beneath Our Feet Project, VCDH; Smith, *They Closed Their Schools*, 47–48.

21. SR, interview by JW, Aug. 22, 1989; OH, interview by Higginbotham, May 25, 1985, 424.

22. Barbara Johns Powell, interview by Richard Kluger, May 14, 1971, Philadelphia, BBEC, MS 759.

23. "Survey Made at Farmville on Segregation," *RTD*, Apr. 28, 1951, 4; B. T. Gillespie, "School Board Inaction Hit," *RAA*, May 5, 1951, 1; "Va. Pupils' Strike Ends," *RAA*, May 12, 1951, 1. In several interviews, Hill suggested that he and Robinson had attended the April 26 meeting on their way home from Pulaski. However, other accounts—among them, Smith, *They Closed Their Schools*, 55, and Stokes, *Students on Strike*, 82–85—refute that memory. It seems unlikely that the *Richmond Times-Dispatch* would have failed to mention the attorneys had they been present.

24. "Segregation End Sought in Schools," *RNL*, May 3, 1951, 1; "Prince Edward Negroes Seek End to Segregation in Schools," *RTD*, May 4, 1951, 1.

25. Virginia State Conference of Branches, press release, May 5, 1951, NAACP Papers, Group II, Box C-212.

26. "Va. Pupils' Strike Ends," 1; Guy Friddell, "Students, Backed by Petition, to End Strike at Farmville," *RNL*, May 4, 1951, 2; Stokes, *Students on Strike*, 93–99; Smith, *They Closed Their Schools*, 58–60.

27. "Pupil Lashes Out at School Principal," *RAA*, May 12, 1951, 1.

28. Ibid.

29. Ibid.; "Va. Pupils' Strike Ends," 1.

30. Joy Cabarrus Speakes, interview by author, Jan. 9, 2015.

31. "'Not Ready'—Gov. Battle; Predicts Bitter Last Stand," *RAA*, May 12, 1951, 1; "State Has No Unsegregated Schooling Plan," *RNL*, May 4, 1951, B1.

32. Complaint, *Davis v. County School Board of Prince Edward Co.*, May 23, 1951, Civil Action 1333, PFRC.

33. Edwilda Allen Issac [sic], interview by Gilliam and Mills.

34. Smith, *They Closed Their Schools*, 71; Bonastia, *Southern Stalemate*, 191;

Cobbs, telephone interview by author, Jan. 13, 2015; RP to members of the Joint Committee, Sept. 11, 1951, OHC.

35. Smith, *They Closed Their Schools*, 72–74; Kluger, *Simple Justice*, 479.

12. Segregation on Trial

1. SR, interview by JW, n.d.

2. "Virginia May Join S. Carolina in Battle for Jim Crow's Life," *RAA*, June 2, 1951, 2.

3. Numerous authors have described the May 1951 trial in *Briggs v. Elliott* and the events leading up to it. See, e.g., Kluger, *Simple Justice*, 313–66; Tushnet, *Making Civil Rights Law*, 156–61; Irons, *Jim Crow's Children*, 43–79; and Sullivan, *Lift Every Voice*, 402–8. The information in the following four paragraphs is from these same sources.

4. Rowen, *Dream Makers, Dream Breakers*, 12; Kluger, *Simple Justice*, 328.

5. *Briggs v. Elliott*, 98 F. Supp. 529 (E.D.S.C. 1951).

6. "NAACP Sues the Mosque," *RAA*, July 7, 1951, 1; "City Officials Offer to Wink at Race Mixing," *RAA*, Sept. 22, 1951, 1; "Mosque Suit Dismissed," *RAA*, Sept. 29, 1951, 1.

7. "Statement by the President on Establishing the CGCC," Dec. 3, 1951, https:// trumanlibrary.org/publicpapers/index.php?pid=570; "Transcript, President's News Conference," Jan. 10, 1952, https://trumanlibrary.org/publicpapers/index .php?pid=603&st=&st1=; "Hill Out of Council Race," *RAA*, Jan. 17, 1952, 1.

8. King, *Devil in the Grove*, 273–82, 219–20, 230–39.

9. "Va. Set to Tighten Jim Crow School Law," *RAA*, Jan. 24, 1952, 1; "Race Violence Flares in Cairo, Ill.," *Jet Magazine*, Feb. 14, 1952, 3; "Illinois City Jails Eight NAACP Fight Leaders," *RAA*, Feb. 16, 1952, 1.

10. District Judge Walter Bastian dismissed the Washington, DC, case *Bolling v. Sharpe* without a trial or opinion on the grounds that the constitutionality of the city's segregated schools had been decided by *Carr v. Corning*, 182 F.2d 14 (1950).

11. Richard K. Perkins, "A Brief History of the Lewis F. Powell, Jr. United States Courthouse, 1858–2012," 6th printing, 2012, www.ca4.uscourts.gov/docs/pdfs /BriefHistoryOfPowellCourthouse.pdf.

12. OH, interview by Kluger, Apr. 4, 1971; Kluger, *Simple Justice*, 396–400; Sullivan, *Lift Every Voice*, 297.

13. Anne Hobson Freeman, *The Style of a Law Firm: Eight Gentlemen from Virginia* (Chapel Hill, NC: Algonquin, 1989), 129–43; Tyler-McGraw, *At the Falls*, 281.

14. Freeman, *Style of a Law Firm*, 132, 135; Irons, *Jim Crow's Children*, 89–90.

15. F. D. G. Ribble, "Armistead M. Dobie: A Reminiscence," *Virginia Law Review* 49 (Oct. 1963): 1079–81; "Remembering the Fourth Circuit Judges," *Washington & Lee Law Review* 55 (Mar. 1, 1998): 490–93; Kluger, *Simple Justice*, 485; "Inventory of the Papers of Armistead Mason Dobie," University of Virginia Law Library, Special Collections, MSS 78–2.

16. "Remembering the Fourth Circuit Judges," 483–87.

17. Trial transcript, *Davis v. County School Board of Prince Edward County,* Feb. 25, 1952, PFRC. The opening day of the trial is also described in "Educational Segregation Suit Opens," *RTD,* Feb. 26, 1952, 1; "Moton School Plant Praised by McIlwaine," *RNL,* Feb. 25, 1952, B1; "Race Case Statistics Provided," *RNL,* Feb. 25, 1952, 1; and "Experts Reject Separate Schools," *RAA,* Mar. 1, 1952, 1.

18. Trial transcript, *Davis v. County School Board of Prince Edward County,* Feb. 26, 1952, PFRC; "Tactics Shift in School Racial Suit," *RNL,* Feb. 26, 1952, B1; "4 Experts in U.S. Court Here, Score Segregation in Schools," *RTD,* Feb. 27, 1952, 1.

19. Trial transcript, *Davis v. County School Board of Prince Edward County,* Feb. 26, 1952, PFRC; note that the original Q and A in the transcript have been replaced here with *Moore* and *Chein,* and colons have been replaced for clarity.

20. Trial transcript, *Davis v. County School Board of Prince Edward County,* Feb. 27, 1952, PFRC (note that in the following two extracts the original Q and A have been replaced with *Moore* and *Clark* in the first instance and with *Clark* and *Moore* in the second instance, and colons have been added for clarity); Frank Walin, "28 Counties Said to Offer 'Equal' Schools," *RTD,* Feb. 28, 1952, 1; "Run-Around on School Issue Denied," *RNL,* Feb. 27, 1952, B1.

21. Kluger, *Simple Justice,* 497.

22. Trial transcript, *Davis v. County School Board of Prince Edward County,* Feb. 28, 1952, PFRC (note that in the following extract the original Q and A have been replaced with *Hill* and *Darden,* and colons have been added for clarity); "Segregation Ban in Schools May Cut Funds, Court is Told," *RTD,* Feb. 29, 1952, 1; William B. Foster Jr., "No Support for 2-Race School Seen," *RNL,* Feb. 28, 1952, 1.

23. Trial transcript, *Davis v. County School Board of Prince Edward County,* Feb. 29, 1952, PFRC; "Job Losses in 2-Race School Seen," *RNL,* Feb. 29, 1952; "School Segregation Case Arguments Completed," *RTD,* Mar. 2, 1952, 1; OH, interview by Higginbotham, May 25, 1985, 425–26.

24. OH, interview by Higginbotham, May 25, 1985, 425–26; Henry Garrett, *IQ and Racial Differences* (1973; reprint, Torrance, CA: Noontide Press & Historical Review, 1980), 10–11; Kluger, *Simple Justice,* 502–4.

25. Rufus Wells, "Death Threat Sent Lawyer in School Case," *RAA,* Mar. 8, 1952, 1. Hill considered the letter to be the work of a crank and did not report the incident to the police. OH, interview by author, Apr. 1994, Richmond.

26. Opinion, *Davis v. County School Board of Prince Edward County,* 103 F. Supp. 337 (1952).

13. Face-Off at the Supreme Court

1. Jack Greenberg, Brown v. Board of Education: *Witness to a Landmark Decision* (New York: Twelve Tables, 2004), 90.

2. Among the many books describing the advent of *Brown v. Board of Educa-*

tion, the most complete include Kluger, *Simple Justice;* Irons, *Jim Crow's Children;* Greenberg, *Brown v. Board of Education;* and James T. Patterson, Brown v. Board of Education: *A Civil Rights Milestone and Its Troubled Legacy* (Oxford: Oxford University Press, 2001).

3. Sullivan, *Lift Every Voice,* 415–17; Greenberg, *Brown v. Board of Education,* 59; Kluger, *Simple Justice,* 534–36.

4. "Court Action and Other Means of Achieving Racial Integration," *Journal of Negro Education* 21 (Summer 1952): 385–86.

5. Ibid., 332–34. Robinson provided additional details in an interview by JW, n.d., JWC. Hill and Robinson each related the farmer story with himself as the questioner.

6. SR to TM, Oct. 1, 1950, NAACP Papers, Group II, Box B-171; JT to RW, Aug. 21, 1952, ibid., Box C-212.

7. Greenberg, *Brown v. Board of Education,* 7; Jack Greenberg, *Crusader in the Courts* (New York: Twelve Tables, 2004), 165; Christopher Gray, "Streetscapes," *NYT,* Aug. 4, 2002; "Demolished Club Casts a Long Shadow," *NYT,* Apr. 10, 2014. Later that year, the LDF moved its headquarters to 107 W. Forty-Third Street, described by Greenberg as more spacious but beset by "bums" and burglaries.

8. Kluger, *Simple Justice,* 553.

9. Klarman, *From Jim Crow to Civil Rights,* 291; Waldo Martin Jr., Brown v. Board of Education: *A Brief History with Documents* (Boston: St. Martin's, 1998), 27; "Public School Segregation Cases," NAACP press release, Nov. 26, 1952, NAACP Papers, Group II, Box B-141.

10. Patterson, *Brown v. Board of Education,* xiv–xvi; "Public School Segregation Cases."

11. Kluger, *Simple Justice,* 642–45; Greenberg, *Brown v. Board of Education,* 92–95.

12. Kluger, *Simple Justice,* 553.

13. Tushnet, *Making Civil Rights Law,* 166–67.

14. "The Supreme Court Building," accessed June 19, 2015, http://www.supremecourt.gov/about/courtbuilding.aspx.

15. Joseph Moore, *Larry Doby: The Struggle of the American League's First Black Player* (Mineola, NY: Dover, 2011), 59; St. Regis, Washington, DC, "Hotel Heritage," accessed June 19, 2015, http://www.starwoodhotels.com/stregis/property/overview/history.html?propertyID=193&language=en_US; King, *Devil in the Grove,* 335; Tushnet, *Making Civil Rights Law,* 173, 177; Greenberg, *Brown v. Board of Education,* 98–99.

16. "U.S. Supreme Court Ponders Fate of Segregated Schools," NAACP press release, Dec. 12, 1952, NAACP Papers, Group II, Box A-625. Another press release, "Public School Segregation Cases," names thirteen additional attorneys who participated in preparing the cases, including Oliver Hill.

17. Trial transcript of *Brown* case, housed in the Supreme Court library, contained in *U.S. Supreme Court Oral Arguments, Case Nos. 1–5, Oct. Term, 1954,*

vol. 1, *Dec. 9–11, 1952* (Washington, DC: Ward & Paul). The *New York Times* and the *Richmond Times-Dispatch,* among other newspapers, provided three-day coverage of the hearings. The *New York Times* coverage, supplied by the reporter Luther Huston, began with "Supreme Court Asked to End School Segregation in Nation," Dec. 10, 1952, 1. The *Times-Dispatch* coverage, provided by the Associated Press, began with "Supreme Court Hears Arguments on Legality of Segregated Schools," Dec. 10, 1952, 1.

18. Trial transcript of *Brown* case, *U.S. Supreme Court Oral Arguments*, vol. 1, *Dec. 9–11, 1952.*

19. Irons, *Jim Crow's Children,* 141, 149–50, 167; Kluger, *Simple Justice,* 115; Tushnet, *Making Civil Rights Law,* 175–77.

20. Trial transcript of *Brown* case, *U.S. Supreme Court Oral Arguments,* vol. 1, *Dec. 9–11, 1952.*

21. Ibid.

22. Ibid.

23. Ibid.; Tushnet, *Making Civil Rights Law,* 181–82.

24. Trial transcript of *Brown* case, *U.S. Supreme Court Oral Arguments,* vol. 1, *Dec. 9–11, 1952.*

25. "U.S. Supreme Court Ponders Fate of Segregated Schools."

26. Trial transcript of *Brown* case, *U.S. Supreme Court Oral Arguments,* vol. 1, *Dec. 9–11, 1952.*

27. Ibid.; Tushnet, *Making Civil Rights Law,* 183.

28. Trial transcript of *Brown* case, *U.S. Supreme Court Oral Arguments,* vol. 1, *Dec. 9–11, 1952.*

29. Greenberg, *Brown v. Board of Education,* 109, 111.

30. Ibid., 132; Hill, *Big Bang,* 165–66.

31. Irons, *Jim Crow's Children,* 147–51; Tushnet, *Making Civil Rights Law,* 187.

32. "Hill & Robinson to Virginia State Conference," 1952, OHC.

33. Lucy Thornton Edwards, interview by author, Sept. 30, 2014.

34. "Pupils Protest Segregated Schools," *RAA,* Sept. 13, 1952, 1; "School Strike Still on at West Point," *RAA,* Nov. 29, 1952, 3; Spottswood Robinson, "Annual Report of the Southeast Regional Counsel, 1955," NAACP Papers, Group II, Box B-77 (Robinson's monthly reports during 1953 also give updates on the West Point case, then styled *Commonwealth of Virginia v. William T. Billups, et al.*); Larry Chowning, "Remembering the Courage of the 'West Point 29,'" May 25, 2011, www.ssentinel.com/index.php/news/article/remembering_the_courage_of_the_west_point_29/; *Dobbins v. Virginia,* 198 Va. 697 (1957).

35. Waldo Martin Jr., "The Supreme Court's Order: The Questions," in Martin, *Brown v. Board of Education,* 156–58.

36. "130 Experts Help NAACP in Research for School Cases," NAACP press release, Oct. 29, 1953, NAACP Papers, Group II, Box A-625; Sullivan, *Lift Every Voice,* 419; Kluger, *Simple Justice,* 645.

37. TM to NAACP Board of Directors, July 16, 1953, NAACP Papers, Group II, Box B-143; "Local NAACP Joins Fund-Raising Drive," *RAA*, July 25, 1953, 1; "Where to Send Your NAACP Contribution," *RAA*, Sept. 19, 1953, 1.

38. OH travel expenses, "*Brown v. Board* Expense Reports, 1953–55," NAACP Papers, Group II, Box D-176.

39. Kluger, *Simple Justice*, 647; John Riely, "*Brown v. The Board:* A Very Personal Retrospective Glance," *Virginia Lawyer* 37 (Feb. 1989): 17ff.

40. Greenberg, *Brown v. Board of Education*, 117–25; Kluger, *Simple Justice*, 623; Tushnet, *Making Civil Rights Law*, 198–99; Patterson, *Brown v. Board of Education*, 39.

41. "Lawyers Confident," *RAA*, Dec. 12, 1953, 8.

42. Irons, *Jim Crow's Children*, 154–55; Tushnet, *Making Civil Rights Law*, 202–3. Frankfurter's widely repeated quote appears without further attribution in Kluger, *Simple Justice*, 656.

43. Greenberg, *Crusader in the Courts*, 34; trial transcript of *Brown* case, housed in the Supreme Court library, *U.S. Supreme Court Oral Arguments, Case Nos. 1–5, Oct. Term, 1954*, vol. 2, *Dec. 7–9, 1953* (Washington, DC: Ward & Paul). The *New York Times*'s three-day coverage of the trial began with "Final Fight Opens in Supreme Court on Bias in Schools," Dec. 8, 1953, 1; coverage in the *Richmond Times-Dispatch* began with "School Segregation is Argued," Dec. 8, 1953, 1.

44. Trial transcript of *Brown* case, *U.S. Supreme Court Oral Arguments*, vol. 2, *Dec. 7–9, 1953*.

45. Greenberg, *Brown v. Board of Education*, 127; Tushnet, *Making Civil Rights Law*, 205; Kluger, *Simple Justice*, 669.

46. Trial transcript of *Brown* case, *U.S. Supreme Court Oral Arguments*, vol. 2, *Dec. 7–9, 1953*.

47. Ibid.; Greenberg, *Brown v. Board of Education*, 127; "School Arguments Ended," *RAA*, Dec. 12, 1953, 1.

48. Trial transcript of *Brown* case, *U.S. Supreme Court Oral Arguments*, vol. 2, *Dec. 7–9, 1953*.

49. Ibid.

50. Greenberg, *Brown v. Board of Education*, 131.

51. SR, interview by JW, Aug. 22, 1989; Nina Govan, interview by author, Apr. 20, 2011.

52. "Spottswood W. Robinson III, Personal Data Questionnaire," June 18, 1963.

53. Muse, "Negro Crusaders Should Relax Awhile"; LB to undisclosed recipients, Dec. 14, 1953, and TM to Rev. James Hinton and Kelly Alexander, Dec. 17, 1953, both in LDF Papers, Box 32.

54. WW to NAACP staff, Mar. 15, 1954, NAACP Papers, Group II, Box A-622.

55. Hill, *Big Bang*, 167; Martin, *Brown v. Board of Education*, 168–74; *Brown v. Bd. of Ed. of Topeka*, 347 U. S. 483 (1954); *Bolling v. Sharpe*, 347 U. S. 497 (1954).

56. Sauder, "Oliver Hill," 1.

14. Rocky Road to a New Day

1. OH, statement before Commission to Study Public Education, Nov. 15, 1954, OHC; "Commission Weighs Segregation Ideas," *RNL*, Nov. 16, 1954, 1; Paul Duke, "Let Localities Set School Course Main Appeal at Virginia Hearing," *VP*, Nov. 16, 1954, 1; Rufus Wells, "Virginia seeking to sidestep court ruling," *RAA*, Nov. 20, 1954, 1.

2. David J. Mays, *Race, Reason, and Massive Resistance: The Diary of David J. Mays, 1954–1959*, ed. James R. Sweeney (Athens: University of Georgia Press, 2008), 191.

3. OH, statement before Commission to Study Public Education, Nov. 15, 1954.

4. Soon after the *Brown* ruling, the Virginia Board of Education advised local school boards that they could continue to segregate public schools for the 1954–55 term.

5. J. Douglas Smith, "When Reason Collides with Prejudice," in *The Moderates' Dilemma: Massive Resistance to School Desegregation in Virginia*, ed. Matthew D. Lassiter and Andrew B. Lewis (Charlottesville: University Press of Virginia, 1998), 33; James H. Hershman Jr., "A Rumbling in the Museum: The Opponents of Virginia's Massive Resistance" (PhD diss., University of Virginia, 1978), 42; Robbins L. Gates, *The Making of Massive Resistance: Virginia's Politics of Public School Desegregation, 1954–1956* (Chapel Hill: University of North Carolina Press, 1964), 30; Muse, "Negro Crusaders Should Relax Awhile"; Benjamin Muse, *Virginia's Massive Resistance* (Bloomington: Indiana University Press, 1961), 2.

6. Kluger, *Simple Justice*, 710; "Virginia," *SSN*, Sept. 3, 1954, 13; Muse, *Virginia's Massive Resistance*, 7. A group of southern newspaper editors and educators launched the *Southern School News* in the summer of 1954 to provide monthly comprehensive coverage of the school-desegregation story. Richmond's Virginius Dabney was elected chairman of the Southern Education Reporting Service, which supplied the reportage.

7. "Dixie NAACP Leaders Map Plans to Implement Court's Ruling," NAACP press release, May 23, 1954, NAACP Papers, Group II, Box A-625; Brian Daugherity, "Keep On Keeping On," in *With All Deliberate Speed: Implementing* Brown v. Board of Education, ed. Daugherity and Charles Bolton (Fayetteville: University of Arkansas Press, 2008), 45–46.

8. Gary M. Williams, *Sussex County, Virginia*, 234; "Virginia," *SSN*, Oct. 1, 1954, 14.

9. Four-day coverage began in the *New York Times* with "High Court Hears Debate on Ending Segregation Now," Apr. 12, 1955, 1, and in the *Richmond Times-Dispatch* with "Court Asked to Order Start on Integration Forthwith in Virginia," Apr. 12, 1955, 1. See also "Urge Top Court to Issue School Order," *RAA*, Apr. 16, 1955, 1; and "Mix Schools Now, Marshall Pleads," *RAA*, Apr. 23, 1955, 1.

10. Trial transcript of *Brown* case, *U.S. Supreme Court Oral Arguments, Case Nos. 1–5, Oct. Term 1954*, vol. 3, *Apr. 11–14, 1955* (Washington, DC: Ward & Paul).

11. Ibid.

12. "Text of the Supreme Court Order on School Desegregation," May 31, 1955, and "Memo by Thurgood Marshall and Roy Wilkins," both in NAACP Papers, Group II, Box A-622.

13. J. Harvie Wilkinson III, *Harry Byrd and the Changing Face of Virginia Politics, 1945–1966* (Charlottesville: University Press of Virginia, 1968), 273.

14. Muse, *Virginia's Massive Resistance*, 48–49.

15. Leslie Griffin Jr., interview by author, July 23, 2014.

16. Mays, *Race, Reason, and Massive Resistance*, 235, 261–62.

17. Ibid., 229.

18. RC to SR, Feb. 9, 1954, and SR to RC, Feb. 11, 1954, both in LDF Papers, Box 32.

19. SR to TM, June 9, 1948 and Jan. 4, 1951, ibid.; Hill, *Big Bang*, 186; "Memorandum: *Davis v. School Board*," OHC; William Foster Jr., "Counsel on Schools Has Cost Virginia More than $100,000," *RNL*, May 11, 1956, 1; Mays, *Race, Reason, and Massive Resistance*, 129.

20. Foster, "Counsel on Schools Has Cost Virginia," 1; "Commonwealth of Virginia: Budget, 1958–60, Part II," Office of the Governor, Budget Records, LVA.

21. TM, memo to Mrs. Waring, Sept. 2, 1948, and TM to SR, Apr. 24, 1951, both in LDF Papers, Box 32.

22. OH, interview by Carrington, Nov. 13, 2002; Wilder, interview by author, Apr. 13, 2011; "S. W. Robinson Jr. is Buried," *RAA*, Jan. 9, 1955, 1.

23. All these letters are in OHC.

24. "Killers Still At Large," *RAA*, Aug. 6, 1955, 4; "NAACP Leader Shot," *RAA*, Dec. 3, 1955, 1; "Details Told of Murder of Boy Kidnapped in Miss.," *RAA*, Sept. 10, 1955, 2.

25. Sauder, "Oliver Hill," 1; OH, interview by "PB," n.d., OHC; Nina Govan, interview by author, Apr. 20, 2011; Oliver Hill Jr., interview by author, July 28, 2011.

26. Sauder, "Oliver Hill," 1; Irving Engel to OH, Aug. 12, 1955, and OH to Engel, Aug. 17, 1955, both in OHC.

27. OH, interview by "PB," n.d.; Mays, *Race, Reason, and Massive Resistance*, 237.

28. OH to Dudley, Aug. 23 and Sept. 30, 1954; OH to Victor Ashe, Oct. 25, 1954; OH to Treble Clef & Book Lovers Club, June 1, 1955; OH to Hotel Alexander, May 25, 1955; and "Reflections of Former National President Beresenia W. Hill," all in OHC.

29. Robert Grey Jr., interview by author, June 3, 2013, Richmond; Oliver Hill Jr., e-mails to author, Oct. 19, 2015.

30. Greenberg, *Crusaders in the Courts*, 34; Jenkins, "Nobody Raises Eyebrows When U.S. Judge Calls His Secretary 'Honey.'"

31. Robert Turpin, interview by author, Sept. 2008, Richmond; Working Man to NAACP, Mar. 13, 1959, NAACP Papers, Group III, Box A-281.

32. "Four of the Disgusted Ones" to Governor Thomas Stanley, Aug. 28, 1956, Executive Papers of Governor Stanley, 1954–58, Box 106, LVA.

33. Irons, *Jim Crow's Children*, 174–75; Hershman, "Rumbling in the Museum," 113; "Lower Court Decrees Mark Busy Month," *SSN*, Aug. 1955, 8.

34. "Virginia Proceedings," *SSN*, Aug. 1955, 10–11; "At Richmond," ibid., 1; Rufus Wells, "Court Orders Prince Edward to Integrate," *RAA*, July 23, 1955, 1.

35. "Virginia Proceedings," 10–11; "At Richmond," 1; "Desegregation Spotty as Schools Open," *SSN*, Sept. 1955, 1.

36. Lassiter and Lewis, *Moderates' Dilemma*, 5; Buni, *Negro in Virginia Politics*, 177; OH, interview by Elwood, Oct. 1987, 914.

37. *Encyclopedia Virginia*, s.v. "Defenders of State Sovereignty and Individual Liberties," by David Neff, accessed Nov. 3, 2015, www.encyclopediavirginia.org /Defenders_of_State_Sovereignty_and_Individual_Liberties.

38. OH to Harry Penn, Oct. 11, 1955, OHC.

39. *Public Education: Report of the Commission to the Governor of Virginia*, Division of Purchase and Printing, Commonwealth of Virginia, Nov. 11, 1955, LDF Papers, Box 144.

40. SR, "Comments on the Report of the Virginia Commission on Public Education," Dec. 17, 1955, LDF Papers, Box 144.

41. "Statement of Oliver Hill," Nov. 30, 1955, OHC.

42. "Hill presented Pro Bono Award by State Bar for civil rights work," *RTD*, Apr. 24, 1992, C4.

43. Gates, *Making of Massive Resistance*, 117–19; "Virginia's 'Gray Plan' Laid Aside," *SSN*, June 1956, 13; "Manifesto Protests Court Act," *SSN*, April 1956, 1.

44. Lassiter and Lewis, *Moderates' Dilemma*, 9–12, providing a helpful summation of various interpretations of Byrd's motivations; OH, interview by A. E. Dick Howard, Dec. 7, 1987, CRLP, 436–37; OH, interview by Elwood, Oct. 1987, 891.

45. Harry Byrd to Sterling Hutcheson, Apr. 26, 1965, CSH.

46. "Two Virginia Districts Asked to Begin School Desegregation," *SSN*, May 1956, 3; "Order Mixed Schools By Fall, Court Urged," *RAA*, Apr. 28, 1956, 1; Daugherity, "Keep on Keeping On," 50.

47. Hershman, "Rumbling in the Museum," 223; OH, interview by Higginbotham, May 25, 1985, 427; Hill, *Big Bang*, 177.

48. Rufus Wells, "Virginia Schools Ordered Open to All Citizens," *RAA*, July 21, 1956, 1; "What They Said in Virginia Case," *RAA*, July 21, 1956, 8; Gates, *Making of Massive Resistance*, 126–27.

49. Gates, *Making of Massive Resistance*, 127–28; Mays, *Race, Reason, and Massive Resistance*, 39, 140; *Tate v. Dept. of Conservation & Development*, 133 F. Supp. 53 (1955), 4th Circ. affirmed, Apr. 9, 1956.

50. Mays, *Race, Reason, and Massive Resistance*, 140; Bonastia, *Southern Stalemate*, 70–71; "Virginia to Keep Separate Schools," *SSN*, Sept. 1956, 8.

51. Muse, *Virginia's Massive Resistance,* 29–30; "Stanley's Plan Faces Opposition," *RAA,* Sept. 1, 1956, 1; Hershman, "Rumbling in the Museum," 188–89; "Virginia's General Assembly Bars State Funds for Mixed Schools," *SSN,* Oct. 1956, 16.

52. "Virginia's General Assembly Bars State Funds for Mixed Schools," *SSN,* Oct. 1956, 16; Bonastia, *Southern Stalemate,* 73–74; Numan Bartley, *The Rise of Massive Resistance: Race and Politics in the South During the 1950's* (Baton Rouge: Louisiana State University Press, 1969), 214.

53. Acts of the Special Session of the General Assembly of Virginia, Sept. 9, 1956, chs. 31–37; Hershman, "Rumbling in the Museum," 256.

54. SR, interview by JW, Aug. 22, 1989; OH, interview by Oliver, June 9, 1999.

15. A Fight to Survive

1. O. R. Phillips to Stanley, Feb. 1, 1957, Executive Papers of Governor Stanley, Box 106.

2. Evalyn Shaed to RC, Aug. 21, 1956, LDF Papers, Box 32.

3. "Louisiana: Legal Action," *SSN,* Apr. 1956, 14; "Alabama Court Enjoins NAACP Units from Activity," *SSN,* July 1956, 10; Bartley, *Rise of Massive Resistance,* 185–86, 212–21; Walter Murphy, "The South Counterattacks: The Anti-NAACP Laws," *Western Political Quarterly* 12 (June 1959): 371–90.

4. *Scull v. Virginia ex rel. Comm. On Law Reform and Racial Activities,* 359 U.S. 344 (1959); "Negro Group, Subsidiary Start Action in U.S. Court," *RTD,* Nov. 30, 1956, 1; "Almond Plans to Resist Bills Attack," *RNL,* Nov. 30, 1956.

5. Bartley, *Rise of Massive Resistance,* 221; OH, interview by Elwood, Oct. 1987, 915; Mays, *Race, Reason, and Massive Resistance,* 191. Mays likely was referring to the Virginia State Bar, which was charged with disciplining lawyers.

6. Boat(w)right Family Genealogy in America, accessed Jan. 23, 2016, http://boatwrightgenealogy.com/johnboatwright9.1.html.

7. "Thomson Claims Status as 'Virginia Gentleman,'" *WP,* Apr. 16, 1957, 17; Karlyn Barker and Paul Edwards, "Thomson Conducts Campaign for Judgeship in Alexandria," *WP,* Jan. 25, 1979, C1–C2; Muse, *Virginia's Massive Resistance,* 33–34.

8. John Boatwright Jr. to LDF, and John Boatwright Jr. to Virginia State Conference of NAACP Branches, both Jan. 14, 1957, in NAACP Papers, Group III, Box A-281.

9. OH to Legislative Committee, Jan. 22, 1957; LB to members of the Executive Board and legal staff, Jan. 23, 1957; and Harold Kelly to Virginia State Conference of NAACP Branches, Jan. 30, 1957, all in ibid.

10. Gregory Swanson to OH, Feb. 8, 1957, and OH to Swanson, Feb. 11, 1957, both in OHC.

11. RW to John Boatwright Jr., Feb. 13, 1957, and Virginia State Conference of Branches, press release, Feb. 14, 1957, both in NAACP Papers, Group III, Box A-281.

12. Richmond Hustings Court, summons to LB, Feb. 14, 1957, and RW to Branch Presidents in Virginia, Feb. 14, 1957, both in ibid.; "Temporary relief won in Virginia probe of NAACP," *RAA*, Feb. 23, 1957, 1; Rufus Wells, "An Editor's Eye View of the Virginia Capitol," *RAA*, Dec. 10, 1955, 19; "NAACP Supplies Assembly Group with Some Data," *RTD*, Feb. 21, 1957, 1.

13. David Longley to RW, Apr. 26, 1957, and RW to Longely [*sic*], May 8, 1957, both in NAACP Papers, Group III, Box A-281.

14. "A Valiant Stand," *RAA*, Feb. 23, 1957, 1.

15. Report of the Committee on Offenses Against the Administration of Justice, Nov. 13, 1957, H. D. Doc. 8, p. 9; OH to State Corporation Commission, Dec. 4, 1959, NAACP Papers, Group III, Box A-281.

16. RC to TM, "Conference on the Virginia Cases," May 23, 1957, NAACP Papers, Group III, Box A-281.

17. Hill's testimony is included in Report of the Committee on Offenses Against the Administration of Justice, Nov. 13, 1957, 16. Note that *A* has been replaced with *Hill*, and colons have been added for clarity.

18. "Boatwright Witness Says Talk Recorded," *RNL*, May 16, 1957, 1; Jean Bruns, "Four Tell State Group of School Suit Origin," *RTD*, May 16, 1957, 1.

19. Bruns, "Four Tell State Group of School Suit Origin," 1; Hershman, "Rumbling in the Museum," 213.

20. Bruns, "Four Tell State Group of School Suit Origin," 1.

21. See, e.g., "Probers May Go to Court to See Personal Financial Records of State NAACP Officials," "NAACP Lawyers Attack Federal Court Ruling," and "Injunction Spurs Return to Schools," in *RTD*, Sept. 20, 1957, 4, 3, 3.

22. "NAACP Losing Members Court Hears in Test Case," *RTD*, Sept. 17, 1957, 4; "Five Negro Plaintiffs Deny Knowing of Suits," *RNL*, Sept. 18, 1957, 1; Alexander Leidholdt, *Standing Before the Shouting Mob: Lenoir Chambers and Virginia's Massive Resistance to Public-School Integration* (Tuscaloosa: University of Alabama Press, 1997), 95; "Legal Maneuver Staves Off Showdown in Virginia," *SSN*, Oct. 1957, 7.

23. Mays, *Race, Reason, and Massive Resistance*, 201; "Alabamian Backs Laws of Virginia," *RTD*, Sept. 20, 1957, 1.

24. Report of the Committee on Law Reform and Racial Activities, H. D. Doc. 9 (1957), 8–11, 18.

25. Report of the Committee on Offenses Against the Administration of Justice, Nov. 13, 1957, 7–9, 14–21.

26. Ibid., 19–20.

27. "Almond Hits GOP, NAACP Role in Dixie," *RTD*, Sept. 20, 1957, 4; "Almond Victor in Virginia Test of 'Resistance' Plan," *SSN*, Dec. 1957, 10; Harvard Sitkoff, *The Struggle for Black Equality, 1954–1992*, 25th-anniversary ed. (New York: Hill & Wang, 2008), 27–28.

28. Bartley, *Rise of Massive Resistance*, 189.

29. W. Ferguson Reid, telephone interview by author, Feb. 2, 2016.

30. Oliver Hill Jr., e-mails to author, Feb. 1, 2016; L. Douglas Wilder, interview by author, Feb. 3, 2016, Richmond.

31. "Statement by Robert L. Carter," Jan. 24, 1958, and "NAACP in Virginia Rejects Demand of Committee for Names of Members," Jan. 30, 1958, both in NAACP Papers, Group III, Box A-282; "Virginia 'NAACP Laws' Invalid, Probe Held," *SSN*, Feb. 1958, 16.

32. J. Douglas Smith, "When Reason Collides with Prejudice," 45; "Virginia's 'Little Rock' Bill Passes," *SSN*, Mar. 1958, 9; "Virginia: Legislative Action," *SSN*, Apr. 1958, 2; Hershman, "Rumbling in the Museum," 271–73.

33. Hershman, "Rumbling in the Museum," 281; "Showdown Near on Issue of School Desegregation," *SSN*, Aug. 1958, 6; "Virginia: Legal Action," *SSN*, Apr. 1958, 2; opinion, *Allen v. County Sch. Bd. of Prince Edward County*, 164 F. Supp. 786 (1958).

34. Hershman, "Rumbling in the Museum," 221; *Hill v. Sch. Bd. of Norfolk*, 282 F.2d 473 (1960); *Thompson v. County Sch. Bd. of Arlington County*, 144 F. Supp. 529 (1958).

35. Muse, *Virginia's Massive Resistance*, 67–71; "Nine Schools Close in 3 Cities," *SSN*, Oct. 1958, 3; *Kilby v. Sch. Bd. of Warren County*, 259 F.2d 497 (1958).

36. "Showdown Near on Issue of School Desegregation," 6; "Virginia: What They Say," *SSN*, Sept. 1958, 7; Muse, *Virginia's Massive Resistance*, 66.

37. "Nine Schools Close in 3 Cities," 4; OH photograph and cutline, *Sunday Star*, Sept. 14, 1958, OHC.

38. Hershman, "Rumbling in the Museum," 304; *Cooper v. Aaron*, 358 U.S. 1 (1958); Sitkoff, *Struggle for Black Equality*, 35.

39. Muse, *Virginia's Massive Resistance*, 73–75; Littlejohn and Ford, *Elusive Equality*, 77–79.

40. Al White to OH, Sept. 15, 1958, OHC; J. E. Fitzgerald to Lindsay Almond, Jan. 30, 1959, Executive Papers of Lindsay Almond, Box 46, LVA.

41. Mays, *Race, Reason, and Massive Resistance*, 232; "Slackening of Massive Resistance Contemplated" and "Virginia Press Views Possible Modification in 'Massive Resistance,'" both in *SSN*, Dec. 1958, 6; Leidholdt, *Standing Before the Shouting Mob*, 94, 106.

42. Leidholdt, *Standing Before the Shouting Mob*, 104.

43. Ibid., 98, 111–12; Littlejohn and Ford, *Elusive Equality*, 101.

44. "1,000 Negroes Walk in Rain to Protest School Closings," *RTD*, Jan. 2, 1959, 1; "1,500 Join Pilgrimage for Schools," *RAA*, Jan. 10, 1959, 1.

45. Murphy, "South Counterattacks," 389; Sullivan, *Lift Every Voice*, 342–43.

46. Hershman, "Rumbling in the Museum," 340–42; Frank Atkinson, *The Dynamic Dominion: Realignment and the Rise of Virginia's Republican Party Since 1945* (Fairfax, VA: George Mason University Press, 1992), 104–5.

47. "Speech of Oliver Hill," WXEX-TV, Jan. 25, 1959, OHC.

48. Mays, *Race, Reason, and Massive Resistance*, 256; Muse, *Virginia's Massive Resistance*, 131–35; Hill, *Big Bang*, 178.

49. "Integration Peaceful in State," *RNL*, Feb. 2, 1959, 1; "Segregation Era Ends in State Public Schools," *RTD*, Feb. 3, 1959, 1; "Law Wins," *RAA*, Feb. 7, 1959, 1; "Superintendent of Public Instruction, Annual Report, 1959–60," Executive Papers of Lindsay Almond, Box 36.

50. "U.S. Circuit Court Reverses District Decision in Prince Edward," *SSN*, June 1959, 6.

51. Hill spoke of this incident many times, including in OH, interview by Elwood, Oct. 1987, 916, and OH, interview by Higginbotham, May 25, 1985, 427.

52. Byrd to Sterling Hutcheson, Jan. 14, 1959, CSH, Box 4.

16. New Directions

1. Mays, *Race, Reason, and Massive Resistance*, 257; Daugherity and Bolton, *With All Deliberate Speed*, 52–53; James Hershman Jr., "Virginia on the Cusp of Change," unpublished paper in author's possession, courtesy of J. Hershman Jr., 1.

2. "Prince Edward Group Opens Private Schools," *RTD*, Sept. 11, 1959, 1; "Prince Edward Schools Open," *RNL*, Sept. 10, 1959, 1; Kristen Green, *Something Must Be Done About Prince Edward County* (New York: HarperCollins, 2015), 92–96.

3. "Whites Concerned about Negro Schools," *RNL*, Sept. 10, 1959, 57; Paul Hope, "Prince Edward Schools to Face NAACP Suits," *Washington Evening Star*, Sept. 11, 1959, C17.

4. Robert Hamlin, interview by author, Jan. 9, 2015, Farmville, VA.

5. "1,000 pupil [*sic*] at fete in Farmville," *RAA*, Jan. 2, 1960, 1.

6. Leslie Griffin Jr., interview by author, July 23, 2014.

7. Virginia State Bar notice and written complaint against S. W. Tucker, Sept. 23, 1959, NAACP Papers, Group III, Box A-282; Mays, *Race, Reason, and Massive Resistance*, 260.

8. OH to RC, Oct. 14, 1959; RC to RW, Jan 7, 1960; and "Background Information on Disbarment Proceedings," Feb. 10, 1960, all in NAACP Papers, Group III, Box A-282.

9. "Background Information on Disbarment Proceedings," Feb. 10, 1960.

10. "Attempt to Disbar Virginia NAACP Attorney Stalemated," NAACP press release, Feb. 12, 1960, NAACP Papers, Group III, Box A-282; "Disbarment trial draws huge crowd," *RAA*, Feb. 20, 1960, 1.

11. Harvard Sitkoff, *The Struggle for Black Equality, 1952–1980* (New York: Hill & Wang, 1981), 62–64.

12. Peter Wallenstein, "To Sit or Not to Sit: The Supreme Court of the United States and the Civil Rights Movement in the Upper South," *Journal of Supreme Court History* 29 (July 2004): 146–48; "150 Negroes Stage Two Sitdowns Here," *RNL*, Feb. 20, 1960, 1; "Sit-Downs at Counters Begin Here," *RTD*, Feb. 21, 1960, 1.

13. Wallenstein, "To Sit or Not to Sit," 148–49; "34 are Arrested in Sitdowns

Here," *RTD*, Feb. 23, 1060, 1; Clarence Mitchell, telegram to Dr. and Mrs. J. M. Tinsley, Feb. 25, 1960, NAACP Papers, Group III, Box A-281.

14. "Negroes to Expand Picketing," *RNL*, Feb. 25, 1960, 1; Al Coates, "Negroes to Spread Boycott," *RTD*, Feb. 25, 1960, 1.

15. Coates, "Negroes to Spread Boycott," 1; "Hill Asks Increased Picketing," Feb. 29, 1960, 1; SR, interview by JW, Aug. 22, 1989; Rise, *Martinsville Seven*, 71.

16. "Virginian New Howard Law Dean," *RAA*, Sept. 10, 1960, 1; Logan, *Howard University*, 463.

17. Ellen Robertson, Michael Paul Williams, and Lindsay Kastner, "Oliver W. Hill Sr., Longtime Civil-rights Leader, Dies at 100," *RTD*, Aug. 6, 2007, A5; Hill, *Big Bang*, 250–51.

18. Hill, *Big Bang*, 256.

19. Ibid., 258; OH, application for federal employment, 1961, OHC.

20. "Oliver W. Hill is Appointed FHA Assistant," *RNL*, May 10, 1961, 1; "Oliver Hill Named to Key Housing Post," *RAA*, May 20, 1961, 1.

21. Hill, *Big Bang*, 261.

22. ST to Princene Hutcherson, Aug. 20, 1961, NAACP Papers, Group III, Box A-282, note added by Shaed to bottom of letter.

23. *Boynton v. Virginia*, 364 U.S. 454 (1960).

24. *Congressional Record* 107, pt. 10 (July 27, 1961); "Robinson, Spottswood W(illiam) 3D," *Current Biography*, Mar. 1962, 33.

25. FBI report on OH, June 30, 1958, and January 31, 1961, OHC; FBI report on SR, June 25, 1963, in author's possession, obtained under Freedom of Information Act; Nina Govan, interview by author, Apr. 20, 2011.

26. SR to TM, June 10, 1961, LDF Papers, Box 32.

27. Wilder, interview by author, Feb. 3, 2016; Henry Marsh, interview by author, May 2011, Richmond.

28. Ackerman, "Trials of S. W. Tucker," W14ff.; "Va. Court Drops Charges Against NAACP Attorney," *RAA*, Feb. 3, 1962; "Emporia Attorney Given Reprimand," *RTD*, Jan. 25, 1962.

29. Ackerman, "Trials of S. W. Tucker," W14ff.

30. Text of OH speech, May 20, 1961, OHC.

31. Bonastia, *Southern Stalemate*, 152–57; *Encyclopedia Virginia*, s.v. "Danville Civil Rights Demonstrations of 1963," by Emma Edmunds, accessed Mar. 19, 2017, www.encyclopediavirginia.org/Danville_Civil_Rights_Demonstrations_of_1963; Brian Lee and Brian Daugherity, "Program of Action: The Rev. L. Francis Griffin and the Struggle for Racial Equality in Farmville, 1963," *VMHB* 121 (2013): 263–73.

32. *Griffin v. County Board of Supervisors of Prince Edward County*, 377 U.S. 218 (1964).

33. RC, background paper, "To Fulfill these Rights," OHC; Daugherity, "Keep on Keeping On," 54.

34. OH, interview by JW, Dec. 17, 1992.

35. *NAACP v. Button,* 371 U.S. 415 (1963).

36. *Gibson v. Florida Legislative Investigation Committee,* 372 U. S. 539 (1963); Tushnet, *Making Civil Rights Law,* 300.

37. Hubert Bennett to Harry Nims, May 23, 1958, Aubrey Bowles Jr. Papers, Series 1, Virginia Historical Society, Richmond; Minutes of the Executive Committee, Virginia State Bar, Oct. 26, 1961, July 20, 1962, Feb. 15, 1963, and Oct. 24, 1963.

38. Report to the Governor and the General Assembly, S. Doc. 17 (1964).

39. "Johnson Plans to Rename Robinson for Judge Post," *WAA,* Jan. 4, 1964, 11; "Robinson Named to Court Here," *WP,* Jan. 8, 1964, B8.

40. "Senate Confirms Robinson as Judge," *WP,* July 2, 1964, B15; memos in FBI Report on SR from agents W. V. Cleveland, June 25, 1963, and Richard E. Brennan, July 3, 1963.

41. Judge Harry Edwards, "Proceedings of the Memorial Ceremony Celebrating the Life and Work of Spottswood William Robinson III"; "Spottswood W. Robinson III," *WP,* Oct. 17, 1998, A20; Stephen Carter, telephone interview by author, Feb. 20, 2014.

42. Hill, *Big Bang,* 261–62; "M. A. Martin, civil rights lawyer, dies," *RAA,* May 4, 1963, 1.

43. Robertson, Williams, and Kaestner, "Oliver W. Hill Sr., Longtime Civil-rights Leader, Dies at 100," A5; Holton, interview by author, May 28, 2014.

44. *Green v. County Sch. Brd. of New Kent County,* 391 U.S. 430 (1968); "New Kent School Plan Is Nullified," *RTD,* May 28, 1968, 1.

45. *Milliken v. Bradley,* 418 U.S. 717 (1974); Hershman, "Virginia on the Cusp of Change," 2; Gary Orfield and Erica Frankenberg, "Brown at 60: Great Progress, a Long Retreat and an Uncertain Future," Civil Rights Project, May 15, 2014, https://civilrightsproject.ucla.edu/research/k-12-education/integration-and-diversity/brown-at-60-great-progress-a-long-retreat-and-an-uncertain-future/Brown-at-60–051814.pdf, 10.

46. Michael Paul Williams, "Hill Rises to Occasion," *RTD,* Aug. 12, 1999, 1; "Oliver W. Hill: A Life of Service to Virginia—and America," *WP,* Aug. 7, 2007, A12; Oliver W. Hill Jr., e-mail to author, Apr. 25, 2016.

47. *Sch. Brd., City of Richmond v. State Brd. of Education,* 412 U.S. 92 (1973); *Bradley v. Sch. Brd. of City of Richmond,* 416 U.S. 696 (1974).

48. SR, interview by JW, Aug. 22, 1989.

49. OH, interview by author, Feb. 6, 1985, Richmond; "Fight for Integration is Clarified by Hill," *RNL,* May 20, 1959, 3, called to author's attention by James Hershman Jr.

Epilogue

1. Author notes on speech by John King, Century Foundation symposium, Apr. 10, 2016, Washington, DC.

2. Gary Orfield, Jongyeon Ee, Erica Frankenberg, and Genevieve Siegel-Hawley, "Brown at 62: School Segregation by Race, Poverty and State," research brief, Civil Rights Project, May 16, 2016, 2, https://www.civilrightsproject.ucla.edu/research /k-12-education/integration-and-diversity/brown-at-62-school-segregation-by -race-poverty-and-state; *Parents Involved in Community Schools v. Seattle School District No.1*, 551 U.S. 701 (2007).

3. Ibid., 3; "K-12 Education: Better Use of Information Could Help Agencies Identify Disparities and Address Racial Discrimination," General Accountability Office Report, GAO-16–345, Apr. 21, 2016, 57, www.gao.gov/products/GAO -16–345.

4. Alan Cooper, "Oliver Hill: Civil Rights Attorney," *Virginia Lawyers Weekly*, Aug. 13, 2007, 1.

5. James E. Ryan, interview by author, Apr. 7, 2016, Cambridge, MA; James Ryan, *Five Miles Away, A World Apart: One City, Two Schools, and the Story of Educational Opportunity in Modern America* (Oxford: Oxford University Press, 2010), 307.

6. Richard Kahlenberg, "Turnaround Schools and Charter Schools That Work," 292, in *The Future of School Integration: Socioeconomic Diversity as an Education Reform Strategy*, ed. Kahlenberg (New York: Century Foundation, 2012); Heather Schwartz, "Housing Policy is School Policy," ibid., 27–55. See also numerous studies cited in Kahlenberg, *Future of School Integration*, 25–29; Curtis Ivery and Joshua Bassett, eds., *Reclaiming Integration and the Language of Race in the "Post-Racial" Era* (Lanham, MD: Rowman & Littlefield, 2015); and Genevieve Siegel-Hawley, *When the Fences Come Down: Twenty-First-Century Lessons from Metropolitan School Desegregation* (Chapel Hill: University of North Carolina Press, 2016).

7. Ryan, *Five Miles Away, A World Apart*, 165.

8. Author notes on speech by Richard Kahlenberg, Century Foundation symposium, Apr. 10, 2016, Washington, DC.

9. National Coalition on School Diversity, school-diversity.org, accessed Apr. 22, 2016.

10. Bobby Scott, interview by author, June 19, 2016, Richmond, and telephone interview by author, Nov. 14, 2016; Richard Kahlenberg, telephone interview by author, Nov. 15, 2016.

11. Cooper, "Oliver Hill," 1; Reid, interview by author, Jan. 18, 2013; Bobby Scott, interview by author, June 19, 2016.

12. Richard Kahlenberg, interview by author, May 5, 2016, Washington DC.

13. Genevieve Siegel-Hawley, interview by author, May 17, 2016, Richmond.

14. Halley Potter and Kimberly Quick, "A New Wave of School Integration: Districts and Charters Pursuing Socioeconomic Diversity" (working paper, Century Foundation, Feb. 9, 2016), 1–2.

15. Descriptions of the five diversity categories and examples of school systems pursuing those strategies appear in ibid., 11–17.

16. Ibid.; Alana Semuels, "The City That Believed in Desegregation," *Atlantic,* Mar. 27, 2015.

17. "Scott, Conyers Unveil New GAO Report on Segregation in Public Schools," press release, May 17, 2016.

18. OH speech, Public Policy Forum, St. Paul's College, Lawrenceville, VA, Feb. 22, 1977, and application for federal tax exemption for Evolutionary Change, Inc., July 3, 1990, both in OHC; OH, interview by Higginbotham, May 25, 1985, 433.

INDEX

Italicized page numbers preceded by "G" denote illustrations in unfolioed gallery (e.g., G1 for first gallery page) following page 160.